THE
SILENT OPTION

Commander Derek Evans—He's been a SEAL longer than most of his trainees have been alive. But with the mission he now faces, and time rapidly running out, he must find a way to turn his unit of tadpoles into a team of sharks. Yet even Evans may not know what he and SEAL Team FIVE are up against. Are they the hunters . . . or are they merely bait to draw out Karpenko?

Major General Dimitri Karpenko—Called the "Alpha Wolf" because of his animal-like instincts, Karpenko has undertaken an operation that could change the course of history. He is a man driven by two obsessions: 1) the quest for unlimited power, which is now within his grasp, and 2) the fierce desire to kill the man who scarred him for life . . . Derek Evans.

Colonel Natila Saraskina—With her cold heart, empty eyes, and ruthless ambition, she makes the perfect partner for General Karpenko. But behind the chilling facade hides a woman of profound sensuality and secrecy. She kills and she loves with an equal passion, and the true nature of her loyalty could prove fatal . . . to Karpenko or to Evans.

"Larry Simmons's *SILENT OPTION* is fiction that could turn into tomorrow's headlines as Navy SEALS—the world's most feared commandos—take on the new threat of nuclear proliferation. As a SEAL team commander, Simmons has been there—done that. In this fast-action novel, Simmons takes the reader along for the ride, from the intrigue-filled Middle East to the dangerous alleys of Southeast Asia."
                    —Orr Kelly, author of *Never Fight Fair!*

Alysin Harris—A CIA Special Agent, she has been assigned to "handle" SEAL Team FIVE's Commander Derek Evans and to terminate Major General Dimitri Karpenko . . . no matter the cost. And she is brilliantly suited to the task, a professional operative skilled in the arts of psychological warfare, sexual seduction, and subtle betrayal.

Vladimir Suburov—The one and only man Major General Dimitri Karpenko truly trusts, Suburov is a killing machine, a murderer with no conscience and less mercy. And there is just one way to get at Karpenko: kill Suburov before he kills you.

Master Chief Steven Saleen—Poised, powerful, and self-assured, he is the epitome of a SEAL warrior. He is also the one man Commander Derek Evans wants at his side—whether sharing a beer or sharing a fight. And when the battle begins in earnest, Evans knows he can count on Saleen . . . no matter how overwhelming the odds.

Lieutenant David Eric Owen—He's come to the SEAL Team FIVE against the expressed wishes of his father . . . Chief of Naval Operations. Now, under Derek Evans's command, Owen has risen to the rank of platoon commander. But word has come down through channels to keep young Owen out of harm's way—an order that goes against everything a SEAL believes in and fights for.

Seaman Lee Loi Lam—Half American, half Vietnamese, the SEAL trainee is driven by anger, hatred, and a desire for revenge. But to succeed in the SEALs, he must let go of the past and all the horrors he suffered as a child. For failing to sacrifice all to the good of the team could become the tool of his destruction.

Sofia Skiathos—An Israeli agent assigned to infiltrate Karpenko's inner circle, she is prepared to go to any length, take any risk, pay any price, to fulfill her mission. And should her cover be blown, she knows that Karpenko will make her pay the highest price of all. . . .

SILENT OPTION

LARRY SIMMONS

POCKET BOOKS

New York   London   Toronto   Sydney   Tokyo   Singapore

An *Original* Publication of POCKET BOOKS

POCKET BOOKS, a division of Simon & Schuster Inc.
1230 Avenue of the Americas, New York, NY 10020

ISBN: 0-671-55281-3

First Pocket Books printing June 1997

10 9 8 7 6 5 4 3 2 1

POCKET and colophon are registered trademarks of Simon & Schuster Inc.

Cover art by James Wang

Printed in the U.S.A.

To those who answer
the call to
move, shoot, and communicate

FOREWORD

Ask any military professional what NBC means and you will get an immediate response: Nuclear, Biological, and Chemical warfare. This book revolves about these social diseases. It is a work of fiction, but the central theme, the problem of the proliferation of weapons of mass destruction, is real.

Perhaps the greatest challenge of our time is to keep NBC weapons out of the hands of fanatics. With the disintegration of the Soviet Empire, the new republics on the rim of Russia have become huge shopping bazaars for trade in fissionable materials and the know-how to build the most horrible weapons mankind has ever devised. In these markets agents of the West have acquired NBC technology and materials such as red mercury, a substance purported to be the crucial ingredient in making lightweight human-portable neutron bombs. Neutron bombs are the ones that kill people and spare buildings. Shopping in these bazaars are agents of the ruler-fanatics of the world, men such as Saddam Hussein, Muammar Qaddafi, and Pol Pot.

The proliferation of NBC technology will eventually result in a new generation of warfare, one that transcends national boundaries. Like the Drug War taken to the fifth power, this new warfare has no easy solution and we as a nation are not prepared for it any more than we are for the war on drugs. But unlike drugs that kill the weak of spirit in the shadows and the back alleys of America's cities, these social diseases have the terrible capacity to destroy entire cities in blazing holocausts or seething contagious infections. They are cataclysmic killers. With the push of a button or the breaking of a vial a madman can seal the fate of thousands of innocent people without seeing the horror of death.

I believe Tel Aviv is one of the primary targets on the short list for destruction. Because of its population ratio, highly Jewish and very little Arab, it is Armageddon waiting to happen. With oppression, injustice, and brutality on both sides of the conflict between the descendants of the children of Abraham, it is only a matter of time until a fanatic unleashes an Armageddon. In the Middle East one man's terrorist is truly another man's hero. A Jewish doctor who murders scores of Arabs praying in a mosque is a hero to the Zionist zealot. An Arab farmer fighting injustice over a plot of barren and parched land becomes a martyr when he kills scores of schoolchildren with a suicide bomb. NBC weaponry introduced into this volatile human equation is absolute madness.

This book is also about making warriors, men whose mission is to take gun in hand and kill the enemy up close and personal. It is a long and laborious process of socializing young men into a subculture of danger and trust where each man's survival is dependent on his teammates. The modern samurai are Special Operations Forces (SOF). They are the warriors of choice for quiet, covert operations that don't arouse public attention, missions such as seizing a ship loaded with missiles bound for Bandar Abbās, or lightning raids on truckloads of contraband bound for Baghdad. SOF is the silent option. They are the pointy end of the national sword, and in many respects they are the most vulnerable. What they are trained to do they might be asked to do. What they are not trained to do is thrust

FOREWORD

upon them. Enjoy this trip into the realm of special operations. Savor this glimpse into the secret world of special operations and become part of the silent option for a few hours of easy-chair reading. It is hoped that this will be the only glimpse you get into this dangerous and mysterious arena.

The Cold War is over. The Soviet Union is no more. The new republics on the rim of Russia have become huge shopping bazaars for trade in nuclear, biological, and chemical (NBC) weapons.

"FOB Sword, FOB Sword, this is Delta One, over."

"Delta One, Delta One, bead window. I repeat. Bead window. This net is for authorized users only," responded the radio operator.

"Screw you!" blared the response.

The generals in the Pentagon scowled at each other. Admiral Arlington recognized the voice and scrunched down in his chair.

"I repeat. Bead window! Remain clear of this net!" responded the operator more sternly.

"Let me make myself perfectly clear, asshole! If you don't shut the hell up, I'm gonna rip out your tonsils when I get back to base. Now! I got one man down. Possible broken ribs. Require medevac *immediately*. Latitude three-five degrees, zero-eight minutes. Longitude three-five degrees, zero-one minutes. How copy, over?" queried Gomez.

"Good copy, Delta One," responded the radio operator.

"Excellent," continued the commanding voice on the

other side of the world. "I have five tangos KIA. They appear to be Russian in nationality." The old men sat up in their chairs in anticipation. Arlington sat up straight and smiled proudly. "For the moment I am in possession of one, I repeat, one nuclear device that appears to be Russian in origin. How copy, over?"

The modern samurai are the Special Operations Forces (SOF), men whose job is to take gun in hand and kill the enemy up close and personal. They are the weapon of choice for quiet, covert operations that don't arouse public attention. They are the silent option.

*The U.S. military has in its ranks some of the finest and most brilliant men in our nation, but as an institution it is brain-dead and powerless to transform itself into a machine capable of efficiently dealing with this new generation of warfare. It is a military marching in ranks in an open field like the Red Coats, kneeling on one knee on cue to shoot at an enemy hidden in the trees. While its enemies fly on American Airlines and dress in three-piece business suits, the U.S. government is busy preparing for World War III and an instant replay of Vietnam. What SOF is trained to do they may be asked to do. What they are not trained to do will be thrust upon them. **The American public must not let the system turn SOF into just another conventional force.***

SILENT OPTION

CHAPTER

1

Rukslav Province, Ukraine
Soviet Union, 1991

The truck convoy was under armed escort as it rumbled by a guarded checkpoint and through the perimeter of a huge military complex deep within the Soviet Union. Men with dogs patrolled the fence line surrounding the facility. From her vantage point in the hills above the arsenal, Colonel Natila Saraskina watched the activity below through binoculars. Through early morning haze she noted the number of patrols and the weapons the guards carried.

Disgraceful, she thought. *Simply pathetic!*

The security of the facility was intolerably lax in view of their mission to secure an arsenal full of nuclear weapons. The guards carried only small arms and they weren't loaded because the sergeant at arms didn't trust his men with loaded weapons. They carried loaded magazines in their ammunition pouches, but it was more for show during security drills than for actual readiness. Like most men of their category they were underpaid and poorly trained. In the crumbling Soviet Empire, bullets were too expensive to waste on security guards.

Colonel Saraskina had studied Perisislav for more than a year. She had assigned her most trusted men to this mission and they had worked the area like a pack of hounds. To gather intelligence, they had infiltrated the local bars in the

1

nearby town of Rukslav and had bought drinks for some of the unfortunate security guards she was watching. Under the influence of large amounts of vodka, they had told her men everything she needed to know about the security of the Perisislav Nuclear Weapons Depot. Physical security was simply a pretense.

Checking the defenses of top-secret facilities was a small but important part of Saraskina's mission. She had administered many such security audits and the laxness at Perisislav came as no surprise. Training of security forces assigned inside the Soviet Union had a very low priority. Saraskina was certain today's audit would change such a practice forever.

"Colonel Saraskina, the convoy is on schedule. The first truck just arrived in the assembly area and they have established a hasty perimeter," whispered Major Voshchanov.

"Very well," she said without looking at the battle-hardened major.

He silently moved back to his concealment, blending into the foliage with the other men in the command element. As she waited for the general's convoy, her mind wondered back to her Spetznaz training and her first meeting with Major General Karpenko.

Success always depends on proper planning and good basic training, she thought. *And luck!*

Her first encounter with Dimitri Karpenko had occurred at a secret training base in the Ukraine. It had been raining for months and the soil of the steppe had turned to a sea of sticky mud. She was assigned to a group of raw recruits who had been training all morning with the Russian spade.

In Russia every infantryman carries a small spade. It is a multipurpose tool that never leaves the soldier's side. When the order to halt is given, the soldier throws himself on the ground and begins to dig a shallow trench eight inches deep to protect himself from enemy bullets. If he remains in the location for any length of time, he continues to dig until he has a foxhole that, in time, he connects to the soldier's next to him to create breastworks. That is the Russian way. Unlike the American military entrenching tool, the Russian spade does not have a folding handle. It has to be a single monolithic object with three edges of the blade as sharp as a razor. Surprisingly, Spetznaz soldiers also carry the little shovel. But they don't dig trenches with it. They use it as a battle ax and learn to throw it on the run like a tomahawk. To the Spetznaz soldier the spade is an instrument of death.

Because of her superior athletic abilities, Natila had outperformed the other recruits in her Spetznaz training class in the run and throw contest and had earned their respect, respect that came hard for Russian men. On the morning she first met Dimitri Karpenko she was covered in mud and blood. The blood was from small cuts caused by the razor-sharp edges of her spade. It was misting rain and everything was wet and limp. Natila's camouflage uniform stuck to her body, outlining curves that identified her as different from the others. Her eyes were vacant as the large Slavic sergeant, who had no pity for trainees, called them to attention in front of a huge rain-soaked tent.

"Get inside, goddamnit!" he yelled after the senior man had reported all accounted for.

There were only twenty men and one woman left of the original lot of sixty-seven trainees. They had been through hell, the most brutal training the Soviet military had to offer, and it was far from over. As they crowded around the entrance of the tent uncertain of what was in store, Sergeant Suburov yelled obscenities. They were just miserable recruits, there to be abused until the weak ones quit. The nearest soldier scrambled to thrust aside the wet tarpaulin and was about to enter when something stopped him momentarily. On the muddy trampled ground just inside the entrance of the tent was a snow-white towel laid down as a doormat. The soldier hesitated. Behind him Suburov was shouting and the other soldiers were pushing.

"Get in the goddamn tent, fools!" yelled Suburov, "or I will kick your asses all the way to Vilnius."

Every man stepped over the towel for fear of soiling it and incurring the wrath of its owner. Every man! Natila was last, not because she was being a good babushka but because she sensed something was going to happen. She saw the snow-white towel, stepped through the entrance of the tent, and wiped her muddy boots on it as if it were a doormat. Then she bravely took her place at the end of the formation.

The men were silent, mouths agape, as a huge, intimidating senior army officer appeared at the other end of the tent. His eyes locked on Natila as he spoke quietly in a voice that betrayed both brutality and ruthlessness.

"Who soiled my towel?" he growled.

For a moment time stood still as the trainees listened to their pounding hearts. Stomachs surged with fear. They had all heard stories about him from their instructors. He was a legend. His reputation was feared throughout Russian Special Forces. Behind his back Karpenko was called Alpha Wolf because of his animal-like instincts. He tilted his head back slightly and sniffed the air as he paced in front of the mud-caked formation. Natila's feminine voice pierced the silence.

"I used the doormat, Comrade Colonel, sir!" she said sharply with more bravado than she felt.

Silence reigned. Karpenko continued his cold stare at her for a full minute before turning his gaze individually on the others in formation. As he passed up and down the line no one looked him in the eye except Natila. His face assumed a countenance of disgust, seeing fear exude from their pores. For two minutes he slowly paced silently back and forth as they stood frozen like statues.

"I hate cowards!" he growled viciously. "I *hate cowards!*"

For the longest time he said nothing more as he slowly paced back and forth, nostrils flaring and eyes piercing their souls.

"I can smell fear like rotten meat!" he boomed out with a fierceness that caused them to flinch. "Fear is your enemy! It makes you weak. It interferes with clear thinking at critical moments of battle. Fear overloads your mind! You must learn to control it or it will kill you as quickly as your enemy!"

He paused for a moment before shouting orders.

"*Sergeant Suburov!* Take charge of these . . . these . . . men!" he said with disgust, "and teach them to wipe their feet before they enter my tent. *Lieutenant Saraskina!* You will report to me at seventeen hundred hours."

At 1700 hours the trainees were driven out into the mud in their bare feet and beaten with belts, sticks, fists, and boots, with anything that would inflict pain. They ran and crawled through the mud all night, and while they suffered, Natila dined with the colonel. That night while the men in her training class suffered, she slept with the colonel. It wasn't personal. It was an alliance, and a new partnership. That night Lieutenant Natila Saraskina had knowingly and willingly joined the inner circle of Comrade Colonel Dimitri Karpenko, the most ruthless man in the history of the Spetznaz.

Saraskina's thoughts were interrupted as the foliage came to life. Like a wolf, Voshchanov appeared from out of the bushes and silently moved to her position. Both stood motionless looking out over the valley.

"Colonel, the last truck is being loaded at the dock. The others are in the assembly area. Should I order the men to final assault positions?" he asked in a whisper that wasn't necessary. The Spetznaz controlled the terrain for ten square miles.

"Nyet!" she snapped without changing position. "But inform the general it is time." Voshchanov returned to his radioman like an apparition in the morning mist.

Dimitri Karpenko was a cossack, a huge, pockmarked, ugly man with an insatiable appetite for power. Had he been born a hundred years early, he would have ridden the endless steppe on horseback, plundering all in his path. It was in his genes. In the Spetznaz he had found his niche. As the supreme commander of a regiment of cutthroats he was the man the Russian government depended upon for covert operations.

Colonel Saraskina understood what motivated Dimitri Karpenko. She had seen it in his eyes in that rain-soaked tent in the Ukraine. It was power. He had two passions in life, collecting human talent and trading secrets. Both were means to the same objective. The acquisition of power. Over the years he had groomed her like a prized racehorse, because secret knowledge was power, and Natila, beautiful Natila, with her cold vacant eyes, empty heart, and ruthless ambition, had no reservations about using her treasures to acquire secret knowledge for the sake of the wolf pack.

Saraskina's thoughts were interrupted again as Major Voshchanov moved quickly to her side.

"Colonel, our convoy is approaching." She turned to face

him and looked the seasoned soldier directly in the eye as if divining the future. Coldly she nodded acknowledgment.

"Final assault positions!" she ordered as she walked calmly toward the road.

At the head of the approaching convoy of covered army trucks was a large black sedan. It carried the plates and flew the flag of a two-star general. Natila stepped out from the trees and walked slowly to the edge of the road. The car stopped momentarily in front of her and she slid into the backseat.

"All is ready, General," she said.

Karpenko stared at her as if probing for unknown details. His nostrils flared and he sniffed the air unconsciously.

"Very well, Natila, very well." Shifting his gaze to the driver in the front seat he growled, "Press on, Vlad; it is time to change the course of history."

Sergeant Suburov slipped the Zil into gear and with a lurch accelerated to match the speed of the trucks approaching in his rearview mirror. With the Zil in front the convoy proceeded down the hill and across an open area to a kiosk that commanded the entrance to the arsenal. The huge facility was buried in trees and wire.

At the gate the guard stopped the sedan momentarily. Nikolos Papov had been warned that the arsenal was having a security drill, and he'd had the misfortune of encountering General Karpenko before during an audit. Papov, a gregarious guard from the small town of Rukslav, knew better than to anger the Spetznaz general. He waved them on without inspection and the convoy proceeded to a staging apron deep within the arsenal compound where six army trucks and two armored personnel carriers were assembled for departure.

The convoy commander had set up a hasty perimeter about the trucks, but it was sloppy and rather unprofessional in appearance. The soldiers were smoking and standing around in the open area inside the trees that lined the apron. Their only concern was to look good for the inspectors. They threw down their cigarettes and picked up their empty weapons at the approach of the general's car. Karpenko and Saraskina got out of the sedan and briskly approached the young army captain in charge of the convoy. He saluted smartly. Recognizing the general, the young captain said politely, "Good morning, General Karpenko . . . , Colonel Saraskina. May I help you, sir?"

"Yes, you can. We are here to assume your mission," said Saraskina.

The captain continued to look at the general's face for clues to his response as he answered Saraskina. "But, Colonel, I have no message concerning a change to my mission. As you know, I must confirm any change of plan with my superiors."

"I am on a top-secret mission, Captain, and I relieve you of your duties," said Saraskina.

"But . . . General . . . , I know of your security audit, sir, but . . . I have no orders to. . . . As you know, sir, I cannot transfer this cargo to you without proper written authorization from my superiors," stuttered the young captain, not sure what to say to satisfy the auditors.

"You are relieved, Captain," said Saraskina with an evil stare.

"But, Colonel, I must insist on contacting my superiors before I allow you to assume this important responsibility," protested the captain in a manner fitting for a junior addressing a colonel. He continued to look at Karpenko while speaking to Saraskina. Captain Boborov wrongly assumed this was part of the game and he was going to play it professionally to impress the shine off the general's stars.

While Captain Boborov stood at attention inside the compound, trying to impress the general, all around the arsenal Spetznaz troops quietly closed the distance from their final assault positions to their quarry. Silently they killed the fence-line guards in Spetznaz style with their spades and took their places patrolling the line. The guards never saw the blades coming. They were struck in the back of the head or neck with the razor-sharp blades, instantly smashing them into unconsciousness. The dogs were harder to kill than the men. Within two minutes the bodies were out of sight and a new guard force with a terrifying mission controlled Perisislav.

Saraskina motioned with a hand signal and the canvas cover on two of the trucks peeled back. Two dozen commandos dressed in battle fatigues fanned out, AK assault rifles in hand. From the back of one of the trucks, two Spetznaz soldiers emerged with electronic equipment hanging from their shoulders. They quickly passed by each of the young captain's trucks while reading their instruments, pausing to peer into the rear of each vehicle for a visual check to confirm their readings. Captain Boborov watched with apprehension. When the soldiers finished their survey, they signaled Saraskina in sign language.

"The weapons are on board, General," she reported.

"General Karpenko, there are real nuclear weapons on board my trucks! And I have no message from headquarters to change my mission. As you know, sir, I cannot relinquish my responsibility without proper authorization," protested the captain more forcefully. Captain Boborov shifted his position at attention and turned slightly to face Karpenko squarely. He clicked his heels together loudly and asked, "Under whose authority are your orders, sir?" He was hoping those were the words the general wanted to hear before ending the security charade.

Natila pulled out a Makarov pistol with a large silencer attached to the barrel and pointed it at Boborov's head. "Here are your new orders, Captain."

Captain Boborov stared at the weapon in total shock. His eyes grew in size.

"I-I do not understand, sir," he stammered, trying to focus his eyes on the general's.

"Silence! You are relieved!" snapped Karpenko, looking around peevishly like a wolf closing in on a kill. He faced the young officer and smiled at the brilliance of his immediate thoughts. "Since you insist on knowing, young Captain Boborov, my authority comes from Comrade Kalesnikof," he said gesturing to his Spetznaz commandos holding their Kalesnikof assault rifles at the ready.

"All is ready, General," said Saraskina, steadily holding the pistol aimed at Boborov's face.

Karpenko grunted acknowledgment and turned to walk back to the Zil. With a motion of her left hand, the Spetznaz began to kill the captain's soldiers with their spades. The first six men fell instantly, petrified by the sight of the swinging blades. In horror several men broke free and ran for the tree line. Two were caught in the back by spades whirling through the air like buzz saws. Three men broke free, running behind one of the trucks before heading for the tree line. Reluctantly, Suburov motioned with his weapon, sending a signal to shoot the fleeing soldiers. The Spetznaz raised their weapons and took careful aim. with short, quick bursts they shot the fleeing men in the back, dropping them on the run like hunters shooting deer. The echo of the automatic weapons fire through the trees shattered the morning calm and further shattered Captain Boborov's vision of a routine security audit.

Boborov's face was white with fear when he stiffly turned his head to face the muzzle of the pistol in Saraskina's hand. She stared at him for a moment and he felt the cold shiver of death run down his spine. The bile in his stomach surged as he looked deep into her bottomless eyes. It was the last feeling Captain Boborov would know. From three feet away Saraskina fired two quick shots from the silenced pistol. The first bullet went through his left eye and into his brain, killing him instantly. The second bullet struck the cheekbone of a dead man in the act of falling down. The impact of the two bullets thrust the body back in a heap on the muddy ground.

Though her silenced Makarov was no longer necessary, she preferred using it, because its limitations forced the action to be up close and personal. The Makarov was almost silent, the sound distinctive when the bullet met bone, like a spade crushing a spine. Killing shouldn't be done from high altitude or by pushing a button from far away. For her, that was too antiseptic, too impersonal. If one was going to commit to killing another human being, one should know the consequence of one's actions.

The bodies were neatly placed on the front seats of the general's trucks and the huge bombs in the rear were armed for simultaneous detonation. With the Zil in the lead, and under escort of the APCs, Captain Boborov's six covered army trucks rumbled off to the kiosk at the entrance to the arsenal. Nikolos Papov waved them to a stop at the gate. The rear window of the Zil rolled down slowly and Papov, the gregarious guard from Rukslav, found himself face-to-face with the infamous General Karpenko. His knees shook. Although petrified of the general, he was alert and wide-eyed because of the sound of shooting from within the facility.

"What happened, General?" he asked in a voice that was crackling from nervousness. "I-I heard shooting," he stammered. "I signaled all my men to high alert!"

Karpenko's index finger slowly traced the line of a deep scar that ran the length of his face. His cheek quivered and his nostrils flared. With an evil, vacant stare he looked out from the back seat of the Zil. "An old cossack lesson from the Steppes, Comrade Sergeant: Being prepared is knowing that your worst shot is good enough."

As Papov stared at Karpenko with bewilderment, the Makarov calmly appeared from behind the general. Saraskina fired two quick shots directly into the face of the dumbstruck guard, who fell back as if hammered in the head by a mallet. Sergeant Suburov blew the horn on the Zil and men along the fence line began to run in all directions. Some disappeared into the foliage, while others boarded trucks in the convoy. Commandos covered every direction in perimeter defense like a huge organism defending itself with spines. The defense posture was more instinctual than necessary. All the Perisislav guards were dead. Two soldiers grabbed the body of the gate guard and threw the corpse into the rear of one of the trucks. In less than three minutes they were mounted and the convoy sped off into the turmoil that was the death throes of the Soviet Union.

The explosion within the Perisislav Nuclear Weapons Depot was enormous. It incinerated the vehicles and the bodies, and it killed most of the people inside the arsenal's main buildings almost a mile from ground zero. It even shattered buildings in the village of Rukslav five miles away. The first thoughts of the survivors inside the storage bunkers and in the village of Rukslav was that their worst nightmares had been realized, the accidental discharge of a nuclear weapon. Moreover, the explosion presented a mystery for investigators that took several months to decipher.

Their first assumption was that one of the weapons had gone off low order accidentally. For months officials struggled to explain the aftermath before accepting the unthinkable. It took another six weeks before the West was notified through diplomatic channels that several nuclear weapons were missing from a Soviet arsenal. By the time the news reached the West it was too late for U.S. satellites to help in tracking the nuclear trails given off by the weapons. The unthinkable now facing the crumbling Politburo was that Comrade General Dimitri Karpenko, the head of Soviet covert operations, had committed himself to capitalism and the free enterprise of the weapons trade. The face of war had changed forever.

CHAPTER
2

Naval Amphibious Base
Coronado Island
San Diego, California

On your feet," yelled Instructor Tim Taufaudy.

Ninety-eight young men scrambled from slumber to alert attention. As they raced to be the first to their feet, chairs and desks clattered on the floor, creating a distinctive sound of classroom thunder that brought Lam back to reality. He had been drooling on his desk. There was no River of Perfumes beneath his head, only a puddle of saliva created during his nap. Slowly his head cleared. Toothless Waa was just a distant memory, a horrible recurring nightmare from his childhood in Vietnam. As his brain slowly cleared from the fog of sleep he remembered where he was, Basic Underwater Demolition/SEAL training in Coronado, California.

Lee Loi Lam looked through a sea of bodies all dressed in green fatigues to see a huge black man in a crisp khaki uniform. He was standing on a platform in front of the class, inspecting the men with a knowing eye. The eight-inch elevation of the platform, combined with his great height, made him appear to be a giant. On his chest he wore row after row of ribbons, and at the top of the ribbons was a shiny, bright, golden medallion. As the big man moved, it seemed to magnify flashes of light like a mirror reflecting sunlight.

12

Lam had worshiped the symbol all through high school and had memorized every detail before joining the Navy. Every boy in his high school in South San Diego had heard stories about the SEALs. They were awesome warriors who were masters of self-defense, diving, parachuting, weapons, and explosives. To Lam, the symbol of the SEALs was a thing of beauty.

The acronym *SEAL* is derived from the words *sea, air,* and *land,* and it is a play on words referring to the sea animal that is more at home in the sea than on land. The insignia of the SEALs is a trident, after the scepter that crosses through the heart of the device. The symbolism that Lam revered had been carefully chosen by men of action to represent the media in which the SEAL warrior operates: sea, air, and land. The central part and foundation of the insignia is an anchor, clearly identifying the branch of service as Navy. Above the anchor is an eagle with its wings outstretched, representing the air as well as the strength and courage of warriors. One of the eagle's talons holds a trident, the scepter of the Roman god of the sea; the other, a cocked flintlock pistol representing the land. It is cocked to indicate a high state of readiness for war.

Master Chief Steven Saleen stood six feet four and weighed 225 pounds. The trident belonged on his chest. It fit his image like hand and glove. In appearance he was awesome, and he was everything the young men in the classroom aspired to be. A SEAL warrior. Handsome with pleasant features, his perfect proportions, muscular build, and athletic glow beamed confidence. Poised and self-assured, he spoke in a deep, sonorous voice that commanded attention.

"Gents, there is too much snoring going on in this room. Wake up!" he bugled. "Commander Evans is going to be late this morning. So I'm going to use this time to talk about a few critically important items that may seem trivial, but I assure you they are as important to your success at BUDS as learning to shoot an M-16."

He looked down from the podium, examining the class with a menacing expression. Seeing they were all wide-awake, he quietly ordered, "Take seats."

Again the distinctive shuffling thunder of men rushing to

be the first to be seated echoed off the bare cinder-block walls. Within seconds the room was dead silent. Every eye in the room was fixed on the master chief.

"Men, the devil is in the details. In special operations even the small things can kill you. What I'm going to talk about may seem like small stuff, but it's critically important information. First and foremost, a trainee must take care of his wheels." He burst into a broad smile.

"I don't mean your car or your motorcycle. You won't need those kinds of wheels for the next six months. I mean your feet! If you get sores or blisters on your feet and you can't run and swim, *you will* be dropped from the course. That's a fact!"

Saleen stomped down on the platform twice like an obstinate mule, emphasizing the importance of the point. There was no mistaking his intention. He always stomped on the platform when he gave out test questions. "Is that clear?"

"Hoo yah, Master Chief Saleen!" they yelled in unison. He waited for silence before continuing his lecture.

"The most important items to the GIs of the Korean War, other than their weaponry, of course, were a good fart sack, a big spoon, and an extra pair of socks. Now, you don't have to worry about a fart sack here at BUDS, or a big spoon, but you better pay close attention to your socks. To prevent sores and blisters you must take special care of your feet. Wash and dry them carefully, especially between your toes. Rub and massage them daily. And always—I repeat, always—put on clean, dry socks whenever you have the opportunity. *Never,*" he said in a raised voice, "never be caught without clean, dry socks."

Saleen stomped twice on the platform and walked the width of the classroom before continuing his talk.

"In pretraining most of you broke in your boots. That's gooood! Ensure that you have two pairs of old boots. If you change your socks frequently, old boots are much easier on your feet. If you don't have two pairs of old boots, go to supply and tell them Master Chief Saleen sent you. Keep a third, new pair of boots, shined to *perfection,* just for *inspections.* The pretty ones will keep the instructors happy and off your ass. Gents, it is important in the extreme that you take care of your feet. Should you develop blisters, see Dr. Poland immediately. He will help you patch your wheel before it becomes a total blowout. *You got that?"*

"Hoo yah, Master Chief Saleen," thundered the class in unison.

"For the next six months you will be constantly on the move. You will run everywhere you go, to class, to the barracks, to chow, everywhere. In the course of a day it will not be unusual for you to run as much as twenty miles and swim four or five miles. Men, your feet must remain healthy or you will fail. I repeat—your feet must remain healthy throughout this course or *you will fail,"* he said with finality. Saleen looked around the class to ensure no one was nodding off.

"Secondly, you must eat well." Again he stomped twice on the platform. It seemed to give way under his enormous weight. "I have arranged for a special healthy diet at the galley. Eat every meal. Keep bread and peanut butter and other high-calorie, high-carbohydrate foods in your rooms. The instructors won't bother you about that as long as you keep things neat and clean. And I will see they don't eat all your goodies during barracks inspections."

The instructors in the back of the class snickered out loud.

"Eat four to five meals each day. *You will need the energy,"* he said just as the speaker in the back of the classroom blared out, "Master Chief Saleen, lay to the commanding officer's office. That is, Master Chief Saleen, lay to the commanding officer's office immediately!"

Saleen paused for a second before speaking. "Gents, take a break. Keep the snoring down to a dull roar until I get back." Saleen knew this routine well. He had put many a boy in training and had graduated some very tough men. He was a master training specialist who knew all the tricks of teaching young men how to move, shoot, and communicate. He used his sleep-learning technique to drive little important details such as foot care and personal hygiene deep into their brains. He never missed an opportunity to teach something. Moments that most instructors considered lost time he turned into what he called "hip-pocket" training. And from his hip pocket he pulled out the survival lessons of a master warrior. As he turned to leave he spoke in a deeply resonant voice with a thick German accent, "I'll be bak!" The men laughed at his perfect imitation of the movie star.

Most of the other young men in Class 168 fell asleep quickly. They had learned to sleep anywhere, anytime, anyplace, especially after a huge breakfast. Lam didn't want to sleep, because he could feel the nightmare just below the surface of his groggy thoughts. His mind was sluggish from a lack of rest and from the strain of the physical screening test they had completed the day before selection. But in a few minutes his eyes closed and his head descended to his arm in jerking bobs until it rested in the crook of his arm. Toothless Waa was waiting by the River of Perfumes. Even under the big oilman's careful parenting, Lam had experienced terrible recurring nightmares of life in Vietnam. Half-American, half-Vietnamese children were treated like animals in the back streets of Saigon. The experiences left lasting mental scars.

Lam's image of horror was an evil, toothless grin on a deeply scarred Asian face. His head shifted in the cradle of his arm as the image of the dragons on Waa's deltoids danced with every movement of his naked arms. His long queue slithered down his back in a thick black braid tied in a knot to resemble a snake's head. With each movement, the queue seemed to snap out like a striking snake. Even in his dream, Lam flinched in fear. He gasped for breath as he felt Waa's hands grasp him about the throat and lift him in the air. Choking in his sleep, he felt near unconsciousness. He could see Waa smile with pleasure with each blow of the bamboo cane, venting the hate generated more than a decade before during the war with the Americans.

"You little American bastard, stay out of Cholon or next time I'll kill you!"

Lam came to with a start. His head raised from his desk as if propelled by a kick in the face. Gasping for breath, he glanced around the room. The others were snoring or whispering quietly, waiting for the big master chief to return from the captain's office, unaware of his personal hell. By the clock on the classroom wall he had dozed off for only a couple of minutes, a short time of recurring hell. He wiped his chin and rubbed his face.

No more sleep. No more Toothless Waa, he begged himself.

With his head in the cradle of his arm he felt a tear roll down his nose and fall on the desk. He thought about the night the enforcers caught them in their nipa-palm hut over the River of Perfumes. He remembered his feeling upon regaining consciousness in the *binjo* ditch partly buried in the soft, smooth mud of the delta. The sound of the others crying had brought him back. They were huddled about in fetal positions sobbing quietly. The mud had plastered the welts on his body and had drawn out the poison in his skin, but nothing could draw out the poison in his mind. Hate. Consuming hate. Beside him lay Skinny Choi, facedown in the mud. He was dead, smothered by the soft, life-giving mud of Vietnam, an unintended victim of Toothless Waa. Lee Loi Lam hated Vietnam. He hated the Vietnamese and he hated Waa. He silently swore a blood oath of vengeance, an oath he had sworn a hundred times before. He could feel the tears washing the mud from his face as his thoughts dragged him back in time. *Why? Why?* he asked himself as he silently swore he would become a SEAL. SEALs were the best fighters in the world. *After I have learned all the secrets of the SEALs, I'll go back and kill them all. I'll kill the killers of children!*

He silently promised Skinny Choi and the others. *I'll get them back. I'll kill them all! I'm gonna become the best fighter in the world and then I am gonna kill Waa, slowly! I promise! I promise!*

Fortunately for Lee Loi Lam, he had always been bigger than the other boys in his gang. It was a gift from his American father, a man he would never know. Each day in Ho Chi Minh City had been a survival lesson that had left a mental scar. Along with hunger, he had endured the scorn of the Vietnamese people. But the wild seeds left by the American Army grew wily and cunning in the hostile back rows of Saigon, or perished. Their curse was a half-American face, something they couldn't hide.

Lam's survival skills were a perfect fit for the culture of

the SEAL teams: Be sneaky, do the unexpected, strike with lightning speed, and fade away into the night. His nightmare always began the same way. He found himself sneaking in the shadows of a dilapidated two-story villa watching the street with his sad half-almond eyes. Dressed in dirty black pajamas and a straw cone hat, he blended into the darkness in near-perfect camouflage. Nearby was his escape route, a narrow unpaved alley the rains had turned to a stream of mud.

The main street of Cholon, the busiest sector of the "Pearl of the Orient," was filled with rice farmers and merchants trying to hustle a living. Hundreds of sidewalk merchants lined the street, selling everything from rice to a trip through the jade gate. The store across the street sold chickens and ducks, all nicely plucked and hung upside down for inspection. A fat man of Chinese ancestry sat guarding the store.

He could be a problem, thought Lam as his dream turned from surreal to real. *Too lazy to get up to see the commotion in the street.*

An old woman squatting down over her rice pot chewing betel nut kept the fat Chinaman company. She spat on the sidewalk. Beckoning to a shopper with a broad smile, she showed one black-purple-stained front tooth. The red betel-nut saliva stained her chin as she spat incessantly on the filthy ground. The betel nut numbed her mouth and eased the pain of rotten teeth and infected gums.

Other shops and street vendors along main street sold fruits and vegetables laid out in open-air stalls on banana leaves. Dried fish hung everywhere from bamboo roof supports. They swayed gently in the breeze like a school of fish feeding on a reef.

So much food. And I am so hungry, thought Lam. *So hungry.*

Music blared from outdoor speakers and hawkers beckoned for shoppers to buy their wares. With the street noise of motorbikes, Lambrettas, and occasional heavy trucks passing down main street, there was an unpleasant blend of sound that assaulted the senses. Lam's head rolled back and forth in the cradle of his arm, an unconscious movement that told his body to wake up before Waa began the torture.

From the shadows Lam surveyed the scene for fifty yards up and down Main Street. His mind rehearsed the plan. *The timing is right. The escape routes are good. There are no soldiers around. It is time,* he resolved.

The gang hadn't hit this area for over two months and he was confident of his plan. He was about to step down from the veranda when a figure swaggered in front of him. His heart stopped and his blood ran cold. Fear rose in his stomach. His breathing stopped. It was Toothless Waa surveying his kingdom.

Waa was the local enforcer who made his living gambling and working the protection rackets. There was no mistaking his profile as Lam looked down from the darkness. He had long jet-black hair that the whores braided into a Chinese-style pigtail. It shone in the streetlight like a black snake running down the length of his bare back. His hair was drawn back so tightly that his slanted eyes were almost V-shaped. A shadow cast by the streetlight accentuated a deep facial scar on his left cheek, the result of a knife fight that had nearly cost him his eye. With his broken nose and the scars on his face, he was a walking road map of violence and a visible reminder of the dangers of life in the back streets of Saigon. The multicolored dragons tattooed on his shoulders seemed to come alive with each movement of his bare arms.

All the street kids knew of Toothless Waa. He was a killer who enjoyed making his victims suffer before they died. Lam had seen him chase down a street kid and beat him to death with his fist. He watched without breathing as Waa swaggered off down the street, glaring at anyone who dared to make eye contact. He relaxed and took a deep breath as Waa disappeared into the crowd. His first thought was to leave Cholon as quickly as possible, but his gnawing stomach reminded him of the plan. He waited another hour before he reluctantly stepped out into the streetlight to give the signal.

Lam watched stoically as a skinny little boy ran into the street and ricocheted off the side of a speeding three-wheeled motor taxi loaded with passengers. His frail body landed in a puddle like a damp rag. Shopkeepers and shoppers stared in shock as he screamed in agony. No one helped him. They were too busy arguing and pointing fingers at the Lambretta driver. He lay in the muddy street clutching his leg, blood soaking his dirty black pajamas. As the crowd gathered, Lam took off his conical straw hat and wiped his forehead. Instantly, five young Amerasian boys moved out of the shadows like cockroaches. They stole a chicken, a loaf of bread, a bag of rice, a string of fish, and a bottle of Ba-Muy-Ba beer. They surreptitiously lifted the goods from their owners with the deftness of a London pickpocket—all but the scrawny plucked chicken.

The old woman saw Nguyen filch the chicken and yelled *"Doe—mae!"*

Alerted by the old woman, the fat Chinaman began to scream, "Thief, thief! He stole my chicken! That boy stole my chicken," he wailed, pointing at Nguyen running down the street.

Lam kicked the stay from under the wheel of an overloaded vegetable cart and gave it a nudge. It rolled into the street, spilling some of its contents in the path of a motorbike. The cyclist veered to avoid the cart and struck several bicyclists. Pandemonium reigned for precious seconds. The Lambretta boy, no longer the center of attention, got to his feet and ran like the wind, snatching a bunch of bananas as he flew up an alley. Stealth and speed meant survival, because street thugs like Waa would kill a kid for a bottle of beer and a trip through the jade gate with their favorite whore.

The gang's rendezvous sight was a nipa-palm *hootch* on the edge of a squatter's village. It was built on bamboo poles and lay out over what they called the River of Perfumes, a fetid privy ditch infested with mosquitos and rats. The rats were an added benefit to the accommodations. If things didn't go well in a foray, they were invited for dinner. The boys had perfected elaborate traps to catch them. But tonight the rats were safe. The take was good.

They boiled the rice and the chicken, and in the Vietnamese style chopped the bird into little pieces, bones and all, which they mixed with the rice. Seasoned with *noucmam* from a previous raid, it was a tasty meal for seven wild seeds of the American Army. Their fathers would have been proud of the way they had conducted the mission.

They ate quickly and in silence, as if at any moment

someone would barge through the door and take the food from them. Trinh broke the silence as the rain began to attack the thatched roof of their *hootch*. "Lam, let's go to America. We can steal a boat and go on the sea."

Tran, the small boy who had bounced off the side of the Lambretta, answered. "It's too far, Trinh. We would die on the sea."

Nguyen, with his moon black face, nodded in agreement.

Lam looked over his scrawny band of boy-men. "We don't have to go all the way to America by the sea. There are refugee camps in Malaysia and Thailand. We could become boat people and go there. In a refugee camp our fathers can find us."

"Let's go, Lam! Let's go tomorrow," said Dong, a scrawny boy of twelve.

Lam thought for a moment before he spoke. "No! We must make a plan. Tomorrow we go to the docks. When we find the right boat . . . we go to Malaysia."

"Lam, where is Malaysia?" said Trinh.

"It's right next to America, you zipperhead," said Dong with a smile.

The boys fell asleep to the heavy smell of joss sticks to keep away demons and mosquitos. Then the rain came in torrential waves, cleansing the squalor of the River of Perfumes running below their *hootch*. When Lam fell asleep, in his dream he always saw the face of the scrawny Vietnamese kid sitting in the shadows of an old French villa with peeling stucco. But he couldn't warn the others no matter how hard he tried. It was just a blurry recurring nightmare that always ended in a cold sweat.

The kid had been sitting there every night for months and he witnessed the entire operation. Quietly scurrying like a rat, he picked up Trinh's trail and silently followed him down the alley. Through the fog of sleep Lam tried to warn Trinh. But Trinh couldn't hear. He was dead. He had died at sea.

They came at three in the morning. They pushed through the thatched door and snatched the boys out of their sleep, holding them by the scruff of their necks like animals. By the light of a lantern Waa scanned the terrified faces until he came to Lam. Pointing a bony finger at him, he yelled, "You are the one! You are the one!" He turned quickly to look at the street waif for confirmation, and the snake struck out like a black hooded cobra.

Lam kicked Waa as hard as he could. But the impact of the blow only angered him. There was nothing he could do. His malnourished body didn't have the strength to fight off a grown man whose business was fighting.

"You little insect. Let's see how you like the cane."

While two men held Lam, Waa beat him with a bamboo cane. The blows waled the bare skin and caused a stinging pain that seared into his brain. With each blow Waa grimaced and cursed and spit, and with each blow Lam swore he would kill them all. Even in his dream the blow of the cane burned like fire. Lam was near unconsciousness from pain when Waa picked him up by his neck and held him suspended above the floor. He growled directly into his face, spitting through the gap caused by his missing teeth.

"Don't ever come back to Cholon, boy, or I will kill you." He viciously threw Lam to the floor and stomped on his chest. In agony Lam listened to the caning of the other boys. Their screams haunted his dreams.

They were fortunate boys. Waa wanted to killed the boys, dump their bodies in the privy ditch, and return to his favorite bar. But his benefactor was a devout Buddhist who wanted only to drive the boys to another district, and Waa couldn't afford to anger him. So he settled for the pleasure of beating the little American bastards to unconsciousness and throwing them in the *binjo* ditch. Skinny Choi's death was unintended. Lam's dream was interrupted as he lay sobbing in the soft, life-giving mud of the delta. Instructor Taufaudy barged into the back of the classroom and yelled at the top of his lungs. "On your feet! On your feet! On your feet!"

As Lam jumped to attention he glanced at the clock on the wall. He had dozed off for only a minute, a brief time of living hell.

"I promise!" he said to himself. "I promise! I'm gonna cut off Waa's balls and stuff them down his throat!"

CHAPTER 3

Commander Derek Evans was in a hurry. He was still ten minutes late when he dropped out of the foothills above San Diego and headed down Interstate 94 at eighty miles per hour. He pushed the Porsche 928 hard through east San Diego and had cut his trip by nearly one hour when he crossed the Coronado Bridge. The car's rack and pinion steering made it a delight to handle as he zipped through traffic, and the eight-cylinder engine gave it enormous acceleration. It was an "E" ticket ride and Evans loved every bit of it. Good guns, parachutes, and cars were his passions. His Porsche 928 was a dream machine that had cost him several years' worth of military pay.

Evans was by nature a punctual man. He hated being late for anything. One couldn't survive in the SEALs without that character trait. His return from the SEAL desert training camp at Niland, California, had been delayed by military politics, a subject he hated with equal passion. Evans could have taken a chopper back to Coronado with the general and earned a few brownie points with his prospective new boss, the commodore of the West Coast teams, but that would have meant trusting his dream machine to one of the enlisted crew to drive back to San Diego. He chose to drive the four-hour trip in three hours

23

and take his chances with the cops. He knew Master Chief Saleen would make good use of lost time. Young men were like molding clay in his hands.

Like most SEALs, Derek Evans was a high-risk taker who always had an alternate plan. He was a handsome man with a Robert Conrad face that added to his natural charisma. In addition to being an expert parachutist, a superb diver, and an outstanding shot with any kind of weapon, he was accomplished in martial arts. In his career in the SEALs, he had seen and done just about everything. With a proven track record of high performance from seaman shooter in a SEAL platoon to commander with two master's degrees, his hard-nosed attitude was tolerated in view of his brilliance as a combat leader. Troops willingly followed him and the brass knew it. Men trusted Derek Evans, and those who could, like Master Chief Saleen and Senior Chief Masure, followed him from command to command whenever he transferred. As soon as the scuttlebutt hit the street that Evans was next in line for command of SEAL Team Five, the detailer was deluged with transfer requests.

Evans slowed his pace in the streets of Coronado. From years of experience he knew where to do the speed limit. The police of the island community made their living off young sailors who didn't know where the speed traps were set. South of the Hotel Del Coronado he made a sharp right turn at twenty-five miles per hour into the ocean side of the Naval Amphibious Base and quickly wheeled around SEAL Team Five, a huge fenced compound with large red signs every twenty feet that read Restricted Area. He pulled up in front of the Naval Special Warfare Center and out of habit automatically began to wheel the Porsche into his parking spot, the one clearly marked Executive Officer. It was occupied by a rental car. Still a few minutes late and annoyed by the offender, he parked directly behind the rental car and walked briskly to the quarterdeck.

"Carroll, find the SOB who parked in my spot and have him report to the master-at-arms immediately," he said to the petty officer of the watch. "When he moves that rent-a-bitch, park my car and put the keys on my desk. And, Carroll."

"Yes, sir!"

"If you put a scratch on it, I'll tear off your . . ." Evans stopped in midsentence and with a grin slammed his keys down on the counter. He turned and crossed the quarterdeck in four quick steps before Carroll could speak.

"Yes, sir, XO, sir! Right away, sir! It'll be a pleasure to park that car, after I get that lady to move her jalopy," he yelled. Evans glanced back at Carroll with a quizzical look as he hurried into the noisy compound behind the quarterdeck. The grinder inside the Naval Special Warfare Center was a large six-hundred-foot-square compound of asphalt almost completely enclosed by buildings. It was a sort of living room for the Center, used for just about everything from calisthenics, which the trainees called PT, short for physical torture, to class graduations. On the façade of one of the buildings was a huge sign painted in big block letters: THE COWARDS NEVER STARTED AND THE WEAK DIED ALONG THE WAY. Underneath was a meticulously polished ship's bell and below it were two green helmets.

Two students have already quit and the course hasn't really started, he thought. When SEAL trainees quit it was customary to ring the ship's bell and place their helmets in a line in front of the First Phase Office. By Hell Week there would be more helmets than trainees.

On his way to the classroom, Evans passed a group of trainees doing PT. A well-muscled instructor was on the podium leading the exercise, and as he counted "Down, up, down, up," the trainees kept a numerical count. The instructor was effortlessly counting off beats when one of the trainees spotted Evans and yelled, "Commander Evans!" A hundred trainees thunderously echoed a traditional greeting. "Hoo yah, Commander Evans."

Evans had a recurring thought. *I would stop this nonsense if I could. I can't go anywhere without half the base knowing where I am.*

Inside the classroom, Saleen clearly heard the announcement as he lectured on the keys to success in SEAL training. Evans entered a narrow room that separated two enormous classrooms and peered through a small window in the door. He saw Saleen on the podium. The room was full of young men dressed in green fatigues. They all sported extremely short haircuts. In fact, they had no hair. Several instructors were standing in the rear of the class listening to the lecture. Then he also saw something unusual for BUDS. Sitting in the back of the room was a woman. Her dress and long hair were clearly out of place in a man's world of short hair and sweat. Petty Officer Carroll's words came back to him: "It'll be a pleasure to park that car after I get that *lady* to move her jalopy."

Who the hell is she? he thought as he opened the door. Saleen had already spotted him through the window. He never missed a thing.

"On your feet!" yelled Saleen. The noise of ninety-eight men thundered as they scrambled to get to attention. Evans couldn't help but notice that the woman jumped up, too. The curve of her perfect figure, dressed smartly in a tight business suit, was strikingly out of place in a room full of green fatigues. As he walked slowly down the center aisle toward the front of the room he caught the scent of her perfume. It was jasmine, and it contrasted sharply with the musty smell of moldy boots, bad breath, and dank seawater.

When silence ruled, Saleen barked, "Take seats!" As soon as they were down he yelled, "On your feet! . . . Take seats! . . . On your feet!" This was a routine that served several functions, but mostly it cleared their sleepy heads. Trainees were always sleepy, even on day one. When Evans reached the platform in the front of the class he turned and faced the attentive eyes of ninety-eight alert young men. "If you're twenty-five years old or older, *take seats!*" He paced the platform as half a dozen men sat down. He noticed out of the corner of his eye that the woman had taken her seat.

"Gents, I have been a SEAL longer than those of you standing have been alive," he said sternly. *"Take seats!"* he commanded.

The instructors in the back of the classroom caught Evans's attention. They were smiling at each other and pointing at the woman. She had been jumping up and down with the trainees with each bark of the orders and they had been watching her with great amusement. It was her butt they were gawking at, of that Evans had no doubt. To the seasoned instructors the sight was hilarious. Caught up in the moment one of them turned his face to the wall, stifling laughter. Evans smiled inwardly as he mentally pictured the

woman acting like a trainee. But he showed no outward sign
of amusement. One had to be a good actor to be a good
leader. He spoke with a confident tone and a cold, unemo-
tional countenance.

"Now that I've established my bona fides, gentlemen, I'm
going to tell you three things. First, you wouldn't be in this
room if you didn't have the physical ability to complete this
course. Ten thousand men applied and you gents are the
ones who get a shot at the brass ring. I repeat, you wouldn't
be in this room if you didn't have the physical ability to
finish this course."

Evans glanced around the room. He paused at a trainee
who was different from the others, a handsome kid with an
Asian face. He knew the Amerasian boy was at the Center.
But he didn't know Lam had been selected to Class 168.
Evans worked the crowd eye to eye for a few moments.

"The second thing, gents," he said, holding up two
fingers. "All the misery and hard work will be worth it a
thousand times over. When you graduate from this course,
you'll have a body engineered by professional trainers.
Women will be crawling all over you." Evans dropped his
hand to his sides, smiled, and gave a little pelvic thrust,
which stimulated the men to scream at the top of their
lungs, "Hoo yah!"

He noticed that the intensity of their reaction visibly
startled the lady. The instructors in Fourth Phase had
conditioned this group well, and when he held up his
clenched fist, the room went from a thunderous din of noise
to instant dead silence.

"You should have to pay to attend this course," he
continued. "For those of you who finish, you will have
earned the respect of every military man in the world.
Everywhere you go, people will know you are someone
special. Who's going to make it, Class One Sixty-Eight?" he
said, raising his voice in intensity.

"*Hoo yah!*" the students roared back at the tops of their
lungs. Evans let them yell for ten seconds before he smiled
and raised his fist to gain silence. It was like flipping a
switch.

"Unfortunately, gents, only about thirty of you will finish
this course. You know how I know? Because thousands of

men have tried. Your class number is One Sixty-Eight. My class number is Thirty-Eight and I have personally put several hundred men through this course."

He paused for a few seconds to let the information sink in.

"Only about thirty of you will be here six months from now. The rest of you will quit. Oh, the quitters will find an excuse to tell their friends and families." In quick machine-gun fashion he ripped off, "Excuses like my knee gave out, or my girlfriend got pregnant, my dog died, or some other cop-out reason for not finishing, and they'll justify to everybody but themselves, that they could've made it but . . . but. *But,* deep down inside they'll know they quit when things got tough."

Evans walked across the platform before he turned to look at the trainees.

"It ain't the size of the balls, gents, it's the size of the heart," he said, raising his voice. Master Chief Saleen stomped on the platform twice. Evans paced back and forth from one side of the room to the other without saying a word. His rack of ribbons, which the trainees called fruit salad because of their multicolors, echoed his years of combat service. His biceps bulged at his short-sleeve khaki shirt. SEALs need great upper-body strength to scale the sides of ships, and years of training had increased the size of his upper body. His neck was thick and his pectoral muscles pushed the ribbon bar and the trident away from his chest.

"The quitters will know they *quit* when the going got tough. Gents, this is physically and mentally the hardest course in the military. Don't doubt that! It is! And there is a reason for it. But no matter how hard it is, if you're mentally strong, you'll do it. You wouldn't be in this room if you didn't have the physical ability to complete this course," he said, shaking one finger in the air for emphasis.

"Make a commitment to yourself." In a machine-gun fashion he rattled off, "Not to me, not to your father, not to your mother, and not to your girlfriend, but"—he paused for effect—"to yourself," he said, shaking his finger. "Make a commitment to yourself that nothing, *nothing* will stop you from finishing this course. *Nothing!*" he yelled. "Not the instructors, not a sore knee, not a pregnant girlfriend, not blisters on your feet, nothing. *NOTHING!*" he yelled with a fierceness that vibrated the windows.

Speaking very quickly, he said, "You know how they make a samurai sword, gents? Master craftsmen take a piece of high-quality steel and they fire it until it glows red hot. They beat the hell out of it until it's flat like a sword and they plunge it into ice-cold water. Then they heat it again until it glows white hot, bend it double, and do it over and over and over again." He glanced around the room with a wild-eyed look. "They do it over and over and over according to a secret process, and with each step the steel gets stronger and stronger and stronger. The fire, the pounding, and the cold water combined with the secret process stress the metal to its limits and make it stronger. Only after the steel is tempered do they shape it into a weapon, a weapon so awesome that even to utter the words gives one a shiver of respect. The samurai sword!" he said with icy calm. "This course is like that."

Evans turned and walked toward Master Chief Saleen.

"For those of you who stick it out, we are going to change you forever. But only those that are truly committed will finish." Evans eyed them with a serious expression. "It ain't the size of the balls, gents, it's the size of the heart that counts," he growled.

For emphasis Saleen stomped on the platform twice.

"We are going to push you to your personal wall so you can see what's there. We'll heat you up physically and mentally until you are red hot, and then plunge you into the cold Pacific again and again and again, until you are strong physically and mentally. I promise you, if you finish this course you will leave as men and everyone will know it by the look in your eye. We have a secret process here at BUDS. Physical exertion is our fire, fear of the unknown is our hammer, and the Pacific Ocean is our cleansing water. If you make it through this course people will know you are someone special just by the way you carry yourself."

Evans paced the platform without speaking. "If you finish, we'll give you a ticket to the game and shape you into an awesome weapon. If you quit we'll get you a clean rack, three squares, and a set of orders out of here. Class One Sixty-Eight, who's going to make it?"

The entire classroom exploded. The men yelled for twenty seconds before Evans held up his fist. As they fell silent he stuck two fingers in the air.

"The *third thing,* gents," he said, shaking three fingers, "it's worth it. You'll lead a life of adventure that most men only read about. From jumping out of airplanes at thirty thousand feet to diving on coral heads in the South Pacific, you'll do it—not just read about it, you'll do it. You'll see the world from Colombia to Korea, from Java to Norway, and not from a porthole or the inside of a bar. You'll see it. If you hang with us, we'll change you, *forever!*" he yelled with finality. "But being a SEAL is not about jumping out of airplanes at thirty thousand feet, or diving on coral heads in the South Pacific. It's about preparing for war. It's about survival in shitty little places your mother never heard of. Before you sign on with us, gents, know this to be true. This is a dangerous profession. Before you break trail with us with a loaded gun in your hand, you'll have to prove yourself. We can't afford quitters in our business. It's not a part of the plan. Teamwork. Teamwork is the key to survival in Special Operations."

Saleen stomped on the platform and the sound of his foot was joined by the ten instructors in the back of the room stomping on the floor like bulls in heat.

Evans searched the crowd for the look he knew was the one of a winner. He glanced at Lieutenant Owen. "He'll make it," he said to himself. He looked at Lam. "This one is definitely a survivor, but is he a team player? Blond will make it. He's got a fire in his eyes." He liked what he saw and smiled deviously, knowing what lay ahead.

"We know you lack confidence in yourself. We'll give you confidence. We know you don't have the skills of a warrior. We'll teach you those skills. We know you need to grow physically. We'll make you strong. If you commit your everything, we'll make you strong physically and mentally. But first you have to show us you have the heart for this business. Do you understand me?"

The class erupted spontaneously with a determined scream of "Hoo yah." They stomped on the floor like their instructors until Evans stopped them with a clenched fist.

"BUDS is like the obstacle course taken to the tenth

power. Some of the obstacles may seem foolish, like drown-proofing. Why would anyone purposely tie a man's hands behind his back, bind his feet together, and make him swim fifty meters like a dolphin? The answer is confidence, gents. Confidence! We'll turn you into a water-breathing mother . . ." Evans paused in midsentence and looked at the woman in the back of the room. She was glued to his every word. He decided not to curse.

"Drown-proofing sounds impossible now. But it'll be child's play in a few months. There are hundreds of obstacles in BUDS, like Hell Week, pool competency, long-distance runs, long swims. There is a reason for each of these obstacles. BUDS is a secret process born of men who have gone to war and survived. Warriors don't love war any more than doctors love cancer; they just deal with it. If you are here for glory, you're here for the wrong reason. If you're having second thoughts about your personal commitment, I want you to see Instructor Masure after class and we'll help you get a decent set of orders."

Evans looked at Master Chief Saleen, then at the instructors in the back of the room.

"Know this to be true. Before you walk the trail with us we'll test every fiber in your mind and body. We don't care how good an athlete you are. We'll stretch your personal rubber band to its limit. Lieutenant Owen. You're a triathlete. Are you going to make it through this course?" he asked, addressing a muscular young lieutenant in the front row. Owen was the class leader and Evans wanted to focus attention on him.

"Yes, XO. I'll be here for graduation," he said shaking his head in the affirmative. Evans stared him in the eye.

"Are you sure, Lieutenant?"

He stared back and responded with calm determination in his voice. "Nothing can make me quit this course, sir. Nothing!"

Evans liked the cool, calculated response. *Maybe that silver spoon he was raised with didn't ruin him after all,* he said to himself.

Looking around, he stopped at the half-Asian face sitting near the back of the room. "Are you going to make it, Seaman Lam?" he asked in Vietnamese.

"Hoo yah, XO, I make it," answered Lam in English.

Evans continued, "This is the most difficult training course in the world and I know from experience that most of you will quit when the going gets tough. It's easy to sit here and say you won't. But unless you have a real fire in your gut, you won't make it. Are you committed, sailor?" he yelled at a kid about to drop off to sleep.

"Yes, Master Chief," blurted out the sleepy trainee.

Saleen exploded. "Hit the surf, maggot! Report to Fourth Phase. You're out of here until you can tell the difference between a commander and a master chief." Evans continued without missing a beat as the kid ran out the door like a frightened jackrabbit.

"The instructors play the part of war. With sleep deprivation, cold water, and brutal physical training they'll push you to your physical limit so you can see what's there. If you quit along the way here in beautiful Southern California, you'll quit in the middle of enemy territory. And, gents"—Evans paused for a long beat—"we can't afford a quitter in our midst. Are you going to make it, Petty Officer Robinson?" he yelled at a stocky, blue-eyed blond who had the makings of a linebacker.

Robinson screamed at the top of his lungs, "Hoo yah!" and continued to yell with a fierceness and intensity that caused Evans to chuckle out loud. Evans had to hold up his fist to stop him.

"Sure kid, sure, but you have to show me, not deafen me." *This one will definitely make it,* he thought. *He's got a fire in his gut.*

Evans looked the men over slowly.

"Now I'm going to ask you one more time. Are you committed to finishing this course, Class One Sixty-Eight?" The classroom thundered with screams of *Hoo yah.* After raising a clenched fist, Evans spoke quietly in grave tones.

"If you're not, I want you to see Instructor Masure after class. If you have any doubt at all, I want you out. We'll help you get a good set of orders. For those who remain and quit before Hell Week, I will personally detail your ass to the most undesirable place on earth."

Evans's problem was simple. The bean counters in Washington. Captain May was under tremendous pressure to bring down attrition. He had drafted Evans as XO to get BUDS under control. Evans knew that good up-front screening could exclude those who didn't have the necessary physical skills to complete the course, so he created a corral called Fourth Phase where sharp-eyed instructors culled the herd before selection to BUDS. Today's speech and veiled threats were an extension of the corral and his last chance to count the losers in another course number. After day one the computer took over and the losses counted against the course the Navy called BUDS, Basic Underwater Demolition/SEAL training.

"Three things, gents, three things," he said, holding up three fingers.

"You wouldn't be here if you didn't have the physical ability to finish this course," said Evans, shaking one finger like a preacher. Shaking two fingers, he continued. "And it's worth all the misery a hundred times over. If you're committed, I'll give you a misery strategy. On your feet!" he commanded roughly. The class quickly jumped to attention. Evans noticed the woman was on her feet and staring wide-eyed at him as he stepped off the platform into the silent room.

"Close your eyes for a moment and visualize this in your mind's eye. When the going gets really tough, visualize this image. Imagine you are seated on the grinder on Graduation Day, your graduation. The sun is shining and the Navy band is playing. Your name is called and you walk proudly to the podium where Captain May hands you a folder that contains your graduation certificate. When you get back to your seat you open it and see your name on the diploma, and"—he paused a few seconds—"and next to it is a check for one million dollars."

Evans raised his voice like an evangelist. "Would that motivate you to complete this course on a broken leg, Class One Sixty-Eight?"

The room exploded and Evans let them yell until the noise fell off naturally. "This course is worth more than a million dollars, gents. Much more. Remember that."

As he walked down the center aisle toward the back door

he looked directly at the woman for an instant. She was beautiful and out of place. *What the hell is she doing here?* he thought.

The sound of his shoes on the floor broke the dead silence in the room. At the door he turned to address the young men frozen at attention, staring at the front of the room. Curious, the woman had turned around to watch him leave. She was studying him like a bug in a petri dish.

"Oh, by the way, gents, the *fourth* thing"—he paused for dramatic effect—*"the cowards never started!"* The room exploded with committed voices, each in their own private way determined to graduate from basic SEAL training.

CHAPTER

4

Evans was satisfied with the talk he had given to Class 168. He made his points and his thoughts quickly shifted to other matters as he headed toward his office. Halfway across the grinder a gorgeous black petty officer, immaculately dressed in a crisp white uniform, fell into step beside him.

"XO, may I have a word with you, sir," she pleaded.

"Certainly, Petty Officer Nixon," he said, adjusting his mind from theory to the real world. "What's up?"

"Sir, I need your signature right away on those messages Linda put on your desk yesterday."

"You bet. Give me thirty minutes, then come pick 'em up."

"XO, you haven't seen your desk, have you, sir?" warned Nixon, shaking her head in pity.

He looked at her with a nod of recognition.

"And sir, the admiral is on board. I saw him with the skipper while you were with Class One Sixty-Eight."

"Thanks, Pam. By the way, you see those two helmets under the bell."

"Yes, sir. I know. Find out who they are and send them to Adak."

"Smart girl," he said with a chuckle.

Evans shunned the thought of his desk. On it lay every

35

kind of problem a man could imagine, from the requirement to give an all-hands lecture on sexual harassment to
a sealed envelope with the name of a young person positive for HIV. He was deep in thought when a burly chief
petty officer approached in a huff. The chief was too heavy
for a SEAL operator and had seen his best days in
the teams. Evans tolerated his excesses and mistakes
because the Junkyard Dawg had proven himself fearless in
combat.

"XO, I'm going to kick the shit outta that fat civilian in
Scheduling. I told him three weeks ago to schedule the Navy
band for next Friday. He says he forgot."

"Did you send him a memo, Junkyard?"

"Nah. You know how I hate to write, sir. All he had to do
was make a call and send out a damn form letter. Shit, sir, it
ain't like we don't have graduation eight times a fuckin'
year." The burly chief shook his head. "One of these days
I'm gonna pound the shit out of that fat son of a bitch. I
know he does this kind of shit just to piss me off."

Junkyard was the master-at-arms and as the command
sheriff he did a good job keeping the troops to standards.
But like most SEALs, he was a disaster when it came to
paperwork. Evans looked at him with exasperation. The
scheduler, a civilian employee, hated Junkyard with a
passion and would do just about anything to jab him in the
eye with a sharp stick. Junkyard Ballard was an abrasive
man who had turned rubbing people the wrong way into an
art form. To Junkyard, if you weren't a SEAL you were a
maggot.

"Rent that damn circus-looking band again," ordered
Evans. "And Junkyard, send Scheduling a memo next time.
Write it on a bar napkin or something. That won't hurt your
image."

"No, XO. That's a great idea," he said, thoughtfully
rubbing the stubble on his chin. "I'll get some from the
Chief's Club with anchors on 'em," he said seriously.

Before Evans could take two steps Senior Chief Masure
caught up with him and kept pace as he continued around
the edge of the grinder. Masure was the class proctor for
168, the trainees' best friend. The instructors took turns as

proctor, because the hours were long and none of them really liked being the good guy. It was more fun playing hard-ass instructor.

"Well, sir, the helmets are already startin' to line up underneath the bell. After your little talk four guys quit. We'll have them out of here before the day's over," he said proudly.

"Seven down, sixty-three to go," said Evans without breaking stride. "Actually, Stick, we need about forty out of this class to feed the losses in the teams. What do you think of One Sixty-Eight?"

"It's a good class, Boss. I think a lot of them will make it. The class leader, Lieutenant Owen, is outstanding. The LPO, Ryeback, is strong. He's got fleet experience. There's a lot of good men in this class. I'm guessing we'll make thirty-eight, maybe forty." Masure smiled deviously. "I'm pickin' out the best for Team Five," he bragged.

Evans stopped dead in his tracks and looked Masure directly in the eye.

"And why would you be stacking the deck at Five, Senior?"

"Well, sir, I'm up for orders in a few months and I only want the best in my command," he said, smiling. "You never know, sir; one of these little bastards might be in my platoon someday."

Masure and Evans had served on many of the same teams, and he was glad a man of his caliber had chosen to serve under his command. Masure had been "one of those little bastards" in training when Evans had been an instructor more than a decade ago. He wasn't a little bastard anymore. *Funny how they grow up so confident and cocky,* he thought, looking at Masure's sly smile.

"Stick, make sure Student Control counts the losses against Pretraining," he said, calling Masure by his nickname, a handle derived from *measuring stick.*

"Roger that," said Masure, heading out for Student Control.

Class 168 began to jog across the grinder in formation. Robinson, the big blond, led a chant that the entire class repeated.

Everywhere we go, oh (Everywhere we go, oh)
People want to know, oh (People want to know, oh)
Who we are (Who we are)

The sound faded as they picked up the pace and ran down the road behind the confines of the grinder. Evans watched in amusement. For some reason, SEAL trainees never sounded as good as Rangers or Green Berets. Halfway across the grinder Evans had a bad feeling about his car so he headed for the quarterdeck to check on Petty Officer Carroll. The boy needed adult leadership. He wasn't above reparking the Porsche by way of Imperial Beach or maybe even La Jolla. At the grinder entrance to the quarterdeck he ran into Carroll struggling at the door with a cup of coffee in each hand.

"Carroll, did you get that SOB out of my parking spot?" demanded Evans.

"Huh, well—huh, no, sir. Not yet, sir."

Evans looked at the steaming coffee. "I'll bet one of those is for me, huh, Petty Officer Carroll?"

"Yes, sir—I mean, no, sir. I mean, ambush rear, sir."

"Commander, I asked Mr. Carroll for the coffee," said a female voice from behind him. The lady who had been jumping up and down like a trainee stepped forward.

"I'll take those, Mr. Carroll. Thank you," she said politely.

"And, Commander, I'm sorry to say so, but I'm the SOB who parked in your spot. Admiral Arlington advised me not to miss your lecture. Unfortunately, I left his office a little late and your space was the only one open. I hope I haven't inconvenienced you," she said apologetically.

Evans found himself staring, mouth agape, at a professionally dressed woman of thirty-something. He couldn't tell her age accurately. She was in excellent physical condition, intelligent by her manner of speech, and beautiful. It was clear from the way she carried herself that she knew it. She had the most perfect teeth and sensuous figure Evans had seen in months. He was just about to say, "And just who are you?" when Petty Officer Carroll interrupted. "Attention on deck!"

"Carry on, carry on," said Admiral George Arlington, a

tall patrician-looking officer dressed in whites. Even without the gold all over his uniform, one could tell he was important. Arlington possessed the air of one who considered himself important, and he was. He was the head of Naval Special Warfare and the most senior SEAL in the U.S. Navy. He approached confidently and smiled elegantly, betraying his Naval Academy background.

"Well, I see you two have met."

"No, sir, not yet!" said Evans emphatically.

"Well then, I'll do the honors. Dr. Harris, this is Commander Derek Evans, soon to be the commanding officer of one of my SEAL teams. Derek, this is Dr. Alysin Harris, from Georgetown University." Harris handed the admiral a cup of coffee and kept the second cup for herself. "Thank you, Doctor," he said. "Nothing like a good cup of Navy coffee to brace up the morning."

"Pleased to meet you, Dr. Harris," growled Evans, lost for words.

"Admiral, I just heard Commander Evans's opening speech to Class One Sixty-Eight and as you promised it was inspirational and insightful to say the least. This is going to be the most interesting Pentagon project I've ever worked on."

Evans was bewildered. "Admiral, am I missing something?" he asked, gesturing with his hands in an amphibious salute Arlington understood.

"Perhaps. I understand you've been in the desert with Captain Cameron, showing General Ashton our new facilities?"

"Yes, sir."

Arlington paused for a moment as if searching for the right words. He looked at Petty Officer Carroll and then back at Evans. "Dr. Harris has been assigned to study leadership in the Special Forces. She will begin her study here at BUDS."

"Admiral, you have got to be kidding me. We've been through . . ."

"No, I am not, Commander!" Arlington interrupted abruptly. "I expect you to extend your full cooperation and courtesy to Dr. Harris," he said, looking directly at Evans in a manner that was all business. Admiral Arlington had other matters on his mind and he was in no mood for brashness. His major interest was hunting down a Russian mafioso. BUDS was on the bottom of his list of problems. For some reason the Chief of Naval Operations had taken a personal interest in reducing the attrition in the course and he was under heat to solve the problem, a minor problem compared with a load of missing nuclear warheads.

"Commander, I have the distinct impression you have reservations about the efficacy of my project," stated Harris politely.

"Well, yes. I can't imagine what you might discover that hasn't already been published. We've been through this before, Dr. Harris," he said, giving her the evil eye.

"Oh, I don't know, Commander. I've already learned a few things I've never seen in publication, like"—she paused for dramatic effect—"it ain't the size of the balls that counts, it's the size of the heart," she said with an arrogant toss of her head.

With that comment Arlington became visibly uncomfortable. He coughed a polite a-hum, and said, "Well, I can see you two are going to get along splendidly. Derek, Dr. Harris will be in your office in thirty minutes to brief you into this program."

"Program, sir?" inquired Evans.

Arlington ignored the question and addressed Harris. "Dr. Harris, please allow me to show you around the Naval Special Warfare Center."

"Thank you, Admiral. I would be delighted."

Evans couldn't help but stare in disbelief as they walked off. And he couldn't help but stare at her posterior.

"Program. Not project? Program?" *Program* was a word used by the military to describe secret-compartmented information that required signing security release forms. *Nothing but trouble,* he thought. *Nothing but trouble.*

Carroll read the worry lines on Evans's face. "Admit nothing, deny everything, and make counteraccusations, sir. Shall I move the commander's car now?"

"Yeah! But don't scratch it!"

Evans was working over a two-foot pile of paperwork when the secretary knocked at his door. As executive officer, he did all the paperwork for the command. Without Linda Hall he would have been constantly late and continuously harassed by visitors. She looked at him and shook her head in pity.

"XO, a Ms. Harris to see you, sir." He decided to make Harris wait.

"Linda, give me five minutes and show her in."

"Yes, sir. XO?"

"Yeah."

"Watch yourself with this one, sir. Call it woman's intuition. She's a man-eater."

Evans looked up again and smiled. His immediate thoughts were carnal but he said nothing. The phone hadn't stopped ringing and he needed two days just to dig himself out from under the pile of paper on his desk.

In precisely five minutes Linda opened the door. "XO, Ms. Harris to see you."

"Linda, get these messages to Petty Officer Nixon right away," he said, handing several folders across the desk.

"Yes, sir. She's outside waiting for them," she said, closing the door behind Harris.

Evans stood and gestured toward a seat across from his desk. When they were seated she spoke first. "Commander Evans, I hope we didn't get off to a bad start this morning."

"Not at all, Dr. Harris. Not at all."

"Please call me Alysin," she said assertively.

"Derek," responded Evans.

"I could tell by your lecture this morning that you're a straightforward man who doesn't tolerate a load of bullshit."

"Correct. So cut to the chase, Alysin," he said in a businesslike manner.

"You would've told me to fuck off this morning if the admiral hadn't been there. Right?"

"Dr. Harris . . . uh . . . Alysin," he stammered. "I'm beginning to like you. Those are most unusual words for a Ph.D. assigned to study leadership." He stood up, walked around the desk, and extended his hand in a friendly manner. She accepted it with a firm and confident grip. When Evans was seated in the chair next to her, she continued in a direct manner.

"I have a Ph.D., Commander, but I'm not here to study leadership."

"Let me guess. That's your cover story, isn't it, Agent Harris?"

"Exactly. You know the procedure, Commander. Please sign the disclosure form and I'll brief you into Operation Fastback," she said, extending a folded sheet of paper.

Evans took it and walked behind his desk to sign it. While he was occupied, Harris perused the pictures and plaques on his office wall.

"Ok! What's this all about?" insisted Evans, extending the security form.

"This picture right here," responded Harris, taking an eight-by-ten photograph off his wall. She studied it for a few more seconds before handing it to Evans.

"You've lost me."

"It's a lousy picture, Commander. Why do you keep it so close?"

"Personal reasons."

"Tell me about it," she demanded brazenly.

"I'd rather not. It's just a reminder of a close encounter of an intimate kind with our opposition behind the Iron Curtain," he confessed with serious eyes that didn't blink.

Evans looked down at the photo. It was a picture of himself standing in the middle of a group of men and women in sweaty PT gear. It had been taken in Indonesia while his SEAL platoon was on a special mission. Shooter, Stick, Wild Bill, and he were hoisting beer bottles with several expatriates of various nationalities. Harris had recognized the Spetznaz among the expatriates. Karpenko, Saraskina, Voschanov, and Suburov were among the crowd.

"What's this got to do with anything, Harris?" demanded Evans.

"Three things, Commander, *three things!*" she said, shaking three fingers in the air, pantomiming his lecture to Class 168.

"First," she said holding out one finger, "some of your old friends are no longer behind the Iron Curtain, or what's left of it."

"I don't have any friends behind the Iron Curtain, Agent Harris," cautioned Evans.

"Second," she said, holding up two fingers, "they've absconded with several nuclear weapons. The way Karpenko feels about you, I wouldn't be surprised if San Diego disappears in a blinding white flash."

Evans's mind was working at warp speed. Everyone knew the Soviet Union was flying apart at the seams and no one knew what was happening to the awesome Soviet arsenal. The realization of what Karpenko and his thugs had done came to him. They had taken advantage of the crumbling Soviet Empire. During his assignment in Indonesia, Evans had learned a great deal about the Spetznaz, and one fact stood out above the rest. They were absolutely ruthless.

"You seem to know a great deal about me, Agent Harris, or is it Dr. Harris?"

"Alysin."

"Yeah. Right."

"Trust me, Commander, I do. It's my job."

"I get nervous anytime anyone says trust me. So what are we doing to get this weapon back?" asked Evans, studying her face for clues. He used the singular case on purpose to see her reaction.

"Weapons, Commander. Weapons."

"How many?"

"Three."

"What type?"

"To answer your initial question, Commander," interjected Harris, "we are doing everything humanly possible. We've formed a coalition of special forces, GSG-Nine, SAS, Delta, Six, and even some Spetznaz. We've formed a special task force composed of members from the CIA, MI-Six, the Mossad, and several other related agencies to help track down every lead. And you, sir, are one of those leads." She ignored his question concerning the type of nuclear weapons Karpenko had stolen.

"I take it the Agency hasn't been able to locate the weapons by satellite?" he pried.

"Correct. They've surveyed every inch of the planet. Nothing. Not a trace. We've even tried to quietly buy them back through third parties. No deal. It seems Major General Karpenko is a very cautious man."

"So how do I fit into the equation, Harris?" asked Evans in an exhausted voice.

"As the CO of SEAL Team Five, you—and your men—will be all over Korea. Right?"

"Correct."

"We have reason to believe North Korea is his primary client. You served in South Korea with the Black Beret. Right?"

"That's right."

"Karpenko served in North Korea at about the same time. Koreans talk to Koreans, even across the border. With your contacts, you may hear something."

"No way. But do go on, Agent Harris," demanded Evans.

"SEAL Team Five is the best commando team in the Pacific Theater. They are assigned as second-string forces for Operation Fastback."

"Why are you briefing me into this program? I'm not the CO yet."

"You will be soon." She smiled.

"Doesn't flush, Harris. Doesn't flush at all. There is something you're not telling me."

Harris ignored his accusation. She was authorized only to brief him into Operation Fastback at a low level.

"Commander, I've read all the official reports about your MTT to Indonesia." MTT was the military acronym for *mobile training team*. "What I need from you is a complete and thorough briefing of your close encounter of an intimate kind, everything in the minutest detail. Let's start this evening over dinner," she ordered with probing eyes. She knew a little food and wine would relax him and soften his belligerent mood. It was all in his profile.

"Sure, anything for the company. The Charthouse, nineteen-thirty. I'll get a table where we can talk privately."

"Great," said Harris, preparing to leave.

"Where do I pick you up?" Evans asked with a sharp-eyed glance.

"The lobby of the BOQ at North Island. Seven-thirty sharp. Don't bother to come in. I'll be ready," she said, walking toward the door.

"OK, Doc . . . Alysin . . . Harris—whatever your name really is. What's the third thing?"

"Wow! You don't miss a thing, do you, Commander," she said in a flattering tone. "I would have told you this evening if you hadn't asked."

"I'm asking you now."

For a long moment she stared at him with a serious expression. "We have it from a very reliable source that General Karpenko intends to kill you personally. It seems he is still suffering from the injury you inflicted with his spade."

Evans was thunderstruck and she could see it written on his face.

"Nineteen-thirty. I'll be ready," she said, before opening the door.

Evans stared down at the picture on his desk. In a flashback he saw the silver glint of a razor-sharp blade as it slashed down his chest, opening up his flesh like a melon. For a moment he could feel it hammer into his M-16. His body jerked as he recalled grasping the handle, kicking, spinning, and chopping out at an unknown assailant in the darkness of a Javanese jungle. The sound of the metal chopping into bone echoed in his mind. He slumped back deeper into his chair and took a deep breath.

I'm the bait, he thought. *They're going to dangle me like a worm all over Korea. I'm a worm and she's my handler.*

For two minutes he sat dumbstruck by his second encounter with Alysin Harris. *Man-eater, man-eater! What an understatement,* he thought as he dug into the pile of folders on his desk. He tried to focus his mind, but he couldn't concentrate on anything but their conversation.

45

CHAPTER
5

Evans whipped the 928 into the parking lot of the North Island BOQ at precisely 1930 and got out of the car. Before he could close the door he saw Harris exiting the building. Dressed in tight jeans and a red blouse that flowed over her body like water, she moved like a model down a Paris runway. She tossed her hair to one side and waved at him. As he watched her hurry down the walkway, beaming a broad smile as if he were a long-lost friend, he had a strange sensation. He felt like an animal in a cage at the zoo and people were watching his every move. It was foreboding. Out of instinct he quickly scanned the surroundings.

Alysin Harris was the perfect woman. Too perfect. She had soft facial features like Jaclyn Smith and a body like one of the girls on *Baywatch*. If Evans had been asked to create his dream girl, Alysin Harris would have been a close fit. She was intelligent, quick-witted, punctual, and obviously dedicated to a cause, all traits he admired.

I'm the bait, he thought. *Usable. Expendable. Why are they wasting so much time and effort on me? I don't get it.*

Despite the verbal fencing, Evans liked Harris. She was straightforward, outspoken, and bold. She fascinated him. He found himself staring at her lasciviously as she slipped into the soft leather seat and put on his Porsche 928 like an elegant pair of silk stockings.

The short ride to the Charthouse was filled with small talk over the rumble of the car's powerful engine. All the way Evans kept thinking, *Remember, she's a handler. She's a can opener, sent to pry into my brain.*

At the restaurant, he was aware of the eyes that followed her to their table. He checked each pair to see if he saw lust or mission. They were all men in heat watching her butt wiggle between tables.

Mistake, he thought. *If I hadn't told her the name of the restaurant I wouldn't be concerned about surveillance.* He mentally filed away the lesson for future reference. *I'm getting paranoid,* he thought. *This is stupid.*

The waiter showed them to a table in the corner that looked out over Glorietta Bay. After they ordered, Evans pressed the conversation. His mind was working overtime and he wanted to know what motivated Alysin Harris. Evans knew how to handle hotshot CIA agents. He had dealt with lots of them and he wasn't impressed by most. Before the evening was over he was determined to find out what really made Harris tick.

"Alysin, excuse me for questioning your credentials, but you seem a bit too young for a Ph.D. in psychology."

"I'm flattered, Derek. I don't usually tell a man my age, but actually I'm thirty-five. I earned my Ph.D. at twenty-seven," she bragged, "and I have been working for the . . ." Harris stopped in midsentence. She had almost forgotten Evans was not Agency. She had complete access to all the records on Commander Derek Evans and she knew he had been involved in numerous interagency operations. But he wasn't CIA. In fact, there were notes in his record that stated that he didn't have much regard for the Agency. She had studied his career like a textbook and in the process had come to know and admire him. His career spanned the gamut from Vietnam to special operations that were never made public.

Evans mentally calculated her Agency experience. *Thirty-five minus twenty-seven equals eight years. Just a novice,* he thought. "I took you for a much younger woman," he said as flattery.

"Oh, please, do go on. Like you SEALs, I work out every day, and I'm glad it shows," she said beaming a smile. Her lips seemed to beckon him.

"It shows. Believe me. It shows," he said with a grin.

After dinner the conversation turned more serious as Harris focused like a radar on her subject. She caught him staring at the lights dancing on the water, and like a clinical psychologist played his mood with finesse.

"Derek, you seem very comfortable here. Is it the wine or the location?" she asked in a soothing voice.

"Both," he said as his mind flashed back to the moment. "The wine is excellent and you are marvelous company." He took a deep breath and exhaled. "I was thinking of the first time I sat at this table gazing out over Glorietta Bay. I was nineteen years old," he said looking back at the water. "In fact, it was the night before I went to Vietnam."

"Bad memories?" inquired Harris, softly working her way to Southeast Asia.

"No. Not at all. In fact, great memories. The company was not nearly so pleasant," he continued, smiling at her. "Just a bunch of guys hell-bent for leather. We ate the biggest steaks in the Charthouse and tried to drink all the booze in the bar."

"You like Asia, don't you," she stated, steering the conversation slowly toward her objective. She knew he volunteered for every mission that deployed to Southeast Asia. "I could see it in your eyes when you said the word *Vietnam.*"

"Yes, I do."

"Me too. It's exotic and alien. Unfortunately, most of my overseas experience has been in Europe. Tell me about Indonesia," she said directly. "I've always wanted to go there."

Evans knew the game. He understood her objective and he read her eyes. "What do you want to know?" asked Evans.

"Tell me the stuff that's not in the official reports, whatever comes to mind. Just let the information flow out. Don't force it. Tell me something interesting, something funny, something scary. I want to know everything about the people in the photograph."

Evans stared out the window for a long moment without speaking. He knew she had read the secret reports describing the incident in Pasir Putih. He figured she knew all about the death of Jack Squires, but he didn't want to revive the memories at the moment. He decided to throw her a curveball, a little personality test to check her mettle. He had caught the clinical tone in her voice. He smiled and recounted a verbal picture of Java, spreading on the color like a thick layer of mayonnaise.

"In the weeks before we went to the secret Indonesian training base called Pasir Putih," he said, watching her eyes for reaction, "the Trimedia took us to El Bromo, one of the largest volcanos in Java. They call Bromo the Indonesian Sahara because the caldera is a vast sand-filled valley that looks like a desert in the Middle East. We traveled all night up the mountainside and across this huge caldera of sand and arrived at the vent just before sunrise, soaking wet with perspiration. Dressed for the equator, we promptly began to freeze our proverbial asses off."

"You're kidding me," she said, wondering what this had to do with Jack Squires's death.

"No. No, I'm serious."

"I'm not sure that this has to do with the subject at hand, but, please, do go on," she said eagerly.

"To keep warm, we had to form a body pile. The Indonesians thought this was hilarious. Even though we were near the equator, we were so high it was freezing cold. To make a long story short, the Indonesians kidded me for weeks that I had to have a warm blanket at Pasir Putih because a cold wind from El Bromo would sweep down to the sea and freeze me. At any rate, I agreed to have a warm blanket at Pasir Putih just in case."

Evans paused to ensure he had her attention.

"I'm not boring you, am I?" he asked with penetrating eyes.

"No, no. Please continue," she said eagerly.

"Well, we arrived at Pasir Putih after a ten-hour ride from hell. My room was right on the edge of the Sea of the Doldrums and from my veranda I could see the sun set over the sea. It was like glass, not a ripple on the sea or a breeze in the air. The temperature was ninety-five degrees and so was the humidity. So I sat on my veranda and waited for the cool winds of Bromo to freeze my ass. And sure enough, at about ten o'clock a breeze came up. The temperature dropped to about ninety degrees, which is cold for an Indonesian, and at about the same time my warm blanket showed up. She was a gorgeous creature. . . ."

Harris looked at Evans, perplexed, not sure if he was kidding.

"You're putting me on," she said warmly with a half-liquid smile that seemed to beg for a kiss.

"Oh, no, I'm not. I wouldn't do that," he said, smiling licentiously. Evans waited until she spoke.

"Well, what?" asked Harris impatiently.

He knew he had her. Now it was time for a little personality check. "Well, the next morning my counterpart asked me if my warm blanket was OK. I told him that the winds of El Bromo had indeed chilled my bones, and that I would need at least two warm blankets every night for the rest of our stay at Pasir Putih."

Evans chuckled as he sipped his wine, watching her carefully for a response. She looked at him, not sure what to believe. She was smart enough not to mention the name of Jack Squires and spoil the moment. Evans's tour in Indonesia was shrouded in mystery and secrecy. He had lost one man and had almost lost his own life in a jungle encounter with Karpenko and his Spetznaz. She had read and reread his daily situation reports until she had memorized every detail. They were clear and concise. However, there was a blank spot in the official record. In fact the official record stopped the day before Evans was evacuated to Subic Bay Philippines for injuries that kept him in the hospital for six months. And unlike the daily SITREPs, the after-action report was dry and uninformative. Evans had been the object of an intense recruitment effort by the KGB, orchestrated by Dimitri Karpenko. She had to gain his confidence before opening up his brain. Harris was pleased with Evans's frivolous mood. She had him where she wanted him.

"Were two warm blankets sufficient?" she inquired with a knowing smile.

"Let's say they were barely efficacious," he responded, using her five-dollar word.

"I'll bet!" she said with a giggle.

He liked her response. On the surface Harris was his kind of woman. Aggressive. Self-assured. Confident. He liked her and he decided to level with her. He knew it was her job to find out everything possible about his relationship with the Spetznaz.

"Tell me about the people in the photo," she said, urging him on.

"Well, most of the people were expates who worked in and around Surabaya. There were French, German, Italian. You name it. To counter the boredom of an overseas posting, they would get together once or twice a month and have a sort of jungle Olympics."

"You mean footraces and such?" asked Harris.

"Sort of. It was more of a social gathering than a race. A couple of guys would be chosen by lot to serve as rabbits. Their job was to blaze a trail with small bits of shredded paper, and like a rabbit lead the pack of runners back to the hole. The rabbits would mark a large circling main trail through the paddies and *campongs,* but would also mark several short dead-end trails to confuse the runners."

"I know what you mean—little false trails to confuse people," she interjected.

"Precisely. Those in front would often end up on one of the false trails and would have to double back as someone in the pack picked up the main trail."

"I see," she commented. "The false trails allowed the young and old, men and women to compete."

"Yes. After running or walking through the rice paddies for a couple of hours everyone would end back where they started and drink a lot of beer."

"Sounds like fun," said Harris.

"That was the objective. They called the club the Hash Hound Harriers because it was more like a pack of hound dogs tracking a rabbit than a footrace. Afterward, someone always cooked up international food for the get-together. All the expates around Surabaya were involved and they invited every round-eye in Java to play."

"You are not going to do the gorgeous-creature routine again, are you?" she asked seriously.

"No, no. Not again!" he said, shaking his head.

"How is it that SEALs and Spetznaz found themselves in the same part of the world at the same time and not on the opposite end of a gun?" asked Harris in a more serious tone. She already knew the answer to the question. It was just her way of leading the dance of conversation.

"After the fall of the Sukarno government, the Indonesians were working both sides of the Iron Curtain for all the aid money they could get. The Spetznaz were the last of the Russians to leave and we were the first Americans to arrive."

"So you actually ate and drank with them at the height of the Cold War?"

"Oh yeah! At first we were on friendly terms. But somehow we managed to turn everything into brutal competition. I beat Comrade Lieutenant Colonel Karpenko in the last half mile of the race and although he smiled for the photograph, he was one pissed-off hombre."

"I take it he doesn't like to lose?"

"That's a fair assessment, Dr. Harris." Evans used her title to let her know he understood the game.

"Would you say he's the kind of man who would trigger a thermonuclear device in downtown Manhattan, if cornered?"

"You bet he would! Without a second thought."

"So beating him in a footrace caused the initial falling-out?" probed Harris, delighted Evans had opened up.

"Noooo! We were mentally and physically testing each other like a couple of bulls in heat. They bought us drinks and we bought them drinks. Even the parties boiled down to competitive drinking events."

"So what happened?" asked Harris.

"I assume you have read my official reports, Dr. Harris?" chided Evans, carefully watching her eyes for a reaction.

"I have. Several times. You indicated that the Spetznaz attempted to recruit you and your men, and that Karpenko became furious when the Indonesians allowed you on board the submarines the Russians had sold them," she responded, proving her bona fides.

"Exactly," responded Evans, convinced she had done her homework. "The Indonesians had purchased two Russian submarines to run covert operations against their neighbors. Karpenko was teaching the little devils to lock in and out of the subs, under way, at night, so they could terrorize their neighbors."

"As I recall, several of them died in a training accident. Did the SEALs have anything to do with that?"

"Of course not!" snapped Evans incredulously. "Russian subs don't have escape trunks like American boats, so they lock in and out of the torpedo tubes. The Indonesians were just too small to overcome the bow pressure of the underway submarine. Several of them drowned in a forward torpedo tube, trapped behind their gear bags."

"And that caused a political schism in the GOI?" she asked. GOI was short talk for Government of Indonesia.

"Noooo! The division was already there. The faction that was trying to make peace in the region used the accident to stop the Spetznaz training program. We were invited to provide proper instruction. Since the U.S. was keenly interested in Russian submarine technology, the ambassador agreed."

"And when you took Karpenko's mission he was furious?"

"Furious, Alysin Harris, is an understatement. The loss of the mission was a huge black eye to Karpenko personally. The situation deteriorated even more when I taught the little devils how to do night dry-deck operations. It's not as dangerous as locking out underwater and in the absence of surface-search radar it is much more efficient."

"Brilliant! The Indonesians didn't need the underwater modus operandi because there was no effective surface search radar in their AO," she volunteered enthusiastically. AO was the acronym for *area of operations*.

"Alysin," said Evans, drawing out her name, "you are beginning to sound like one of Admiral Arlington's Intell weenies."

"Oh! Sorry," responded Harris with a slight blush. She was getting into the story like a high school kid seeking vicarious adventure. "Karpenko's covert mission was intelligence, wasn't it?"

"Yes. And so was mine."

"Tell me about the Spetznaz. What were they like?" she asked, eagerly leading the conversation.

"They were a friendly, boisterous sort of people who liked to drink and joke around. And they were totally ruthless when it came to getting their way."

"Your reports stated that one of them—I believe her name was Saraskina—tried to recruit you by seduction?" she asked carefully.

"Yes, that is correct," responded Evans abruptly, shutting up like a clam. Harris caught the tone in his voice but decided to press the issue.

"I'm extremely interested in their methods. Would you tell me what happened? Please," she pleaded.

Evans picked up his wineglass and sipped it. He looked at the boats tied up at the dock and collected his thoughts. Harris watched his facial features, wisely letting him ruminate the past.

"Natila Saraskina is a very beautiful woman, and very cunning. I was never sure"—he paused for a moment, gathering his thoughts—"if she . . ." Evans stumbled, looking for the right words. "I'm not sure what motivated her. For a while I actually believed she wanted to defect, and of course we were very interested in that possibility. We played the game and I met her in Denpasar for a few weekend excursions. The bottom line is, she tried to recruit me and I tried to recruit her and neither of us succeeded."

"What was she like? I mean, how did she come on?" asked Harris softly.

Evans smiled. "She was a gorgeous creature who warmed the winds of El Bromo."

Harris laughed at his pun and waited for him to continue.

"She acted like a tigress in public and came on like a fluffy, frightened little pussycat when we were alone. She was full of passion and when she had my complete undivided attention, which isn't all that hard to get, Alysin Harris, she told me that if I didn't help her Karpenko would have her parents killed. She pleaded with me to help her by providing some bullshit unclassified information to please him."

"What did you do?" asked Harris.

"If you read my reports, you know very well what we did, Alysin Harris," snapped Evans with eyes ablaze. "We strung her along. They were trying to hook me and I was trying to hook her. They photographed our little liaisons in bed. They even had pictures of me giving her the unclassified publications Karpenko wanted."

"You actually saw the photos?"

"Yes! That was their game, *blackmail*. That's how it works," he said, gazing into her eyes. "She told me that if I didn't cooperate, Karpenko would send the photos to the CIA. By the way, did he?"

Harris blushed slightly, giving away her thoughts. "I know a great deal about you, Commander. That's my job. And—how can I say this? I really appreciate all the things you have done for our country. Colombia, Bolivia, Korea, Afghanistan, Vietnam, all the others."

Evans stared at Harris until she spoke out of discomfort.

"Did you care for her?" she probed gently.

"I don't know! It was a long time ago, Harris. I was young and dumb."

"So was she. Has she ever tried to contact you?" asked Harris like a lawyer teasing a witness.

"No," he responded emphatically.

"Did she love you?"

"Hell, I don't know, Harris. Maybe."

"You said maybe, Derek. Why?" she probed gently. Harris was close to her objective. She needed to know if Evans was still in contact with Saraskina and how deep the relationship between them had been.

"Someone sent me a warning. The night before our big training exercise with the Russian subs, a scrawny little street girl handed me a dirty scrap of paper. There was only one word written on it, barely legible. But it spooked me because the word was misspelled and it looked slightly Cyrillic."

"And you think it was Saraskina who sent you the warning?" she asked gently.

"Who else?"

"What did you do?" she asked eagerly.

"After we left port, I moved the infiltration time up five hours and we locked and loaded with live ammunition. I followed the same plan, just early. My point man, the man who was killed, walked right up on them huddled over a map with a red-lens flashlight. He must have thought they were a group of our trainees who were lost. The best I can figure is, they were just as confused as we were. Karpenko must have divided his men into two groups, one to hit us and one to ambush our trainees."

"That doesn't make sense, Derek. How could he get away with killing Americans and Indonesians in the GOI?"

"I had a lot of time to think about it while I lay in the hospital at Subic. I believe he intended to ambush us, put live rounds in our weapons and make it look like someone mixed up the ammunition in the dark."

"Brilliant and devious! Since you were training with blank ammunition, it should have been easy to cut you down and make the scene look like a training accident," she volunteered.

"Well, it wasn't so easy," snapped Evans. "All hell broke loose when Squires walked into their formation. It was dark and we couldn't shoot because we couldn't tell friend from foe. The situation quickly deteriorated into voice-activated hand-to-hand combat."

"And Karpenko tried to kill you?" she asked.

"Let's say we traded scars!" he bristled.

After working over the thought, she responded almost clinically. "Commander, I know you have a busy schedule tomorrow. Let's call it a night."

"OK." He nodded agreement. He stood up to leave without taking his eyes off her.

The short trip to the BOQ was filled with small talk about SEAL training. When Evans stopped directly in front of the BOQ at North Island, he knew the evening was over. He could tell by the look in her eyes. He wanted to take her to his apartment and make wild, passionate love to her all night.

"You know something?" he asked.

"What?" asked Harris, locked on Evans's eyes.

"It's not fair. You've seen pictures of me naked in bed and I don't know a damn thing about you."

"Derek, thank you for opening up to me tonight. I really, really enjoyed your company. You are one of the most impressive men I have ever met." She reached over and touched his cheek lightly. "I wish I had met you ten years ago," she said sincerely.

"Oh, I get the picture, Doc," he said. "You're married."

He looked into her eyes, trying to read her thoughts. He couldn't.

"Will I see you in the morning, Commander?" she asked as she turned to open the car door.

"Sure, Doc. Sure," he said, disappointed. Evans didn't take his eyes off her as she walked toward the entrance of the BOQ.

Man-eater, he thought. *Man-eater! The understatement of the decade.*

CHAPTER
6

Dresden, East Germany

Abdul Salim strolled into the Lodz Bakery at 1316 Dusseldorf Street in Dresden, East Germany, at precisely one o'clock as specified in his communiqué. His mission was to make face-to-face contact with General Karpenko and negotiate terms favorable to his client. Salim was a frequent traveler to Germany and he knew the country well. His Syrian import-export business was the perfect cover for special projects such as smuggling weapons and explosives in and out of Europe. He went directly to the bread section and examined a huge loaf of dark German bread. He strolled around for a while, waiting for the clerk to make contact. The proprietor watched him out of the corner of his eye and when they were alone he asked the Arab the most obvious question.

"May I help you, sir?" he said, politely watching the Arab's eyes.

"Perhaps," responded Salim. "Perhaps. I was told you could bake a special cake for me."

"Yes. We can. What do you have in mind?"

"Oh, a very special cake, one made from an old cossack recipe," whispered Salim discreetly.

"Ah," said the clerk with a nod. "For that you must speak with our management. Please follow me."

Salim followed the burly man through a door in the back of the store and across the floor of the old bakery. It had survived Hitler and communism, and from the look of the machinery had operated continuously for sixty years without any replacements. The heat from the ovens warmed the room and the smell of baking bread warmed his senses. At the back of the bakery they approached a nondescript door, dark-aged with years of use. Salim heard deep voices inside talking boisterously. The German looked at him with a knowing eye and gestured for him to enter. For a fleeting moment Salim felt the chill of death. His heart skipped a beat, warning of danger. Reluctantly he knocked lightly on the door and opened it to peek inside.

Karpenko and three of his men were playing cards at a table in the center of the room. Saraskina was working at a desk in the corner. They all stared at the Arab with cold, vacant expressions. With a glare, Karpenko sized up the frail Arab in a heartbeat. He motioned with a condescending wave of his hand for Salim to enter the room and continued playing his card game. Salim's eyes shifted about the room like a radar as he closed the door and eased his way toward the card players.

He cleared his throat. "I was told I could have a special cake prepared at this establishment, one made from an old cossack recipe," he murmured nervously.

Karpenko looked up from his game. His eyes pierced Salim's soul. With a deep guttural sound he growled at the Arab. "For the right price, my towel-head friend, you can have any recipe you want." His lips snarled and one cheek quivered as he stared menacingly without blinking. The pockmarks and the scar on his face were shadowed by the poor light in the room. They stood out like craters on the face of the moon.

"But this is a very special occasion and my clients want a very special product."

"You have come to the right place, Arab. First, I require sufficient funds for the ingredients."

"If you are the baker I seek, you already have the proper ingredients," said Salim politely.

Karpenko looked at his cards. He took one from his hand and threw it down hard in the center of the table. "You bore me, Arab," he said, looking up with a glare. The deep resonance of Karpenko's voice seemed to vibrate Salim's sinus cavities. The hairs on the back of his neck stood at attention.

"Forgive me, my baker friend, but I must have assurance you can deliver the product my client desires," he said politely.

Karpenko lifted his chin slightly. His nostrils flared and he sniffed the air unconsciously. He slowly ran his finger down the deep scar that bisected the right side of his face.

"Of course I have the proper ingredients, *towel-head!* What I require is for your client to wire transfer one half the cost in advance. Deposit *two* million dollars in this Swiss account by this time next week or there will be no deal." Karpenko took a small envelope from his pocket and threw it at Salim's feet.

"That is a very large sum of money," complained Salim, picking up the envelope.

"You want the weapon, you pay the price," stated Karpenko flatly.

"But once you have our money how do we know you will deliver the product as agreed?" inquired Salim politely.

"Now you are boring the shit out of me, camel breath," snarled Karpenko. The big Russians playing cards with Karpenko chuckled at the disparagement. Karpenko's eyes locked on to Salim and he sat absolutely motionless for several seconds. "Tell your client that I will deliver on my terms and at the time of my choosing. You know I have the weapons or you wouldn't be here, *errand boy!*" He continued to stare at the Arab until Salim looked down at the floor. "You want it delivered to Syria, right?"

Salim looked at Karpenko and swallowed hard. "Yes," he answered nervously.

"Half the money in advance. And if your client doesn't pay his balance promptly, I will deliver him a second weapon absolutely free of charge. Of course, the only thing he will see is a blinding white flash." Karpenko showed a sinister grin. "You are dismissed, errand boy."

Salim glanced around the room, noting the details of the office. He saw the gun in the shoulder holster of the big Russian seated next to Karpenko, but it didn't bother him.

He wasn't frightened by the sight of guns. Guns and explosives were his business. What frightened him was the look on Saraskina's face. When he made eye contact with her he felt the icy shiver of death run down his spine. It was like looking into the eyes of the Jewish spy he had killed in Lebanon the month before his trip to Germany. They had tortured her male companion to death in front of her. After gang-raping her for hours, Salim had pointed a pistol at her, thinking she would beg for her life. Instead she spat at him. He had stared into her eyes for several seconds before pulling the trigger. Those were the same eyes. Eyes filled with anger and hate and rage. The feeling spooked him and his legs began to tremble.

"Allah, protect your humble servant from these infidels," he uttered to himself as he backed slowly toward the door.

"It will be as you say, Russian, but if you do not deliver as agreed . . ."

Karpenko interrupted him in midsentence. "Don't threaten me, towel-head," he yelled, aiming his finger at Salim as if sighting down the barrel of a pistol, "or I will kill you where you stand." Karpenko slowly lowered his hand. "I said, you are dismissed."

Salim opened the door without taking his eyes off Karpenko. As he turned to leave he felt the eyes of the woman piercing the back of his skull.

When Salim had gone, Karpenko looked around at his men and laughed. He knew how to intimidate and frighten men. It was a game he loved to play. "Now it is time for the iced vodka. Vlad, would you do the honors?"

As Suburov stood up to fetch the bottle, the gun hanging from his shoulder holster caught on the table, rattling the ashtrays.

"Vlad, you are getting fat. We must find some appropriate exercise for you," said Karpenko jovially. As Suburov crossed the room, he continued his discourse.

"We will take this deal, but that one dies. I don't like him. I don't like him at all," he mumbled almost to himself. He sniffed the air unconsciously. "Natila," he ordered. "Get someone close to that Arab. Learn his personal habits and weaknesses. I want to know better whom I am killing."

"Yes, General. I know he likes blond women. That's why

he comes to Germany so often. I hired a German whore to sleep with him last night." She smiled cleverly.

"Natila, you always amaze me with your prescience. How did you know I would want this?"

"I know, General. I know how you think. I don't trust Arabs either. They make my skin crawl."

"You don't trust anybody, Natila," Karpenko said, chuckling jovially. "Maybe not even me?" He gave her a hard look and continued. "What I wanted to know is this," he said gruffly. "Is he an important player in the Arab cause?"

"Sir, he thinks he is important, but he is only an errand boy," answered Natila with a degree of assurance.

"Very well. I don't like him and I don't trust him," grumbled Karpenko. "We change safehouses tonight," he ordered, "and we kill the Arab at our next meeting."

Karpenko looked at Suburov. "Suburov needs exercise. He is getting fat," he said, studying the old sergeant. "Vlad, I want you to . . ." He paused, watching Suburov pet his pistol like a cat. Karpenko shook his head no. "No. No. No. No. No. I want you to strangle him with his greasy head towel." He smiled cleverly, pleased with his decision, as Suburov and Voshchanov laughed out loud. As they toasted to free enterprise with iced vodka, Natila protested the decision.

"General, let me kill the Arab?"

Karpenko glanced at her with a grin but didn't respond.

Karpenko had sensed the beginning of the end of the Soviet Union when he had returned from deployment in Afghanistan. The satellite states had become insubordinate and he felt the vast empire tremble beneath his feet when the Politburo failed immediately to crush the first open defiance of central authority. In self-interest he had set in motion a plan he had formulated years before. Using one of his legitimate missions, which was to evaluate and audit the security of secret facilities, he had exploited the very weaknesses he was charged with correcting.

The Soviet Union possessed more than thirty thousand nuclear warheads and numerous black programs designed to develop weapons of mass destruction. With the breakdown of political, social, and economic order, it was impossible to maintain control over the enormous arsenal. Nuclear, chemical, and biological weapons capable of horrendous destruction were being dispersed like cards in a poker game to various power brokers in several Soviet states. Karpenko's objective was to be the first high-ranking officer to enter the arms market. He had stolen the smallest, lightest, and most destructive nuclear weapons in the Soviet inventory and he had raided the black programs for other weapons even more destructive than thermonuclear devices.

The regiment he commanded possessed enormous firepower and the freedom to move about the Soviet Union unchallenged because of its secret mission. Using selected personnel, he simultaneously raided several facilities and simply disappeared like a phantom into his secret agent network on the rim of the empire. It was easy because he controlled all three branches of the Spetznaz.

The Spetznaz were the most feared fighting units in Russia. Outsiders, even those within the Soviet Army, didn't know much about them or that there were actually three distinct Spetznaz organizations. First and foremost were the fighting units like the one Natila Saraskina commanded. Such teams were known for using a file to rasp the teeth of their prisoners to make them talk. Second, and of little importance, were the professional sportsmen who competed for the motherland. They were a pampered lot who performed no real military duties. He used them to spot vulnerable people for use as spies. Then there was the Secret Agent Corps. Their mission was to recruit spies and manage spy networks.

In numerical terms, the fighting units of the Spetznaz were the largest and most notorious. Only the toughest, strongest, and most loyal were selected for duty with the fighting forces. In the Soviet Union there was an unspoken system of segregating troops into categories that carefully screened and divided men according to physical and mental abilities, and political reliability. The fortunate soldier was selected into the lowest category and forced to perform two years of military servitude in some remote and godforsaken pioneer battalion where there was no discipline or supervision, or in a unit where the officers drank away their authority. The higher-category soldiers were the unfortunate ones. They were selected for duty with such units as the Spetznaz. Their training was harsh, brutal, and dangerous. The pay was low and their assignments were extremely perilous.

When recruited into the Spetznaz the soldier signed a disclosure statement and with it signed away his life and what little freedom he possessed. Disclosure of the secrets of the Spetznaz was treated as high treason, punishable by death according to Article 64 of the Soviet Criminal Code, or punishable by death at the hands of the men with whom he served. Karpenko had his choice of the most ruthless and highly trained commandos behind the Iron Curtain.

As a general rule he never let the three distinct units of the Spetznaz mix, nor were they aware of each other's existence. Saraskina was an important exception. She had served in all three branches. Women in the Soviet military were generally not taken seriously as leaders and were not assigned to positions of great responsibility. But Saraskina had mastered the corrupt Soviet system and with Karpenko's backing had advanced despite her gender. Her career was most unusual. It began in the Spetznaz Athletic Corps. She was a world-class athlete who possessed superior physical abilities. After a minor injury took her out of competition for the biathlon, an injury caused by a comrade who wanted her position, she was assigned to the Secret Agent Corps, partly because of her good looks and partly because of her intelligence. It was there that she had caught Karpenko's eye. Her transfer from the Secret Agent Corps to a fighting unit had been planned in meticulous detail.

Natila Saraskina was unusual for a Russian. She had a mixture of Oriental, Turkish, and Slavic heritage in her face that covered a deep, dark family secret. Her raven black hair, dark skin, and full lips attracted men the moment they laid eyes on her. But when an admirer looked into her eyes his heart stopped momentarily, not from passion but from fright, like that experienced when looking into the eyes of a predatory animal. It wasn't that her eyes weren't beautiful; they were. It was that they were empty, unfeeling, and bottomless. They emanated the coldness of death, piercing the soul and warning of danger. She was his special agent and the only one in the pack with experience in all three branches of the Spetznaz.

The symbol of Karpenko's Spetznaz was a patch depicting a pack of wolves on the hunt, and no other animal in the world could have served as a better symbol. The wolf is a strong, proud animal that can run for hours through deep snow and then muster an incredible burst of speed to bring down prey five times its size. It has a powerful intellect and is strong, wise, and indomitable. And it lives in a pack. A wolf pack is a loosely knit but well-organized fighting unit of frightening predators that live on the move. Their tactics are flexible and daring, a collection of tricks, a mixture of cunning and strength, confusion and maneuver, and lightning sneak attacks that result in the death of their prey. Karpenko was called the Alpha Wolf because of his animal-like instincts; Suburov was called the Mad Wolf because he would mutilate his enemies in a blind rage; Saraskina was called the She Wolf because of her personal allure and beguiling nature.

Karpenko designed his Spetznaz training after the wolf's tactics. A wolf lives on its legs, and on that premise he modeled his training program, which began and ended with the legs. Sambo was a compulsory feature of their daily routine when not on maneuvers. Sambo, or *samooborrona bez oruzhiya,* was a unique system of fighting that brought unarmed combat up to date. It involved the use of weapons such as bottles, sticks, knives, knuckle-dusters, pistols, rifles, and razor-sharp spades. Sambo, combined with running, swimming, and long field maneuvers, toughened his men until their legs were like spring steel.

The process of psychological training was inseparably linked to the physical toughening. Their association was a closed society living permanently at the limits of human existence. It was an eat-or-be-eaten world, survival of the fittest. Risk taking was a major part of their existence and killing was part of the job. The continual psychological training developed a spirit of self-confidence and independence and a feeling of superiority. But within the wolf pack there is a continual running battle to gain a higher place in the hierarchy. Within Karpenko's select group the bitter battle went on for a place at the table of the leader, closer and closer to the top, and even to take Karpenko's place if possible. They defended their positions of respect within the hierarchy in ways ranging from sambo to shooting. A man who waited longer than the others to pull his parachute earned respect. A man who could shoot better than anyone else earned respect. A man handy with the spade and the knife was respected. There were many ways, both physically and mentally, to earn a seat at the table and a place in the pack.

Suburov was a old *stariki* who had earned his reputation with his bare knuckles. At one time he had been called the Beast, because he would fly into a rage and lash out at anyone within reach. In bare-knuckles fighting he could beat any man in the regiment. In a tournament fight Suburov had beaten to convulsions a man known to be an expert in sambo fighting. As he gained status in the hierarchy and experience overseas, he grew more and more like a subordinate wolf dependent upon the alpha. Like Karpenko, he was a big man who had found his niche in the Spetznaz. Now in his early fifties, he had gained a paunch, but he was still a formidable killing machine and Karpenko's strong right hand, the only man Karpenko truly trusted.

Suburov's credo was, Don't trust, don't beg, and don't show fear, a dogma he had learned in a Russian prison. It was a doctrine now common to the pack. They were skeptics, cynics, and pessimists who didn't believe in justice, goodness, and honor among men. The extremes in which they lived molded their thoughts. They believed profoundly in the depravity of human nature and that under extreme conditions any man would become a beast and sell out his brother for a mouthful of food. In the Spetznaz soldier's mind, the most dangerous thing he could do was to put his complete faith in his comrades, who in a critical moment would turn out to be beasts. That was human nature. It was simpler to accept the fact that when each was cornered, self-preservation would prevail. The relationships within Karpenko's gang were very similar to those within a wolf pack. They were subordinate to the whole for existence but strong, independent, and ruthless when operating alone.

Before going to Germany, Suburov had followed Karpenko's orders to the letter. He stood on the exact corner at the exact time the general had specified. And at precisely the moment he indicated, two men in a covered truck picked him up.

"Where do you want to go, comrade?" asked the driver, a middle-aged man with a receding hairline.

"Belgrade," snarled Suburov like an old *stariki* growling at raw recruits.

"Ah, good. That is on my route."

As the truck bounced along on the back roads of Romania the men tried to make conversation, but Suburov would only grunt his replies. After they had crossed the border into Yugoslavia he stopped them in a wooded area.

"Stop here."

"But, comrade?"

"Stop here. Now. I have to piss."

As soon as the truck stopped, Suburov got out and walked quickly into the woods. He waited patiently until the younger man came to look for him. He caught the youngster from behind and snapped his neck in a heartbeat. Before the body had stopped quivering, he walked back out into the open where the driver could see him and enthusiastically motioned him to come see. He disappeared into the foliage and waited. When the driver came upon the body of his companion he tried to run, but Suburov clubbed him in the back of the head with his huge fist. Placing his knee in the man's back, he broke his neck with one grunt. Without remorse he covered both bodies with brush and continued his journey. Suburov didn't know the reason for the mission. He didn't care. He just executed the orders to the exact detail in a way that would make Karpenko happy. In Belgrade he stopped long enough to have a drink, and a woman, before continuing his journey to rendezvous with Alpha in East Germany.

Karpenko had traveled to East Germany to make deals with Arabs. In East Germany he owned numerous businesses that provided him legitimate cover. Posing as a

German couple, he and Saraskina had crossed several international borders without arousing attention. The safehouse in Dresden was a bakery he had financed ten years before with KGB money. Using the Secret Agent Corps, Karpenko had created a vast network of agents and business enterprises such as the Lodz Bakery. There were cells within cells throughout the world, including the Soviet Union. Some he shared with Saraskina or Voshchanov or Suburov, and some he kept to himself. Saraskina and Suburov had eliminated the controllers within the KGB and the GRU who had knowledge of the Spetznaz intelligence system, so they alone knew the load signals and dead drops needed to activate the nets. In every location the Spetznaz had ever served, they had agents they could activate clandestinely, and Karpenko was pulling the strings like a master puppeteer.

He used his enormous network of clandestine cells to transport the weapons and other materials he had stolen to remote locations in the mountains of Romania. There, near a Black Sea port where he had significant financial holdings and immense agent influence, he stashed most of his treasure. He knew that American satellites were designed to hone in on the faint radiation signal given off by nuclear materials and that once notified they would sweep the surface of the planet for any signal that did not fit the coordinates of known emitters. Any unknown glow would receive a visit from a fleet of helicopters full of armed commandos spoiling for a fight. So he had moved the weapons under the cover of lead blankets and stashed them deep within an abandoned coal mine to hide their nuclear signals from the prying eyes of American satellites.

Suburov had eliminated the only men other than Karpenko himself who knew the exact locations where the weapons were stored. With that information he trusted no one. Karpenko set himself up like an alpha wolf without whom the pack could not survive. They would attend to his every need or perish.

"Vlad, come with me. I want some fresh bread."

Once on the bakery floor amidst the noise of the machinery, Karpenko pulled the old *stariki* close.

"Vlad, you like little Filipino pussies?" he whispered.

"General, I love them almost as much as I like vodka." Suburov smiled deviously.

"In a few days we will change our headquarters to Varna. While everyone is on the move, I want you to go to the Philippines by way of Iran. Tell no one of this trip. No one," he raised his voice. "In addition to getting laid, this is what I want you to do." He pulled Suburov close and whispered in his ear. The old *stariki* chuckled out loud. He loved *maskirovka* too.

CHAPTER

7

Lieutenant David Eric Owen was keeping a secret only three people in the city of San Diego knew, and he was one of those people. His father had warned him about the SEALs and had tried to persuade him to choose another career.

"The SEALs are ruthless knuckle-draggers, David. If they find out about you, they'll harass you until you quit and then your career will be over," he pleaded. "Your future will be ruined. Is that what you want?"

Jonathan David Owen wanted more for his son than what the SEALs could offer. He wanted him to command a ship and achieve high rank. But David Owen already possessed the most essential trait of the SEAL character: tenacity. He refused to give up.

Owen had wanted to be a SEAL since his junior year in high school. A SEAL recruiter had shown his gym class a Navy propaganda film and had told them about life in the teams. He showed slides of men parachuting, locking out of submarines, and shooting all sorts of weapons, and at each image he told an adventure story. As David Owen stood in front of Class 168, Chief Ronald Savarese's words replayed in his mind.

"Men, in our society there's a false image of the warrior

as some sort of Rambo character, rough and tough, and ready for any mission, anytime, anywhere." Savarese had put his pointer between his teeth like a knife and briefly pantomimed a Hollywood character moving through the jungle. "Armed only with cunning and a knife, this guy single-handedly overcomes all odds. That's an exciting image, men." He called them men, which was the first time anyone had ever called them that. "But it's a false image. A warrior is a team player. We're looking for teammates, men, not rogue warriors. You see, men, a warrior is like a fireman. We don't love war any more than a fireman loves a fire. We just put out the fires of human conflict. Someone's got to do it."

Lieutenant David Owen stood in front of Class 168 as a senior petty officer, a large man named Ryeback, addressed the class. Ahead of them was the most difficult training imaginable, and unlike the others in the class he knew what lay ahead. He had done his homework by spying on BUDS. He had even observed parts of Hell Week by hiding in the sand dunes. Owen knew the elements of the SEAL curriculum and he was wondering if it was better to know or not, when Ryeback reported.

"Sir, the men are ready for barrack inspection."

"Very well, Ryeback. Carry on."

Ryeback dismissed the men and they scurried back to their rooms to wait for the instructors.

Class 168 was divided into fourteen boat crews of seven men per boat. Each crew had an officer or petty officer in charge who steered while the others paddled. More often than not, they ran around with the boats bouncing on the tops of their heads. Trainees still used the IBS, an acronym that stood for *inflatable boat small,* despite the fact that the teams hadn't used them since the Korean War. It was a cumbersome raft that weighed over three hundred pounds and it was the source of a lot of fights between SEAL trainees and the Marines. The Marines would jeer them as they ran around the base with the boats on top of their heads.

"Hey, you dumb-ass swabs, boats are for water, not for land."

Owen knew that the IBS was a catalyst and that in the process of paddling and carrying the boats, bonds would be formed that would last a lifetime. The weight of the raft broke some men mentally and others physically, but it made a team of those who survived. Those who endured the cold of the Pacific and the chafing of wet sand on raw skin would come to know the IBS as a place of refuge. The long paddles would soon be opportunities to escape the torment of instructors. Owen had spied on several classes and they all started out the same, a long line of boats snaking about the Naval Amphibious Base. By Hell Week, the fifth week of training, there would be only about ten boats. After Hell Week, there would be only five. Owen shivered as he thought of what lay ahead.

The enlisted men were assigned six to a room in the old barrack behind the Center. It was located right on the Silver Strand Beach on arguably the most expensive real estate in Southern California, but it was worn down like a Chicago tenement. Thousands of sandy boots had scoured the floor like sandpaper for decades, pockmarking the concrete in the hallways. Sand clogged drains and backed up toilets. With nearly a hundred men on each of the three decks, the building smelled of urine, sweat, and dank seawater.

They struggled to meet the impossible demands of instructors who performed daily white-glove inspections. The instructors expected the floors to be gritty, because the barracks were only thirty yards from the Pacific Ocean. They expected the bathrooms to smell, because there was nothing the trainees could do about it. But everything else had to be perfect. A belt buckle that was not shined to perfection resulted in a quick trip to the cold Pacific and another wet, sandy body tracking through the old barracks.

The six men in Lam's room were all assigned to Mr. Owen's boat crew. They were stacked in the room in double bunks that were nearly adjacent to one another. By the fourth week of training they were used to the crowded conditions and had learned to tolerate each other's little quirks.

At breakfast, Lam had spotted Simons lifting a bottle of

Tabasco sauce from the galley. He assumed he was adding to the food cache the men shared and he forgot about the incident until he saw the bottle reappear. While Jackson was in the bathroom, Simons slipped it out of his pocket with a mischievous grin and rifled through Jackson's locker. With a snicker he quietly closed the locker door and put the hot sauce in the food cache.

Just as Jackson entered the room, a lookout hollered, "Stand by for inspection!" The men quickly stood at attention at the end of the bunk beds, ready for a dose of daily torment.

Instructor Wild Bill Williams strolled through the door dressed in his knee-length green fatigue shorts, a blue-and-gold instructor shirt, and a blue baseball hat. He was built like a fireplug, with a low center of gravity that supported a massive linebacker neck. Williams was a novice weight lifter and even in the poor light of the barracks his huge leg muscles rippled. He unconsciously flexed his biceps and pecs, bulging out his shirt.

"Good morning, tadpoles. And how did we sleep last night?"

"Great, Instructor Williams," responded the men in unison.

Williams's boots reflected the dim light like a mirror. They had been shined to perfection by Robinson, the best spit shiner in the class, for having an imperceptible scuff on his perfectly shined boots. Of course, only Williams could see the microscopic scuff, a contrivance that resulted in Robinson's shining Williams's boots.

"Well, let's have a look here, tadpoles," he said, stopping in front of Jackson, whose bunk was closest to the door.

"Well, well, well, Jackson, you fucked up again. Hit the surf, maggot," he yelled.

Jackson ran out of the room like a jackrabbit spooked by a coyote and headed for the surf zone for a dip. This routine had gone on for weeks. Williams didn't like Jackson and every time he inspected he sent him to the surf like clockwork. Williams was more of a tugboat than a racing boat and he secretly envied guys like Jackson who effortlessly ran through the obstacle course like a springbok.

Williams identified with guys like Robinson, who was built like a football player. Both Williams and Robinson were practical jokers.

Williams turned to Simons. "Life jacket," he snapped.

Simons handed him his life jacket and Williams fooled with it for two minutes trying to find a grain of sand. Finally he gave up and yelled, "Drop down, maggot." Simons dropped down into a push-up position the instructors called the leaning rest, while Williams tore into his locker like a Tasmanian devil. He dumped everything on the floor and ripped the covers off his bed before turning his attention to Robinson, who passed without a hitch. Being the best spit shiner in the class paid huge dividends.

"The next time I inspect, you'd better all look as good as Robby," he threatened.

Just as he turned his attention to a tall, lanky kid named Larry Larson, Jackson ran into the room dripping with saltwater.

"Get dressed, maggot. Hurry up. It's almost time for class." Jackson automatically began peeling off his wet fatigues to put on a fresh uniform.

"Men! I remind you, in my team we are together in sickness and in health, until death do us part. When one man fails we all fail. Simons, recover," he said interrupting himself. Simons jumped up from leaning rest and stood at rigid attention. "When one man doesn't do his job correctly he destroys the teamwork we need to *overcome,"* he said, raising his voice.

"Hardship," yelled the trainees in unison.

"Endure," yelled Williams.

"Adversity," responded the men.

"Destroy," sang Williams, cupping his hand to his ear.

"The enemy," yelled the trainees as loud as they could.

Williams ripped everything out of Larson's locker and threw it on the floor. When he came to the *Playboy* magazine he stopped for a look at the cover girl. Then he turned on Larson like a pitbull.

"Larson, why are the pages stuck together?"

"Simons bet me I couldn't stick all the pages together before graduation, Instructor Williams."

Williams dropped the magazine like a chunk of contami-

nated beef as the realization came to him that four weeks'
worth of pages were stuck together.

"What do you mean, Larson?" he growled with a sour
expression.

The others started to snicker.

"OK, OK, I get it. Drop down, you perverted son of a
bitch. Give me fifty," he yelled, referring to push-ups.
"Maybe a little exercise will reduce your sexual frustration,
boy."

Jackson finished putting on a fresh uniform and jumped
into rank at the end of his bunk. Williams turned on Lam.

"Lam-san, you are going to be the cause of some serious
flashbacks if you make it to the teams."

"Tank you, Instructor Williams. It'll be nice to be noticed."

"Like Swiss cheese. You'd better be careful how you walk
up on some of those old geezers in the teams. They might
take you for a Charlie."

He fiddled with Lam's life jacket. "Say, Lam-san, do you
like LBFMs?" he said seriously. LBFM was Williams's
acronym for *little brown fucking machine.*

When Lam didn't answer, Williams continued, "I love
gooks . . . gook women, that is . . . really I do," he said
with a phony English accent. "I like them two at a time.
How 'bout you?" he asked derisively.

"Yes, Instructor Williams. I like LBFM too, but like a real
man. Tree at a time."

"Ooouuh," responded Williams as the other men chuckled. "I hit a raw nerve. Drop down and knock 'em out,
Lam-san." Lam jumped down and started pumping out
push-ups.

Williams looked down the line and saw Jackson squirm-
ing like a child that had to pee. His knees sort of pucked in
as he reached down with his left hand and pulled at his
shorts. The hot sauce in his BVDs had coated his testicles
and they were moving like Mexican jumping beans in a
Tijuana sideshow.

"Jackson, are you scratching your balls?" he asked, walking down the line to stand directly in front of his face.

"No, no, Instructor Williams," he blurted.

Jackson had perspiration beads on his forehead and a

glazed look in his eyes. Williams stared at him for a few seconds. He cocked his head to one side before speaking.

"Jackson, you gotta piss or somethin'?" he asked seriously.

"No, no, Instructor Williams," insisted Jackson in a jittery voice.

Williams stared at him for a few more seconds before turning to leave. "In the classroom in five minutes, tadpoles. Clean up this mess," he snapped as he headed out the door.

As soon as Williams rounded the corner Jackson made a beeline for his locker, grabbed his K-bar, dropped his trousers, and cut off his shorts with two quick slices like a chef at a Japanese restaurant. He threw the knife in his locker with a bang and made for the john, holding up his pants with one hand.

"You sons o' bitches! Paybacks are hell! You *assholes!"* he yelled, running down the hall.

They looked at each other and began to laugh in uncontrollable fits while gathering up the mess Williams had made on the floor.

Class 168 was recovering from a six-mile soft-sand run and a mile surf swim when Evans, Harris, and Saleen walked over the sand dune to observe log PT. As they approached, they could hear Instructor Taufaudy yelling out instructions.

"How is it going, Stick?" asked Evans as they reached the top of a ten-foot sand dune overlooking the beach.

"Great, XO. Taufaudy's busting their rumps," responded Masure. Evans nodded acknowledgment and looked down at the men on the beach.

Log physical training was the kind of exercise only the SEALs could dream up. It began with calisthenics performed by teams of six or seven men holding two- and three-hundred-pound telephone pole logs. Overhead lifts, chest presses, and sit-ups with the log required total team commitment from each man. After calisthenics the evolution finished with log races. Taufaudy had them drenched in sweat and seawater and panting from exhaustion as he smoothly counted cadence to log sit-ups.

"Listen up, ladies," barked Taufaudy when one of the teams faltered. "If you don't start working together we'll repeat this entire evolution from the beginning. Do I make myself clear?"

"Hoo yah, Instructor Taufaudy," roared the class, sounding exhausted.

"Ready. Begin," he ordered.

Jackson had a bad hangover and it was affecting his performance. He had the fastest four-mile timed run, the fastest O-course, and the best swim times in the class, and he let everyone know it at every opportunity. Over the weekend he had tied one on, thinking he was such a superior athlete that a wild night chasing skirts wouldn't affect his performance. He had conducted a Bataan death march, drinking and prowling for women at every bar in downtown San Diego. He found what he wanted and all day Sunday he bragged about his sexual exploits to anyone who would listen. Wisely he had left out the part about the car wreck on the Coronado Bridge. During the beach run Jackson had thrown up his breakfast, spewing little chunks of egg on the guys behind him in ranks. On the ocean swim he had swallowed a lot of seawater. His face was a pale shade of green as he struggled with the heavy log. Lam noticed Jackson was slacking off. Not wanting to carry Jackson's share until he was totally exhausted, he slacked off, too. When Lieutenant Owen's end of the log rocked up, Lam's end collapsed.

"You better pull your share of the load, you little yellow-dick bastard," whispered Jackson in misery.

"*You* not carry your share of the load, jack*ass*," sassed Lam. He hawked up a big lunger and spat it on the log right in front of Jackson's face. The phlegmy glop caused Jackson to succumb to a fit of dry heaves and the log collapsed a second time.

"OK, ladies," yelled Taufaudy. "OK. I see you need a lesson in teamwork."

Taufaudy was an excellent instructor and he could sense when the trainees were at their physical limit.

"It's time for *Pays to Be a Winner*," he said, sounding like a game-show host. "Listen carefully and don't screw up or

77

you will—I repeat, you will—start over again. On my command you will pick up your logs together." He paused and looked at Owen's group. "That means at the same time, Mr. Owen. You will run down the beach through the soft sand and run around Instructor Masure. You will enter the surf with your logs, whereupon you will flop around like mating grunion until you are thoroughly cooled off. After your little bath you will exit the surf zone, pass behind Instructor Masure, and, like Marines raising the flagpole at Iwo Jima, lift the log end over end, until you return to the starting line."

Taufaudy drew a line in the sand with his boot as Masure and the others walked down the beach.

"Do you understand, One Sixty-Eight?"

"Hoo yah, Instructor Taufaudy," roared the class without enthusiasm.

"And, ladies, it pays to be a winner. The first team to cross this line can hit the showers," he said with a grin. "The remaining teams will race again and another winner will be allowed to hit the showers, and so on and so forth, and, ah, you know what I mean."

Taufaudy looked down the beach and signaled Masure, who responded with a thumbs-up.

"OK, ready. Go!"

Their green fatigues were wet and clung to their bodies as the men ran down the beach with the heavy logs on their shoulders. The sand invaded their uniforms, and with the moisture of sweat and seawater it was acting like sandpaper, rubbing knees, elbows, and crotches raw. Owen had secretly prepared his class as best he could. Under their fatigues they wore tight-fitting bikers' shorts to repel the invading sand. They had put large squares of surgical tape on their nipples to minimize chafing. But nothing but guts and determination could overcome the combination of sea, sand, and exhaustion. On the return trip two men quit, abandoning their teammates to struggle with the heavy log without them.

Owen's crew was slightly in the lead twenty-five yards from the finish line when Jackson began to dry-heave. Without his full effort another crew edged them out in the last ten yards. Even Lieutenant Owen, who was wise beyond his years, looked daggers at Jackson. They all knew they wouldn't have another chance of winning for several more races.

As Masure counseled the quitters, Harris began to work on Master Chief Saleen. All the men who had gone to Indonesia with Evans were being questioned, even those who had gotten out of the Navy. Evans, Saleen, Masure, and Wild Bill Williams were loose ends and a gold mine of information about the Spetznaz. As Harris asked questions vaguely related to leadership, she carefully ingratiated herself with them. When she had their confidence she delicately brought up other Special Operations forces, and then the Spetznaz.

"The men who quit look like Olympic athletes," commented Harris.

"We get a lot of Rambo types around here, ma'am," responded Saleen. "The ones with the huge biceps who are attracted by the SEAL mystique usually quit in the first few weeks."

"Like those two?"

"Yes, ma'am. They can run all day and do push-ups for hours, but they don't have what it takes."

"You mean the desire to succeed against all odds?" asked Harris.

"Exactly, Dr. Harris. If they'll quit here they'll quit on a real-world Op," argued Saleen.

Evans watched her carefully weave a web to capture the big black man. All of them liked her. She was smart and beautiful and knew what buttons to push to flatter them. For a while he even forgot she was Case Officer Harris of the Central Intelligence Agency, sent to pick their brains. The admiral had given her an office at his headquarters and for several weeks she had been in and out of the Center like an instructor, clipboard in hand.

"Stick, see the trainee beside the Amerasian kid in Mr. Owen's group?"

"Yes, boss, Master Chief and I need to talk to you in private about Jackson. He's the best athlete in the class, but he's too cocky."

"He's going to need some hydration. He's as green as his uniform," said Evans as the group thundered around them and headed for the surf.

"I've been watching him closely, boss, hoping he'd quit and solve the problem," interjected Saleen.

Evans looked at the big black man. "Trouble, Master?"

"Yes, sir. You remember O'Malley in Class One Fifty-Nine?"

"Yeah."

"Same-same problem," said Saleen, raising his eyebrows.

"OK, I got the message. Keep me informed," ordered Evans.

"Yes, sir," said Saleen, watching the crew of trainees running with a huge log at shoulder carry.

As log PT drew to a close, three crews were left. Lieutenant Owen's group was among them. Jackson was a deeper shade of green, but he wasn't a quitter. Lam, Robinson, Simons, Bailey, Larson, and Owen were visibly angry as Taufaudy made a circling motion above his head with his hand.

"It pays to be a winner, doesn't it, gentlemen?" he commented as he looked over the exhausted faces.

"Hoo yah, Instructor Taufaudy."

"Well, let me tell you why it pays to be a winner. You ladies are going to repeat the four-mile soft-sand run before you hit the showers," he said seriously.

"Hoo yah," yelled the weary men without zest. Robinson continued to yell at the top of his lungs. "Hoo yah, let's go, men. We can do it!"

Taufaudy formed them up to run, and when no one quit, he bellowed out, "Listen up! This evolution is over."

"Hoo yah, Instructor Taufaudy," they yelled with renewed vigor.

"Hey, Jackson, you're green, man," said Taufaudy. "Go see Doc Poland before the next evolution."

"Yes, Instructor Taufaudy," responded Jackson without looking him in the eye.

"OK, this afternoon we'll have a lecture on surf passage, and tomorrow a little fun in the sun. Mr. Owen, take charge, stack your logs, and hit the showers. Class dismissed!"

"Hoo yah, Instructor Taufaudy."

As they stacked the logs, Simons gave Jackson a hard look. "Jackass Jackson, we're going to kill your sorry ass when we get you to the barracks."

Jackson didn't have the energy to respond. He collapsed on the log pile. Robinson helped him to his feet and, using his belt as a handle, half carried him the fifty yards to the barracks.

As Evans and the others walked back to the grinder, Harris asked a question that was directed at Wild Bill Williams. "Would it be possible for me to speak with the quitters this afternoon? I'd like to examine the weaknesses in their personalities."

"Certainly," responded Evans, thinking she was going too far with her cover story. Then he remembered that Wild Bill was in charge of the quitters. He was her next target.

"I'll arrange it, boss," volunteered Williams.

"Thanks, Bill," said Evans.

How about right after chow, Dr. Harris, First Phase Office?" suggested Williams pleasantly.

"I'll be there!"

Williams smiled deviously as he walked to his office. He liked Harris. She was a gorgeous woman who distracted his attention. Given the opportunity, he would jump her bones in broad daylight right in front of the troops. But he didn't like women hanging around the Center. They interfered with his style, his choice of words, and his comportment around the men. And she was asking too many stupid questions about Green Berets, Rangers, and Spetznaz. "Time for a little attitude check," he chuckled.

Harris arrived promptly at 1300 at the First Phase Office. There were several trainees at parade rest standing outside near the ship's bell. The two quitters stood in a separate rank like pariahs. They were already dressed in navy dungarees and blue shirts with white Dixie Cup hats awaiting orders to some faraway place. They were standing above their own green helmets lined up under the ship's bell with the others that had quit. The rest of the men waiting to see Williams were dressed in clean, starched green uniforms topped with shiny green helmets. Harris knocked and proceeded into the office where several instructors were busy at their desks.

"Ms. Harris," said the stocky, muscle-bound instructor, "please excuse me for a moment. I have one more student to counsel before we interview the quitters. Please have a seat," he said, gesticulating toward a large conference table.

"Thank you," said Harris politely, taking the seat at the head of the table.

"Next!" boomed Williams so loudly Harris flinched.

She recognized the student who stepped through the door and stood in front of Williams with his helmet held in his right hand like a waitress holding a platter. It was the loudmouthed blond kid.

"Seaman Robinson, reporting as ordered, Instructor Williams," he screamed at the top of his lungs.

"Robinson, step up here, *now,*" snapped Williams.

Robinson took two steps forward as Williams came out from behind his desk and stood twelve inches from his face.

"Robinson, I want to see your goddamn life jacket and K-bar. Right now!"

With each inflection Williams projected a little saliva into the kid's face. Robinson's eyes were wild with fear. He extended his life jacket and knife with his left hand without moving the trunk of his body. Williams took the life jacket, quickly removed the CO_2 cartridge, and checked the actuator with his pinky finger. He held his small finger directly in front of Robinson's nose and screamed.

"Sand! Sand! You know what this is, dumb shit? *This is sand,"* he yelled as loud as he could. "Your life jacket won't work with sand in it, you dumb ass!" he screamed, spitting saliva on Robinson's face.

Slowly Williams put the life jacket over the petrified trainee's head and then struggled to remove the knife from its sheath. With great show he banged the knife and sheath on the floor and finally succeeded in withdrawing a knife so corroded with rust that it looked like a relic from World War II. William's eyes blazed with fire as he screamed at the horrified trainee.

"Robinson, you are the sorriest piece of shit I have ever

seen in this course. Your life jacket doesn't work and your knife is a rusty piece of shit."

Williams paused and with an icy voice that could kill said, "They won't let me kick your sorry ass out of here for this, but there are other ways of getting rid of garbage."

Williams drew back the knife and screamed.

"I'll stab your sorry ass and give you gangrene," he said, plunging the knife down toward Robinson's chest. He stopped two inches from the kid's clavicle.

Robinson deftly flipped the catch of a clip he held in his right hand, secluded under his helmet. It was connected to a thin tube that ran down the length of his arm. With the movement the entire contents of a large saline bag rigged under his armpit flooded the front of his fatigue pants in the general location of his penis. The liquid poured down his leg and formed a large puddle on the floor. He stood frozen, eyebrows up and eyes wide open as if he had seen a ghost. Williams replaced the knife in its sheath and slowly walked around trainee, shaking his head in amazement.

"Well, well, well. I'll be goddamned, Robinson. You've gone and pissed yourself. Get your sorry ass out of my sight, maggot!"

Robinson did an about-face and waddled out the door and across the grinder like a four-year-old child with a load in his diaper. The instructors in the office were roaring with laughter when Williams turned to face a smiling Alysin Harris.

"Ms. Harris, I'm so sorry about this . . . ah . . . this unfortunate accident. Perhaps we should use the Training Officer's Office while I have someone clean up this mess," he said sincerely.

Harris got up and headed out of the office, nonplussed. She had noticed that the liquid on the floor was clear and that the volume was too great for one human being. As they walked out, Williams yelled at the trainees standing at attention.

"Get inside and clean up that mess. You two quitters. Yes, you two. Follow me," he snapped.

They walked a few paces to an office that opened onto the grinder and he politely held the door for her like a perfect gentleman. Harris stopped and looked Williams directly in the eye. Standing ten inches from his face like an angry instructor, she said, "Great show, Instructor Williams. Great show. Please thank Trainee Robinson for me. You both deserve an Oscar."

Williams's eyes twinkled and he smiled sheepishly.

"OK. You two! One at a time. See Dr. Harris, and you'd better level with her or I'll bust your asses."

"Instructor Williams, when I'm finished with the quitters, I'd like to speak to you, one-on-one," said Harris with a serious expression.

"What . . . what about, Dr. Harris?" stammered Williams nervously.

"I like your sense of humor. You epitomize the essence of the SEAL character and I want to get to know you better. You were with Commander Evans in Indonesia, weren't you?"

"Yes, ma'am. Twice."

"Twice?" Harris's mind did a double back flip. Evans's file recorded only one trip to Indonesia.

"Yes, ma'am."

"I'd like to ask you some questions about operating overseas. You know, leadership as it relates to foreigners."

"Sure thing, Dr. Harris," responded Williams with a relieved expression. "Just yell when you're ready, ma'am."

As Williams walked back into the First Phase Office he gave Harris a new name.

"She's a seafox, man! She knew it was a fucking gag," he said, laughing with the other instructors. "One cool bitch, man. One cool bitch!"

CHAPTER
8

Congressman Larry Ackers stomped hard on the raised curb that marked the world's last Cold War border before stepping into South Korea, suitcase in hand. He smiled at the North Korean border guards who were giving him the evil eye.

"Partner," he said to the closest soldier who spoke no English, "it's a short walk down a real long road."

He took off his baseball cap and extended it to the border guard as a sign of friendship. The stone-faced figure didn't move a centimeter. He just stared at the *mee-gook* with his inscrutable Asian eyes. Ackers shook his head, gesticulated with his eyebrows, and put the hat back on on his head.

"How was your trip, Congressman?" asked a reporter running up to stick a camera in his face. Before he could answer, another reporter rushed up and asked, "Did you meet Kim Il Sung, Congressman Ackers?"

"Congressman Ackers, do the North Koreans have a nuclear weapons program?"

Ackers was the chairman of the Asia-Pacific Foreign Affairs Subcommittee. He looked at the reporters and smiled a big Texan grin.

"Ladies and gentlemen, I'll answer your questions in due time. Please allow me to cross back into the free world," he said, walking away from the demarcation line. He went twenty paces into South Korea and held his press conference.

"I'm the first U.S. official since the Korean War ended in 1953 to cross that truce line and travel from one Korean capital to the other. This is a historic occasion."

An anxious reporter interrupted his carefully worded speech.

"Did you meet with Kim Il Sung, sir?" he asked.

"Yes. On Tuesday, I met with Kim Il Sung and his son Kim Jung Il."

"How would you characterize the meeting, Congressman?" asked a female reporter representing CNN.

"I would characterize the visit as icebreaking."

Ackers wasn't about to tell her that Kim Il Sung had railed at him for almost an hour about the underhanded deceit of the United Nations' nuclear watchdog agency, the International Atomic Energy Agency. And for good reason. The IAEA had been given a sample of nuclear material during an inspection that had proven conclusively that Kim had been pursuing a nuclear weapons program since the mid-1970s. By measuring the half-life decay of nuclear particles, UN scientists had determined the exact year Kim had begun his nuclear weapons program. When confronted with the evidence, he denied it. He held a press conference and told the world the evidence was contrived by IAEA, and he refused to allow the organization to conduct further inspections, violating the nonproliferation treaty he had signed just a few years before.

"Our discussions were useful and productive," continued Ackers.

"Congressman Ackers. Wouldn't you agree that the United Nations and South Korea have already offered too many face-saving gestures to North Korea to woo them back into NPT compliance?"

"Since the division of this peninsula more than forty years ago the international environment has never been more conducive to the establishment of a lasting peace," stated Ackers.

"Congressman Ackers. Isn't that just double-talk? North

Korea has refused to allow the IAEA to inspect and they continue to violate South Korean borders. How can you say peace is at hand when most analysts believe North Korea has, or is close to, producing a nuclear bomb?" asked the lady reporter.

Ackers parried questions for half an hour, practicing his political double-talk before continuing his journey to Seoul. That night he slept like a baby in the free world, thirty miles from the DMZ where two hundred thousand men had died for the ugly little finger of land Mother Nature had robbed of most natural resources. North and South Korea were still at war and still shooting at each other, forty years after the armistice was signed. As Ackers snored on the seventh floor of the Hyatt Hotel in Seoul, Korea, a North Korean 737 pierced the liquid black sky thirty-seven thousand feet over Mongolia. It was a modern aircraft with all amenities, but it reeked of human waste and tobacco. The crew tried to copy the services offered in the West because they had VIPs on board, but it was an impossible task. The North Korean people had been isolated from the world too long and they simply didn't know how to use a western-style toilet. Within a few hours after leaving Warsaw, the aircraft was trashed and the air inside the cabin was insufferable.

The smell of black tobacco, kimchi, and its aftereffects sickened Saraskina. She didn't like the people or the food and she didn't want to go to Pyŏngyang. The inner circle of the wolf pack had discussed the issue at length. For some reason, Karpenko had insisted upon personally dealing with the North Korean government. He knew that word of his presence in Pyŏngyang would quickly leak back to Moscow and to the West, but he didn't care and he refused to listen to alternative plans. Karpenko had insisted on visiting North Korea as a VIP, a fact that unnerved Saraskina.

She belted down a couple of drinks and slept for a few hours, wishing away the smell of kimchi and tobacco. When she awoke she had to use the bathroom, but decided against it when she recalled the scene during her last visit. She could wait until the aircraft landed and she was in her hotel room. Saraskina yawned and looked around the first-class cabin. Voshchanov and Suburov were playing cards in the back row. It was a pastime they enjoyed. They were tough, brutal men, unaffected by their surroundings. Nothing seemed to faze them. She stretched and pulled herself up so she could glance around the seats in front of her to where Karpenko was seated. He was having another one of his attacks. He was writhing in pain with both hands covering his face and head where the spade had entered his skull. Most people would have died from such an injury. But not Karpenko. He lived by sheer force of will. The blade had cut through the skull and into his brain. As it chopped down his face it had shattered his sinus cavities and severed the jaw bone. The best surgeons in Moscow had repaired most of the damage, but they couldn't stop the pain. He lived in constant pain and the descent of the aircraft was exacerbating his condition. Sometimes it came in debilitating waves, like his current seizure. Sometimes it drove him into fits of rage and like a madman he would smash everything in sight. He had tried every form of treatment from acupuncture to electric shock, but nothing had worked.

Saraskina grabbed a glass of water from the galley and a handful of pills from her bag. The narcotics she carried always worked, but the aftereffects scared her. He was capable of anything when he was coming down off the medicine. She grasped one of his wrists and pulled his hand away. Agony, pure agony filled his face. His eyes were glazed in pain as he took the pills and water from her and gulped down the medicine in one motion. He assumed a different countenance when he saw the look of pity in her eyes. He stared at her as if in a trance, using his finger to trace the scar that bisected his cheek. The motion seemed to calm him. It was a sort of mind control mechanism. By concentrated hate he could control the outward appearance of pain.

"I'm going to kill him," he growled. "I'm going to kill him with my bare hands. I swear, I'm going to personally split his fuckin' skull."

He turned and looked out the window so Saraskina couldn't see his pain. She had heard the oath a thousand times. Karpenko seemed to live for the moment when he could personally face Derek Evans and kill him with his bare hands. He could have contracted for Evans's death years ago, but he hadn't. He existed for the moment when he could look him in the eye and rip out his heart.

"Dimitri, we are beginning our descent into Pyŏngyang," she said gently.

She always called him Dimitri when they were alone or with the general public. When the others were present she called him General to show greater respect. Karpenko ignored her report and continued staring out the window at the lights of North Korea. It was a horrible place of extremes but he knew the people. He spoke their language and he knew their cunning ways. He knew they were flying into an ambush.

Saraskina had pleaded with him not to go, and when he refused to listen to her reasoning she argued with him brazenly in front of the others. It was a dangerous move and she knew it.

"General, the North Koreans are a desperate people, a horrible, smelly people. This is an ambush, sir. An ambush! They will imprison us in a filthy cell and torture us. They will inject us with drugs and learn all our secrets, then they will kill us. General Kim cannot be trusted. I can sense treachery, sir."

The look in his eyes froze her blood and ceased her objections. Karpenko had just leered and shook his head knowingly. Saraskina was afraid to go to North Korea. She had almost fled the pack. If she had known where the weapons were hidden she could have ended the madness and escaped Karpenko's grip. She watched his reflection in the aircraft window. Pain, hate, and rage exuded from every pore. For a moment, a brief moment, a handsome face stared back at her from outside the window. It covered the hate and rage with confidence and poise. Her imagination was going wild. How long had it been? Almost ten years since she had last seen that handsome face. So confident. So strong.

Ebans. Ebans. You haunt my dreams, she murmured deep within her mind.

He was the only person she had truly loved in her entire miserable existence and she had no explanation for it. She had done for Derek Evans something she had never done for any human being. She had put his life before her own and warned him Karpenko was going to ambush him.

Why? she thought. *Why? Why should I care for a man who only wanted to recruit me as a spy?*

Evans was a fantasy. To escape her reality she used his memory like a drug. Through the years he had become more handsome, stronger, more intelligent, more understanding. She needed him to survive. What she had created in her mind didn't exist. Derek Evans was just a way to escape a world gone mad.

If Karpenko knew, he would . . . Her thoughts leapt forward like a record skipping a track. *Suburov would break every bone in my body, one at a time. They would torture me for days. No, maybe they wouldn't let me die. They would just keep torturing me. If they find out what I have done all these years . . .* She took a deep breath and closed her eyes and dreamed of Palestine. Then the plane touched down. *There is no escape,* she thought. *No escaping this madness.*

The jet landed with a screech and quickly taxied up to the terminal. It was little more than another military base under heavily armed guard. North Korea was a paranoid police state starved by the West. It was broken morally and monetarily. Its leaders were desperate and isolated. For the life of her she couldn't understand Karpenko's strategy.

At the bottom of the steps, Karpenko was greeted warmly by General Kim, the head of North Korean intelligence. He had met with them on two occasions in East Germany and had arranged their itinerary. Kim had laid out a red carpet from the steps of the aircraft to the awaiting limousine. It reminded Saraskina of a trail of bread crumbs to catch an animal.

As they rumbled along the cold, dark, wet streets of Pyŏngyang, Kim proceeded to brief Karpenko on the agenda.

"Minister Yoon will meet with you at ten in the morning to discuss the conditions of your proposal. . . ."

"Cancel the meeting," ordered Karpenko, cutting him off in midsentence. The Korean general stared at the big Russian in shock.

"But, Deetree, he is the Minister of Defense. I cannot . . ."

"I said, cancel the meeting," snapped Karpenko. "We will deal on my terms and at the time of my choosing. Do you understand me?" he snarled.

"Yes, Deetree, but I cannot . . ." stammered Kim. Saraskina and Voshchanov were as stunned as General Kim.

"Reschedule the meeting for ten o'clock the day after tomorrow. At ten in the morning send me three little kimchi pussies. It has been a long time since I was in your country and I am hungry for their company. Now, enough talk. I am tired." His head was splitting open and he had no tolerance for argument. Kim was stunned by the affront and frozen with fear. Protocol was a way of life in North Korea and he knew that such an affront to the Minister of Defense could cost him his head just for delivering the message.

To Saraskina's surprise Karpenko got his three Korean women. What he really wanted was to set the tone of the negotiations, and he had succeeded. When the motorcade screeched up in front of the Ministry of National Defense, he was greeted like a visiting head of state.

The honor guard snapped to attention as an old moon-faced sergeant yelled, *"Pill sung!"* at the top of his lungs.

They were escorted down an austere stone passageway by an entourage of goose-stepping guards and up a broad staircase. It was impossible to hold a conversation over the sound of boots clopping on the cold stone floor. Soldiers yelled attention and others bowed low as they opened the minister's door. Inside the conference room they were greeted warmly by the minister, who emerged from an adjacent office. He was dressed in civilian clothes and surrounded by high-ranking officers.

"Welcome back to Korea, Major General Karpenko," said Yoon, eyeballing Karpenko. Karpenko only nodded as he locked eyes with Yoon. "Please have a seat. We will have tea while we discuss business," Yoon said, waving his hand toward a huge conference table. Karpenko arrogantly took a seat at the head of the table, the one with the minister's nameplate. After an awkward moment Yoon took a seat at the other end of the table.

"General Kim informs me you have an interesting proposition for my government."

"That is correct," bellowed Karpenko too loudly. "I have several one-hundred-kiloton weapons which I will make available to you for two million dollars each."

"General Karpenko, you have three ninety-five kiloton weapons, one of which you have promised to the Arabs for four million dollars," interjected Yoon, demonstrating his superb intelligence. He smiled a "gotcha" smile and watched Karpenko closely for a reaction. Karpenko sat motionless, glaring at the minister. Out of desire to end the stare, Yoon continued. "Every intelligence organization in the world but mine is looking for you, Major General Karpenko." Karpenko continued to stare like a man in a trance. His face twitched on one side of the facial scar and his nostrils flared. "I am prepared to offer you sanctuary in Korea for the weapons," said Yoon, softening his tone.

"Minister, Minister, do not underestimate me. I lived in your miserable fucking country for two years and I have a great fondness for kimchi pussy, but I do not want sanctuary here. I prefer warmer climates with little brown women. As for the weapons, I believe four million U.S. is a fair price for two, seeing as how the Arabs are paying four million for one."

"General, U.S. currency is very difficult for us to acquire. Sanctuary is more appropriate, seeing as how you are a guest in North Korea."

"Four million! You have gold reserves. I know this," snarled Karpenko, pointing a finger at Yoon. It was a deliberate affront. The senior officers at the conference table reacted with a gasp.

"General Karpenko, North Korea does not need your weapons. We have our own program."

"Yes. I know this. You have a program, but it has not been so successful. That is why you want my weapons."

"Four million is too much!" protested Yoon, showing anger. The game was beginning and Yoon knew he had the upper hand. If Karpenko refused he was going to throw him in a cell to rot for a few years to loosen his tongue.

"Take it or leave it! The Arabs have lots of money and they get more every day from stupid Americans who drive big cars."

When Yoon made no counteroffer, Karpenko stood up

and glanced at his men. With a nod of his head he indicated for them to leave. As they stood Yoon nodded to the guards. They braced their body posture and yelled, *"Pill sung"* in unison. They barred the exit, weapons at the ready.

"General Karpenko, I could have your men killed and make you tell me where the weapons are located," said Yoon with a smile. His round face showed a degree of pleasure and it caused Karpenko to laugh out loud. Karpenko's face turned deadly serious as he glared down at Yoon like a madman.

"You cannot make me do anything, you little pissant. If you kill me you will be killing every man, woman, and child in this stinking city, *including yourself, you fucking fool!"*

"What?" burst out Yoon with blazing eyes. He sat up erect in his chair, believing Karpenko was stark raving mad. He was about to order one of the guards to shoot him when Karpenko spoke in voice that was barely more than a growl.

"Have your spies not told you of the Russian program called Airborne Warrior?"

Yoon sat motionless, his mind working at lightning speed. He glanced quickly at General Kim, who had no idea what Karpenko was talking about.

"I know how your little kimchi minds work, so I have prepared a small demonstration for you. *Everyone* inside my shitty little hotel is now dead."

General Kim jumped up from the table and walked into Yoon's office. Slowly Karpenko pulled an amulet from under his long leather coat. It was a glass vial suspended from a heavy gold chain.

"This, kimchi-breath, is a mistake of Airborne Warrior. Unlike the virus I left in my hotel, it has no cure. *It has no half-life.* If I break this vial, the virus inside it will spread over the earth like pollen on the wind. Inside this vial are trillions of tiny airborne warriors who will kill anyone they meet. Perhaps one in a million will survive their attack. Perhaps no one will survive."

Karpenko walked toward Yoon as if he intended to grab him by the throat and strangle him. He stopped directly in front of the small Korean. Towering over him, he growled in his face, "No, no, no, pissant. You will not attack me because I have planted a device in your city that will kill every human being for fifty miles around." Karpenko's lips snarled and his cheek quivered. "I will take it with me, of course, when I tire of kimchi pussies. *Shall we deal?"* he snarled, smiling like a madman.

Saraskina looked at Voshchanov. There was surprise in his eyes. He was shocked by Karpenko's revelation. Then she looked at Suburov. His eyes were smiling. He knew, and because he knew, she knew Karpenko wasn't bluffing. She had heard rumors of Airborne Warrior. It was a black program designed to produce a viral weapon that acted like a chemical compound with a half-life like a nuclear particle. But something had gone wrong, terribly wrong, and the program had been abandoned.

Kim returned to the conference table, looked at the Minister Yoon with a grim face, and nodded his head. Karpenko wasn't bluffing.

Yoon smiled. His inscrutable eyes hid the terror he felt inside. "Three million and we will provide transportation for the weapons," he said in a defeated voice.

"Very well. The money must be deposited up front in a numbered account in Liechtenstein."

"Of course, General Karpenko. Of course. Let's have *soju* to celebrate our agreement," proposed the minister with a false smile.

Servants appeared at the snap of his fingers, serving shot glasses of the clear fiery liquid the Koreans treasured.

"To old friends," toasted the minister.

"To free enterprise and to beautiful kimchi pussy," toasted Karpenko.

"We-hi-yo!" they saluted as they all downed the liquid at the same time, in one large gulp.

"Let us have another," proposed Yoon.

"No," ordered Karpenko. "General Kim promised to introduce me to your karate champion." Karpenko leered at Yoon, playing the hand they had dealt him. He knew exactly what Kim and Yoon had planned. "I want to meet this man."

"Minister Yoon," interjected Kim. "General Karpenko won our national championship when he was assigned to our special forces. I told him about Lee Su Wong's victories and arranged for him to pay his respects," said Kim. Yoon pretended to be surprised by the information. The carefully orchestrated trap was falling into place just as he had planned.

"It is most unusual for a barbari—for a non-Korean to win such an honor," he corrected himself. "You must be very good at tae kwon do," probed Yoon, goading Karpenko.

"I don't know anything about tae kwon do fighting. I fight Russian style, sambo."

"Ahhh! I have heard of this sambo fighting. It is a primitive form of boxing, is it not? Perhaps you would like to make a small wager, my champion against your champion," challenged Yoon.

"What do you have in mind, Minister Yoon?" asked Karpenko, reading his mind like a book.

The Korean ordered another round of *soju* with a motion of his hand. "If my champion beats your champion, we get both weapons for one million."

"And if my champion wins?"

"We pay you four million," said Yoon with a smile.

"Hah! General Kim has told you how much I like to wager. I see you have studied my file in great detail." Karpenko looked at Kim with a brutal expression that made his legs tremble. "General Kim knows me too well, I think. Maybe you have a plan to take advantage of my . . . my gambling weakness?"

Kim shook his head no.

"Before I make a decision, I want to meet this champion of yours," he said with a wave of his hand. He looked at Voshchanov, Suburov, and Saraskina and raised one eyebrow.

"Shall we go? The dojo is nearby," suggested Kim nervously.

"I warn you, Minister. Sambo is not like game-playing karate, jumping and bowing like a ballerina. It is combat."

The dojo was a large open room with polished wooden floors. Fighting weapons of all types hung on the walls. Near the entrance was a large glass case filled with trophies. The huge championship cup sat at the center, surrounded by lesser trophies. The Korean champion was grunting commands at a group of students doing floor exercises when the entourage entered. All of the students were wearing black belts of high degree. Karpenko's head tilted back and he sniffed the air as the massive moonfaced Korean champion waddled in their direction. He was stocky, powerfully built, with a low center of gravity that was perfect for karate fighting.

"General Karpenko, this is Lee Sue Wong, three-time Korean national champion," said Kim proudly.

Karpenko and Lee locked eyes. Lee's face was so round his eyes were barely visible through his epicanthic eyelids.

"I remember you, old sambo-man," grunted Lee. "If you had fought me you would have lost." Lee was playing his part like a champion fisherman, baiting Karpenko like a big marlin.

"Is this your champion?" asked Yoon, gesticulating at Voshchanov, who looked like a world-class fighter. Karpenko ignored him, locked in a death stare with Lee.

"Do you accept my challenge?" asked Yoon.

"Yes. But only under my conditions," growled Karpenko, continuing to stare at Lee.

"What conditions?" asked Yoon eagerly.

"First, there will be no rules. Agreed?"

Yoon looked at General Kim and Voshchanov. "OK, OK."

"Second, the fight is to the death. *Agreed?*" snapped Karpenko loudly. Lee's eyes widened slightly. Yoon looked at Lee and then at Voshchanov.

"Ahhh! I agree if your champion has no objections," said Yoon, looking back at Voschanov. Voshchanov tipped his head to the side and shrugged his shoulders.

"OK! OK! When is the tournament?" asked Kim nervously.

"Now," growled Karpenko, removing his long leather coat without taking his eyes off Lee. He circled slightly to his right while fixing the amulet under his sweater for better protection. He widened his stance quickly, causing the Korean to assume a fighting stance. Lee stood confident and massive, waiting for Karpenko to attack. Using his leather coat for distraction, Karpenko clicked his right boot against his left, releasing a three-inch blade from the toe of his boot.

As the coat flew at the Korean, he parried it with a classic outer block. With the coat obscuring the Korean's vision, Karpenko swept the razor-sharp blade across the back of Lee's lead leg, cutting his calf muscle to the bone and partially severing the tendon that runs up behind the knee. The Korean stared down at the wound in complete shock, at first not believing what had happened. Blood began pumping from his leg. As soon as Karpenko had recovered to a fighting stance, he kicked out with his left leg, only to pull it back quickly for leverage in a chicken kick with his right. The boot blade plunged into Lee's forearm block. Blood flowed from the Korean's arm as the serrated edge sliced through muscle and tendon.

Karpenko circled, forcing the Korean into his own pool of blood, which was gathering on the polished wooden floor beneath him. With lightning speed Karpenko faked another kick that went halfway to its target. Lee slipped to one knee in his own blood, trying to stop a blow that never arrived. Before he could recover, Karpenko smashed the boot knife into his kneecap. The sound of the bone crunching made Suburov and Voshchanov grimace with sour expressions. Then Suburov laughed out loud.

"Stop! Enough!" yelled Yoon.

"No! *I said, no rules and to the death!*" yelled Karpenko like a madman. Covered in blood, Lee used the distraction to scoot across the slippery floor to the wall. He grabbed a staff to defend himself. Seeing Lee with a stick drove Karpenko into a rage. He yanked a weapon off the wall and threw it at Lee with no apparent regard for its intended use. He continued grabbing weapons and throwing them, with no concern for their function. When he had exhausted the supply of weapons he stomped through the front of the glass trophy case and began throwing trophies like an angry wife throwing dishes. Exhausting the supply of trophies, he grabbed the champion's cup and, like an ape with a large rock over his head, hurled it at Lee. He followed it in for the kill. Planting a knee in Lee's chest, he grabbed him by the throat and crushed his Adam's apple. As Lee clawed with his bloody fingers at the death grip, Karpenko ripped at his eyes with his free hand. Like a rodeo rider who had just tied up a calf's legs, he stood up and began plunging the boot knife into the Korean's back and sides. The big man rolled and squirmed on the bloody floor, trying to protect himself. His situation was hopeless. When Lee ceased to move, Karpenko stomped on his neck with such force he nearly severed the head from the body. Karpenko looked down at his victim and saw Derek Evans lying in a pool of red. It made his senses soar.

"Four million in advance, or I will destroy this entire miserable fucking country!" he yelled, shaking his finger at Yoon.

CHAPTER 9

Evans looked up from his desk. It was dark outside and he was mentally exhausted. Grabbing his coat and hat, he abandoned the large stack of folders in his In basket. As he crossed the grinder he noticed the classroom lights were still on. Peering through the small window in the door he saw Lam, head down, laboring over his notebook. Evans entered.

"On dang lam zi da?" he asked in Vietnamese.

Lam jumped to attention.

"Carry on, carry on. Sit down."

"I fine, XO," responded Lam in English, resuming his seat.

"You're working late."

"Yes, sir."

"Do your classmates help you study?" inquired Evans.

"I not need help, sir," snapped Lam.

"Everyone needs help once in a while." Evans studied the boy's face. "How old were you when you left Vietnam?"

"Thirteen, sir."

"Tell me about it," ordered Evans.

"I escape in a boat," responded Lam flatly.

"Escape from what? What was it like in Vietnam?" pressed Evans.

99

"It was bad, sir. I not like to talk about it. It makes me dream bad."

"Perhaps talking about it will make it better."

"No, not better," snapped Lam. "You think I Vietnamese. The Vietnamese think I American. I not belong to anyone. The Vietnamese people were bad to us. They starve us so we steal food. If they catch us they beat us."

"You said us. How many?" asked Evans.

"It change. Sometimes ten, sometimes more," answered Lam.

"All like you?"

"Like me? American? Yes!" answered Lam.

With Evans's persistence, Lam recounted the beating by Waa and his thugs.

"How did you escape?" asked Evans, visualizing the third-world streets of Saigon after the war.

"When the night come for a big boat to leave, we hide on the wharf until the people come by. We joined dem like children and go on the boat with the people. No one know who we belong to, so no one ask."

With Evans's prodding, Lam relived his experience at sea. Disease, lack of sanitation, and storms took many of the refugees. Seasickness and squalor turned the vessel into a hellish nightmare. On the evening of the tenth day in heavy seas they came upon an oil rig off the coast of Malaysia. They begged for help from the oil workers on the platform, but they were ignored. The workers were under orders not to help. To do so would have caused a deluge of people seeking asylum. In desperation the captain used his remaining fuel to ram into the oil rig and scuttle his craft. Lam had been lucky. He was fished from the sea by a huge oilman with a red beard and carried to the main deck where the survivors and dead were gathered.

Lam didn't tell Evans that for the first time in his young life he had cried like a little boy when he saw the tiny bodies of his friends lying on the cold steel deck. He didn't tell the commander that he had sworn a blood oath of revenge against the Vietnamese people. Jack Saunders, the burly rogue of Texaco, plucked Lam out of the sea and carried him topside. He couldn't understand a word the boy said, but he could feel his anguish. With a tear in his eye the big man made a silent commitment that he would adopt one kid. Lam's luck had changed. He was on his way to the Golden Land.

"Hit the rack, Lam," ordered Evans, turning to leave.

"Yes, sir!"

Three days after the Tabasco sauce incident, Jackson struck back at Robinson and Williams, whom he thought were in cahoots. For two days he carried a Ziploc baggy in his trousers waiting for just the right moment. His chance came at lunch after a two-mile ocean swim. Williams loved to eat and he couldn't resist raiding the students' box lunches while they ate. He would walk among them, looking here and there for something to filch. Jackson saw him making his rounds and slipped the bag into Robinson's box lunch when he wasn't looking. Williams rifled Jackson's lunch first but couldn't find anything worth pilfering. But in Robby's box he spotted something different. With a curious look he opened up the bag and took in a big malodorous sniff of dog crap. Jackson could hardly contain himself as Williams exploded with a contorted look on his face.

"Robinson, you twisted, perverted son of a bitch! You have dog shit in your lunch!" he yelled, dumping the contents of the bag on Robinson's head. Robby was lost. He hadn't a clue what Williams was talking about, so he reached up and pulled a chunk of the offal out of his hair. When he smelled it he recognized his mistake.

"Hit the surf, you maggot!" yelled Williams with a sour expression. As the class roared in laughter Robinson made a dash for the surf. For twenty minutes Williams had the entire class doing push-ups in the surf zone. Lam had seen it all and he was tired of childish pranks. Simons, Robinson, and Williams were pains in the butt. Jackson was a total self-centered jerk.

On Friday, 168 passed drown-proofing and the fifty-meter underwater swim and they were pumped at having completed a major hurdle with a record unbeaten by any previous class. Their spirits were high as they ran through the amphibious base on their way back to the center. Robinson's voice boomed out the words the class repeated in rhyme.

> To my left, to my left,
> Hoo, yah, hoo yah, hoo yah
> One sixty-eight
> Feeling good, how 'bout you,
> Fired up, motivate,
> Dedicate, graduate,
> Ah ha, ah ha.
>
> Hey, army, backpacking army,
> Pick up your packs and run with me.
> We are the sons of UDT.
>
> Hey, marine corps, bullet-sponge marine corps,
> Get in your tanks and follow me
> We are the sons of UDT.
>
> Hey, air force, low-flying air force,
> Get in your planes and follow me
> We are the sons of UDT.
>
> Hey, navy, world's finest navy,
> Get on your ships and follow me
> We are the sons of UDT.
> Wake up, wake up NAB.
> We've been up since half past three,
> Runnin', swimmin' all day long.
> That's what makes us tadpoles strong.

They were still on an emotional high when they entered the grinder for their last class of the day. Taufaudy met them at the ship's bell hanging in front of First Phase.

"Jackson, Lam, report to Senior Chief Masure immediately," he said gruffly, and disappeared back into the office.

Ryeback looked at Lieutenant Owen. As the others filed into the classroom he commented, "They are going to pay hell, sir. You can bet on that. Senior Chief Masure saw what happened at the swimming pool."

During the underwater swim test, Williams had grabbed Jackson's leg and held him for a few seconds. Cocky Jackson had attempted the fifty-meter swim anyway and had passed out underwater right in front of Lam. With contempt in his eyes, Lam had just watched him sink to the bottom of the pool. Lieutenant Owen and Simons, who were farther away, had saved Jackson's life. Masure had seen it all, including the argument in the locker room.

Harris had been in and out of the Center for several weeks, observing and questioning, mostly Saleen, Masure, and Williams. They had added small bits of information but nothing worth her time and effort. The object of her assignment was Evans, who might in time become a small scrap of bait to lure Karpenko out of his den and, it was hoped, away from the weapons he had stolen. Her mission was to keep tabs on him, to evaluate him until his every habit was predictable and then do whatever it took to control him during the mission to capture Karpenko. She was confused by a small scrap of information Williams had let slip. Evans and his men had made two trips to Indonesia and only one was described in the official record. As Evans crossed the grinder she fell into step beside him.

"Hi, Commander. How are you?" she said pleasantly.

"Busy."

"Going to check on the underwater knot-tying class?"

"Yeah. Just a quick look-see."

"Mind if I join you?" she asked.

"Not at all."

"I was amused when I saw the word *Seafox* written by the underwater knot-tying class," she said, trying to keep pace.

"A seafox is a type of boat, Alysin."

"Not in this case. Didn't you know? Seafox is my new nickname."

He chuckled. "Somehow that doesn't surprise me."

"At first I thought Williams was up to one of his tricks until I figured out the knots are specially designed for tying explosive cord for simultaneous detonation."

"Spoken like a true frogman. How is your project—excuse me—program going?"

"I've about exhausted my sources. Your men are sick of

my questions. There are a few things, however, I need to clarify with you before I go back to Washington. You think we might have a little chat this evening?"

"Sure thing. Meet me on the quarterdeck at seventeen forty-five. We'll take your car."

"May I ask where we are going?"

"To the races," he said with a smile.

Harris drove the rental car seventy yards to the end of Trident Way and parked. Without moving they had a perfect view of the obstacle course.

"What's up?" she asked.

"That's what I've been wondering."

"Derek, I'm not authorized to talk more about Operation Fastback."

"So, I gather we've made no progress in recovering the weapons," he pried.

"The Coalition has chased down several false leads. I shouldn't tell you this, but the Russians have been extremely open. They've even provided us with photographs of the men in Karpenko's gang."

"I'll bet they are plastered at every border crossing in the world."

"That would be a good bet," she responded.

"No clues as to his whereabouts?"

"The Russians think he is in North Korea," she said, looking through her binoculars at the O-course.

"A SEAL masochist must have designed this thing," she commented. There were numerous behemoths devised to exercise and abuse every part of the human anatomy. The obstacles were arranged in a circle about three hundred meters in diameter. She judged that a good athlete could run the course in fifteen minutes.

"How fast can you run the course, Commander?" she asked, trying to steer the conversation.

"Don't change the subject," he ordered. "Where do you think he is?"

"North Korea, East Germany—who knows? The man is a master of *maskirovka*."

"That's Russian for camouflage or trick, or something like that, isn't it?" he asked.

"Yes."

"I still don't see how I fit into this."

"I told you, SEAL Team Five is assigned as a second-tier force."

"I roger that, Harris. But I'm not the CO of SEAL Team Five yet," he stated.

Harris lowered her binoculars and looked him directly in the eyes. "We've been over this, Derek."

"You know something, Harris?"

"What?"

"You're a bad liar. When you try to deceive me, your pupils constrict and your eyes shift slightly to the right."

"Give me a break, Evans. You know they put me on the box periodically. I've already told you more than I should have."

"Does your boss think Saraskina has been in contact with me all these years? Is that it? Or does he think Karpenko will just walk up to me on the street and try to remove my liver with his spade?"

"Yes. No. I don't know. All we know is he wants to kill you. That's all I'm authorized to tell you."

"How do you know that?"

"I can't tell you that. I can't tell you the source of such information," argued Harris incredulously.

"Why are you hanging around here, Harris?"

"Did you bring me down here to interrogate me?" she demanded.

"Nah. I already know what the score is, Harris. Forget it. Watch the races. You'll find this interesting."

"Tell me about your second trip to Indonesia," she demanded, looking right at him.

"I only made one trip, Harris. It's in the record."

"You know something, Evans?"

"What?"

"You're a bad liar. When you try to deceive me, your pupils constrict and your eyes shift slightly to the right."

Evans smiled broadly. "Simple, Harris. You people can't keep a fuckin' secret. I went back on my own."

"Why did you go back on your own? Saraskina?"

"Harris, I don't owe you an explanation."

"Yes, you do," snapped Harris with a vicious expression. She stared in his eyes until he answered.

"I went back on vacation."

"Bullshit, Evans. You know tradescraft. I know you do. You used to teach it. Did you communicate with Saraskina?"

"Harris, you've got a dangerous fixation on Karpenko's vicious bitch. I'll level with you, which is something you're not doing with me. I went back to kill the crazy bastard and the vermin that surrounded him."

She studied his eyes. "He was gone?"

"Yes. If he had been there, there wouldn't be an Operation Fastback, Harris. You got that?"

"Yes, sir. I believe you," she said seriously. She saw it in his face and it was in keeping with his character. He'd gone back to kill the Spetznaz, not to save Saraskina. Evans had no idea she was Jewish, that she had been feeding the Mossad information for years.

Harris stared at the O-course in relief. With rope swings, balancing logs, and barbed-wire trenches, the SEAL obstacle course looked like a cross between a relic from World War II and machines used during the Spanish Inquisition. She was determined to change the subject.

"How long does it take you to run the course, Derek?" she asked softly just as Saleen, Masure, Jackson, and Lam jogged up to the starting line.

"Ahhh, about nine minutes."

After stretching, Masure, Jackson, and Lam began to run the course. At first they ran neck and neck, at times one taking the lead and then another, but after about six minutes Jackson began to pull ahead of Masure while Lam paced slightly behind. Saleen was at the finish line when Jackson completed the course a full thirty seconds ahead of Masure. He bent over in front of the big black man and threw up. Harris glanced at her watch. He had completed the course in a little over eight minutes.

"The student just beat the teacher," she commented.

"Just like the Company. Jump to a conclusion. It ain't over till it's over, Alysin."

Masure didn't stop at the finish line. He ran right by

Jackson and proceeded to do the course a second time. She watched Saleen shouting at Jackson and pointing in Masure's direction. Jackson tried to catch up, but he only succeeded in catching Lam, who had fallen a full minute behind the experienced instructor. Forty minutes later both Masure and Lam lapped Jackson on the fourth run through the course. In the dusky light of a beautiful California evening Harris watched Saleen pick Jackson up and throw him over an eight-foot vertical wall. She couldn't see what happened on the far side but Jackson burst into view like a dog with its tail on fire. Five minutes later he was crawling in the sand at the base of the Burma Bridge when Masure finished the course the fifth time. Masure and Saleen jogged off, leaving the students on the course. Lam finished five minutes behind Masure, staggering like a dying man in the desert. He looked around for an instructor as he recovered his strength and, seeing only Jackson, whom he despised, he jogged off toward the barracks, leaving his teammate crawling in the sand like a man dying of thirst.

As they drove back to the Center Evans said, "Be in my office at ten hundred on Monday if you want to observe the mast, or should I say observe me administering a mast. I'll warp around Jackson's personality or shit-can him."

"I'll be there."

"Don't be late. Point number one about my character. I don't like being late."

"And you sure as hell don't like to lose either, do you?" she volunteered.

"Make that point number two. On second thought, make that point number one and punctuality point number two," he said gruffly.

Harris was prompt on Monday morning. When she entered the outer office, five people and their entourage were nervously waiting for mast. They were all dressed in their finest blue uniforms and gleaming with spit and polish. Jackson was physically and mentally beat up. Owen, Ryeback, and Robinson were with him to support his case. Robinson kept looking at Jackson and giving him a thumbs-up. Ballard burst through the door and gruffly ordered a sailor out of Evans's office.

"Jackson, you're next," he said without mercy. "Step inside and stand directly in front of the commander. I will order hand-salute, ready, two. On two, you drop your salute. Then I will say, uncover, ready, two. On the word *uncover* your hand goes to your hat. On ready two, you remove your hat. You got that, Jackson?" Ballard spoke as if he had repeated the directions a thousand times. He had.

Jackson's eyes were open wide like a man who had seen a ghost, or was about to. Ballard looked around the room and motioned Owen, Ryeback, and Robinson into the office with a quick jerk of his head. He was turning to reenter the office when he saw Harris.

"Harris, the commander requests your presence for this case. Please stand in the rear," he said in a gruff voice with a touch of annoyance.

"Jackson, forward march," snapped the Junkyard Dawg.

Evans sat behind his huge desk with his hat on. On the desk were several service records and files. He stared at Jackson without a hint of emotion as Ballard went through the motions to set the mast. When he finished, Evans began in an equally harsh manner.

"Jackson, you are charged with a violation of the Uniform Code of Military Justice, specifically, drunk and disorderly. You have a right to remain silent. Anything you say may be used as evidence against you should this case be referred to court-martial. You have a right to a lawyer, one appointed by the government or one retained by you at your expense. Do you understand your rights, Jackson?"

"Yes, sir," responded Jackson in a whipped, trembling voice.

"Very well, do you wish to see a lawyer?" asked Evans.

"No, sir," he answered feebly.

"Speak up, Jackson. I can't hear you."

"No, sir," he responded, still barely audible.

Evans picked up the charge file and perused it. "Master-at-arms, what did you find out from the Coronado police?"

"Sir, the cops arrested Jackson for public drunkenness and disturbing the peace on the Coronado Bridge. However, according to Old Red Foster, he could have charged him with DUI, assault on a police officer, public drunkenness, and pukin' in his squad car. Jackson sideswiped a small car on the Coronado Bridge. One of his lady friends claimed she was driving, though witnesses testified otherwise. After detainment, Jackson told the police he was on a secret mission for SEAL Team Five and was working as a special agent for Commander Evans. Old Red knew he was lying and called Master Chief," said Ballard like a slick lawyer laying on the schmooze.

"Master?" said Evans with a growl. His eyes began to blaze.

"Sir, that is correct. I received a call from Red at three in the morning on the twelfth of September. He explained the situation and agreed to turn Jackson over to me. I ordered the watch to pick Jackson up and restrict him to barracks," responded Saleen. "And, sir, Jackson told Red he was a SEAL stationed at Five. He was lucky Red was once a frogman or his butt would still be in the Coronado jail," he concluded.

Evans was visibly angry.

"Jackson, keeping in mind you don't have to talk to me, and that anything you say may be used as evidence in a trial by courts-martial, what can you tell me to help me make up my mind *not to shit-can your sorry ass?*" snapped Evans.

Jackson mumbled, stuttered, and eventually said, "Ah, sir, I'm sorry."

"Sorry, sorry," bellowed Evans. "I'm going to ask you one time, and one time only, and if you lie to me I will rip out your liver before I send your ass to Adak. Were you driving that car?"

"Sir, yea-yeah . . . yes, sir," stuttered Jackson almost inaudibly. He was shaking so hard his voice was trembling.

"Jackson, let me understand this. While drunk, you drove a three-thousand-pound missile across the Coronado Bridge in complete disregard for the safety of other human beings. Is that right?" he asked grimly.

"No, no, sir. I mean, yes, sir. I mean, I wasn't thinking, sir," he responded weakly.

"What if you had hit Master Chief Saleen's wife and children on that bridge and killed them?" asked Evans in a demanding voice.

Jackson didn't answer. He was bent over like an old man, looking at the floor. Evans jumped up from his chair and snapped, "Look me in the eye, Jackson!" When Jackson looked up, his heart froze. He was looking at a Colt 1911 .45-caliber pistol.

"Jackson, you were a drunken slob bragging about being a SEAL warrior. An unguided missile ready to go off at the slightest twitch."

The sound of the safety clicking reverberated through the room.

"A sneeze, an unexpected noise, and *bang*," he thundered.

The room was dead silent except for the pounding of Jackson's heart, which was skipping beats. Evans's eyes were boring holes into Jackson's skull as he examined the weapon in his hand. The phone rang, shattering the stillness of the room. Jackson flinched and Harris heard his bladder break loose momentarily. Unlike Robinson and the saline bottle, this was no act. When the phone stopped ringing, Evans slowly put the pistol back in his desk drawer. He rubbed his hands over his face as if wiping off salt spray from the deck of an underway boat.

"Jackson," he said calmly, "if you'd hit Master Chief Saleen's family he would have snapped your neck like a chicken and fed your body to the sharks."

Evans sat there for a moment with his hands folded like Solomon before speaking. "Jackson, you were honest with me. I'll give you that. I have made my decision. Look me in the eye."

Ballard yelled, "Aten *hut!*"

"If I see you drinking any form of alcohol while in my course I will personally rip out your heart. This case is dismissed," he said, picking up the next file.

With that the Junkyard Dawg went into action before anyone had the opportunity to think. "Jackson, cover, ready, two. Hand salute, ready, two. About face. Follow me."

It was over so quickly Harris found herself standing dumbfounded with her mouth open. Owen, Ryeback, and Robinson, who had expected to speak on Jackson's behalf, followed him out the door, wide-eyed. Harris smiled as she left the office.

"Shooter, Stick, watch this kid closely. If he is still a troublemaker after this, we get rid of him."

"Boss, what about the gook kid? He's no damn good," said Saleen.

"He copped out on a teammate twice," advised Masure. "I recommend we dump him."

"Look, guys. He's as hard as nails, been through the school of hard knocks. He speaks five languages. Watch him, work him, and mold him into the makings of a SEAL," he ordered.

"I don't know, boss. The school of hard knocks has screwed up that kid so badly, I don't think we can help him," said Masure sincerely.

"Hey, guys. He reminds me of a little orphan girl I saw in Korea. I handed her a cookie and you know what she did? She bit my hand, grabbed the cookie, and gobbled it up in two seconds. She had to fight for her food or die. Today she is a straight-A student in a class for gifted children. Hang in there with me on this one," he said, picking up the next file.

"Remember, she bit your hand before she took the cookie, sir," cautioned Saleen. "This one will have an M-16 in his hand."

CHAPTER
10

Mindanao, Philippines

Lieutenant Alex Gomez and three of his most experienced men had been on the move for almost twenty-four hours. They had left Luzon under cover of darkness in the cargo bay of a C-130 Hercules, along with a group of Filipino commandos who had been in isolation for days planning a routine military exercise. The aircraft had taken them to a small island off the coast of Mindanao, where they had boarded a fast patrol boat for a quick trip across the channel to the main island. There they had rendezvoused with several old trucks that had transported them into the interior of the huge island. Several miles from the target they split into two elements and patrolled on foot through the jungle. It was an elaborate route, skillfully planned by the Philippine Counterterrorist Group to maintain absolute secrecy and the element of surprise. It was almost one in the morning when they finally reached their lay-up point and stopped for a short break.

Gomez whispered to his senior enlisted man, Master Chief Ronald Savarese. "Boomer, see anything?"

"Nah. Just a few critters looking for dinner."

"Things are going just too damn good. I should've known better. I should've sent Decker and Johnson with the other platoon," commented Gomez in a whisper. He brushed a mosquito off his cheek and continued searching the jungle with his nightscope.

"You're wasting your time, boss. I can see a mouse fart with this thermal imager and there ain't nobody out there," whispered the burly master chief. He was scanning the jungle with a night vision device that detected body heat. It was so sensitive it could detect a quarter of a degree of change from the background temperature of the jungle. Savarese could see birds roosting in the trees and small rodents scurrying along the trail ahead of them, but no men. The image he saw was black with blurry white-red images scurrying about. The body heat of a man would have showed up like a flashlight on a dark night. He was comfortable in the darkness, protected by an M-16, a load of 40mm grenades, and the firepower of the United States military.

"I know. I know no one is sneaking up on us, damnit," whispered Gomez, incensed. "The show hasn't started yet. The dicey part begins when we try to link up with the other group. How far do you make us from target?" he asked, already knowing the answer.

"Oh, 'bout a half-click," whispered Savarese, spitting out a gob of tobacco juice.

"We'll know where they are, but they won't know where we are," worried Gomez out loud. "How are we going to make contact?" Gomez wasn't really asking a question. He was thinking out loud.

"Without the use of hot lead, I hope," responded Savarese.

"When we spot 'em with the NVGs, Mangonong can use a red-lens flashlight to signal 'em," suggested Gomez.

"Yeah, and he can send one of his little zipper-heads over for a powwow. If they start shooting at each other we'll kill anyone who comes near us before daylight," said Savarese coldly. The gnarly master chief was serious about defense.

The American ambassador had personally requested the SEALs' assistance on behalf of the government of the Philippines. It was an unusual request that normally would have been ignored, except that the request came from the Philippine Counterterrorist Group, a crack unit of commandos specially trained to combat terrorism. The PCG trusted Alex Gomez and Boomer Savarese. Gomez's wife was Filipino and he had lived among them for three years while assigned to the PCG. During his tour, he had proven himself in action on numerous occasions and in many respects he was considered a charter member of the unit.

"Boomer," whispered Gomez.

"Yeah, boss."

"Something big is going down," volunteered Gomez, making hushed conversation. He took a swig of water and offered Saverese his canteen.

"Like what?" asked Saverese, taking the canteen. He took a big swallow and made a face Gomez could see in the moonlight.

"Damn, sir. Don't you ever clean this thing out? It tastes like iodine. Don't you know that shit will kill you?" complained Savarese. The white of his teeth reflected the dim light filtering down through the thin canopy. Gomez ignored the comment.

"The teams are deploying to Egypt," he continued.

"What the fuck for? There's nothing over there but camel turds and sand."

"Some big combined exercise," whispered Gomez.

"You buying it?" asked Savarese. He raised the thermal imager and scanned the jungle around them.

"Hell, no," answered Gomez in a hushed voice. "It's got to be a cover."

"Cover for what?"

"I don't know. All I know is, shit is being deployed all over the place and for no apparent reason."

"What the hell are we doing here, if the team is headed for Egypt?"

"The PCG asked for us."

"Yeah, I know. Like that carries a lot of clout."

"Boomer, there's a lot of guys back in Guam on a real short string backing us up. There's more to this than meets the eye."

"Like what?" asked Savarese curiously.

"The admiral asked me to be on the lookout for special weapons. He had a weird look in his eye."

"That pompous fuck always has a weird look in his eye," commented Savarese derisively.

Gomez was an ex-enlisted officer of Cuban ancestry who spoke Spanish, English, and Tagalog. Because of his fluency in Spanish he had seen action in Central and South America. In his career with the SEALs he had amassed enormous operational experience. Even men like Boomer Savarese, who had seen action on every continent, respected him and trusted him with such intimate comments. Gomez was considered to be both officer and enlisted.

While assigned to the PCG, Gomez had done more to develop the unit into an effective counterterrorist force than any individual in either government. As a Cuban he was respected. As a SEAL he was venerated. When the PCG began receiving unusual information from reliable sources that something big was happening on Mindanao, the Director of Philippine Intelligence, at the insistence of the PCG, requested Gomez on special assignment.

What they really wanted was the use of specialized night vision and communications equipment that only the Americans possessed, and they wanted the backup of the U.S. government without telling the ambassador why. Ordinarily the U.S. ambassador would have ignored such a request, especially for a junior officer, but the Director of Intelligence had mentioned an intelligence report alluding to a weapon of mass destruction being transported to Mindanao. It was this small scrap of information that had energized the ambassador.

Gomez carried on his person a satellite radio that gave him instant access to his headquarters in Virginia. Men and aircraft were on standby in Guam to assist if he needed them. Three platoons of SEALs and two Green Beret A teams were on standby in a hanger on the runway. General Ashton and Admiral Arlington had personally briefed Gomez on the rules of engagement. In private, Arlington had asked him to be on the lookout for special weapons and to contact headquarters immediately if he came across information on any special weapon or equipment not indigenous to the area. The admiral didn't brief him into Operation Fastback, but Gomez was smart enough to know that a lot of unusual troop movements in the Special Operations community meant big trouble brewing.

The PCG operated American-style in large part owing to

Gomez's influence during their formative years. The assault units had been in isolation at a secret training base on Luzon for more than a week when Gomez and his men joined the mission two days before launch. His special action team was still suffering from jet lag when they departed Luzon. But they were experienced men who had learned to sleep anywhere, anytime, anyplace. They caught a few winks on the C-130 and a few more on the patrol craft before bouncing along the jungle roads of Mindanao in the back of the old trucks. By the time the mission was near climax they were acclimated.

The PCG were good operators for Filipinos but they were no match for a crack unit of professionals. They dressed in American camouflage and they looked the part, but they lacked the specialized weaponry, communications, and night vision equipment necessary for a major operation against a well-trained and well-financed terrorist group. They carried M-16s, M-60s, and 40 Mike-Mike, so they lacked the surgical capabilities of the Brits, the Germans, or the Americans, who used MP-5s for close-in work. The 9mm weapons didn't penetrate walls as easily as the M-16 and the M-60. Such weapons could easily pass through the body of a terrorist and continue through the wall of a hotel room to kill a friendly on the other side. Less powerful, lower-velocity weapons like the 9mm MP-5 were needed for surgical operations like shipboarding and urban assaults. Without sophisticated communications equipment it was almost impossible to choreograph the movements of several men in combat action in a congested urban or shipboard environment.

But what the PCG lacked in equipment they made up for in good intelligence, cultural knowledge, and experience in the terrain. Their commander, Colonel Mangonong, had decided to use twenty-four shooters, plus Gomez and his crew of three men, for the mission. Alex Gomez was worried about the tactics Mangonong had chosen. He was approaching the objective from two separate directions in two groups of twelve men each. Gomez didn't like dividing the assault forces unless absolutely necessary, and then only at the last moment. He had insisted that he and his crew join Mangonong's group so they could watch out for each other. It was a decision he now regretted.

Gomez's major concern as they moved up a jungle trail toward their initial assault position was that the two groups would get confused and hit each other by accident. Two heavily armed trigger-happy groups of commandos operating independently in enemy territory was his worst nightmare. Two hours after they left the trucks they lost communications with the other group. As they neared the target area unaware of the location of the other unit, the hair on the back of Gomez's neck was beginning to stand at attention in preparation for the horrible crack of an M-16 that would spell mission disaster and perhaps death from friendly fire.

But Gomez's years with the PCG paid off. Both groups coolly approached the target and calmly set up observation points to survey the area. After establishing verbal communications, a feat made possible by Gomez's night vision equipment, short-range radio communications was reestablished by sharing American equipment. The main bodies approached the target in an L-shaped fashion and settled in to wait for dawn.

Gomez was beside himself with pride. From experience he knew that operations as complicated as this one rarely went as planned. Something always went sour. Either a plane or boat or truck or radio would fail, sending the operation into chaos. The PCG had flawlessly executed the plan even without radio communications, and from the movement within the village the insurgents were completely unaware of their presence.

The guerrillas had chosen their rendezvous location well. It was a small village deep in the mountains of Mindanao. The locals were supportive of the revolutionaries and the few government controls that existed on the island were miles away in Zamboanga. Moreover, they had infiltrated the local forces with informants so every move the government made was telegraphed to them well in advance. They were secure in the mountains and they controlled a sizable chunk of real estate surrounding the village. The circuitous route planned by Mangonong had been designed to avoid detection by spies.

The bar the insurgents were using as a meeting place was the local watering hole for miles around. There were four ways in by vehicle and numerous ways out on foot. Colonel Lim, the Director of Intelligence, had uncovered the location of guerrilla observation posts along the approach corridors. Using this information, Colonel Mangonong had deftly avoided detection by abandoning the trucks and taking to foot patrol.

From Gomez's position he could clearly see people inside the nipa-palm bar. There were ten to twelve men and women sitting around drinking and talking without a concern for security. The village around them consisted of a few shacks and about ten nipa-palm-thatched *hootches* nestled around the bar and a ramshackle gas station located at the crossroads. The bar was typical of the area, little more than a palm-thatched roof over a group of tables. From a distance, it looked like an open-air beach cabana, with large palm-thatched shutters that could be lowered to keep out wind and rain. It was the dry season and the windows were all wide open, giving the commandos a clear view through the bar from every angle. As he slowly crept up on the target, Gomez used his binoculars to observe the people inside the bar. They were drinking beer and talking loudly over the sound of music blaring from a radio. The music sounded more Arabic than Filipino.

At three, Colonel Mangonong gave the order for the main bodies to close in to final assault positions. The men slowly inched their way toward the target like cats closing in for the kill. Occasionally a dog would spook and bark sporadically, alerted by odors beyond the senses of humans. From his advanced position Gomez could clearly see the faces of the people inside the bar. He could even hear some of the small talk over the sound of the music. By the lamplight in the bar he counted the pistols and assault rifles that were visible. In his mind he began to question Mangonong's decision to use only twenty-four men, but then he decided that with the element of surprise, twenty-four to twelve was damn good odds. Secrecy was much easier to keep for a small force in a land filled with numerous suspicious factions spying on one another. He liked small groups. It was the SEAL way, a methodology that had been abandoned by the U.S. military, in favor of U.S. Army methodology. The U.S. would have used an entire ranger battalion for a mission of this size and they would have approached like a herd of water buffalo. The army method was like killing flies with sledgehammers. Recently, Gomez had been involved in a huge American operation in Bolivia dominated by the army and the DEA, and he didn't like the feel of it. By the time it was planned and geared up, the bad guys were gone. Even with his concern for the PCG's choice of tactics, Gomez was comfortable in his ability to fight his way out of a bad situation. He had a SATCOM radio and the power of the Seventh Fleet at his disposal if he decided to go his own way.

Gomez searched for lookouts and heavy weapons up and down the roads using Savarese's thermal imager, but he couldn't spot any. There were several beat-up vehicles parked alongside the roads but no one was in them.

They must have left their heavy-caliber weapons in the vehicles or put them on the floor of the bar, he thought.

The insurgents were bunched up with no barricades to hide behind but the thin palm thatch. As he sized up the situation he couldn't help but think that it was just too easy. There was only one problem, the damn M-16s and M-60s. They were great for the approach but too destructive for a surgical operation like this one where capture was a major objective.

The PCG's stated mission was to surprise the insurgents during a coordination meeting between cells, capture as many prisoners as possible, and gather intelligence to be used for quick follow-on strikes that could destroy the entire insurgency on the Island of Mindanao. Philippine Special Forces on exercise in Luzon would be diverted to Mindanao to conduct search and destroy operations based on the information they gathered during the mission. Multiple intelligence sources indicated that this group of terrorists was planning a major offensive and that they had amassed large caches of weapons and supplies in the mountains of Mindanao for transhipment and use on the islands of Cebu and Luzon. The GOP hoped that several quick follow-on strikes would destroy the insurrection completely.

Savarese heard the grinding of gears first, then the sound

of engines straining up the mountain road. Several minutes later an old '63 Chevrolet followed by a beat-up Ford of fifties vintage screeched to a halt in front of the bar. Mangonong became excited as several armed men piled out of the cars, looking suspiciously up and down the street. They walked in the bar and were greeted warmly by the occupants.

Gomez looked through his binoculars and the face of a beautiful Asian woman about twenty-eight years old filled his view.

"Boomer, look at this shit, man," he whispered, handing Savarese his binoculars.

"Well, she's definitely not a Flip. Tits are too big," whispered Savarese, forgetting in the heat of the moment that Gomez's wife was Filipino. He handed the binoculars back. "High cheekbones, boss. I think I smell kimchi."

"Me too. What the hell are Koreans doing in Mindanao?" he asked.

"Beats the shit out of me, but they're sure as hell walkin' in harm's way," commented Savarese, looking around at the trigger-happy commandos. Gomez's first thought was that they were selling arms to the Filipinos and had blundered into the ambush by sheer bad luck. His ruminations were interrupted when a soldier near him shifted position for a better shot-angle and lost his footing. He hit the ground with a distinctive metallic clatter that alerted the village dogs. They began to bark ferociously and everything went downhill. The new arrivals were still fidgety and a couple of them got up to investigate the noise. As the lead man stepped through the door, one of the colonel's men spooked and squeezed off a round that caught him squarely in the chest. For several seconds there was silence and disbelief as the report of the rifle echoed through the jungle and slowly registered in the minds of insurgents and commandos. Then all hell broke loose.

"Fire," yelled Mangonong as he cut loose with his M-16 on automatic. A stream of red tracers streaked into the bar like a ray gun from space.

For four full minutes the PCG rained absolute hell on the insurgents. Red tracers ripped through the walls of thatch and bamboo as if through paper. Showers of wood splinters, glass, and hot lead flew throughout the bar. The crack of 40 Mike-Mike grenades rumbled up and down the roads like thunder. There were only a few effective rounds returned from behind the vehicles and they fell silent after the first grenade exploded. Between the four M-60s and the 40mm grenades, there was sufficient firepower for total destruction in thirty seconds.

Colonel Mangonong finally gained control and halted the fusillade of lead. He deployed perimeter teams to cover the four exits and sent in search teams. Gomez and Savarese entered the bar two minutes after the shooting stopped. The dirt floor was covered in blood and guts. Dead and dying littered the floor in body piles. The beautiful Korean girl was missing half her head from a direct hit by a 40mm grenade. She lay in a tangled mass of bleeding bodies that had congregated near the bar for cover. The ones that were still alive were not long for this world. They were gurgling in blood and moaning the wail of the dying. Next to the Korean woman was a Korean male. He had a sucking chest wound that bubbled and frothed with each gasping breath. His eyes were vacant in death despite the involuntary movement of his chest.

Savarese grabbed Gomez by the shoulder and roared, "Boss, check this gear out! It looks like the shit carried by those infiltrators the ROKs smoked up near the DMZ last fall."

"Yeah. It's North Korean, all right," responded Gomez, checking the equipment markings.

"All of the arms are knockoffs. Look at this one," said Savarese excitedly.

Gomez took the rifle and shone his flashlight on the receiver. There were no serial numbers and no sign that serial numbers had been removed. It was a perfect copy of an M-16 and it wasn't American made.

"Same-same as the ones we saw in kimchi land, boss," suggested Savarese.

"Yeah. It's counterfeit, all right," agreed Gomez, puzzled by the mess around him.

They looked over the other weapons. The AKs were knockoffs, as were the pistols. All the gear was North Korean forgery. The intelligence gain from the flotsam was of minimal value. There were no prisoners to question or documents to read. Gomez looked through the tangled mess of bleeding bodies and just as he suspected, discovered several Korean males. But what was on the back side of the bar nearly knocked him off his feet.

"Hey, Boomer! Look at this guy!" he yelled.

Savarese worked his way around the mess on the floor and shone his flashlight down on the body, combining his light with Gomez's.

"Son of a bitch if it isn't Muammar Qaddafi," exclaimed Savarese.

"It certainly looks like his brother. I don't know what to make of this shit, Master," commented Gomez. He searched around and found another Arab. "Hey, here's another one."

"What are Arabs doing on Minda-fuckin'-now?" commented Savarese.

"Bleeding profusely from massive sucking chest wounds. Too bad we can't have a little chat with them," retorted Gomez, searching the pocket of a dead Arab.

"Maybe their camels took a wrong turn at India," said Savarese, making light of the situation. It was his way of blocking out the gore.

"Nothing on this guy," said Gomez.

"This one's clean too, boss," reported Savarese. "I need some air. Let's get the fuck out of here."

The search teams quickly stripped the bodies of weapons and documents, most of which were useless. In the back of one of the old trucks they found what they had come for. It was a map case that led to ten strike missions, everything the GOP had hoped for.

Colonel Mangonong had the bodies photographed before he torched the village. Just after daylight the helicopters came in one at a time to a small field on the edge of the abandoned village and extracted the commandos and their booty. Gomez and his crew took the first bird out. They stayed on Luzon for the analysis of the intelligence and the launching of phase two of the operation, but within thirty-six hours of his initial report to headquarters they were recalled to Washington, D.C., for debriefing.

Gomez was assigned the worst seat in the economy class

of the Northwest Orient 747 among several crying orphans on their way to the Golden Land. Their cries kept echoing through his exhausted half-sleep like the sounds of the dying on Mindanao. His mind kept replaying the significant events over and over again, thirty-six thousand feet above the Pacific. But the pieces just wouldn't fit together. North Korea was too poor to sponsor guerrilla warfare in the Philippines and the insurgents were too poor to buy arms from North Korea. The Arabs had money, lots of money, but no reason to be on Mindanao. Gomez didn't know the Russian term *maskirovka*. It was camouflage, disinformation, trickery, subterfuge, and ruse all rolled into one concept. In his wildest dream he could not have imagined that the carnage on Mindanao was *maskirovka*. But Suburov could.

CHAPTER

11

The atmosphere in the Pentagon conference room seemed very British—stuffy, polite formalities and mild disagreements over semantics and procedure. It was the third in a series of conferences chaired by Lord Alfred Norton-Taylor on the subject of future technologies assessment. Their overt function was legitimate and it served as excellent cover for the combined task force of experts whose covert mission was to track down Major General Karpenko and recover the missing nuclear weapons.

Preventing nuclear proliferation was a subject of endless discussion in political circles, which was followed by little or no action. Efforts mostly devolved to attempts at blocking the transfer of critical technology and material necessary to the construction of nuclear weaponry. With the breakup of the Soviet Union, the new republics on the rim of Russia had become huge shopping bazaars for trade in nuclear, biological, and chemical weapons. But Karpenko was selling finished goods in a demand market to customers who were more than willing to provide him with intelligence and assistance.

Behind the chair members were the most experienced men in the world in special operations and intelligence. The German chair was held by Klaus Von Kessler, who brought with him the Chief of German Intelligence and the Commander of the GSG-9, the crack German counterterrorist unit that had successfully defeated several terrorist organizations. Behind Norton-Taylor was the Director of MI-6 and the Commander of the Special Air Service, the British counterterrorist unit that had successfully taken down the Iranian embassy in London. Norton-Taylor himself was a professional diplomat, but he had risen up through the ranks of British intelligence before entering the diplomatic corps. He was an expert in solving international intelligence problems. Mosha Habberman was the only Israeli in attendance at the meeting, but he was the Israeli Prime Minister's personal advisor on terrorism and he had direct access to all the resources of the Israeli government, including the Mossad. The Israelis had the best intelligence sources in the Middle East. Habberman had shocked his colleagues during their last executive secession with information that a radical Arab faction of the PLO was going to purchase one of the stolen weapons.

Miles MacFarlane, the U.S. Assistant Secretary for Special Operations, was the lowest ranking of the diplomatic players, but he had the most resources at his disposal. Behind him were his military subordinates. They sat quietly, grim faced and bored, like their counterparts from the other countries, waiting for the politicians to ask technical questions about military matters. General Ashton had brought all five of his principal players from the Rangers, the SEALs, the Green Berets, the Air Force Special Operations Squadron, and the Joint Helicopter Task Force.

The politicians sat around a huge conference table listening to endless briefings from various intelligence specialists. MacFarlane had requested that the third meeting be held in Washington, D.C., because he knew that Maksim Litvinov would be embroiled in internal Russian politics and unable to attend. Litvinov was the Russian envoy personally appointed by Boris Yeltsin, who had given specific instructions to share all the information the Russians possessed. In the first meeting Litvinov had provided a comprehensive briefing and an in-depth analysis of General Karpenko's career, his organization, and the types of weapons he had stolen. He also provided a list of possible customers based on the contacts Karpenko had made during his military career. During the second meeting Litvinov had even provided personality profiles and pictures of the members of Karpenko's organization. But even with this forthrightness, no one fully trusted the Russians. Their country was in turmoil and it was likely that Karpenko had friends in very high places within the Commonwealth of Independent States. Each chair member was holding a different hand of cards and was playing them as he saw fit.

Norton-Taylor and MacFarlane suspected that Habberman was holding back valuable intelligence because he distrusted the Russians. So the third meeting had been strategically planned to exclude Litvinov by circumstance and thereby work Habberman into a more open partnership.

A U.S. Intelligence officer dressed in a crisp air force uniform took the floor first to brief the committee. He pushed the button on the slide projector and a huge screen at the end of the room filled with a satellite photo of Russia and Eastern Europe. It was marked all over with little red dots that looked like measles.

"Gentlemen," said the razor-sharp air force colonel, "this overhead depicts all the known emitters in Central Asia. The one with a tail like a small comet is Chernobyl. All these emitters," he said, circling the photo with a light pointer, "have been correlated with previously charted emissions. From time to time we lose track of an emission, such as during a reactor overhaul or during a deep dive by a nuclear submarine, but we soon regain contact, classify, and replot the emission. All current emitters correlate with the information provided by the Russians, as well as our own intelligence data bank."

The briefer flipped to the next slide and continued through his fifteen-minute monologue. The incident on Mindanao was a small bullet buried among thirty briefing slides. Only Habberman questioned the information.

"What precipitated U.S. involvement in the Philippine operation?" he asked curiously.

MacFarlane responded. "The GOP requested our assistance on a counterterrorist operation on the island of

Mindanao. They have been having a lot of trouble in that area lately. The U.S. ambassador thought it prudent that we provide the requested assets because of an unusual intelligence report, propaganda to the effect that the insurgents had a weapon of mass destruction." He looked at General Ashton, who took over the response.

"I assigned a SEAL officer who served a tour of duty with the Philippines Counterterrorist Group," stated Ashton. "Combining all sources of information from the CIA, NSA, DIA, and his report, we concluded that the information about a weapon of mass destruction was propaganda on the part of the rebels."

"May I speak directly with the action officer?" asked Habberman. The other chair members turned to Mac-Farlane, who turned to General Ashton, who looked at Admiral Arlington.

In his most patrician manner Arlington said, "I have thoroughly debriefed the action officer and his senior enlisted, and I am prepared to answer your questions."

Habberman looked at the admiral for a short moment before responding in a politically correct tone. "Admiral, it is my policy to speak directly to the men who actually participate in a mission whenever possible. May I speak with them personally?" he asked pleasantly.

Habberman had learned from experience that admirals and generals were too far removed from the action. When the Israelis wanted to execute a mission the political leaders insisted that the commanders of the action units plan and execute the mission, not their senior administrative superiors. Their experience had proved that field commanders were the ones with the necessary knowledge to avoid the costly little oversights that lead to disaster. The major blunders in U.S. military history could be attributed to planning that failed to incorporate the men who were charged with carrying out the missions. Operational security was a double-edged sword. If the soldiers who executed the mission knew, there was a chance of a breach of security. If they didn't know, there was an opportunity for disaster by planning oversight.

"Yes, of course," responded Arlington. "Lieutenant

Gomez and Master Chief Savarese are in the building."
Arlington was pleased with himself for anticipating the
possibility. He might be dressed in a military uniform, but
he was a consummate politician.

When the series of briefings ended, an aide handed
Norton-Taylor a folder, which he perused briefly before
speaking. "Gentlemen, before we adjourn for lunch I want
to read a cable I just received from MI-Six. I think you will
find it very interesting and somewhat related to the problem
we face. I quote. 'Ukrainian President Leonid Kravchuk
fired off an angry cable today to Boris Yeltsin, calling the
unauthorized flight of six long-range bombers from the
Ukraine to Russia last week a hijacking. Kravchuk demanded that Russia return the planes, their crews, and the
regimental banner they took with them.' End quote. Also,
and I paraphrase the cable for brevity, neither the Russians
nor Ukrainians have any new information to report on the
Karpenko mafia. I suppose we are bloody lucky Karpenko
wasn't an air martial or the weapons would already be in the
hands of the enemy. With that, gentlemen, this meeting is
adjourned. There will be an executive secession immediately following lunch."

At 1255 Gomez and Savarese sat down outside the
conference room on a sterile bench that had sat in the same
location since the construction of the Pentagon. The surface
of the bench was as smooth as glass, polished by countless
nervous asses waiting to brief important men who were
struggling with the difficult issues of their time. The face of
war had changed drastically since the bench was placed in
the huge hallway, from trench warfare with clear national
battle lines to intercultural conflicts that transcended national boundaries. The modern-day enemy wore civilian
clothes and flew on United Airlines with fake passports.
Pandering to public emotion, terrorists played the news
media. And now a drug war raged, pitting men in uniform
against international mafias of rich narco-merchants operating with impunity from dozens of countries.

Two armed marines assigned to guard the entrance eyed
Gomez and Savarese with disdain. They didn't like SEALs.

SEALs were swabs who got too much attention. As high-ranking officers and political appointees returned from lunch, the marines saluted smartly. The important people walked by the marines as if the young men should recognize them personally. They couldn't. To the marines they were just a crowd of important people, paper-pushing assholes who didn't know one end of a gun from the other. They were reading their name tags and checking them off a list. Only Admiral Arlington noticed that the two most decorated men in the immediate area of the Pentagon were sitting in the hallway shining a bench with their asses. He smiled at them and gave a sort of backhand British salute as he entered the conference room.

"What gives, boss? What the fuck are we doing here?" asked Savarese too loudly.

"Shooo," said Gomez, motioning toward the marines glaring at them.

"I say again, what the fuck are we doing here?" whispered Savarese.

"I don't know, Boomer," said Gomez, motioning with his eyes to the sign over the conference room door, "but I'll bet it's got nothing to do with future technologies assessment. What the hell would Arlington and Ashton have to do with that kind of ethereal bullshit?"

"What does *ethereal* mean?" asked Savarese with a sour expression.

"Something to do with ether—you know, sky-high brainy stuff that gets you high," whispered Gomez.

"Well, I'd much rather be humping an LBFM in the PI than shining this goddamn bench with my ass," said Savarese, forgetting again that Gomez's wife was Filipino. Savarese had a great sense of integrity when it came to most things, but when it came to sex there were no rules as long as it was female. He liked his LBFMs two and three at a time. Gomez didn't take offense because he had a similar appetite that had been thoroughly whetted in the PI before he got married. That part of Savarese just never changed.

Savarese's voice was deep and booming and he soon forgot there was a conference going on inside the room. One of the marines pointed a finger at him and shook it. He put it up to his lips in a gesture ordering Savarese to be quiet. His manner of gesticulating set Savarese off. He gave the marine a finger and silently spoke the words "Fuck you," daring him to take further action. The marine looked down at his clipboard, defusing the bomb that was about to explode.

"Get me out of this fucking place. I wanna go back to Bolivia or the PI," complained Savarese, angry from the exchange. He wanted to kick the shit out of the marines, or anybody, just for the action.

"Boomer, we ain't going back to the PI, pal."

"Then where we goin'?" demanded Savarese.

"Shit, I don't know. The whole damn command's on standby. In fact, all Special Operations Forces are on standby. My guess, something big is going down in Europe."

"Hmmm, I wonder if that fur-lined fräulein of mine still lives in Hamburg."

"Forget it, Boomer," Gomez said with a chuckle. "The only thing you're going to see is a fur-lined fart sack laid out on a cot inside an empty aircraft hanger."

The executive session started like a poker game. There were a few pleasantries and then a little verbal fencing over nothing in particular until Norton-Taylor busted through the ice.

"Gentlemen, we know that Libya, Pakistan, Syria, Iran, Iraq, and North Korea are on Karpenko's short list of customers. Then there is the PLO, Abu Nidal, and Hezbollah. I don't believe there are any other organizations with sufficient finances to buy one of the weapons," he challenged in a thick British accent.

"I agree," said MacFarlane.

Kessler nodded his head in agreement. "Since Intell has been unable to fix the location of the weapons we must be prepared for immediate action in each area," volunteered Kessler.

"I agree," said MacFarlane. "We have sufficient resources in place to interdict any suspected shipment by sea, air, and land."

"But how long can we sustain such a posture? And do we

have sufficient forces to cover the entire planet?" argued Kessler like an arrogant Prussian.

"If we pool our resources and keep them strategically positioned, we can cut off all lines of communication between Karpenko and his clients. But we cannot maintain such a posture indefinitely," argued MacFarlane.

"Karpenko has limited options, too, gentlemen," interjected Norton-Taylor. "The signature of the weapons, for example, restrict him to seagoing vessels or large trucks."

"Why?" asked Kessler.

"He knows he has to cover the weapons under a thick layer of shielding to prevent detection by satellite; otherwise, we would have spotted them by now," responded MacFarlane.

"But what about aircraft? He could move the weapons so quickly we might not be able to respond," commented Kessler.

"If he moves the weapons by aircraft, it must be done very quickly. We are prepared to challenge any aircraft that strays from flight plan," Norton-Taylor commented.

"But we don't know where the weapons are," stated Kessler flatly. "They could be stashed in the Urals, the Caucasus, or, for all we know, Outer Mongolia. In which case he could truck the weapons to Iran or Iraq. We might not be able to spot the emissions or respond in time if we did see the signature," argued the German.

"The Russians are searching all road traffic carefully. If Litvinov is correct, Karpenko is still in the area of the eastern Black Sea, and if he is there, his first customer is either Libya, Syria, Iraq, or Iran," volunteered Kessler.

"If the Russians are correct," MacFarlane interjected, "Karpenko is in North Korea making a deal as we speak."

"If they are correct," interrupted Habberman. It was the time he had spoken and they all looked at him curiously.

"Karpenko might wait for years before he moves a weapon," said MacFarlane.

"Oh, I don't believe so. I should think his bloody ego wouldn't allow him to hold off. He will move soon," said Norton-Taylor confidently.

"Then we must be prepared to launch a mission on any new emitter," Kessler chimed in.

"Yes, of course. But we agree we can't cover the entire planet indefinitely. We have to gamble on Northeast Asia," urged MacFarlane.

"Habberman, what do you think?" asked Norton-Taylor, carefully watching the Jewish man's eyes.

"I want to talk to the men who went to Mindanao," responded Habberman, deep in thought.

MacFarlane looked at Norton-Taylor and exchanged a silent agreement. "Sure," said MacFarlane, pushing a buzzer that summoned an armed marine.

The marine closed the door behind Gomez and Savarese as they entered the anteroom.

MacFarlane motioned them to have a seat. "Gents, we just have a few questions about your mission in the Philippines." He looked to Habberman to continue.

"How would you rate the quality of the intelligence?" asked Habberman.

"Outstanding. They knew exactly where they were going and exactly what they were going to find," Gomez responded.

"Wouldn't you say that was unusual for the Philippines?" suggested Habberman.

"Well, yes, sir. I spent three years with them chasing Sparrows and we only caught a few," responded Gomez. He knew that Habberman was an Israeli by his accent and if he was a pro he knew that a Sparrow was a Filipino hit team. If he didn't know, he wasn't worth talking to.

"So, their intelligence was unusually good," stated MacFarlane.

"Yes, sir. It was outstanding," answered Gomez with conviction.

Habberman turned his questions toward Savarese.

"Master Chief Savarese, did you notice anything unusual while you were on the mission?"

"Yes, sir, I did. Three Koreans walked right into the kill zone, one female and two males. And there was a shit-pot load of North Korean gear, all new, everywhere," answered Savarese.

Habberman raised his eyebrows. "Master Chief, how do you know it was North Korean equipment?"

"The gear had the same milling and factory markings we saw on the five North Korean infiltrators the ROCs shot last year near Kisamoon. I examined the scene personally," answered Savarese flatly. "And that's not all that was unusual. There were a couple of dead Arabs in the body pile."

Habberman furrowed his brow. "Lieutenant Gomez, doesn't it seem strange that after years of searching, they achieved such a degree of success?"

"Well, I can only surmise that they lucked into a good intelligence source and it paid off."

"Any sign of Russian involvement?" asked Habberman.

"No," responded Gomez with a puzzled expression.

"What do you think about the rumor of a nuclear weapon on the island?" asked Habberman.

Gomez looked at Savarese. "Nuke? On Mindanao?" growled Savarese. "No fuckin' way! The Flips on that island can barely pick coconuts!"

Habberman looked at MacFarlane and nodded his head that he was satisified.

"Thank you, gentlemen," said MacFarlane as he pushed the buzzer to summons the marines.

After the door had closed, Habberman spoke to the group. "The Philippines is just a ruse. One of several false trails Karpenko has created. We have information that he will deliver one of the weapons to a radical Palestinian group in Syria sometime in the first part of November. Their target, gentlemen, is Tel Aviv."

Kessler, MacFarlane, and Norton-Taylor were stunned. Even their poker faces had deteriorated to furrowed brows. Norton-Taylor was the first to break the silence.

"Mosha, is your bloody mole inside the Karpenko organization or the Arab alliance?" he asked.

"I am not authorized to disclose our sources, Alfred, but I assure you the information is very reliable. We must prevent this weapon from being delivered to Syria, or Israel will be forced to conduct a preemptive strike that will precipitate another war in the Middle East. Miles, I invite you to send Lieutenant Gomez and Master Chief Savarese to Israel to join with a special unit we have formed." Habberman had read intelligence reports on the crazy

Cuban provided by a Jewish American officer stationed in the Pentagon. He needed an experienced American for the Mossad's next move. He wanted the cover.

"Done deal," said MacFarlane without reservation.

As Gomez and Savarese walked down the huge Pentagon corridor, their steps echoed in unison off the bare concrete walls.

"What the hell was that all about, boss?"

"I think I know why everyone, including the FBI, is on such a short string, Boomer."

"Let me guess. Someone is missing a fuckin' nuke," growled Savarese.

"That'd be my guess."

"Fuck me to parade rest. But who?" asked Savarese.

"I'd bet it's the Ruskies," said Gomez.

CHAPTER

12

The flags of all fifty states stood neatly arranged around the perimeter of the grinder in freshly painted navy blue stanchions. They fluttered in the wind flowing off the Pacific like a field of tall flowers swaying in a lazy breeze. Lam gazed at the large speaker's platform in awe. The deck was covered in dark blue carpet and surrounded by bright red, white, and blue bunting. Behind it hung an enormous American flag that covered the entire surface of the two-story building. The bottom rippled gently in the breeze. In front of the platform were four hundred folding chairs neatly arranged in rows.

Lam just couldn't believe BUDS was finally over. It had all gone by so quickly, and so slowly. One of those four hundred chairs was for Jack Saunders, the big oilman from Texaco who had plucked him from the South China Sea. As he waited for his burly foster father, he thought about the incident that had almost resulted in his dismissal from the course. It began during Hell Week and came to a head with a simple prank Robinson played on Simons several weeks later.

Hell Week, the common denominator of all SEALs, was founded on the theory that men are capable of superhuman performance and that once pushed to that limit they would gain the confidence and courage to face the horrors of World War III. It was six days of continuous hell designed as the ultimate test of physical and mental motivation. For 168, it began with the blast of a machine gun, and it ended with a handshake on the beach.

At precisely midnight, Williams exploded through the door of the barracks with an M-60 on full automatic, yelling at the top of his lungs, "Welcome to Hell Week, gentlemen. Welcome to Hell Week."

They had bolted from the barracks like a panicked herd of wildebeest to face a barrage of water spraying through a cloud of theatrical smoke. Then grenade simulators hammered them, like the concussions that slammed into the men who braved the beaches of Normandy and Omaha. Several men quit in the first five minutes. After breakout, Williams began whistle drills and for more than an hour they wriggled in the sand, following him to the ocean as he snaked his way like the Pied Piper, up and down the sand dunes. Parachute flares lit the night sky as they crawled into the surf.

Hours later, cold and miserable, they were still linked arm in arm, singing songs in the surf zone. Williams ordered them in and out of the ocean over and over to exercise on the beach. Leny Thompson, a skinny boy from Kansas, collapsed from hypothermia on the fourth trip to the beach. All he could do as the corpsman dragged him off stiff as a board was yell, "Hoo yah, One Sixty-Eight!" They yelled back, knowing it was over for Leny Thompson. As Williams ordered them back into the cold surf, another man quit.

"Get back with your class, Kaiser," ordered Williams.

"No, Instructor. I quit!"

"Kaiser, if you don't get back with your boat crew, I'll make them carry me to chow in the IBS," he screamed.

"I don't care what you do! I quit!" cried Kaiser.

"Ring out, traitor. You're out of here," growled Williams.

Kaiser had walked to the pickup truck and rung the ship's bell three times. Lam could almost hear the bell ringing as he looked at the huge flag rippling in the breeze.

Ding! Ding! Ding!

The pickup truck had followed them all week. All they had to do to end the misery was ring the bell. It was a symbolic act of abandoning one's teammates to the enemy. They watched silently, standing as close together as men could stand, as Kaiser abandoned them. As he walked up the beach, they sang him a song.

"Happy trails to you, until we meet again. Happy trails to you . . ." Kaiser had given them the finger.

"You like surf appreciation, gents?" yelled Williams.

They answered with a spirited roar and a song. "We like it here, we like it here, you fuckin' aye, we like it here."

Back in the surf zone they began to taunt the instructors with "It's toasty warm. Come on in. We like it here, we like it here, you fuckin' aye, we like it here."

The instructors liked their spirit. They waded into the surf and swam around behind the men, diving under the waves like seals. Even Williams got in the water, but he refused to get his hat wet. When he tired of the waves he ordered them out and made them do two thousand jumping jacks and fifty push-ups to warm up.

"About face! Forward march!" ordered Williams, sending them back into the surf to see if anyone else would quit. They were numb and shaking so hard their teeth rattled, but no one quit. At the waters edge he hollered, *"And halt! About face!"*

"It pays to be a winner, gentlemen. The first boat crew ready for chow rides in the ambulance."

Monday had bled into Tuesday and Tuesday into Wednesday without sleep. The water in Glorietta Bay was dark and icy cold as they stood at the end of steel pier, a floating dock used to tie up small craft. Taufaudy ordered them to jump off fully clothed and for ten minutes he let them tread water. Finally he ordered them to remove their clothing and make water wings from their pants, knowing that someone would lose their boots. When he ordered them out of the water he was looking for a missing pair of boots.

"There are not enough boots here, gentlemen," yelled Taufaudy.

"Instructor Taufaudy, you mean to tell me someone has been so careless as to lose their boots?" yelled Williams. "Who? I want to know who, right now," he demanded like a game show host.

The men shivered in spasms as the instructors poured bootfuls of cold bay water on their bodies. Finally Robinson confessed that he had lost his boots. Williams accused him of covering up for a quitter and ordered them back into the bay to search for the missing boots. Then a student named Johnny Clinton shouted in a hoarse voice, "I quit, Instructor Williams. I quit." That started an avalanche of quitters, muttering and shivering down steel pier to the ambulance. One kid collapsed dramatically. Williams hated the kid because he was always putting on a show of misery. After a little warmth the green in his face disappeared and he tried to join the men in the bay who were diving in the muck looking for the missing boots.

"No, Mabry!" shouted Williams. "You quit while you were passed out. You're outta here!"

When steel pier ended, Class 168 numbered fewer than forty men.

Thursday went by in a blur. The instructors kept them on the move with surf passage and IBS races. All week they had been keeping score and Lieutenant Owen's crew was winning the biggest race of all, Hell Week. As Thursday dragged to a close they were well ahead on points and a sure bet to be secured early Friday morning, six hours ahead of the other crews.

All the students were walking a bowlegged BUDS shuffle as they entered the classroom. The sand had rubbed areas of their skin completely raw. Starved for sleep, their bodies surrendered. They lost toenails. Knees swelled like melons. Limbs waled, fingers and joints puffed up, and because of the severe chafing in the crotch and armpits, sores began to ooze. They held their arms stiffly away from their bodies and hobbled about in a shuffle that minimized the pain of the chafing. Men hallucinated and they all carried the blank look of prisoners released from Auschwitz. During one of the long paddles Lam fell asleep while rowing the boat and fell overboard. Jackson and Robinson had to haul him in the boat because he lacked the strength to help himself. At last light Williams ordered them into the classroom.

"You will not sleep. You will write an essay on the importance of Hell Week, and why you want to be a SEAL."

He dimmed the lights and put soft elevator music on his

radio. Their minds couldn't focus and one by one they keeled over and fell asleep only to be awakened by the shrill sound of a whistle and the yells of the instructors.

"You will not fall asleep! You will write an essay! Your subject is, describe your last moments of life as a lobster placed in a pot of boiling water," screamed Williams.

The mental torture went on for two hours but no one quit. All the quitters were gone. Finally he gave them a mission. The objective was to launch their boats through a heavy surf, paddle down the coast, land on the rocks in front of the Hotel Del, and run back to the grinder.

"It pays to be a winner, gentlemen. The first crew back to the grinder gets to rack out for half an hour," Williams said with a grin.

There were only five boats left of the original fourteen as they patiently waited in the dark for Williams to give the signal with a parachute flare. Timing, teamwork, and luck came into play as the groggy men used their maximum effort to launch the heavy rubber rafts between sets of waves. Owen and crew made it through the surf without a problem and proceeded parallel to the beach. When they reached the turning point they were well ahead of the other crews. All they needed to cinch early relief was a good landing and an easy trot down the beach.

Lam could hear the surf pound on the rocks and he could see the white water in the moonlight. Lieutenant Owen timed the approach so he could jump on the rocks and hold the boat with the bowline until the others could scramble ashore and pull the raft out of the water. But Lam froze for critical seconds. While the men in his boat crew were sitting on an IBS in the rough Pacific Ocean, Lam was on an old Vietnamese junk crashing into an oil rig in the South China Sea.

"Now, Lam!" yelled Owen. "Now!"

But Lam couldn't respond. He was frozen in the past.

Robinson shook him and yelled, "Jump, Lam! Jump!"

But he couldn't move. Robinson finally grabbed the bowline and leapt off the boat. But it was too late. A wave hit and washed the IBS back to sea, pulling Robinson off the rocks. As he struggled to climb back on the rocks, another wave caught the boat broadside and flipped it over in the boiling surf. They all abandoned boat and swam for the beach. Then Lam made a second mistake even more critical than the first. He had crawled up on the sand without his swim buddy, eyes wide with fear. As Masure ran toward Owen's boat crew he heard Jackson yelling in an angry voice. He stopped and let nature take its course.

"You sorry son of bitch! You chickened out!" screamed Jackson.

Lam lashed out with a tired punch that knocked Jackson on his can. Just as Lieutenant Owen grabbed Lam, Simons punched with all his might. "Larson's got a broken arm, you fuck," yelled Simons.

Masure broke up the fracas and called an ambulance to take Larson to the hospital. Hell Week continued without a break and it was assured that Owen's crew wouldn't win. When daylight broke, Williams gathered them on the beach behind the Center.

"Aten *hut!*" he yelled. "It pays to be a winner, gentlemen. It pays to be a winner!"

Evans stood in front of the exhausted men and secured boat crew number five with a handshake while the men in Owen's crew stared at Lam with hate.

"I promised you we would stretch your personal rubber band," said Evans. "Are there any quitters left in this class?" he asked.

"No, XO, hoo yahaaaaa!"

"Then carry on. This mission is not over," yelled Evans.

For eight more hours they paddled and dragged the boats. Every second turned into an hour's worth of hell. Then Evans appeared again. Williams had them lined up facing the ocean for another trip to surf torture.

"About face!" he ordered.

They turned to face Commander Evans, dressed in a fresh khaki uniform, looking like a recruit poster. The trident on his chest reflected the afternoon sunlight in flashes as he moved in front of their bedraggled formation. The sound of the surf broke the silence.

"What's this all about, men?" he asked.

"Preparing for war," said Owen calmly.

"War! war! war! war!" chanted the class hoarsely.

Evans held up a clenched fist. The winning boat crew

walked over the dune, dressed in fresh, clean uniforms, and joined the line of wet, soggy men.

"What's this all about, men?"

"Teamwork," said Owen.

"Teamwork! Teamwork! Teamwork! Teamwork!" chanted the class until Evans held up his fist.

"I've got some good news and I've got some bad news," he said with a look of concern.

"Hoo yah!" yelled the class.

"The good news is, *the cowards never started.*"

"Hoo yah," they yelled until he stopped them.

"The bad news is, *the weak died along the way.*"

"Hoo yah!" they roared, sensing the end was near.

Holding up his fist, he said, "It ain't the size of the balls, gents. It's what's in the heart that counts. And you have what counts. *This mission is over!*"

They raised their fists in victory and hugged one another, jumping up and down with renewed energy. Crying and blowing mucus from their cold, wet noses, they looked up at Evans with shivering faces like starved POWs being liberated from a prison camp. When Evans shook Lam's hand, he couldn't look the commander in the eye. He looked down at the beach. Even in his exhaustion he knew there was a price to pay for Larry Larson.

It came a few weeks after Hell Week when Robinson played a practical joke on Simons. Williams punished both Simons and Lam for the prank and Lam was irate when he entered the barrack. He threw his swim gear in the corner so hard it bounced out of his locker like a rubber ball.

"You always playing games," he shouted. "You always playing games. Now I pay for you, two thousand squat thrust. Two thousand! For nothing but damn games!"

"Fuck you, Lam! It's no big deal," argued Jackson, shoving Lam on the bunk. "You fucked up in Hell Week and caused Larson to get his arm broke!"

Lam jumped up from the bunk and shoved Jackson, who took a swing. Lam ducked and knocked Jackson on his butt just as Senior Chief Masure walked through the door.

"Attention on deck!" yelled Robinson.

Masure stood in the doorway. He stared coldly at Lam. "You know something, Lam, if you kicked the shit out of the guy responsible for most of your problems, you wouldn't be able to sit down for a week. All of you, in the XO's office at thirteen hundred!"

Mast had been a frightening ordeal. Ballard had ordered the two of them into the commander's office like prisoners going to an execution. Reading from a file, Masure recounted every incident against them from day one, concluding with the scuffle in the barracks.

"Sir, these two men have not shown the qualities required of a SEAL. I recommend they be dropped from the course."

"Master Chief, your thoughts?" asked Evans, seated behind his desk like a hanging judge.

"Sir, Jackson has shown great improvement since the incident on the Coronado Bridge. I think we should retain him. Lam, on the other hand, has not shown the team spirit required of a SEAL. I recommend he be dismissed."

Lieutenant Owen broke the silence. "Sir, if I may. All of us have learned a great deal since,"

"Excuses bore me, Lieutenant!" roared Evans viciously.

"Williams! Lash these men together at the hip until I say otherwise. Master Chief, have a buddy line made up from the hawser of the USS *Independence*. Williams, you see to it that these men wear it twenty-four hours a day. They are to run together, PT together, swim together, eat together, sleep together, even use the john together, until I say otherwise," he ordered. "Lieutenant Owen. I expect you to take charge of these men and whip them into shape, even if you have to sleep with them. You got that?"

"Yes, sir." responded Owen.

"Now, with the exception of Lam, you are all dismissed."

When the others had gone, Lam had faced the commander alone. His heart was racing when Evans asked softly, "What happened during rock portage?"

"I cop out, sir."

"What happened?"

"I cop out."

Evans had shouted at him in Vietnamese, *"Ang dang lam zi da, doe mae?"*

"I think too much about escape from Vietnam. I think about crashing into oil rig."

"So you froze?"

"Yes, sir."

Evans leaned back in his chair and stared at Lam with a look that pierced his soul.

"Lam, all of us carry a seabag full of good and bad memories. Bad memories destroy the weak, but they make the strong stronger. You must exercise your mind and your body."

Lam was wearing his Asian mask of empty feeling despite the fact he was about to collapse inside.

"The way of the warrior is not easy. It is discipline and control, not just of body but of mind. You must learn to control your fear and your anger or they will destroy you."

"I not afraid, sir," snapped Lam.

"I don't doubt that. Your people are disciplined."

Then came the statement that had almost cost him his career.

"Who are my people, sir?" Lam had blurted out. "I hate the Vietnamese. They think I American. You think I Vietnamese. I part this! I part that! What am I, sir? You might be my fadder!"

Evans was stunned by the outburst. For a long time he sat staring, boring holes into Lam's head. Lam could sense he was thinking of dropping him from the course, so he softened his expression. "I sorry, sir. I sorry," he pleaded.

"You can't change the past, kid. No one can. But we can change the future. Do you want to be a SEAL?"

"Yes, sir!"

"Why?"

"Because I want to kill dem!"

"Kill who?" yelled Evans.

"The ones who beat us. The ones who call me dust of the earth."

"All the wrong reasons, *boy!*" snapped Evans with a roar. "You understand Buddhism?"

"Yes, sir."

"Then you had better understand this. A Buddhist can only attain enlightenment when he is free from all worldly passions, like anger, greed, fear, lust, and desire. *Right?*"

"Yes, sir."

"Like Buddhism, warrior enlightenment is discipline of mind and body. I *will not let you* become a SEAL until you have learned mental discipline. Do you understand me?" he yelled.

"Yes, sir." Lam had responded like a spanked child.

Then Evans softened his tone.

"Lam, in Vietnam the Americans seldom saw their enemy. They were constantly shot at by an unseen enemy. One day a river patrol boat returned with the body of a sniper they had killed along the river. They dragged the body behind their boat with a rope and when they got to the base they pulled it up on the pier where everyone could see the hated enemy. Everyone came down to see. Some even kicked the corpse and yanked on the rope. An old warrant officer put a stop to the ugliness. Do you know what he said?"

"No, sir," answered Lam calmly.

"He told them there were two enemies in Vietnam. The one outside and the one inside. The one outside is the one that can kill you. The one inside is the one that can turn you into an animal. He pointed at the dead soldier and said, 'This is not your enemy. That is the shell of a man who was fighting for a cause, *just like you!* Treat what's left of him with dignity and respect, for there, but for the grace of God, go you.' Lam, do you understand the enemy inside you?"

"I understand what you saying, XO. I understand. You have bad scar on your body. I see dem when you run on the beach and I think they are the scar of your enemy. You are saying my enemy leave a scar on my mind."

"Yes. Exactly. And it will always be there, like it will always be on my body. But the scars are not the enemy. Fear is not the enemy. Not understanding is the enemy. You must come to grips with how your past influences your life."

"I understand what you mean, sir. If you see the man who makes the scar on your body, will you kill him?"

Evans looked at him with a mean expression. He couldn't lie. "Yes. I would kill him, but with discipline, control, and for a cause greater than myself. You want to kill because of revenge, selfishness, ugliness, because of hate."

"Sir, in my world it is kill or be killed. I can take care of myself," blurted Lam.

"This is your world now, *boy!* You'd better get that

through your head, or I will shit-can your ass from this course."

"Yes, sir!"

"You'd better get the message, loud and clear. There are two enemies, Lam. The one out there which can kill you with a gun or a knife, and the one inside *here,*" he said, pointing at his temple with his finger like a pistol. "Teamwork, Lam. Teamwork. Do you understand?"

"Yes, sir."

"Good. Then I'll tell you what I want you to do to gain enlightenment. Go down to the beach and think about these things. Then, run to Imperial Beach and think some more. And after you have meditated on these thoughts, run back. And if you don't get it, do it again, and again, and again, *until you do get it!* Your mind is clouded by impure thoughts of anger and hate. Leave your seabag of woes along the beach and press on with your life. Dismissed, sailor!"

Lam had to run a marathon to get it. What Jack Saunders saw when he crossed the quarterdeck of the Naval Special Warfare Center was a strong and proud man. He noticed the difference right away. It was in the handshake. It was in the look in his eyes. Lam introduced his foster father to Senior Chief Masure, showed him to his seat, and made a beeline for the barracks to change clothes for graduation.

CHAPTER

13

Derek Evans sat anxiously in his office going over the speech he had written for the occasion. It was his last graduation at the Center before assuming command of SEAL Team Five, and he was tense. Captain May usually presided over ceremonial functions, but he was in Washington on urgent business. Evans was tense because the guest speaker was the Chief of Naval Operations, the most powerful man in the United States Navy. He finished his mental rehearsal and headed for the quarterdeck to greet the four-star admiral. As he walked down the stairway, the faint smell of jasmine assaulted his senses. He quickly scanned the crowd for Alysin Harris, but he didn't see her.

"Front site focus," he said to himself. "Front site focus."

The CNO arrived in a motorcade with an entourage of attendants. In the reception area Evans briefed him on the ceremony and nervously glanced out the door for the Junkyard Dawg. Ballard was there with a thumbs-up indicating everything was in order. With the band playing, they took position at the rear door of the quarterdeck and waited for Ballard's signal to begin the ceremony.

"Admiral, I'd rather jump out of a C-One-Thirty at thirty thousand feet in enemy-held territory than give a speech in front of four hundred people."

"Nothing to it, Commander. I do it twice a day, whether I want to or not," responded the admiral with a tired expression. "By the way, thanks for taking care of my boy."

"Man, Admiral. Man. We didn't cut him any slack. All we did was keep his identity secret. He did the rest."

"Thanks," repeated the admiral just as the band stopped playing.

Evans peeked out from the quarterdeck through the fluttering state flags and Ballard gave him a thumbs-up. He was first to join the chaplain on the platform. He paused at the sideboys for the announcement by the master of ceremonies, and waited for the bonging of the ship's bell before saluting as he walked up on the platform. The Navy Band played their best ruffles and flourishes for the CNO before he took his seat beside Evans.

On cue, Evans walked to the podium and looked at the crowd. He spotted the Junkyard Dawg standing in the back and decided he was the only person on the grinder. Ballard was going to get the speech of his life.

"Admiral, ladies and gentlemen, staff, men of Class One Sixty-Eight," he said, looking at the class, "good morning and welcome to the Naval Special Warfare Center. On behalf of Captain May, who is away on orders, I want to welcome you to the graduation of Basic Underwater Demolition SEAL Training Class One Sixty-Eight. I'd like to extend a special welcome to all the lovely ladies for coming to this place of sweat and pain. Your presence adds grace to this special occasion."

As Evans glanced over the crowd he saw Alysin Harris seated near Admiral Arlington. She smiled at him, realizing he was looking directly at her.

"This ceremony marks the end of six months of the most intensive training in the free world. Why so difficult? What's it all about?"

As he spoke he looked down from the podium directly at Lieutenant Owen, and then from man to man.

"It's about war and peace. It's about preparing for the common defense. It's about preparing for the most difficult of all operational environments, the sea, on it, in it, under it, one foot in and one foot out of it. Why so difficult? Because the sea has no mercy. It is unforgiving."

Evans turned to briefly look at the four-star admiral sitting in the high-back royal navy chair behind him, and then back to the crowd. They were listening.

"Competent leaders have always sought to enhance their straightforward activities by a variety of special operations behind enemy lines. Over the years, changes in technology have affected the form but not the substance of special operations. Aircraft have replaced horses and explosives have replaced fire, but sabotage still has the same crippling effect. And intelligence still reigns supreme, as it did in the days of Sun Tzu."

Evans paused to catch his breath.

"Admiral, the difference between conventional forces and special forces has its basis in training. Special forces must be more physically and mentally fit. Their equipment and training must emphasize mobility and self-reliance, more than firepower. They must be special men developed by special training, operating with special equipment."

Evans had to stop his speech as two F-18s flew low overhead on final approach to North Island.

"Ladies and gentlemen, I surrender to the sound of freedom flying overhead," he said, pointing up at the jets. The crowd smiled.

"SEALs are special because of their special training, which begins here at BUDS. Unless you've been through this course you cannot imagine what it takes to succeed. Behind you is a bell." He pointed to the bell to the rear of the audience, causing them to turn and look. The big block letters on the side of the building stood out: THE COWARDS NEVER STARTED AND THE WEAK DIE ALONG THE WAY.

"Our students spends six months with that bell haunting them. All a student has to do to end the course is ring that bell *and abandon his teammates.* The tenacity it takes to stay the course is beyond my ability to describe in words." He paused as if searching for a way.

"Imagine it's a cold morning and reveille occurs at oh-four-thirty. It's still dark and the wind is blowing off the ocean. You're wet and cold, so cold you shiver down to your bones. You're sore, with an ache that hurts to the depths of your joints. And you find yourself lying on your back, wet and miserable, *right there by that bell.* An instructor is yelling in your face, one of those awesome men," he said, pointing to a gallery of instructors bedecked in medals. Evans raised his voice like an instructor working a student at PT.

"Hold your legs up, Evans! What are you, some kind of wimp! Get 'em up or you hit the surf, boy! You hear *me!*" He softened his voice and spoke with grave seriousness. "He has no mercy, because he knows the sea has no mercy. You hear the words, 'Hit the surf, Evans!' and your mind screams no, and there is the bell, haunting, tempting, a hot shower, rest, just three rings away. These men," he said, pointing at Class 168 and raising his voice like a preacher, "spent six months with that bell haunting them, testing their mettle. Some of the worst moments occur during Hell Week. Let me read the words of a trainee during the fifth night of Hell Week. At this point the young man has undergone tremendous stress, almost no sleep. He is tired, cold, wet, and miserable, but indomitable. He falls asleep twice while writing this simple note. I quote," said Evans, reading from a dirty scrap of yellow notepaper. " 'Hell Week is an important evolution because it separates those that have the mental capacity for special operations from those that don't. Everyone who comes here wants to be a SEAL but not everyone can handle the job. Hell Week tests your ability to handle pressure. No sleep, cold, yelling, screaming, death.' The young man fell asleep here," commented Evans. "I can tell because there is a long jagged pencil line to the edge of the page. When he woke up he wrote, 'screaming, death, and confusion are the realities of war. Hell week is designed to push a man to his limit so he can see what's there.' End quote." Evans handed the paper to the CNO. "These are very profound words written by Lieutenant Owen, Class Leader of One Sixty-Eight, Thursday night of his Hell Week.

"Admiral Owen, on our left are some of the most outstanding men in our navy. One of them is your *son.*"

A hush went through the crowd. The men of Class 168 turned to look at their lieutenant, son of the top man in the navy. Admiral Arlington had a look of utter shock on his face. No one at the Center had put the pieces together. Only three people in San Diego knew that Lieutenant Owen was the only son of the CNO. Captain May and Commander Evans had sworn an oath of secrecy.

"Admiral Owen, on our right are some of the most outstanding warriors in the U.S. military. Class One Sixty-Eight's instructors. These are men who care. Behind the harsh words are individuals who care about their profession. They are SEALs who come here to teach the skills of their craft. They know that the men on our left will soon join them in some thankless brushfire conflict. They know that when they return to the teams their lives may depend on the men they've trained."

Evans looked back at the graduating class.

"Class One Sixty-Eight. Soon the gun, the man, and the mission come together in the real world. The certificate the CNO is about to give you is only a ticket to the game. On the ball field of life you must prove yourselves at the bar of your peers. Don't forget the lessons you've learned here and remember, *training is never over!* The sea, and the enemies of your nation, are unforgiving of errors. Now it is my pleasure to present a man who needs no introduction, a man who carries a heavy load of our nation's problems. Ladies and gentlemen, please join me in welcoming the top man in the United States Navy, Admiral Jonathan Owen, Chief of Naval Operations."

The CNO made a short speech about the problems in the world and he passed out the graduation certificates. With the formalities over, Lieutenant Owen stood and saluted Evans.

"Permission to ring out Class One Sixty-Eight, sir?"

"Permission granted!" responded Evans

Owen ran like a springbok to the ship's bell. Grabbing the clapper he rang it with the familiar sound of *ding! ding! ding!* and Class 168 threw their hats in the air with joy. It was a simple end to a grueling navy course.

Behind the grinder, Class 169 sprinted to get ahead of Class 170. They were tired of standing in rank watching the ceremony. They fell back into step in front of the junior class and began a running chant that could be heard on the grinder.

I had a dog and his name was Blue,
Yeah! Blue wanted to be in a SEAL team too,
So we bought him a mask and some tiny little fins,
And took him to the ocean and threw him in,
Blue came up to my surprise,
With a shark in his teeth and a gleam in his eye,
Hoo yah, swimming day, running day,
Another easy day!
It's the SEAL team way,
Ah haaa! Ah haaa!
Hoo yah, One Sixty-Eight!

Class 170 burst into a sprint and took the lead back from
169. Some of the men ran with the bow-legged Charlie
Chaplin shuffle, struggling to keep up. They had recently
finished Hell Week and were still feeling the effects. Falling
into step in front of the senior class, they sang back:

I don't wanna be no Green Beret,
They only PT once a day.
I don't wanna be no fat RECON.
I wanna stay till the job is done.
I wanna be the best I can,
And that's what makes me a SEAL team man!
Ah haaa! Easy day!

"Hoo yah, One Sixty-Eight!" they yelled as the two
formations approached the signal light in front of SEAL
Team Five. Their turn would come.

The graduation party started out semiformal, but as the
parents retired, spirits enlivened to the mood most enjoyed
by young people. Evans usually left along with the parents,
but he had escorted Harris and she was looking good. They
were talking about the trick Williams and Robinson had
played on her in First Phase office when the music stopped
abruptly. A group of men moved out onto the center of the
dance floor and took seats on folding chairs.

Ryeback, in blackface, yelled, "On your feet, take seats,
on your feet, take seats," until they were out of sequence.
Some of the men were going down as others were jumping

up. Then out of the darkness appeared a man dressed as a Japanese ninja, brandishing a samurai sword. He jumped around with grunts and groans, slicing at them while the men yelled *hoo yah* to every combination of grunts.

"I'ma gonna tell you tree tings," he grunted.

"Hoo yah," they yelled.

"First athink! You not-a here, if you not-a have *big balls,*" he grunted.

"Hoo yah," they yelled. The ninja sliced over their heads with the sword and achieved silence.

"Second ting: It not-a size of the balls that count, it the size of . . . of . . . of veapon."

"Hoo yah."

The ninja sliced at them again.

"Ona your feet!"

The ninja walked off a little ways and said, "Oh yeah! Third ting: Prease forgive! I forget third ting!"

The crowd roared with laughter as the men disappeared off the dance floor.

Next, Robinson took center stage and sat on a folding chair. He appeared to look down at an imaginary desk. Two men came up wearing UDT life jackets over their heads and K-bar knives on web belts.

"Simons and Lam to see Instructor Williams," they yelled.

"Enter!" yelled Robinson.

As they stood at attention Robinson grabbed Lam's life jacket and pulled on it. With his tongue out Lam acted like a man being hanged as Robinson extracted the CO_2 cartridge.

"Sand! You know what this is, knucklehead!" he yelled.

"No, Instructor Williams. I can't see anything," shouted Lam. Robinson pulled a big magnifying glass from his back pocket and aimed it between Lam and his index finger.

"You see that, knucklehead?"

"No, Instructor Williams," yelled Lam.

"Drop down, knock 'em out, knucklehead," yelled Robinson.

Robinson turned his attention to Simons's K-bar knife. He feigned trying to pull it from the sheath, but it wouldn't budge. Taking it off the belt he beat it on the floor and pulled out a chrome-plated knife that shone like a mirror.

Looking at it with the huge magnifying glass, he said, "You see that, Simons?"

Simons peered through the magnifying lens at the knife. "No, Instructor Williams."

"That's a microscopic flake of rust. You could get me killed, knucklehead. Hit the surf."

Four guys appeared out of the dark and threw pitchers of beer on Simons and Lam. The crowd roared with laughter. The skits went on until everyone was laughing so hard the waiters stopped service.

When the crowd settled down from the skits, the music turned soft and sensuous. Wild Bill Williams bought a handful of beers and sauntered over to the table where Jackson, Simons, Robinson, and Bailey were sitting with three lovely girls. Williams whispered something in Robinson's ear and sat the beer bottles on the table.

"I just wanted to say congratulation, teammates. I'm glad you guys got orders to SEAL Team Five. The Commander, Master Chief, Stick, and me, all got orders to Five. We're gonna be teammates, teammates," he said passing out the beers.

"Hoo yah," responded the troops with questionable enthusiasm. As Williams pulled up a chair, Robinson said, "Excuse us, Instruc—Wild Bill, but we gonna do the slow grind," he said with an undulating pelvic motion.

"Yeah, yeah," said Williams with a devious smile. "Here you go, teammate," said Williams, passing Jackson a beer.

"No thanks, Bill. I don't drink. That shit can kill, man," commented Jackson, looking around for Commander Evans. He spotted him on the dance floor. Williams saw his roving eye.

"Yeah, I know what you mean. It took me two years to get over the ass kicking Commander Evans gave me when he was my XO at Five. You'd better steer clear of Colt .45 for a couple of years. Hey, good buddy, hold this!" he said, handing Jackson three chemlites of various colors. He smiled deviously. Breaking the vial in an orange chemlite, he shook it vigorously under the table before cutting off the top. About that time, Robinson danced his girlfriend up close to the table and maneuvered her so he could hold out one hand without her seeing. Williams surreptitiously handed the glowing liquid to him. One by one he repeated the procedure with red, green, and blue chemlites until all his troops were armed.

When the slow music began, Evans asked Harris to dance. He held her close and she responded sensuously. He could feel his excitement rise as she moved next to his body.

"Alysin, you're a fascinating woman," he whispered. "I'd like to get to know you better," he said, breathing slightly next to her ear.

"Derek, the attraction is mutual, but," she said, pulling away from him far enough to look him in the eyes.

"Do you want to tell me about it?" he asked.

"Yes, but . . . The timing is all wrong," she said, laying her head on his muscular shoulder. "When this is over I'll have to try and fix my personal life, if I can."

"Sounds like a husband-job conflict to me," he said, fishing.

"Yes. We're separated. It's my fault. I put too much in my job and not enough in my marriage."

"I guess I have a similar story to tell," he said soothingly. "Speaking of your job, how are things going?" he asked, deliberately changing the subject.

"OK, I guess."

"Can you tell me about it?"

"No," she answered flatly. "I've already told you enough to get me sent to jail."

"I guess I should feel flattered that you care enough to jeopardize you career for me."

"You know how serious this is, Derek. I'm just doing my job."

"Yes, I know," he said, whispering in her ear. She responded by pulling him closer.

"Things are not moving as fast as we thought they might," volunteered Harris.

"So why are you here?"

"Derek, please."

"We're on the same side, you know," he pleaded.

"I'm not authorized to brief you on the details. Ask the admiral. He's on the inside."

"OK. But after today, he'll probably just chew my ass," Evans said innocently, smiling.

"There is one question I need to ask you, Derek."

"Shoot," said Evans, whispering in her ear. He squeezed her tightly. The heat in her body was rising.

"Are you sure Saraskina hasn't tried to contact you in some sort of way?"

"Yes. I'm positive. Alysin, do you have a fixation on her, or what? You've already asked me that question three times. If anyone makes contact with me, I'll tell you." He thought for a few seconds and said, "You know something, Alysin?"

"What?"

"I'm liable to march into your director's office and grab him by the throat, after I remove Karpenko's liver with his spade." Shocked by his abruptness and the power she felt surging through his body, she pulled away.

"I care about you. I respect you. And like you, I'm only a small piece of a very big puzzle. Please remember, I'm just doing my job the best I know how."

"I understand that. But I don't like being a mushroom," Evans growled with a hurt expression.

"No one is using you to lure Karpenko. If they do I'll tell you, even if it costs me my job."

He looked deep in her eyes and saw the sincerity. "Thanks, Alysin." He couldn't help himself as he looked at her. He tenderly kissed her.

Alysin Harris caved in to her desires and kissed him passionately like a women starved for love. She had sworn an oath not to get emotionally involved, but she couldn't help herself. When the kiss ended they danced quietly for a few minutes, enjoying each other's embrace.

"You know it's going to be hard to keep tabs on me after I assume command. As the captain, I'll be spending most of my time on the road training the troops."

"What kind of training?" she asked pleasantly as the music stopped.

"Shooting, diving, insertion, and extraction, you name it."

"I think you've already done quite well in the insertion-extraction department," she said, laughing.

155

Every woman on the dance floor except Harris was covered in glowing iridescent handprints that were all over their butts and boobs. The men held up their glowing hands in victory. Harris saw Williams at the edge of the dance floor with a grin that looked like the Grand Canyon.

"That arrogant bastard!" she said, chuckling.

After the party Evans drove her back to the BOQ and stopped the engine of the 928. For a long moment he looked at her and for the first time saw a glimpse of insecurity. He liked her and he didn't want to push her. So he waited for her to make the next move. Finally she pulled him close and kissed him passionately.

"I have to leave in the morning so you'll have to get me back by five."

He looked at her gorgeous face, seeing through the beauty to the fear and desire in her eyes. He started the engine and sped through the back streets of Coronado to his apartment. Evans made love to Harris until daylight and then hustled her to her plane.

At the gate he kissed her good-bye.

"I'll see you soon," she said when the kiss ended. "If not, I'll see you in Korea."

Korea! he thought, waving good-bye. *If it is going to happen overseas, I'm glad it's Korea.*

CHAPTER

14

Ahmed El-Sayed Farouk could feel the heavy boots approaching his dark prison cell as he lay facedown on the fetid stone floor sprawled out in the same position they had thrown him several hours ago. It was wet with his own urine, saliva, and blood, which mixed with the odors of prisoners who had soiled the cell continuously since the days of the pharaohs. As the boots clopped down the labyrinth toward his cell he briefly opened one eye. Pain seized his brain as the dim light coming from the crack beneath the heavy wooden door pierced his soul and returned him to reality. For the past few days they had come at odd hours and dragged him away for interrogation.

With short, shallow breaths like a mortally wounded animal, he tried to roll on his side. Every joint in his body had been racked and twisted and was swollen twice its size. In agony he slumped back on the filthy floor, praying for death.

"Allahu Akbar! O Lord! Have mercy on Your humble servant. Deliver me from this torment. Embrace my soul and allow me to enter Your Kingdom."

His interrogators had done unspeakable things to make him talk. His fingernails and toenails had been removed. Blood oozed from stubs on his hands and feet where digits had been traumatically severed. The broken stumps of his teeth sent showers of searing pain with each involuntary swallow. His testicles were numb from numerous electrical shocks. But Farouk wouldn't talk. He had kept the secret. His cheek flinched as images of mutilation seized him. To block them out he mumbled another prayer.

"Allah, have mercy on Your humble servant. Embrace me in Your arms and allow me to enter Your Kingdom," he mumbled without moving his lips. Blood and saliva drooled on the stone floor.

The face of the Egyptian he had killed to keep the secret invaded his mind before he finished the prayer. The gunman on the motorcycle in the lead element had drilled a twelve-inch circular hole in the bullet-proof glass with an MAC 10 submachine gun on full automatic. It had hammered away until only the plastic bonding remained intact. Taha Ahmed Mohammed, in the second element, had thrust a twelve-inch blade through the Mylar and opened up a hole as if carving a melon. Then Farouk had shoved in the pistol. The face he saw through the gaping hole was filled with terror. He flinched as he felt his missing finger pull the trigger over and over. Farouk had emptied a 9mm pistol through the outstretched fingers of the Egyptian magistrate.

The man he had killed in the backseat of the car had ordered the torture of his comrades. They all had to die to keep the secret. He had learned of the plan to cleanse Palestine of the Jews and he couldn't be trusted with such information. Through torture he had learned that al-Gamaa al-Islamiya was planning an attack on the secret Israeli nuclear weapons depot at Beersheba. The interrogators, the agents, his comrades, they all had to die to keep the secret.

The plan was simple. Explode a nuclear device in Tel Aviv and attack Beersheba while the Jews were still reeling from the explosion. It was so simple. The weapon was a gift from God. The Russian weapons could destroy Tel Aviv in one blazing holocaust. Once al-Gamaa al-Islamiya possessed the secret arsenal at Beersheba, they would control the Middle East. It was payback for the massacre at Deir Yassin. It was justice for the theft of a country by an invasion force of illegal Jewish immigrants.

Farouk opened one eye and stared at the crack under the

door, waiting for the monster to drag him away to unspeakable torture. Death begetting death, retribution and retaliation, to al-Gamaa al-Islamiya it was the same. In the Middle East one man's terrorist was another's freedom fighter. Members of al-Gamaa swore a blood oath of revenge for the death of their comrades in the struggle for freedom from the Jews, and Farouk was sure they would avenge his death, too.

"Allah, merciful Allah, end the pain of Your tortured servant. Allah, have mercy."

The heavy boots halted outside his cell and Farouk stopped breathing as he waited for the door to open and the monster to drag him off to more torture. He could see the toe of one menacing boot as the man stood outside his cell. Then it disappeared.

"Allah, You are a merciful God," he mumbled through swollen lips.

As the boots clopped away down the stone corridor, he heard an unusual sound, a faint, almost inaudible tinkle, like the sound of a sliver of glass striking the stone floor of his cell. Then he saw a glint of light reflecting off the surface of a small, irregular fragment of glass no more than inch long. He stared at the object of mercy for a long time, not believing it was real. His interrogators were Arab. Arab beating Arab. The small sliver of glass slipped through the crack at the top of his door was a gift of mercy. Arab helping Arab. Gathering his remaining strength he strained his swollen joints enough to roll onto his side in a position where he could grasp the gift from the stranger wearing the boots.

"Allah, God of mercy. You have answered my prayers. Oh, Allah, soon You will deliver us from the Jews. Your angel with the slanted eyes will deliver the instrument of Your justice. Oh Allah, we will be free to worship Your greatness in the land of our fathers. Allah, God of mercy, with Your blessings we will be free."

With his remaining fingers Farouk struggled to grasp the slender sliver of glass. When he held it in his mangled hand and knew that it was real, he thanked God again, and then with all his strength he drew himself up into a fetal position. Waves of torment from his distended joints flooded his brain with agony. The pain was so intense Farouk passed out for a few precious seconds of painless life. When he regained consciousness, he inched his right hand, his clean hand, slowly to the wrist of his unclean hand, and with the sliver from God he slit the veins on his wrist. He watched the blood ooze out slowly, bathing his arm in the warmth of his ebbing life.

"Allah, merciful Allah, accept Your humble servant into Your Kingdom. Deliver my people from the hands of the Jews. Oh, Allah, with Your instrument of justice we will burn the Zionist capital from the face of the earth and end the Jewish oppression of Your people. Allah, merciful Allah, they have tortured my body with unspeakable crimes but I did not reveal Your yellow angel with the slanted eyes and his gift of power and freedom. With the blood of the lamb we will mark the doors of our Arab brothers in the city of Tel Aviv and then we will scorch the cursed city from the face of the earth. Then we will seize Beersheba. Allah, accept this humble servant into Your Kingdom. O Lord! Grant our land veneration. O Lord! Grant those in the struggle for freedom, peace and forgiveness. Peace is from Thee. So greet us on the Day of Judgment with the greeting of peace. Here we come, O Allah! Here we come! No partner have You. Praise and blessings are Yours. . . ."

Ahmed El-Sayed Farouk felt the heavy boots on the stone floor. They came down the corridor from the opposite direction and passed by his cell without stopping. He thanked God again for his mercy. As he watched the crimson pool at his wrist grow larger, the light from the crack under the door grew dimmer until blackness covered his soul.

Salim was under pressure. He had deposited two million dollars in Karpenko's account and had made all the necessary arrangements for transfer of the weapon to Syria, but the Russian had failed to deliver. His warning about a leak to the Mossad had failed to materialize during the testing phase of the operation. Salim had personally paid off every official, from Adapazari on the northern coast of Turkey to Halab on the Syrian border, and had succeeded in transporting a large box of worthless machinery parts. It was a security test the Russian bitch had insisted upon and it had cost his Saudi benefactor a huge sum of money to bribe all the officials along the route. The same box could have contained a nuclear weapon.

The leaders of the Arab alliance knew their organization had been penetrated by Jewish agents and they had done everything within their power to maintain operational security. Knowledge of the weapons was compartmentalized. Salim knew of the plan only because of his position as a middleman. The cautiousness of the Russian worked to the disadvantage of the Arabs. Every day the PLO's precarious situation got worse. Several Palestinian operatives working out of Egypt had died in the cause of maintaining security. To seal the leaks, the Yassinist had mounted a major offensive in Cairo and a number of people had been terminated.

In addition, Salim was getting pressure from Hamas and Abu Nidal. They were afraid the CIA or the Mossad would get to the weapons before the Russians or the North Koreans could deliver. Even the top-secret agreement they had signed with the North Korean government failed to appease the radical elements of the PLO.

Shortly after the successful delivery of the machinery parts to Syria, Salim arranged a personal meeting with Karpenko to pressure him into speeding up delivery. Unfortunately he had few tools with which to coerce the Russian, except threat and bravado. He intended to unnerve Karpenko with a veiled threat of exposure, and if that didn't work, to offer him a bonus for speeding up delivery. He was mentally working on his strategy in a small park in northern Istanbul when an old man in a threadbare coat shuffled by, eyeballing him like a stray dog eyeing a piece of meat. Salim stared up from his paper as the old man passed his secluded park bench and disappeared up the winding path into the foliage. Moments later Karpenko appeared out of the bushes like a phantom and sat down beside him.

"Do you have a light?" he said to Salim while tapping a cigarette out of his pack. The Arab lit the cigarette and one for himself before speaking.

"You have a problem," said Salim.

Karpenko interrupted him abruptly. "No. You have a problem. I canceled your party because you mailed out too many invitations."

"*You* have a security problem. Your intelligence is incorrect. *You* have taken our money and not delivered as promised," said Salim anxiously.

"Calm down, my towel-head frie-e-end," Karpenko said, chuckling.

"We want to know when you will deliver our weapon," he said emphatically and with the most verve he could muster.

"Restrain yourself, my greasy towel-head friend. The security problem is on your side, I assure you," argued Karpenko with a devious look in his eye. He slapped Salim on the back so hard Salim dropped his cigarette. Salim felt the power of the big Russian and lost some of his nerve.

"You talk but you do not deliver," he said calmly. "There are many factions of the PLO and many of them are most impatient. They are capable of—"

"I always make good on my business transactions," interrupted Karpenko. His cheek quivered and his eyes narrowed. He took a deep drag on his cigarette and blew the smoke in Salim's face.

"The Mossad, the CIA, the KGB—every agency in the world wants to know where you are, my big, Slavic baker frie-e-end, and if you do not deliver soon they will find you," he said with more confidence in his voice than he felt.

Karpenko glared at him. He tilted his head back and sniffed the air as he looked up and down the path. "So, now you threaten me again, you greasy, unshaven asshole. You Arabs are infiltrated with Jews like shit complected with piss. You dare to threaten me. You pissant!"

"We have no evidence of a leak on our side," lied Salim lamely.

"Of course you don't, you fool. But I do. All your Arab organizations are infiltrated with Jewish swine." Karpenko pointed a huge finger in Salim's face. "Why did you ask for this meeting?" he demanded.

"My clients are—are very anxious," stuttered Salim. "They . . . ah . . . some of the Arab organizations are worried the CIA or the Mossad will find you."

"Why are they worried?" Karpenko studied Salim's face.

"I'll tell you why. You are infiltrated with Jewish spies and you know it," snarled Karpenko.

"Someone may inform on you if you do not deliver soon," threatened Salim weakly.

"So that is the reason you asked for this meeting? To tell me you have spies in your midst, that some of your crazy Arab boys will rat on me to the Americanskis?"

"I am prepared to offer a bonus," blurted Salim.

"I don't want your bonus, *Arab!*" growled Karpenko like a wolf at its prey. "I will not allow your Arab incompetence to ruin my business." His face turned from deadly serious to a large, phony Slavic smile.

"A half million more if you deliver the weapon next week."

"A deal is a deal, towel-head. Your client will get his weapon for the agreed price, but . . ." Karpenko stopped in midsentence.

"But what?" asked Salim, alarmed by the look in Karpenko's eye.

"He will need a new errand boy," growled Karpenko.

Karpenko backhanded Salim on the chest so hard Salim sat up straight on the bench. Behind him, Suburov moved like a cat out of the bushes and quickly pulled off Salim's head cloth. Pinned by Karpenko, Suburov easily wrapped the cloth around the Arab's neck and strangled him. When Salim ceased to flail, Suburov reached around, grabbed his chin, and snapped his neck. As Suburov arranged the corpse in a sitting position on the park bench, Karpenko picked up Salim's cigarette and put it between his lips.

"Enjoy," he said to the dead man. Suburov chuckled at the gesture.

As they got in the back of a black Mercedes at the edge of the park, the old man in the threadbare coat took the cigarette from Salim's lips and inhaled deeply. He looked around nervously and began rifling the Arab's pockets.

As the car sped through the streets of Istanbul, Karpenko addressed Suburov and Saraskina, like a general thinking out loud in the presence of his staff.

"Excellent job, Vlad," he said. Suburov beamed like a dog patted on the head by its owner.

"Natila, send a message to our Arab friends that towel-head was an informer, and tell them I am not angry with them for their poor security. Inform them I will deliver as promised but on my terms, directly to Syria. Then leak a trail for the Jews like we planned for a Red Sea transit to Bandar Abbās."

"Yes, General," responded Saraskina in a businesslike manner.

"The Jews and the Americans need a little chase to make them feel important. So we will give the hounds in the lead a few false trails to follow, huh?" He looked out the window of the speeding car, deep in thought.

"Vlad," he babbled. "I have a special mission for you. I will tell you about it later."

Suburov nodded with a knowing expression. *Maskirovka.*

Karpenko, Saraskina, Voshchanov, Khasanov, and Suburov were living in several safehouses scattered throughout the outskirts of Varna, Bulgaria, a medium-size seaport on the Black Sea. They were working out of a motor transport company that specialized in moving medium and heavy cargo throughout Bulgaria, Romania, and Yugoslavia. It was a GRU cell Karpenko had developed to provide heavy transport for the Soviet army in case of war in the region.

A few weeks after they had eliminated the Arab, Suburov loaded the dead drops of the major players and ordered a meeting at the Varna Transport Company office. After greetings and coffee Karpenko began with a statement and a question, which stimulated the intelligence reports he demanded from his senior officers.

"It is time to deliver the towel-heads their weapon," said Karpenko. "Natila, have you tested the land route through Turkey?"

"Yes, my general." In the presence of her contemporaries she always addressed Karpenko formally. "I have dispatched a consignment of cargo weekly from Varna to Adapazari by ship and from Adapazari to Halab by truck. The cargo was inspected only one time and that was by the Turks in the Adapazari shipyard. We bribed the Chief Customs Inspector, and since the payoff, we have had no further problems."

"What kind of cargo, Natila?" asked Karpenko.

"Heavy pipe, steel, and machinery. I also ran several consignments across the Bulgarian border through Turkey using a ferry to cross over the Bosporus."

"Excellent. Any problems with the ferry?"

"No, sir. The land routes have been thoroughly conditioned," she responded, like an intelligence analyst giving a briefing to a senior officer at regimental headquarters.

"Very well, Saraskina. As usual you are thorough in your actions and concise in your briefing," he said. "Did you work all the shipments with our Arab friends?"

"No, General—only the one that was inspected in Adapazari," responded Saraskina.

"Ahhh! So they are infiltrated with spies." Karpenko shifting his gaze from Saraskina to Khasanov. Khasanov was small for a Spetznaz officer but he had the kind of face that no one could remember. He was an outstanding operative and competition for Saraskina in the wolf pack.

"Viktor, how goes the sea transport?"

"Sea transport is less responsive than motor transport, General. I have two suitable vessels homeported in Varna. Both are small and old, and fit our profile perfectly. They frequently make transit from Varna around the Black Sea ports and have entered the Mediterranean many times with cargo for Libya, Egypt, and Syria."

"What is the transit time from Varna to the Suez Canal?" asked Karpenko.

"Sir, the transit time from Varna around Turkey, staying just outside Turkish territorial waters, is about two weeks. Both vessels have delivered cargo to Cyprus, Lebanon, and Syria in the past two years. Last month I dispatched a consignment of large cement drainage pipes to Syria. The deliveries were made without incident," responded Khasanov in proper military fashion.

"Very well, Viktor," said Karpenko, nodding his head in approval. "Did you have any problems with customs?"

"No, sir. None," responded Khasanov.

"And your Arab contacts were not aware of your actions?" pressed Karpenko.

"No, sir. The shipments were arranged through the Varna Transport Company."

"Good." Karpenko shifted his gaze to Suburov. "Vlad, what have you discovered about air transportation?"

"Sir, I reconnoitered the airports very carefully. The ones in this region are under heavy guard. It will be extremely difficult to hijack a plane of sufficient size to reach Syria."

"As I suspected, Vlad," said Karpenko, starting to pace the office floor. He walked to the window and peered out at the yard where several large trucks were parked at a loading dock. A light rain was falling on the oil-caked dirt. He watched silently as a large covered truck pulled away from the dock, leaving tandem tracks in the mud. Karpenko lit a cigarette and inhaled deeply while observing the bleak scene outside the office. For several minutes they were silent, leaving him to think. Natila looked at the deep scar that ran down the length of his face. It seemed to grow with each drag on the cigarette. Out of habit he ran his finger down the length of the scar, tracing the line the SEAL had chopped with the spade. Unconsciously his face furrowed with anger. When he turned from the window he spoke quickly. "If we do not deliver soon the Arabs will make problems. But if we move the weapons now we run the risk of exposure."

"Why, General? We control all of the Black Sea contacts," said Khasanov.

"Because the Americans are watching this region closely with their satellites, Viktor." He paused and walked back to his chair at the table. Reading the look on Khasanov's face, he continued. "Khasanov, the Americans have satellites that can see radioactive materials. They can see nuclear reactors and big nuclear weapons. If they see the weapons from their satellite, they will launch a mission on them."

"Ahhhh," said Khasanov with a nod, obviously unaware of the capability.

"So," he snapped, looking from person to person, "we will use speed to defeat the Jews and the Americans. This is what we will do. We will ship the weapon by truck just after the satellite passes overhead and we will drive it through Turkey to Syria before they can respond." Karpenko paused to gather their reactions. Saraskina spoke first.

"But, sir, the transit by truck will take more than a week. They will attack the trucks long before they reach Syria," she protested.

Karpenko smiled with a degree of pride. He had trained her well. "We will shield the weapon in lead blankets and use the faster ferry route across the Bosporus. That way we will not waste time in the shipyard at Adapazari. Natila, ensure that our men are on duty at the Bulgarian border just after the satellite passes overhead on the thirty-first of October," he ordered.

"Yes, General. That will not be a problem," she responded.

"Also, arrange for a consignment of machinery parts by ship and truck through Adapazari as you described earlier," he continued. "Viktor, you will arrange two consignments of cargo, one for each of the vessels you described. One shipment will be for Syria and one for Libya. On the ship bound for Libya we will plant a beacon that gives off a signal similar to a nuclear emission," he said, smiling.

They all stared at him as the realization dawned that he was planning a ruse.

"Maskirovka!" said Khasanov out loud.

"Yes, Viktor. *Maskirovka,"* Karpenko said, smiling again. Then he continued. "Natila, you will also plant a beacon on your Adapazari vessel. We will give the Jews and the Americans two good targets to play with, and when they commit, we will quickly move up the middle of Turkey to Syria." Karpenko's smile broadened.

"General, what are the other vessels for?" asked Saraskina with a puzzled look on her face.

"Ah, that is our insurance, Natila. If anything goes wrong with your land route we will shield the weapon and ship it by sea. The primary route will be by truck convoy through Turkey. The secondary route will be the vessel to Syria," he said, as if explaining the strategy to his favorite junior officer.

Karpenko lit another cigarette and took a deep drag. "You have three weeks to make preparations for the transfer. Check your load signals daily and ensure you are not followed when you service your dead drops. Use this time wisely to exercise your men in clandestine affairs," he said with a deadly serious expression. He paused momentarily in thought. His cheek muscles twitched and his nostrils flared like a wolf sniffing the air. "Natila, you will activate and test all cells in Albania. In three weeks we will move our base of operations to Tiranë. Now, before my guest arrives we will toast to the success of free enterprise. Vlad, iced vodka, please," he ordered.

Suburov fetched a bottle of vodka and after the toast he stationed himself at the window while the others made small talk. When he saw two of his men drive up in the black Mercedes, he drew the shade tightly and left the room. When he returned he was leading a stocky man dressed in a heavy, dark overcoat. His breath smelled of garlic and even through the hood he wore over his head, Saraskina could tell he was Korean. With a wave of his hand, Karpenko ordered Saraskina and the others to leave the room.

Suburov removed General Kim's hood and offered him a chair.

"General Kim, my slanty-eyed frie-e-end. How long has it been? A month, two months?" said Karpenko pleasantly.

"On yong ha shim ni ca, General Karpenko, mongrel friend," said Kim with an oriental bow. "Not long enough."

"I have no *soju* to offer you but I do have iced vodka," said Karpenko politely.

"No, no," mumbled the Korean. "I have no time for party."

"Without alcohol and women, life would be boring," said Karpenko, handing him a small glass of vodka. "How are the little slanty pussies these days?"

"As I said, I have no time for party. These days I must deal with the devil just to eat," said Kim, eyeballing Karpenko as he took the small glass.

"I hope you do not think of me as the devil, Kim. There are many secrets between us, no?" said Karpenko seriously.

"Deetree, I do not tink of you as the devil, just as his favorite disciple," responded Kim, looking Karpenko in the eyes.

Karpenko laughed. "I am flattered. Let's do business."

"We are prepared to offer you sanctuary and help with transportation if you turn the weapons over to us immediately."

"What is your hurry?" asked Karpenko, eyeing the Korean with renewed interest.

"We have our source. They tell us your friends in Moscow know where you are and they are planning to . . ."

"To what?" Karpenko smiled. "Mount a mission against me? Have no concern about this, General Kim. Moscow is my home. Someday I will rule it from the Kremlin. I will know long before they launch an operation against me."

"Maybe, maybe not," said Kim emphatically. "Every intelligence organization in the world is looking for you, Deetree. You have a very big price on your head, and money motivates. Even your friends in Moscow. The Arabs have very big mouths, you know. And Deetree, even Minister Yoon knows you are in here."

"Careful, my slanty-eyed frie-e-end, or I will feed your kimchi breath to a Bulgarian wolfhound," growled Karpenko.

Kim sucked air across his teeth and laughed as was his custom. He sipped his vodka before speaking. "I don't tink so, Deetree. You will need us for a place to hide when the Americans find you."

"I do not tink so," said Karpenko, mocking the Korean. "What is your interest in the Arabs, Kim? Why would you give them one of your weapons?" Karpenko asked, playing his hand. Kim wasn't about to answer the question. He changed the subject.

"Deetree, you cannot hide behind your Airborne Warrior forever."

"And why not?" demanded Karpenko.

Kim studied Karpenko's face. "They will launch on you. They do not know about this Airborne Warrior. Not the Americans or the Russians. Someday you will need us, Deetree."

"I don't tink so," mocked Karpenko.

"We do not want you to deliver the weapon to the Philippines," stated Kim flatly.

"It does not matter to me. Anywhere you want," responded Karpenko.

"We pick dem up here?" suggested Kim.

"How do you know they are here, my friend?" asked Karpenko.

"I know," chuckled Kim.

"And where is here?" asked Karpenko.

"Why, Romania, of course," he said with a devious oriental smile.

"Maybe I should feed your ass to a Romanian wolf-hound," laughed Karpenko. "When do you want to make the transfer?"

"Next week!" grunted Kim.

"Impossible," snapped Karpenko. "Six weeks. And I choose the airport and the time. Agreed?"

"Nay," agreed Kim.

"You are worried about the American satellites, no? OK. OK. You don't have to pay the money now," said Karpenko. "I trust you."

Kim wanted to say that money was not the problem. The Saudi who was providing the money didn't care about the price. He wanted action. And if the North Korean government did not produce, he would find another client to deliver a nuclear weapon to the PLO.

"Minister Yoon has forgiven you, Deetree. We place no obligation on you. He extends his greetings. Kim Il Sung has agreed to the price and to providing sanctuary if you turn the weapons over to us next week."

"You will put the money in my account when I tell you the time and place."

"OK. OK. No problem!" agreed Kim. "But it must be soon," he pressed.

"OK. Soon," agreed Karpenko. "I will let you know soon."

The Korean accepted his hand and a toast of Vodka while Suburov prepared for his departure. Before Suburov placed the hood over his face, he looked at Karpenko with exasperation.

"Mongrel friend, why you insist on this coat-and-dagger ting?" asked Kim.

"That's cloak-and-dagger, Kim," chuckled Karpenko, warmed by the vodka. "I will see you in Pyŏngyang in a few months and I expect *soju* and slanty pussy at my reception," he said in jest.

"But no more sambo. And no more killing everyone in your hotel, OK?" Kim glared.

"OK," agreed Karpenko with raised eyebrows and a smirk.

After Kim left, Karpenko loaded Saraskina's dead drop with orders to lease a freighter from Athens, Greece. When she picked up the communiqué two days later, she understood the importance of the message. It was more *maskirovka,* compartmentalized from the others in the pack. With typical thoroughness she assigned Voshchanov to go to Athens to lease the freighter. The mission was so simple any of her men could have accomplished it. She chose Voshchanov because by nature, he kept a low profile and he had worked Athens previously.

CHAPTER
15

Voshchanov accomplished his mission in two days. There were hundreds of shipping companies in Athens that managed thousands of ships and he was authorized to pay top dollar. He arranged for the shipments and sent a coded message to Saraskina providing the details. Then he thought of Sofia and delayed his departure. At first Voshchanov was all business, leaving his room only to make calls and to eat, but when his mission was complete he thought of Sofia. From the moment he had laid eyes on her he had not had a moment's peace. He couldn't stop thinking about her. He had met her on a similar mission just after Karpenko had moved their headquarters to Varna, Bulgaria.

As he sat on the veranda outside his plush room overlooking the Aegean Sea, his mind flooded with desire. She was the most passionate woman he had ever met and she kindled in him a flame that raged. He couldn't wait for her to arrive so he could feel the softness of her touch and taste the sweetness of her breasts. As he sipped his vodka his mind replayed the passionate love song she sang while in orgasm: "Oh, Yuri, nobody makes love to me the way you do. Oh honey, it feels so gooooood." He could smell the musk from her vagina and feel his tongue run up the length of her thighs to the delight that satisfied all his fantasies and desires. He licked his lips out of reflex and the taste of vodka broke his trance.

"I want to keep those thoughts," he said to himself. "Forever." As he shifted in his chair he felt the hardness of his dick bulging against his trousers.

Voshchanov looked at his watch. Another hour before she arrived and he would make his daydream reality.

"The hell with Saraskina and Karpenko," he said out loud.

Voshchanov would have been happy just to live in Europe and enjoy the good life. He took another sip of his drink and lay his head back on the patio chair. Again he heard her soft and sultry voice haunting his thoughts. "Oh, Yuri, Yuri, ooooh," she moaned in pleasure. He could see her large, dark nipples rise and fall in spasms with each wave of pleasure he gave her. Thoughts of long nights of passionate lovemaking tortured him. He lit another cigarette and fixed himself another drink, but nothing could take his mind off his Greek goddess. He intended to make love to her all weekend beginning the moment she walked through the door. He knew she wanted it as badly as he did. Staying at this beautiful beach resort was her idea.

When Sofia finally arrived several hours late, Voshchanov was wild with desire. Before she could speak a word he grabbed her in his arms and kissed her passionately. She responded with equal passion, wrapping one leg around him and pushing herself on the bulge under his trousers. He picked her up in his arms and carried her to the bed. In one easy motion he peeled off her skirt.

"Yuri, we have all weekend," she pleaded softly. But Voshchanov would have none of it. He was so excited he was beyond self-control. He grabbed her panties and pulled them aside. With his tongue flicking wildly he worked his way up her thighs until she sighed passionately. She sucked in her breath in a huge gasp of delight.

"Ohh, ohhh, oh, Yuri, I love the way you eat me. Oh, Yuri, nobody makes me feel like this but you. Oh, Yuriiiiii," she moaned in pleasure. "Oooh, Yuri, I want to feel you inside me," she pleaded. He pulled himself up, breathing hard, and ripped off his pants. When he thrust himself into her wet vagina a frenzied shiver ran up and down his spine and it was all he could do to prevent himself from reaching orgasm. As her fingernails dug deeply into his back an image of Saraskina flashed through his mind. She would kill him if she knew what he was doing. Underneath him Sofia squirmed in pleasure. Voshchanov had found heaven on earth in the West and he had enough money stashed to live comfortably with Sofia anywhere he wanted, compliments of the former Soviet Union. It was time for Voshchanov to leave the security of the wolf pack.

Gomez and Savarese slipped silently into the cool waters of the Aegean and waited for the four Israeli commandos to roll off the Zodiac. They looked at one another in the darkness and without a word or motion communicated that it was time to start swimming toward shore. The coxswain lost sight of them six feet from the boat. His job was to wait for their signal and then motor quickly to shore to pick them up. They were all dressed in black, like Japanese ninjas, but they carried deadly 9mm MP-5s with suppressors. The weapons were so quiet one could hear the action of the weapon cycling and the bullet smack the target without the report of percussion.

With only their faces protruding above the surface of the sea they silently moved closer to an outcropping of rocks. For ten minutes they lay submerged in the mild surf, watching the silhouette of the rocks in the dim moonlight. Satisfied they were alone, they climbed out of the water and took defensive positions within the rocks, each covering a different direction like one protective organism. For another ten minutes they watched the beach. Then five of them scurried across the sandy beach and disappeared into shadows. Gomez looked in Savarese's direction. All he could see was the whites of his eyes and a glint of light reflecting off his white teeth. Boomer was smiling.

One of the Israelis appeared out of the shadow and moved quickly toward the building adjacent to the beach. In three heartbeats he materialized and vanished into the shadows of the building, crossing the lighted area in a sprint. When he reappeared five minutes later, he motioned for Gomez and Savarese to join him. They closed the distance to the building and hid in the shadows. Gomez and Savarese took defensive positions on each side of a sliding glass door. As the Israeli slowly slid the door open, they heard the sound of a woman moaning in pleasure over the drone of a fan. The dim light coming from an open bathroom door illuminated a male and a female deeply involved in delirious lovemaking. The male was thrusting himself up and down wildly, completely unaware of the world around him. He was holding the woman's legs up in the air as he worked out on his knees at a fevered pitch.

The commando moved silently into the room and thrust the cold head of the suppressor on his MP-5 into the man's back. The man gasped, instantly recognizing the cold feel of death at his spine. He froze deadly still, still engaged in the woman. Dropping her legs, he slowly raised his arms above his head in a show of nonresistance. As he slowly backed out of the woman, the commando viciously shoved him down on the bed with the can on the MP-5. The man grunted as if struck in the kidney by a boxer. The woman got up and the commando tossed her a small waterproof packet.

Standing naked in the dim light shining from the bathroom, she checked the contents. Her perfect breasts gleamed in the dim light. Her long, brown, slender legs came together in a fluff of black pubic hair that was luxuriant and inviting. Savarese couldn't see her face clearly but what he could see was beautiful. The woman adroitly removed a syringe from the pack and held it up against the available light. When she was satisfied, she nodded to the commando to back off. When he was clear, she planted a knee in the man's back and plunged the needle into his white ass. As she bent over, the perfect curves of her butt stared Savarese in the face. He was looking directly into the chasm of delight. Savarese forced himself to scan the room and its exits, but his eyes kept returning to the depth of desire. In a few seconds it was over and she stood up, leaving the naked man motionless on the bed.

Still excited, the woman paced around the room naked as if she were alone. When she calmed down, she lit a cigarette. The lighter illuminated her face and for the first time Gomez and Savarese clearly saw her face. She was young and beautiful, so beautiful she could have been a cover girl on any magazine. She drew deeply on the cigarette and spoke to the commando through the smoke of her exhalation.

"You took your time getting here," she complained. "I thought he was going to fuck my brains out."

"Didn't sound to me like you were suffering," snapped the commando lewdly.

"Fuck you!" she said loudly.

"Not on your life," he snapped back.

"Screw you, jerk!"

"Not a chance!" responded the commando.

Taking another deep drag on her cigarette, she said, "Get this asshole out of here so I can get some sleep. And tell that shithead Habberman to send me my bonus."

"You'll get your money, bitch," responded the commando contemptuously.

The Israeli motioned Gomez and Savarese to help. The three men dragged the naked Russian outside, where they were joined by the other two commandos. One of the men grabbed the Russian and threw him over his shoulder in a fireman's carry and followed the others across the beach as fast as he could move. At the beachhead next to the rocks, they joined the rear security and signaled the coxswain to the beach. When the boat reached the rocks, they threw Voshchanov in the Zodiac like a seabag full of operational gear and motored slowly to sea. When the coxswain was out of earshot of the beach, he opened up the throttle and skimmed across the surface of the Aegean Sea at full speed. They rendezvoused with an Israeli fast patrol boat twenty-five miles offshore. Voshchanov was on his own.

The secure telephone distorted their voices with a metallic sound as MacFarlane and Norton-Taylor talked across the Atlantic Ocean.

"So the Mossad has one of Karpenko's men?"

"Yes. A Major Yuri Voshchanov, Saraskina's man from the Razvedupr," responded MacFarlane.

"As I recall Voshchanov was GRU for more than ten years before he entered the Spetznaz," said Norton-Taylor.

"Yes."

"How did they catch him?"

"One of their informants spotted him at a border crossing in Greece. They put a lovely young agent on him, or perhaps I should say put him on her, and snatched him right out of her loving arms," answered MacFarlane.

"You don't say," responded Norton-Taylor with a hint of levity in his voice.

"They even allowed my two SEALs to participate in the snatch operation," continued MacFarlane.

"That's interesting." Norton-Taylor paused for reflection. "I suspect they were invited along to provide cover if anything went wrong. The Mossad is big on plausible denial, you know."

"Of course. If anything had gone wrong, I'm sure the incident would have been reported as American interventionism," said MacFarlane introspectively. "It was a relatively low-risk operation for my SEALs. I had an SSN standing by offshore just in case they needed a way out."

"And I would venture a guess that the Israelis didn't know about your submarine?" asked Norton-Taylor.

"Correct," said MacFarlane.

"Miles, you Americans are so clever. I must remember this conversation before our next joint operation."

MacFarlane ignored the comment. He waited for Norton-Taylor to continue the conversation in a more productive direction. After a decent interval, the red phone blurted out the metallic question he had anticipated.

"Did they get anything out of Voshchanov?" asked Norton-Taylor almost unintelligibly. The metallic distortion was worsening. He sounded like a man with a clothespin on his nose yelling through a long metal pipe.

"Not much. He was in North Korea with Karpenko and claims to have witnessed some extraordinary events. They didn't find the story credible, however. After hours of interrogation and a pantry full of drugs, they concluded he doesn't know where the weapons are hidden."

"What part of his story didn't they believe?"

"Something about a Russian black program called Airborne Warrior. Know anything about it?"

"No. I've never heard of it," lied Norton-Taylor. "How about you?"

"No. I don't know a thing about it." MacFarlane continued without further mention of Airborne Warrior. He suspected the Brit knew about the Russians' biological warfare program, but he didn't want to press the issue. It was top-secret, closely held information. "The Mossad concluded that Voshchanov believes Syria is Karpenko's customer," continued MacFarlane.

"With the way the Palestinians are scattered throughout the Middle East, I doubt that the country really matters," volunteered Norton-Taylor. "We must redouble our efforts in Northeast Asia and the Eastern Mediterranean."

"I concur. I've already maximized the number of U.S. special forces in the Eastern Med using exercise Urgent Tracker as the cover. You have to get the SAS in place right away so we can work them into the CONPLAN."

"I understand the urgency, Miles."

"I can cover Northeast Asia using Exercise Warrior Spirit in South Korea as a cover." MacFarlane paused for a moment and breathed into the receiver with a sigh. "Alfred, if my gut feeling is correct, we may have to take down three widely dispersed targets simultaneously."

"Yes. I suspect you are correct, Miles," responded the Brit. "I'll have the SAS in Egypt within twenty-four hours."

"Very well, then. I'll see you next week in Berlin," concluded MacFarlane.

"Yes. Of course. Let me know how it goes with your channels, Miles. If things go badly I'll ask the prime minister to give your president a ring."

"Thanks," responded MacFarlane.

Unlike MacFarlane, Norton-Taylor had direct access to the prime minister and clear lines of political and military responsibility. Miles MacFarlane had the dreary task of working the issues with the JCS, the OSD, the CIA, and the NSC before someone else, who wanted the face time, briefed the president. MacFarlane was surprised the operation hadn't already leaked to the Washington press.

"Miles?"

"Yes, Alfred."

"What did they do with the poor bugger?" asked Norton-Taylor.

"Voshchanov?" said MacFarlane incredulously. "Locked

him away in a cell where daylight will never penetrate, I suppose," answered MacFarlane.

"Cheerio!"

MacFarlane stared at the red phone for several minutes after Norton-Taylor hung up.

Airborne Warrior, he thought. *A diabolical cross between germ warfare and chemical warfare. No wonder Litvinov hasn't briefed the coalition on its existence. He probably doesn't know anything about it.*

Airborne Warrior was a weapons program the Russians would never admit existed.

Karpenko was angry when he loaded Saraskina's dead drop and instructed her to meet him in Vlorë, a small town on the Albanian coast directly across the Adriatic from Brindisi, Italy. Brindisi was his checkoff. It was the central hub for ferry operations in the Eastern Mediterranean and an easy passport to obscurity. Karpenko actually owned the small hotel where he was staying, but he paid as if he were a guest. From his table in the restaurant atop the hotel, he watched the fishing boats in the harbor depart with an evening tide. He relished in the pleasure of owning the largest private fishing boat in Vlorë. He mused as she got under way.

Private ownership is a powerful state of mind, he thought as he sipped his coffee. *It motivates. It creates pride and results in toil for the sake of pride.*

He made up his mind to order the captain to have his boat freshly painted, all 120 feet of her.

Saraskina arrived precisely at the hour he had directed. He watched as she stood outside the restaurant reading the menu. She was using the window as a mirror to see if anyone was following her. She casually scanned the premises looking for her contact. When she failed to locate him she entered and took a table by the window, which overlooked the street. She deftly maneuvered the waiter into seating her where she had a clear view of the entrance, the kitchen door, and the back exit. Karpenko could see her through the large windows that opened the view of the restaurant up to the street that descended down to the harbor.

Excellent, he thought, *thorough, brilliant, and beautiful.* He watched her for ten minutes, scanning the street for evidence of a tail. For a moment he caught himself thinking about her as if she were a possession like his fishing boat.

One can't own another in a free society, can they? he mused. He decided that it was possible to own a human being if one were rich enough and smart enough. Karpenko tilted his head back and sniffed the air. Waving his hand, he signaled a young boy who was standing by at the back of the restaurant. Pointing out Natila in the restaurant across the street, he handed the boy a flower to give to her. He watched the boy closely as he crossed the street and entered the establishment. Handing her the flower, he pointed up in Karpenko's direction. Saraskina's reaction was quiescent, as if she intended to ignore some secret admirer. He waited patiently as she casually read her paper and finished her coffee. After paying her bill she walked out of the restaurant and nonchalantly paused to smell the flowers that decorated the entrance. She instinctively scanned the block before crossing the street and quickly climbed the stairs to the small restaurant atop the hotel. Her experience told her where Karpenko was seated, but she still had trouble locating him. His manner of dress, his hair, and even his facial features had changed since their last meeting in Varna. As he stood to greet her she marveled at the wonders of western medicine. The deep facial scar he had worn since their mission in Indonesia was gone.

"Dimitri, you look marvelous. You have changed everything."

"You like my new look?" he asked pleasantly.

"Yes. You look ten years younger. I must have this secret."

"Ahhh. Natila, now you are being too kind. You look magnificent without the benefit of a plastic surgeon."

Over wine and to the sound of a violin, he softly interrogated her about Voshchanov and what information he might have known. Saraskina was one of the few people whom Karpenko half-trusted and somewhat respected. He had reliable information from informants in Moscow that the Russian government was cooperating with the West and he knew that their faces were posted at every international border crossing. He expected losses. But he expected Saraskina to anticipate such problems. It was part of the game. Proper compartmentalization prevented disaster and he trusted her to carry out her responsibilities without error. And she didn't disappoint him. Not only could she change her own appearance like a chameleon, but she had already ordered her men to alter their dress, safehouses, and dead drops. Satisfied after she had opined his own thoughts about the missing man, he shifted the conversation.

"We will move the consignment as planned," he said, looking at her for reaction. As she stared at him blankly, he wondered what feelings were at the bottom of those mysterious eyes.

"Vlad will deliver the electronic equipment personally to you at the Varna Transport Company. You ensure all shipments are in motion and then leave immediately for Southeast Asia. I want you in Jakarta before the ship clears the Bosporus."

He unconsciously rubbed his hand along the now invisible scar on his cheek, and for the first time Saraskina noticed the slight swelling that remained from the surgery. Under the makeup the skin was still red. Karpenko observed her face for reaction to his comment. But there was none. She was still in awe of the surgeon's skill.

"Yes, Dimitri."

Suddenly Karpenko's face grimaced and his eyes squinted shut from the burst of pain that racked his brain. For several seconds Saraskina watched silently while he slowly regained his composure. When he spoke she could tell the pain was still there because his eyes were glazed.

"I want you to activate and test every cell from Jakarta to Hanoi," he continued. He looked at her with a new fire in his eyes and growled. "Activate the cell in Tijuana. I want to know what your lover boy is up to."

Her stomach surged and her heart skipped a beat.

"Did you know he is now the commanding officer of SEAL Team Five?"

"No, sir."

"You should've killed him while he slept," growled Kar-

181

penko. "If you had done as I directed, I would not wear this scar." He traced his finger along the invisible line down his face.

Evans was the only man who had ever penetrated her soul. There was no explaining it. She had tried to analyze her feelings a thousand times and there was no explanation. Natila's parents had been killed in Stalin's pogroms and she had grown up the hard way on the streets of Moscow. To survive she had learned to steal and kill without compunction. Her assignment to the Spetznaz was a perfect fit for her personality. She had always followed Karpenko's orders to the letter, except for one time. He had ordered her to kill Evans in Denpasar. She had given Karpenko a plausible excuse and had lived in fear for two years that he blamed her for the pain in his head. She changed the subject for fear that her inner feelings would show.

"Dimitri, do you want me to sterilize Voshchanov's trail?"

"Of course, Saraskina!" he said using her last name to indicate annoyance with the question. "Abandon the money in his primary accounts. And do not let anyone go near any of his safehouses or dead drops. They will be watched. Let the shipments he arranged go as planned. It's good business."

"How long do I stay in the orient?"

"Natila, you must learn to enjoy yourself. If I want you I will contact you," he said with a look of surprise. "Have we not done this before, Saraskina?" he said in a scolding tone.

"Yes, sir. I was just wondering if there was anything more you wanted me to do."

Karpenko sniffed the air in an unconscious reaction before speaking. "Prepare a complete report on Derek Evans. Everything. I want to know his deployment schedule. I want him taken alive the first time he leaves U.S. soil. I want him, Saraskina. I want him," he growled. His fists tightened and his knuckles cracked. "Is that clear?"

"Yes, sir."

"Now, I want you to enjoy life, Natila," he said, changing his mood like Jekyll and Hyde. "Lie by the pool. Eat good food. Find yourself two or three young men and make them sweat. Life is short, bloody, brutish, and mean, you know?"

he said in English with a perfect British accent. She stared at him in fascination, startled by the revelation. In all the years she had known him she had never heard him speak with an English accent. The face was the same, but it was at the same time unfamiliar. And now the voice. So different and so strange. He smiled as he read her thoughts.

"You women have been able to fool men with your changes since time immemorial," he continued with his British accent. "I have simply learned from you."

"No, Dimitri. No. You have truly mastered *maskirovka*," she said sincerely.

They enjoyed a fabulous meal and drank two bottles of wine before he dismissed her gently.

"I would invite you to stay with me in this lovely place, Natila, but you must return to Varna immediately," he said salaciously. He had long ago grown tired of her, not because she lacked sex appeal but because he needed great variety for stimulation. When he could predict a woman's orgasm, he no longer wanted her. Karpenko preferred younger women, the younger the better, and several at a time.

"We must be very careful in the next few days, Natila Saraskina. They have information that our clients are North Korea and Syria and they know the weapons are near the Black Sea. We will conclude this transaction and lie low in Southeast Asia for a few years. Perhaps we should buy part of Burma or Cambodia"—he smiled—"before I return to Moscow. Thoroughly test our assets in the region. We may need them."

"Yes, Dimitri. I will check everything thoroughly."

When Natila left the restaurant, Karpenko checked out of his hotel and moved to a country villa just north of the Greek border. It was little more than a small, rustic farm that raised grapes for local wine consumption, but he owned it.

CHAPTER
16

The art of war is simple. Find out where the enemy is and destroy him. When the Soviets sent Sputnik into orbit on October 4, 1957, they launched more than a 184-pound sphere. They launched a space war. U.S. military planners immediately recognized the significance of the event. The satellite placed the spy in the sky, profoundly altering the ancient craft of espionage. A camera in orbit could photograph the enemy.

Satellites revolutionized the art of warfare, from reconnaissance and surveillance to navigation and communications. The U.S. pursued a course of remote sensing. Over time, a system of ferret satellites were developed to monitor and photograph enemy activity. Some listen in and record enemy radio, telephone, television, and radar transmissions. Others provide real-time telecommunications, telemetry, telephone, and navigation data links. Still others remain top secret, remotely sensing enemy activity by spying on esoteric emissions. Big Bird was the first program to go public. It wouldn't be the last.

Of the hundreds of satellites in earth orbit, Staff Sergeant Steven Lynn Chaffin was assigned to just one. Its job was to track nuclear emissions. His assignment was so secret he wasn't allowed to tell his wife the phone number on his desk or the building address where he worked. When Steven hung up his uniform for civilian clothes and grew his hair too long for military service, Angella Chaffin began to think he was working on a secret mission for the CIA and for some reason he let her believe it. His job, after all, was top secret. It just wasn't for the CIA. For the past twelve months he had been staring at a computer monitor linked to a satellite in geosynchronous orbit twenty-two thousand miles above the surface of the planet. Chaffin's boring but important job was to chart and monitor all nuclear emissions emanating from one-quarter of the earth's surface. He reluctantly reported for duty at midnight to relieve Staff Sergeant David Hasemyer, who was anxious to leave.

"Anything new, Dave?" asked Chaffin, expecting a half-assed debrief of the last eight hours.

"Yeah. Mostly the same old shit, but there's been a faint intermittent signal from this area of Romania," he said, pointing to a map on the wall by the desk. "It's probably a ghost."

"How long and how strong?" asked Chaffin.

"Just a intermittent flicker, man, on and off for less than a minute. Very faint. It's happened twice in the last hour."

"Did you call it in?"

"No. I wanted to confirm with EMSAT before calling the lieutenant. She has been such a bitch lately."

"It's all the pressure she's been under to turn up a new firefly in Eastern Europe," defended Chaffin.

"PMS, if you ask me," retorted Hasemyer, gathering his belongings to leave. "EMSAT will pass over in about two hours and you can get a good look at the area. I recorded and logged the events."

"Any units operating near the signal?" asked Chaffin.

"Nothing, man. Not a damn thing! Mountains, mountains, and more mountains," he exclaimed, pointing at the lower Carpathian Mountains. "There's not a military unit within a hundred miles of the flicker, which is why I didn't call it in," argued Hasemyer.

"Anything moving in the surrounding area?" asked Chaffin.

"Yep. It's in the log, partner," responded Hasemyer like a cowboy in a western movie. "But it's that Tango-class sub you tracked out of Odessa the other day. It's too far away to cause ghosting."

"Maybe the space aliens shanghaied Blinky again, huh?"

"Probably, but you'd better call the lieutenant if it winks in again," he said, tilting his head to one side as if listening to the sky.

The men called the old geosynchronous satellite Blinky because from time to time it would wink in and out with false signals as if some unknown space alien was sending a coded message. Usually the signals paralleled a known emitter. For some unknown reason the signal split while traveling back and forth through the atmosphere, which caused a ghost signal near the actual nuclear emission. The EMSAT bird was different. It was a new and more reliable spy satellite and, unlike the old bird that was fixed above the earth in geosynchronous orbit, it was in low earth orbit, circling the globe at high speed. Its services were passed from desk to desk to other personnel responsible for different sectors of the earth. Hasemyer circled the area on the wall map beside the desk with a grease pencil and briefed Chaffin on several U.S. submarines operating in the Eastern Mediterranean. The U.S. submarines were always a problem to track because their reactors were efficiently shielded. During deep dives the Space Trackers, as they called themselves, always lost contact and had to work to positively identify the emission when it surfaced in a new area. That was the only part of the job that was exciting. Russian reactors weren't much of a challenge. Their computers could identify the name of the vessel from the nuclear fingerprint of the emission.

Hasemyer finished his debriefing and left Chaffin to sort out the dilemma. Steve took a big gulp of his lukewarm coffee and fell back into the desk chair, mentally preparing himself for eight hours of boredom. He slowly scanned the computer monitor, which projected all the emitters in his sector on a rough map of Earth. Nothing new. He reached up and keyed in a password that activated a private program he had been working on for more than a year. A sexy feminine voice softly projected through the speaker.

"Oh, Stevie, it is you! I have missed you so much!"

announced the computer with a slight French accent dripping with sex.

He smiled and keyed in the word *vigilance*.

"Oh, Stevie, I am always vigilance for you," responded the computer suggestively.

"Damn bug," he said out loud. He had worked for two weeks on the subroutine that should have converted *vigilance* to *vigilant* and it had failed. He took another gulp of his coffee and sat back to think about the problem. He was deep in thought when the computer activated.

"Oh, Stevie, I have something to show you!"

He sat up straight in his chair and keyed in the strokes that zoomed the screen in on the new emission. He quickly correlated the signal with those logged by Hasemyer and keyed the computer to search its memory to identify the emission. The screen projected "EMISSION NOT IDENTIFIED," as the sexy voice sounded out the words. He turned off the private program and stared at the screen. Chaffin watched the signal for two more minutes before he nervously picked up the phone and called Lieutenant Vernon. Two hours later EMSAT confirmed the sighting as a nuclear emission of unknown origin. For eighteen hours Chaffin remained glued to his monitor as he tracked the target from the mountains in Romania to the small Black Sea port of Varna, Bulgaria. There the strong signal separated into three faint but distinct emissions.

The discovery of the signal created a flurry of activity throughout the world, but when it separated into three distinct emissions activity took on the appearance of hysteria. One signal slowly moved offshore and into the Black Sea. Twenty-four hours later a ROARSAT passing directly over the target identified it as a small freighter wallowing slowly in a light sea, its course apparently the Mediterranean. On the other side of the world this mission was assigned to Task Force Blue, a coalition of sea commandos from the U.S., the UK, and Germany who had been training for weeks for board-and-seizure operations. One emission moved down the coast through Bulgaria to northern Turkey, as if transported by vehicle. Contact was broken briefly in Istanbul but was regained a few miles south of the city. This mission was assigned to Task Force Red, a coalition of ground commandos supported by a helicopter support battalion. The third target remained stationary in Varna, Bulgaria, for almost two days. While the old men in the War Room at the Pentagon drank a lot of coffee, looked at a lot of satellite photography, and argued incessantly over the best method for commandeering the weapons, Russian agents quickly closed in on the Varna signal. But near the end of the second day it, too, moved quickly down the coast and disappeared in the city of Istanbul beyond the reach of the Russian commandos.

On the Space Tracker's monitor, the emissions appeared to intersect briefly as the old freighter slowly passed through the channel connecting the Black Sea to the Mediterranean. Shortly after it cleared the Sea of Marmara, the body of water separating Turkey from Europe, a fourth weak, ghostlike signal appeared to shadow the old freighter. Its significance was soon overshadowed by a strong signal that appeared in Istanbul and quickly moved southward following the route taken by the first emission. Task Force White, composed of ground and sea commandos, quickly changed plans from seizure at sea to air-land road interdiction. When Sergeant Chaffin relieved Hasemyer on the third day, he replayed the video recording of the event at high speed. It looked like a dance of fireflies on his screen, separating and crossing, appearing and disappearing.

Even in November it is insufferably hot in Egypt, especially inside an aircraft hangar. The interior of the huge building looked like a disorganized flea market laid out inside a large convention center. Gear was stacked in pallets three tiers high. Interspersed among the pallets of food, ammunition, weapons, and shipping crates were cots separated by poncho liners strung on makeshift clotheslines. Clothes, boots, and gear bags full of personal operational equipment lay strewn about among the cots where men slept amid a constant drone of aircraft and helicopters moving about on the hot deck outside the hangar.

The inhabitants of this pseudo-city had been working twenty-four hours a day for weeks participating in Exercise Urgent Tracker, a combined special operations exercise designed to improve interoperability among special forces. The Forward Operating Base, dubbed FOB Sword, was located only a hundred miles from the famous Pyramids of the Nile, but none of the people at FOB Sword had seen them. They were restricted to the airfield compound, which was closely guarded by their own forces.

Combined teams of British, German, and U.S. commandos had successfully planned and executed numerous building and ship takedown operations throughout the eastern Mediterranean operational area they called Oparea Amphora. *Takedown* was a working term for seizing control of buildings and vessels under the control of terrorists. A controller cell, consisting of a large opposition force called the OPFOR, played the part of terrorists. The OPFOR had created challenging mission scenarios throughout Oparea Amphora to drill and test the commandos and airmen in the skills needed to combat terrorism. Every day, one of the three task forces code-named Red, White, and Blue would fly off to an unknown location to seize a difficult objective controlled by the OPFOR. Exercise Urgent Tracker at its peak employed more than three thousand men and women. Sleep was a luxury.

An entirely new vernacular had been created to describe this new kind of warfare, called low-intensity conflict, or LIC for short. Terrorists were called tangos. Weapons were discussed by colloquial acronyms such as MP-5s and M-60s. Functions were described by letters strung together haphazardly. A forward air refueling point became a FARP and a radar surveillance aircraft became a tracker. Such odd-sounding words as HUMINT, SIGINT, and COMINT were used as everyday terms to discuss human, signal, and communications intelligence. To the uninitiated, the inhabitants of FOB Sword spoke a foreign language.

Operating at night and sleeping during the day amidst the constant drone of helicopters and cargo aircraft would have been impossible for the average person. But to the inhabits of FOB Sword it was life as usual. Both men and women shared the same primitive facilities and ate the same bland packaged foods called MREs, which in military jargon translates to "meals ready to eat." They were tolerable for one week. After a month of field operations they were horrible. Despite the appearance of disorganization, FOB Sword was the most organized city in Egypt. Everyone had a job and everyone was a highly trained professional. Assignments ranged from intelligence analysis to commando.

Gomez and Savarese sauntered into the fray of this strange environment as if they had the keys to the city. Deployment exercises were a way of life for SEAL commandos and they subconsciously saw order in the chaos. They had caught a courier aircraft from Haifa to FOB Sword to borrow some equipment the Israelis lacked for intersquad communications. They quickly located Task Force Blue among the confusion of gear in the hangar and made a beeline for the SEALs' bivouac. Task Force Blue was set up in the center of six incredible fiberglass racing boats circled like wagons in an old western movie.

"Hey, guys, what's happening?" asked Savarese as they approached a group of men studying a chart lying on the table.

"Hey, Boomer, why aren't you kicked back on the beach in Haifa soaking up rays?" asked one of the men with a sly smile.

"Too many women on the beach, man. Grabbing me and touching me." Savarese pushed out his jaw with his tongue in a vulgar manner. "You know how women are when I wear my Speedos," he said, grabbing his privates and hitching up his pants. He ignored the female intelligence officer who was glaring up from the chart table. She was so ugly the men actually thought of her as one of the boys.

"Commander, we need a couple of SATCOM radios and some intersquad equipment," said Gomez to the officer in charge of Task Force Blue. "The Israelis have some kind of bullshit junk that won't work half the time."

"Sure, anything for my Crazy Cuban, seeing as how you're going to miss the first real-world op in the last two years," sassed Commander Thompson.

"Sir, the lieutenant and I saw action in the PI and in Greece," reminded Savarese.

"You didn't have to bring that up, Master Chief Asshole!" snarled Thompson jealously. Gomez and Savarese had been on special assignment with the Israelis for more than two months, and they were sorely missed by their teammates, but there was no way Thompson would admit such heresy.

"I wouldn't be so sure about this op, Commander. The Israelis think this Karpenko character is some kind of a magician or somethin'," stated Gomez.

"Bullshit! He's just a damn thief," snapped Thompson.

"So what's the plan, sir?" asked Gomez.

"We're going to take down a freighter halfway between Crete and Libya. Red and White will hit two truck convoys simultaneously in the mountains, here and here," he said, pointing to the Taurus Mountains of southern Turkey. Gomez noted that the two ambush sites were located within helicopter range of the southern coast of Turkey. "Tracker has our baby right here, just west of Crete," he said, pointing out the ship's position. "We'll drop in at last light and take her down just before dawn. Too bad you're playing footsie with the bagel-eaters."

"I like bagels," commented Savarese, pushing out his jaw in an undulating motion.

"Boss, the Israelis think it's all a big ruse," responded Gomez, raising his eyebrows.

"Horseshit! We've been tracking three strong signals for four days and this one's mine!" he said emphatically with a broad grin. "You're just pissed cause you have to lay around with your Israeli buddies waiting for a mission," bragged Thompson. Gomez gave him an amphibious salute with both hands and said, "Sir, we have to catch the courier flight back to Haifa in twenty minutes. I'd like to have Radio check out the equipment before we leave."

"You bet! Hey, Radio!" snapped Thompson gruffly. He nodded his head at an eager petty officer who turned to a large box full of electronic equipment.

Seizing an underway vessel at night is one of the most difficult military operations ever undertaken, but for the men of Task Force Blue it was routine. The mission began with a clear objective and clear rules of engagement. After a thorough study of the situation and a careful briefing, half the men boarded specially equipped helicopters, which ferried them to awaiting assault ships stationed in the Mediterranean. The ships served as lily pads for the helos to stop and refuel. They were shadowing the freighter from over the horizon, keeping within helicopter range. The other half of Task Force Blue loaded four high-speed boats in the cargo bays of the two C-141 Starlifter aircraft. They waited until just before H-hour before taking off to rendezvous with the ship's track.

Precisely on schedule, Tracker, an aircraft specially configured with state-of-the-art radar and communications equipment, vectored the C-141s to a drop point over the horizon in front of the freighter. The men followed the boats out of the cargo bay of the airplanes and descended lightly to the sea in large, maneuverable, square parachutes. They quickly sank their parachutes and put on their operational gear, which was stored inside the boats.

The special operations craft, or SOC boats as they were called by the SEALs, produced twelve-foot rooster tails as they took off across the moonlit Mediterranean Sea. In calm seas they could make seventy knots at full throttle. The coxswains held them down to forty knots, flanking and circling the slow-moving freighter.

Just before dawn, the crewmen aboard Tracker earned their pay. In pitch dark they vectored the SOC boats, two big helicopters, and two little helicopters to precisely the same point in the sea. The first to arrive on target were the little birds. They took station off the beams of the old freighter. Sitting outside the aircraft, strapped in special jump seats, were sharpshooters, experts at shooting from the moving helicopters. Their rules of engagement allowed them to shoot anyone who threatened the boarding parties. Simultaneously with the arrival of the little birds came the SOC boats, screaming up from behind the freighter at angles from each side. The boarding parties reached up to the deck of the ship with painter's poles and hooked caving ladders to the railing, as the coxswains maintained station at the side of the underway ship.

Next, the big birds swooped in one at a time dead on the bow of the ship. The pilots came in low and fast, flaring at just the right point to break speed and hover thirty feet above the deck. The blast of air from rotor wash was so strong a man couldn't stand on deck without holding on. Under cover of the sharpshooters in the hovering little birds, the commandos in the big birds fastroped to the deck of the moving freighter. One man per second hit the deck, like firefighters sliding down a fire pole. They instantly scurried off into the darkness, taking defensive positions.

Commander Thompson arrived on the second big bird and coordinated maneuvers with the leaders of the SOC boat teams. There was no resistance. Advancing carefully from cover to cover, using the cargo containers littering the deck of the freighter, he maneuvered his men in position to seize the pilothouse at the stern of the ship. The horrified seaman on the dog watch stood petrified as the SEALs stormed into the pilothouse, pointing MP-5 submachine guns in his face. Step by step, compartment by compartment, they advanced throughout the old ship until every hold and every compartment was secure.

The *Gregor-Yavlinski* was taken without a shot. There were deep worry lines on the faces of the old men in the Pentagon when Commander Thompson radioed FOB Sword that the source of the emission was some sort of electronic device placed in the forward hold of the ship. Like armchair quarterbacks, they sat drinking coffee, listening to and watching the action on the opposite side of the planet. SATCOM radios allowed them to intercept the field commanders' conversations with FOB Sword in Egypt. Imagery projected on a huge screen allowed them to watch the action in comfort. With the failure of Task Force Blue, their attention turned to Task Forces White and Red, already on the ground in Turkey.

The eight big birds carrying Task Forces White and Red had lifted off from two helicopter assault ships stationed north of Cyprus. They had marshaled above the ships and flown in formation until they went feet-dry over the Turkish coastline at one hundred feet. There they split into two formations and proceeded up separate canyons to isolated ambush points along the desolate mountain road. Since the trucks were moving targets, several LZs and ambush points had been selected. Using the data transmitted from Sergeant Chaffin's fixes in Washington, D.C., Tracker selected the two most efficient landing sights along the routes of the moving convoys. The first helicopter of Task Force Red landed just as Commander Thompson's men made their final approach on the *Gregor-Yavlinski*.

The fifty men of Task Force Red rushed off the still-turning helicopters and ran to preselected positions at checkpoint delta. By SATCOM radio the OIC was continually updated from Tracker using information transmitted from Sergeant Chaffin in Washington, D.C. When the heavy Russian trucks rumbled up the hill and around the curve there was nothing left to chance. The highway patrolman spikes placed in the dark road slowly deflated the tires of the laboring trucks struggling up the mountain grade and they came to a stop in the dead center of the kill zone. There was no resistance from the drivers, who were completely taken by surprise. They climbed down from their cabs with eyes wide open, surrounded by professional soldiers whose faces were covered with black balaclava masks. The British officer in charge of Task Force Red ordered his search party into the kill zone and at the same time he cordoned off the road five hundred meters on each side of the ambush. It was four-thirty in the morning and the only traffic on the mountain road was in his kill zone.

The deep worry lines on the faces of the old men in the Pentagon War Room turned into chasms when the limey voice of the British officer reported to FOB Sword that he had seized three truckloads of machinery parts. They were not surprised when he reported that the source of the emission was an electronic device the size of a portable computer.

Task Force White created even more anxiety for the senior officers in the tank. They ran into trouble almost immediately upon landing at checkpoint three. All of the checkpoints from alpha to foxtrot, one to six, along the convoy routes had been simulated during Exercise Urgent Tracker. However, the mock targets were not precise. They were simply the closest match the OPFOR could find in Oparea Amphora. The pointman of Task Force White became confused by the terrain and set up in counterproductive position. By the time the German officer in charge of the task force had corrected the ambush formation, the trucks were almost in the kill zone. He initiated the correct orders, but the U.S. Special Forces soldiers were young and inexperienced. They were out of breath and pumped up on adrenaline. The young rocket soldier with the AT-4 misunderstood the orders and fired off his rocket dead into the radiator of the lead truck.

The blast shattered the darkness and the explosive flash blinded the soldiers. Instinctively they opened fire and for three minutes rained pure hell on the helpless truck drivers. When the German officer regained control, the trucks were engulfed in a blazing inferno. Fearing the worst, he quickly cut loose three choppers full of men and bravely stayed behind to face the radiation cloud with the experts manning the monitoring equipment. He remained well into the morning light before he was satisfied there was not a hint of radiation in the area. In Washington, Sergeant Chaffin confirmed that the signal had disappeared. Reluctantly Capitan Ruderger Claus boarded his remaining helicopter and returned to the USS *Guam*. The GSG-9 was not accustomed to mission failure. He took consolation in the fact that this one would go down in history as an American failure.

CHAPTER
17

"Delta One, this is Delta One Niner, over?" whispered Savarese in a hushed tone. When there was no reply in his earpiece he waited two minutes before he keyed his radio and repeated his interrogation through his throat mike.

"Delta One, this is Delta One Niner, over?" Savarese whispered out of instinct. He waited but there was no response. There was no need for the hushed tone. Savarese was seventy miles off the coast of Syria in a rubber boat with four Israeli commandos and not a vessel in sight. The sea lay calm in a quarter moon that rippled across the surface from low on the horizon. As the Z-bird in which he sat rocked gently with each passing wave, he moved effortlessly like the stylus on a seismograph, letting the energy pass through his body without fighting it. He was in a resting trance when his earpiece sounded off.

"Delta One Niner, this is Delta One, over?" crackled Lieutenant Gomez's voice, broken up by the pounding of the waves as his Z-bird skimmed over the Mediterranean at full speed. An Israeli fast patrol boat half the size of a U.S. destroyer had dropped him off thirty miles ahead of the track of a small merchant ship that was headed for the Syrian coast. Two hours after launch the merchant had changed course slightly, putting him out of position. He was racing across the surface at full speed, being vectored by the patrol craft to an intercept point with the ship's track. Unlike the fast American SOC boats, which could effortlessly circle a merchant ship at fifty miles, the Israelis used large Zodiacs with souped-up outboard engines. They were seaworthy little craft but not in the same league with the sleek racing boats Gomez and Savarese were accustomed to using.

Gomez had to threaten the life of the firstborn of the Israeli commander in charge of the operation to get a mission. The Israelis intended to board and search seven merchants, so the SEALs were assigned the one with the lowest priority. Savarese keyed the switch on his left breast and whispered a response through the microphone strapped around his neck.

"Delta One, this is One Niner, roger over."

"Delta One Niner, this is Delta One. What's your posit, over?" queried Gomez.

"Delta One, this is One Niner. I'm at IP, locked and cocked."

Savarese picked up his NVGs and quickly scanned the horizon to the northeast. There was a glow on the horizon right where he expected it. Gomez came back.

"One Niner, this is One. I'm about two thousand meters from IP. How copy, over?" he said as the boat bounced off the water and returned with a *whoosh*. Reading his GPS signal was difficult in the bucking boat. As the coxswain piloted the Z-bird, Gomez checked the vectors provided by the patrol craft against his own plot calculated by the global positioning system.

"Roger, good copy, boss. I've got a glow on the horizon right where it should be," said Savarese.

"Roger," returned the crackling voice in the earpiece. "I'll be at IP in five Mikes."

"Roger, out," said Savarese. He checked his position again with his GPS and scanned the horizon with his NVGs. The merchant glowed like a candle against the night sky. When Gomez and his crew took station at his initial point, he immediately began to survey his equipment and ready his weapons and climbing gear. Years of experience had taught him to take survey repeatedly throughout a mission. His primary weapon was an MP-5 with a silencer. Like the commandos in Task Force Blue, it hung low from his shoulder with a harness that allowed him hands-free movement. A 9mm Sigsaur pistol backed up his MP-5. It was slung low on his right leg in a special plastic holster that locked the pistol down with a snap strap. The M-14, which lay against the transverse tube under his leg, backed up the 9mm. The MP-5 and the Sigsaur were excellent weapons for use onboard a ship, if they made it onboard. But they were of little use if they were caught in the open. The M-14 was there just in case they didn't make it onboard. Small-caliber, low-velocity weapons like the MP-5 were an absolute necessity when working inside steel compartments of a ship, where a shooter's own ricochets were a hazard to life and limb. But in the open a .556 or .762 could mean the difference between life and death. The M-14 with the new commando-style plastic stock and grip could reach out and touch someone from long distance with .762 caliber, long enough for the cavalry in the fast patrol boats to arrive. Gomez was a careful man. He felt his ammo pouches and radio fasteners for security, mentally rehearsing their use. He and Boomer had been taught by the best, Commander Derek Evans and Master Chief Steven Saleen.

The Israelis were all carrying 9mm Uzis, a fact that had not gone unnoticed by Gomez. Gone were the MP-5s used in the Greek mission. He had noted the weapons switch but had said nothing to Boomer, who was more interested in seducing one of the female soldiers supporting Task Force Green. During the second week of their stay at Haifa, Boomer had succeeded in his primary mission and was a happy guy. The Israeli change in weapons tipped Gomez off to the real reason why they had been invited along on the Greek body-snatch operation and why General Ashton had insisted upon the secret "American-only" submarine standing by offshore. The general was no fool. He suspected that Gomez and Savarese were along for the ride to take the fall if the op went sour. Gomez also realized it was his superior communications and navigation equipment that were the deciding factors in the present operation. That, and the fact that they had acquitted themselves well in Greece.

"One Niner, this is One, over?"

"This is One Niner, roger, over."

"Locked and cocked, Boomer," said Gomez without procedure, his voice now clear and unmolested by the speeding boat.

Ten miles of deep blue water separated the two Zodiacs when they began to close on the ship's track. They slowly motored toward the oncoming merchant to minimize the phosphorescence in their wakes. The old vessel was wallowing in a following sea making no more than eight knots as she approached them without her running lights on. Merchant vessels lack the radar to pick up small boats, so Gomez wasn't concerned with anyone seeing them. Using their NVGs to illuminate her and their throat mikes to communicate with each other, they guided the coxswains to a point one hundred meters off the starboard and the port quarters of the old freighter. Only the stars lighted the sea as it foamed about the hull of the wallowing freighter.

The two Z-birds approached the vessel at angles slightly off the rear beam on both the port and the starboard quarters, maintaining a constant bearing and a decreasing range until they took station underneath the curve of the stern. Weapons at the ready, Gomez and Savarese coordinated their engagement by constant communication through their throat mikes. As soon as they were on station Gomez queried Savarese.

"Boomer, ready to hook?" whispered Gomez.

"Roger."

"Ready, hook," he ordered.

Timing the motion of the waves, Gomez on one side and Savarese on the other reached up with long, extendable aluminum poles and hooked small cable ladders to the railing of the moving ship. As the coxswains carefully steered parallel courses at the sides of the freighter, a commando in each boat held the bottom of the ladders, using them like sea painters to steady the bows of the rubber boats.

"Boomer, ready to climb?" whispered Gomez.

"Fuckin'-aye, sir! Let's do it!" he whispered in his throat mike.

"Ready, climb."

"Roger," whispered Savarese, acknowledging the order.

They climbed up both sides of the ship simultaneously and slid on deck without a sound. Once onboard they took up defensive positions facing forward on each side of the rusty old vessel. Six commandos quickly followed them up the ladders. Together they slowly inched their way forward and peered through a passageway that crossed through the superstructure of the ship. She was shaped like a banana, with the pilothouse and living quarters placed at the stern of the ship, leaving the forward deck clear for cargo. Above and between them was the superstructure and pilothouse. At 0430 there appeared to be no one on deck and only a single watch in the pilothouse with the quartermaster, who was steering the vessel. Through his NVGs Gomez scanned the foredeck. It was littered with cargo containers and large cement pipes stacked in racks of three.

"Boomer, foredeck clear port side. How starboard, over?"

"Negative, boss. I got one tango smoking on the starboard side fifteen meters from the bow," he whispered.

"Roger." Gomez leaned out from the port gangway and spotted the night watch on the opposite side of the ship. He was sitting on a cargo hatch smoking a cigarette.

"I got him, Boomer. You take the smoking tango. I'll take the pilothouse."

"Roger, boss."

Gomez and his three men eased into the passageway and slowly inched their way to the center of the ship where one ladder ascended to the pilothouse and one descended to the galley. While Gomez guarded the ladder two commandos closed the hatch to the galley and chained it shut. They slowly opened and checked each room on the 01 level. When they were satisfied that the crew was locked below, Gomez whispered into his throat mike. "Boomer, ascending to pilothouse."

"Roger, boss. I'll drill this asshole if he so much as farts."

Gomez climbed the stairway to the pilothouse, followed by two commandos. The compartment was lighted with a red light, casting dark shadows about the huge room that opened to both sides of the ship. They stood in the shadow of the hatchway behind the quartermaster for two minutes, carefully watching him pilot the vessel. One sleepy guard sat in the captain's chair smoking, his AK slung carelessly at his side. Nodding directions at the others, Gomez entered the room like a cat, startling the guard with his appearance. His hand reached down for his weapon out of instinct, but he didn't bring it to the ready. Gomez motioned for him to get down on his knees. One of the commandos handcuffed him and the quartermaster with nylon zip ties and duct-taped them to a steel support stanchion.

"Boomer, pilothouse clear," reported Gomez.

"Roger, good copy. Pilothouse clear," repeated Savarese.

As Gomez moved to one side of the vessel where the hatch exited to the bridge wing, he was startled by the appearance of an armed guard approaching the hatchway. They both raised their weapons out of instinct, but the oncoming watch was still sleepy. The brief instant of hesitation made the difference. Using his silenced MP-5, Gomez put two rounds through the man's forehead. In less than two heartbeats the man lay dead on the bridge wing. Cautiously moving outside, Gomez checked for others. Motioning one of the commandos to chain the aft hatch, he turned to cover Boomer, inching his way up the starboard side of the vessel. Gomez took a bead on the man and waited. Boomer stepped out from the side of a cargo container and walked nonchalantly as if he were a part of the ship's crew. In the darkness it was impossible to tell. The guard spoke something in a language that sounded like Russian but Savarese just coughed a couple of times as he continued walking toward the man. The guard brought his weapon up slowly as the realization came to him that Boomer was not a part of the ship's crew. He caught two rounds in the head before he could get his weapon to a firing position. The impact of the bullets knocked him off the hatch and he thumped loudly on the steel deck.

Startled by the clatter on the deck, a guard appeared from between two cargo containers on the port side of the ship. Seeing Savarese standing over the body, he raised his AK and cut loose with a burst that ruptured the night with sound and flame. Two rounds caught Savarese directly in the chest, knocking him back into a cargo container. It reverberated like a empty oil drum. From the bridge wings and the foredeck Gomez and four commandos sprayed the man with half a dozen rounds, killing him in a hail of bullets. Gomez began shouting orders to seal all hatchways. All the commandos threw grenades inside the nearest hatch and bolted them shut. The deck of the old vessel reverberated as the concussion rumbled through the steel decks.

With the ship secure Gomez made his way to Boomer, fearing the worst. He found him sitting on the foredeck, coughing up phlegm and cursing. His body armor had stopped the bullets, but the impact had broken several of his ribs.

The high-ranking officers and civilians drinking coffee in the Pentagon War Room listened to the chatter on the other side of the world with deep concern. Task Forces Red, White, and Blue had expertly taken down their targets and found nothing but devices that simulated nuclear emissions. They knew Karpenko had fooled them and that along with the slight of hand was a real move. The question was where. MacFarlane suspected the Israelis knew more than they had shared with the coalition. He sat grim faced with Ashton and Arlington. When the SATCOM speaker crackled with a man's voice, everyone listened up, hoping for good news from the Israelis. Admiral Arlington recognized the voice that projected through the speakers and sat up straight in his chair.

"FOB Sword, FOB Sword, this is Delta One, over," crackled the voice.

"Delta One, Delta One, bead window. I repeat. Bead window. This net is for authorized users only. Please remain clear of this net," responded the radio operator at FOB Sword. Delta One was not one of the call signs on his list of authorized users. *Bead window* was a term that meant violation of radio procedure.

"Screw you!" blared the response.

The generals scowled at each other, offended by the transmission. Admiral Arlington scrunched down in his chair.

"Delta One, I repeat. Bead window! Remain clear of this frequency!" challenged the radio operator at FOB Sword.

"Let me make myself perfectly clear, asshole! If you don't shut the hell up and listen, when I get back to base I'm gonna rip out your tonsils, *pal*. Now! I got one man down. Possible broken ribs. Require *medevac immediately*. My posit is latitude three-five degrees, zero-eight minutes. Longitude three-five degrees, zero-one minutes. How copy, over?" demanded Lieutenant Alex Gomez.

"Good copy, Delta One," responded the radio operator.

"I have five tangos, KIA. They appear to be Russian in nationality." The old men sat up in their chairs in anticipation. "For the moment I am in possession of one, I repeat, one nuclear-looking device that appears to be Russian in make. You'd better get the cavalry here on the double. My Israeli friends want to haul it off to Haifa. I will impede their progress by all means at my disposal. Delta One, out."

Just after first light, Thompson and the troops of Task Force Blue arrived. Gomez escorted him to a hold that contained a large metal shipping container. Inside it Thompson saw a nuclear bomb stored in a short section of cement pipe.

"Son of a bitch!" was all he could say.

CHAPTER
18

Evans wheeled the Porsche around SEAL Team Five and screeched to a stop in front of his reserved parking spot, the one clearly marked Commanding Officer, SEAL Team Five. It was occupied by a rental car. The visitor's spot on the opposite side of the quarterdeck walkway was also occupied, so he parked directly between the two cars on the sidewalk leading to the quarterdeck. Perturbed, he sat back in the bucket seat, refusing to move until he collected his thoughts. The CD was playing Chicago 17, "You're a Hard Habit to Break," so he pumped up the volume and waited until the song finished before he reluctantly crawled out of the comfortable leather seat and walked into the building. The duty officer was waiting at the door.

"Good morning, Skipper," he said with a smile.

"Morning."

The quarterdeck watch yelled, "Attention on deck," and everyone within the vicinity of the quarterdeck snapped to attention. Evans responded with the traditional, "Carry on, carry on," then followed the order with a growl. "Petty Officer Carroll, who's the SOB that parked in my spot?" he demanded with anger written on his face.

"It's that woman who did it down at BUDS, Skipper. You

know, the one everyone called the Seafox," he answered. Evans looked at the duty officer.

"She's in with the Master Chief, sir," he said defensively.

"Very well," he responded with a snarl.

As Evans's heels clicked on the highly polished passageway, he heard the PA system announce, "SEAL Team Five, arriving," alerting the command that Captain Derek Evans was onboard. From the condition of the deck he could tell the XO had been working the homebodies hard.

Halfway to his office Evans ran into a chief petty officer everyone called Horsecock, because of his fondness for the navy luncheon meat with the same nickname. Horsecock wasn't alone. He was escorting a beautiful young Mexican girl. Men up and down the passageway were rubbernecking.

"Good morning, Skipper," said Horsecock, pleasantly. "Sir, I'd like to introduce you to my fiancée, Maria Diaz," he said with a smile.

"Please to meet you, Ms. Diaz," said Evans, shaking her hand.

Horsecock was an awkward-looking man. In fact he was downright ugly. Evans stared, mouth agape, trying to fix the face of the lovely young girl when it dawned on him that the car parked in the visitor's spot had Baja plates. She smiled with grace and charm.

"Mucho gusto en conocerlo, Señor Capitán," she said pleasantly.

"The pleasure is mine, I assure you, Ms. Diaz." Evans faced Horsecock and again the thought crossed his mind, *What is this gal up to?*

"Chief, I'm late for a meeting. I'm sorry, but I don't have time to chat."

"Sure, Skipper. I was just walking Maria to her car."

Evans walked down the hall and into his office, still trying to place the face. Before he could hang up his hat, Saleen appeared.

"Captain, Ms. Harris to see you, sir."

"Send her in, Shooter."

Harris walked in with a smile and shook his hand warmly. She looked tired.

"I'll just keep you a minute, Commander," she said as

Saleen closed the door with a inquisitive look. He didn't trust Harris and it showed on his face. Evans studied her for a few seconds before speaking.

"How are you, Alysin?"

"Fine. And you?"

"Great. Alysin, you look tired," he volunteered. "Jet lag?"

"Yeah. Too much time in the friendly skies," she responded with a yawn.

"How are things in Europe?" he asked.

She leveled a steady look at Evans before walking over to his TV, which constantly played the news channel. She turned up the volume before answering the question.

"We've had a degree of success," she said with a smile. "But nothing to really crow about."

"Excellent," he said, coming out from behind the desk. "That's good to hear." He took her hand and held it for a moment, studying her face. Finally he pulled her close and kissed her lightly on the lips. "Have a seat," he said, motioning to the plush chairs sitting around a coffee table.

"OK. But just for a few minutes. I have a meeting at WARCOM at nine," she responded.

"So. What's up? To what do I owe the pleasure of this visit?" asked Evans, tuned to her eyes.

"When are you deploying to Korea?"

"In a week or so. We're playing in Exercise Warrior Spirit. But you already knew that, right?" he asked, raising his eyebrows.

"Yes, I did. We are using Warrior Spirit as cover for Operation Fastback. Sometime in the next few weeks you will need to be briefed into the next higher level," she volunteered.

"Why hasn't Admiral Arlington briefed me in?" asked Evans, concerned.

"You are one of just a handful of people on the West Coast who has knowledge of Operation Fastback. I believe he was hoping for greater success in the European theater."

"The task force that is operating out of Okinawa is Operation Fastback?" he asked.

"Yes. That's part of it," she responded with a focused expression.

"They have OPCON of my two WESTPAC platoons," he explained. Evans had two operational platoons operating in the Western Pacific at all times. They had been chopped to the operational control of a task force on Okinawa and had been training with other special operations forces that had gathered in the area.

"Yes, I know. Derek, we are going to establish an FOB in South Korea and Warrior Spirit is the cover."

"Are the ROKs a part of the task force?" he asked with a touch of surprise.

"No. The operation is U.S. only in Asia."

"Makes sense to me," he said, nodding.

"How good are your contacts in Korea?" asked Harris.

"Let's say I have a lot of friends there, a lot of friends. Some in very high places."

"Good. In recent months South Korean special forces have been conducting some unusual exercises. We'd like to know the nature and reason for those exercises."

"And you want me to find out?" he asked, astounded.

"If you can."

"Alysin, I'm not a spy."

"We are not asking you to spy. Just pay attention to what's going on. Ask a few pointed questions."

"No. I'm not going to use my friendships in that way. Has anyone thought about asking the ROKs what they're doing?" he asked suspiciously. "They will level with the U.S. ambassador."

"They haven't so far. Don't you think you are being unreasonable, considering the nature of the problem we're facing?" she retorted, incredulous.

"What is the problem, Alysin? The Company doesn't have the human resources to figure out what the South Koreans are doing, *in their own country?* Too many computers, not enough field agents?" he asked sarcastically.

"You don't think much of the Agency, do you?"

"No, I don't," he confessed. "And I'm not going to spy on people who trust me."

She knew he was going to be pigheaded about the issue. "So that's your final answer?"

"Yes," he declared. After an awkward pause, he continued. "However, I know some expates who live in Korea who will be more than happy to help you for the right price."

"I'm leaving in the morning. Are you free tonight to discuss the issue?" she asked with a look in her eye that said she needed company all night.

"Wow!" He let out a deep breath. "Alysin, I'm sorry. I'm leaving for the desert this afternoon."

"Well, I'll see you in Korea," she responded with a hurt expression.

"Alysin, if you had just called me, even yesterday, I would've planned an evening for the two of us. It's too late to change my schedule now. Rain check?" he asked with a look of concern.

"Sure."

"I know some great places in Seoul," he continued. "If you have the time."

"I'll hold you to it," she said, standing to leave. "And the contacts."

"You got it," he said, and smiled, hoping she wasn't angry. He kissed her good-bye, but it lacked passion. At the door he said, "I'm really sorry, Alysin. I'd love to spend the evening with you."

She smiled and kissed him lightly. "Korea?"

"You bet," he said, opening the door for her.

Evans was motionless, in deep thought, when Saleen knocked and entered.

"Captain. The XO is ready for the morning briefing. I'll have the watch take in your coffee."

"Thanks, Shooter," Evans said with a look of concern. "Shooter, do me a favor?"

"Sure, Skipper!"

"Get down with Horsecock and feed him a load of beer. Find out everything you can about his Mexican girlfriend."

"Captain! You're not interested in the man's woman, are you?" asked Saleen with shock.

"No! Of course not, goddamnit," he said, chuckling. "At least not like you're thinking. Pervert!"

"Right, Skipper, right. I saw you looking at her ass."

"Shooter, she doesn't seem like his type. And her face." He paused, searching for the right words. "I know I've seen her before. I can't put my finger on it. Sort of like a face in a crowd. And her car . . . yeah. That's it. Her car. I know I've seen it in Coronado, parked near my apartment. Find out if she has been asking questions about me, or my comings and goings. But do it quietly."

"I'll look into it, Captain," said Saleen. "Before we go to the meeting, you'd better wipe the lipstick off your face."

Evans smiled and shook his head. "Thanks."

As they walked to the conference room, Saleen cautioned Evans. "You'd better watch that Harris woman closely, Skipper. Something about her bugs me. You know, she's asked me a shit-pot load of questions about our trip to Indonesia."

"Oh?" responded Evans.

"Yes, sir. And a lot of questions about you. Things that go beyond a personal interest in you or a study of leadership."

"What do you think she's studying, Shooter?"

"You, boss. You, and not for prurient reasons."

"As usual," said Evans, looking Saleen in the eye, "your instincts are right on target."

The SEALs are the only unit in the military to begin their day with a two-hour workout. Evans was the only person in the whole command wearing a uniform when he walked into the conference. Sweat glistened off the Junkyard Dawg's forehead as he held the door and yelled, "Attention on deck!" Everyone jumped to their feet before Evans could say, "Carry on!"

It was the way of the navy. Whenever the CO entered a space, the men jumped to attention until he said otherwise, even in the SEALs. Without Saleen and his trusted enlisted advisors, Evans would have been isolated by protocol. He took a seat at the head of the conference table as the watch handed him a steaming cup of black coffee.

"Thanks, Petty Officer Carroll," he said, taking the cup.

"Captain, do you want me to park your car?" asked Johnny Carroll with a devious smile. Evans cut him a grim look.

"Nah. I'll take care of it, Hot Rod," he said with a grin.

The principal leaders of the command sat around the conference table prepared to brief him on their area of responsibility. A sharp lieutenant commander named Steve Miller took charge. Miller was Evans's first pick as XO. He was a superb officer in whom he had absolute trust to run the command in his absence. As XO, Miller made 90 percent of the decisions, deferring only policy to Evans, who spent his time on the road with the operational platoons. When Evans had been a young phase officer at BUDS, he had put Miller through basic SEAL training.

"Good morning, Captain," said Miller. Evans nodded his head, having just taken a sip of coffee. "There's quite a bit of business on the agenda this morning, sir. First, I'll quickly brief the locations and missions of all our overseas platoons. Then Lieutenant Oakley will give you an intelligence briefing on items of interest in our AO." AO was short talk for *area of operations.* "Following that, each of the department heads will update you on the budget. Finally, Warrant Officer Patton will run down the training schedule for Lieutenant Owen's platoon."

"Steve, I've already reviewed Alpha's schedule. Why are we doing it again?" asked Evans.

"Two reasons, sir. First, Alpha is the only platoon available to deploy with you on exercises Warrior Spirit in Korea and Cobra Fang in Thailand."

"Captain," interjected Saleen, "the XO and I wrestled with this decision for several days. There are just no other options. Your first bitch is going to be that they are just a bunch of new guys right out of BUDS. True. But we don't have any other platoons that aren't already committed."

"Skipper, our schedule is airtight. Our two WESTPAC platoons have been gobbled up by some special task force operating out of Okinawa. Alpha is the only platoon that fits the window for Warrior Spirit and Cobra Fang."

"Captain," argued Saleen, "with Senior Chief Masure assigned as platoon chief, Williams as LPO, and Taufaudy and Gibson as old hands, I believe they'll do OK." He was trying to help Miller sell the idea to Evans.

"I concur, Skipper," said Miller.

"At first the assignment pissed off the old hands, the homebodies who like to do their shopping in Korea. You know the deal, envious of a bunch of new guys deploying to Korea and Thailand just after reporting from BUDS. To stop the bitching, we fleshed out your task groups with old guys entirely from SEAL Team Five. You're going to catch some flack from the other COs," warned Saleen with a grin. It was customary to fill out the task groups with old hands from all the SEAL teams, as well as the staffs, on the West Coast. Miller and Saleen had filled the positions with men from Team Five.

"Good decision, XO," growled Evans. "You said there were two reasons?" he asked.

Everyone stared at the skipper in amazement. They expected him to react negatively to the decision because of all the politics involved with deploying overseas task groups to desirable locations.

"Yes, sir," gulped Miller, surprised by Evans's response. "This afternoon, you and Master Chief Saleen have a meeting with the commodore to discuss predeployment training for the next two cycles. I thought a thorough discussion of our problems, assets, and resources would prepare you for the meeting."

"Excellent. Let's do it."

After the briefing, Saleen walked back to Evans's office and closed the door behind them. With a serious look he said, "Skipper, the meeting this afternoon is about mine clearance training," he said gravely. "Master Chief Humbert gave me a heads up yesterday."

From the tone in his voice Evans concluded something was brewing.

"So what's the problem, Shooter? We've been through this bullshit before."

"This time they want EOD to conduct an MRCI on our platoons to certify readiness to deploy."

An MRCI was a mine readiness countermeasures inspection and EOD was the acronym for *explosives ordnance disposal,* a separate unit of experts specially trained to render safe explosive devices. Evans knew the mine warfare issue all too well, having faced it as the XO of SEAL Team Five. It had come full circle.

The major power brokers in the navy are admirals who specialize in surface warfare, submarine warfare, and aviation. In the scheme of things, the fast movers, silent runners, and surface combats got most of the money. Small organizations like mine warfare and special warfare were continually underfunded. Mine warfare in particular was an intractable problem the navy had swept under the carpet since Farragut had damned the torpedoes in Mobile Bay. The problem stemmed from the navy's neglect of mine warfare.

Military doctrine called for seizing a beachhead in enemy territory with the marines so the army could be transshipped ashore. To counter this strategy, Hitler had simply fortified the beaches of Europe with obstacles and mined the offshore waters, giving genesis to the NCDUs, the UDTs, and minesweepers. Amphibious warfare strategy had remained essentially unchanged since World War II.

While the strategy remained constant, mines had increased in sophistication. Hybrid mines crossed with torpedo technology could lie on the bottom disguised as sea mounds waiting for just the right propeller signatures to come along before waking up and seeking out their targets like torpedoes. There were contact mines, magnetic-influence mines, pressure-sensitive mines, and acoustic mines with devious counters and time delays that defeated conventional minesweeping. Mines could be disguised as the sea floor and lie dormant for weeks or even months. There were bottom mines, moored mines, floating mines, antiship mines, and antipersonnel mines. To beat metal detectors and magnetometers, some mines were engineered with nonferrous cases. Neutralizing an underwater minefield was insurmountable with current technology, and the SEALs and the EOD knew it. All of them.

Evans and Saleen arrived punctually and took their assigned seats at the commodore's conference table. Commodore Cameron was a sarcastic man with a caustic personality. In his younger years he had been an outstanding SEAL who possessed the SEAL spirit. Now in his early fifties, he was more of a politician searching for middle ground, trying not to make waves that would be deleterious to his chances for promotion. Cameron had forgotten what it was like to be a operator crawling along the bottom in a Draeger closed-circuit oxygen scuba rig.

When Cameron strolled into the conference room, Master Chief Humbert called the room to attention. All rose until he told them to take seats, like an instructor talking to a group of trainees at BUDS. He slumped down at the head of the table and with a peevish look began shuffling through the papers in his folder, like a man trying to avoid a minefield. Finally he spoke. "I received a message from PAC Fleet last week outlining the desired skills required for deployed SEAL platoons. In your folder is a list of those requirements," he said as a yeoman passed out a red folder containing a secret message.

"Please note that shallow-water mine clearance is at the top of the list of priorities. I want each of you to restructure your platoon training programs to reflect this new requirement."

All the COs and master chiefs knew that PAC Fleet was a huge bureaucracy that wrestled with enormous problems. Young staff officers looked into hundreds of issues for overburdened navy captains who struggled to please admirals and politicians. They staffed-out reports ranging from fuel and ammunition to war plans, most of which they didn't fully understand. The PAC Fleet staff relied on the fleet for expertise for complicated problems such as mine warfare, and it was not uncommon for experts in the operational commands to challenge an issue in a politically correct fashion. In fact it was expected.

"Commodore, shallow-water mine clearance is impossible with SEALs," piped up Evans.

"You tell that to PAC Fleet," snapped Cameron, coming unglued. Cameron knew mine clearance was impossible with SEALs. He just didn't want to hear it. He didn't like Derek Evans and he let it be known at every meeting.

"Sir, Desert Stroll proved unequivocally that mine clearance is a waste of time. We couldn't land in Kuwait because of the mines. We have to prepare for the next war, sir, *not the last one!*" said Evans louder than he should have.

"And what, pray tell, does your crystal ball tell you we should be preparing for, Commander Evans?" Cameron asked sarcastically.

Evans took a deep breath before he answered. "Commodore, we have a moral obligation to provide our men with life insurance. For a SEAL, that comes in the form of synergistic training focused on real-world missions like shipboarding and hostage rescue operations. We must be able to *move, shoot, and communicate* in a close-quarters environment."

"Are you through? What I want you to do is to relook your priorities and put shallow-water mine countermeasures at the top of the list. I'm not going to tell you how to do that, Commander. That's why you're the commanding officer. I'm just going to tell you the goddamn priorities. Is that clear?"

"Commodore, terrorism and nuclear proliferation are the real problems of our time, not landing on the beaches of Normandy or Kuwait. CQB and shipboarding will train our men for challenges we face. Why don't we send a message to PAC Fleet outlining the problem involved with training for mine clearance," responded Evans inquisitively.

"We! We! Have you got a mouse in your pocket? You mean *me!* And just what would those problems be, Commander Evans?"

Evans was now as exercised as Cameron. "First, *sir,* shallow-water mines scour up and disappear in the sand. We have no way to find them. Second, if we did have a way of locating them, *we don't have a way of neutralizing them under water.* It would take *tens* of thousands of pounds of explosives to clear a small area of beachfront and we don't have that kind of manpower. For Christ's sake, Commodore, there are mines out there that can wipe out an entire SEAL team in the reconnaissance phase of a mission, not to mention the fact that if we train for mine clearance there will be no time left for *crucial mission training!"*

"Get down off your soapbox, Evans, and read my lips. Put shallow-water mine countermeasures at the top of your list of priorities," cut Cameron sarcastically. "You got that?"

"But, Commodore, it will take eight months of our nine-month training schedule to prepare a platoon for the basics of mine warfare. We need that time for CQB and shipboarding," pleaded Evans.

"Again, Commander, I'm not going to tell you how to do your goddamn job! I'm just telling you the goddamn priorities! Now, I've heard enough whining. This meeting is over!"

Cameron pushed himself back from the table and stormed out before Humbert could call attention on deck. They all sat shell-shocked for a moment before the CO of SEAL Team One broke the silence.

"How does it feel to slit your own throat, Evans?" asked Commander Stubbert, smirking.

Evans started to respond with a hostile remark, but thought better of it. "Simply marvelous, partner. Simply marvelous. At least I'll be able to look myself in the mirror tomorrow morning. Let's go, Shooter. We have to restructure our platoon training program."

As Evans and Saleen walked back to SEAL Team Five on the ocean side of Highway 75, Saleen pressed the question. "What are we going to do, boss?"

"Put mine warfare at the top of our list, Shooter," he snapped. "That was the order."

"I was hopin' you wouldn't say that, Skipper. The men deserve better than to crawl around the bottom feeling for mines that are buried up in muck," he said with a disappointed expression.

"Well, Shooter, the way I see it is, we start with mine warfare at the top of our list. We'll have a one-week class on mine recognition, a three-week combat diver course that culminates in boarding a cargo vessel loaded with mines, and then we'll press on to move, shoot, and communicate in a hot urban environment."

With a big, toothy grin, Saleen burst out, "That bastard is gonna have your balls, boss. You know he don't like you."

"Yep, I know, Shooter. I just don't know why."

"I'll tell you why, Captain. 'Cuz people say 'sir' to you, even when they don't say *sir*. And they don't say 'sir' to him, even when they do say *sir*."

"I think I get your gist, Shooter," chuckled Evans. "Pack your bags. Let's go to Niland."

"Hell, I'm always packed, Skipper," responded Saleen with another huge grin.

"Then check out two sets of NVGs and some BINOs, and leak information we're headed up to Camp Pendleton to observe Bravo Platoon at CQB."

Saleen chuckled. "While Bravo Platoon puts on the dog, we're gonna sneak up on Alpha with their pants down, huh?"

Evans just smiled deviously.

CHAPTER

19

Niland is one of those backcountry California towns a truck driver could miss if he blinked his eyes twice. More than a hundred feet below sea level, it sits in a vast desert bowl on the edge of the Salton Sea. The temperature in the summer can rival that of the Sahara for misery. The SEALs had chosen the area for training because no one wanted to live there. Only lizards and coyotes were comfortable in the heat. The lizards made good target practice for pistols and the coyotes were excellent sport for an M-16. Over the years they had learned to avoid the SEALs' camp.

The camp at Niland wasn't really at Niland at all. It was ten miles from town set back in a vast, open tract of empty land that backed up against the Chocolate Mountain Range, a sunburned pile of rocks that jutted up from the desert floor like pinnacles of broken lava. The camp had settled like water to the lowest level. The buildings were warped and ramshackled. The johns smelled of urine and gun oil. Naked pictures of fat women adorned the walls along with sleek models from Fifth Avenue. Niland was a place of men, unshaven, rugged, and armed to the teeth. It was a place where SEALs concentrated on the small unit tactics of move, shoot, and communicate with live ammunition.

Evans didn't want to interfere but he wanted to know the

platoon's progress. The advanced training that went on night after night served to focus the men together like drawing light through a magnifying glass. When he visited Niland on a schedule, the men cleaned the camp for days in advance, which made little difference in the dusty desert. They shaved, cleaned their gear, and in general paid more attention to impressing their CO than learning to fight. Saleen leaked word they were going up the coast to Camp Pendleton, but as soon as they came down off the Coronado Bridge they headed east down Interstate 8 for the desert.

Three hours later the tires of the Blazer were humming along the hot desert roads of Imperial County. Heat shimmering off the road created mirages in the depressions. They pulled into the dusty desert town of Niland just after sundown and stopped for a drink at the Lonestar Saloon. Saleen looked at the temperature gauge over the door as he entered the building. It was 103 degrees and the sun was below the horizon.

They took a seat at the bar and Evans quizzed the old man behind the counter about the SEALs training at the camp.

"Hell, I don't see those rascals much anymore. I hear 'em shootin' and blowin' stuff up now and again, but they don't drink like they used to," said the old man. His skin appeared to have melted in the hot sun. "Come to think of it, I don't see much of you anymore, Commander. Where you been? Fightin' commies?"

"Oh, I been around, Lizard. We just don't drink as much as we use to," responded Evans.

"Yep, them damn MADD women, been bad for business."

The old guy told them that Warrant Officer Patton had bought a couple of cases of beer and four bags of ice before sundown and made off down the dusty road like a rooster with a coyote on his tail. Evans figured the beer was for breakfast. The SEALs operated at night and slept in the day for two reasons. First, SEALs operate at night, and second, it was cooler. Even at night it was not unusual for the temperature to hang in the nineties.

The SEALs' hours were reversed. Beer for breakfast at about 0400, and eggs or burritos at dusk just before they went out on field exercise. Evans went over the platoon's training schedule and plotted their movements. Alpha Platoon was scheduled for a parachute infiltration by C-130 that would launch from El Centro thirty miles to the south. After insertion they would hump across the desert floor and conduct a live-fire ambush on a mock target.

He could tell from the schedule that the live-fire mission would go down at 0330 because of the number of training cell personnel assigned to support the platoon at that hour. The training cell built the targets, acted as an aggressor force, and controlled safety during live-fire operations. Tonight was the convoy strike operation. A smart SEAL named Barron had perfected a sled pulled behind a jeep with a long slender cable. Using pulleys, plywood, battery-powered lights, and sound effects from an old boom box, the training cell could simulate just about anything from a tank to a station wagon. They graded the operation by counting the holes in the target and by firepower, surprise, and timing. From experience Evans and Saleen knew where to go to stay out of sight and out of the kill zone.

They drove to the DZ and watched as the men exited the C-130 at twelve thousand feet. At first the platoon was scattered all over the sky, but within a few minutes they were flying in a wedge formation toward the DZ. Against the dark sky the parachutes would have been invisible without NVGs. The actual landing spot didn't make much of a difference because there was little difference between the DZ and the surrounding desert for twenty-five miles in every direction. The large, square MT1-XX parachutes allowed the men to glide with their heavy loads of weapons, ammunition, radios, food, and water.

Just before landing they released their equipment, dropping it down below them twenty feet on a tether line. The heavy bags hit the ground first, reducing the impact of landing on legs and ankles. They landed in a tight formation on the northern edge of the DZ not more than twenty meters from Evans's op. Even through the distorted light of his NVGs, Evans could pick out Masure, Williams, and Taufaudy by their professional landings. The platoon quickly formed a defensive perimeter and gathered up their parachute equipment. Within minutes they marched off toward the Chocolate Mountain Range ten miles to the north. Evans waited for the DZ crew to police up the parachutes and leave the area before returning to the Blazer they had hidden in a draw.

"Not bad, Shooter. Not bad at all."

"You know something, Skipper? Lieutenant Owen reminds me of you, when you were just a whippersnapper," commented Saleen.

"Doom on him," chuckled Evans.

They drove without headlights, using their NVGs to Pipeline Road, and stopped in a location where they thought the platoon would cross the road. They watched from a distance as they scurried across the road, one at a time in a good defensive posture.

"They move pretty good for a bunch of new guys, Captain," said Saleen.

"Yeah. Let's see how well they cover their tracks," ordered Evans.

Saleen drove down the road to the location where the platoon had crossed and stopped so they could study the sandy road.

"Good job covering their tracks," he said, flipping up the goggles on his NVGs. "Spot any?" he asked Saleen.

"No. Nothing, Skipper."

"Let's go back to Niland and have a cup of coffee while we wait for them to patrol to the ambush site," suggested Evans.

"You buying?" asked Saleen.

"You bet."

"You're on," said Saleen, shoving the truck in gear.

They drove back to town for coffee and waited until two-thirty in morning before returning to Pipeline Road. Waiting in a gorge for the training cell to come along, they fell in behind them with their truck and split off at the last moment to take up a position at a frequently used observation point that controlled the high ground. A few minutes after they had settled into position, the platoon moved into the ambush site like lions on the hunt. Their movements were slow and deliberate, cautious like big cats closing in on prey. Once in position, Warrant Officer Patton walked up behind them and yelled three words that shattered the desert night.

"Lock and load!" he yelled and disappeared back behind the line.

For a few seconds the desert quiet was racked by the sound of magazines clicking and bolts cycling rounds home as the men exchanged blank ammunition for live rounds. Then silence reigned. Dead silence. For thirty minutes the hot wind moved across the desert floor as deer mice played and rattlers hunted to the sound of coyotes calling their mates. Evans was pleased that there was no sound or movement from the platoon. They were invisible. Sound and movement attracted attention and got people killed. One of the first lessons was not to move, even if you think a bad guy sees you. Don't move. If you move, move to kill.

The sound of trucks grinding up the canyon came and went as the chief, with his hand on the volume control of the boom box, turned the knob up and down. In the distance the speakers gave the impression of approaching army trucks. Behind Evans and up the draw came the sound of a jeep starting up, clueing him to the timing of the ambush. As the jeep pulled off, the sleds with the mock truck silhouettes crawled slowly up the canyon and into the kill zone. When the target was dead in the kill zone, Lieutenant Owen opened up with an M-14. His men followed suit immediately, some on automatic and some on semiautomatic to avoid a lull during magazine changes. Robinson worked out with the M-60, blasting away in bursts with the linked ammunition. Simons threw an illumination grenade that lit up the front side of the target. The firepower was awesome and sustained. The M-16s and M-60s blazed into the target with amazing accuracy for new guys. From time to time, a 40mm grenade would burst against the side of the plywood targets. Then Ryeback stuck an AT-4 rocket directly into the side of one of the trucks, completely obliterating the silhouette. At just the right moment, the moment Evans knew by feel, the firing died off.

Owen's voice pierced the night. "Set perimeter. Search parties in!"

They searched the targets for intelligence and departed the kill zone in less than two minutes, only to return several minutes later for a debrief by training cell. Step by step, the most experienced men in SEAL Team Five verbally walked them through the operation from warning order to the ambush. They even counted the number of rounds used and the number of holes in the targets. When the formal debriefing ended, Masure gathered the men around to pass on the wisdom of the teams. They built a campfire and below the light of crystal-clear desert sky discussed the mission in more detail. He waited for the training cell to leave before he brought up the biggest mistakes Evans had observed. After a couple of beers and a few good points from the others he asked, "Simons, you know what you did wrong with that illum?" he asked in joking manner, referring to the illumination grenade Simons had thrown during the ambush.

"No, Senior. I don't," he responded.

"Listen guys. Illum is real tricky. You have to stick it up the other guy's ass or you blind yourself. Don't let it get between you and your target. Always throw it behind your enemy and backlight him or use parachute flares to light the whole area from above."

"Ahhh, I got it, Senior," said Simons.

After they had downed several beers, Williams turned to Jackson and threw him an ice-cold one.

"No thanks, Wild Bill. I'm duty driver," he said as he tossed the beer back.

"Jackson, we're in the middle of the fuckin' desert and it's ninety fuckin' degrees!" blasted Williams.

"You know I don't drink no more, man," grumbled Jackson.

"You're not still gun-shy around .45s, are you?" groused Williams with a chuckle.

"You're damn straight I am, and for good reason," retorted Jackson.

"Jackson, the old man's up at Camp Pendleton. I got a lock on his posit from the team. Lighten up, man. He'll never know, and beside he'd drink it himself in a heartbeat."

"Nah," insisted Jackson.

"One ain't gonna hurt you, dude," argued Williams.

"I'm sticking to water, man," said Jackson.

As Evans watched the interchange from the shadows he had to restrain himself from walking into the camp and guzzling down the ice-cold beer. The water in his canteen was hot and it failed to quench his thirst.

"Hell, just thinking of the Skipper with a .45 in his hand makes me wanna piss my pants."

As the others laughed at Jackson's expression, Owen spoke to Masure.

"Senior, let's go for a walk. There's some things I want to discuss."

"Let's go, boss," he said, tossing the lieutenant a beer.

They left the group and walked off down the trail, passing within ten feet of Evans and Saleen. After they were out of sight, Williams began to work on the boys.

"Hey, you guys ever seen the dance of the flaming assholes?"

"No! What the hell is that?" chuckled Simons.

Evans almost laughed out loud. He looked over at Saleen and all he could see was the whites of his teeth in the shape of a big smile. Williams told the men stories about his exploits in the Philippines and he explained that they weren't really frogmen until they had done the dance of the flaming assholes on top of a bar in the PI. A cold one later, he had them talked into practicing the infamous dance. When Owen and Masure walked back up the road, Simons and Bailey were dancing around the fire without their cammie trousers.

Masure said, "Hold on, L.T. You'll want to watch this from a distance. This is not for officers."

They moved closer to the campfire, taking to the bushes, and almost tripped over Saleen. When they squatted down, Evans had to lean over to see around them to observe the commotion around the campfire. Williams had talked the two youngsters into dancing through the fire with a string of toilet paper held between their butt cheeks. Owen watched in astonishment as Simons danced through the fire. The toilet tissue dangling behind him caught ablaze and began to burn like a fuse toward his butt. Bailey followed suit and was soon being chased by a flame as they ran around the camp. When the flame began to singe the hair off Simons's rear end, he started yelling obscenities and flailing at the paper to remove it from his cheeks. By then, Williams and the others were laughing so hard they were rolling around in the sand like scorpions in a skirmish. In the roar of laughter Bailey took the opportunity to release his bomb before the flame reached his butt. Evans just shook his head in the dark and stifled a laugh. He thought about his youth as he watched the men roll around the ground, laughing uncontrollably. Masure put a stop to the frivolity.

"Ambush, right!" he yelled out of the darkness.

Out of instinct they responded to the command, trying to retrieve their weapons. Owen and Masure stepped out into the firelight, wearing grim faces.

"Simons, Bailey," snapped Masure. "I think I saw the skipper out there with a pair of NVGs. If he sees you dancing butt naked around this campfire, he'll kick your sorry asses out of the teams for being queer."

"Oh, shit!" said Simons, grabbing his trousers.

Williams was still laughing when Masure snapped at him. "Williams, saddle up, goddamnit!"

"Jackson, go get the truck," ordered Williams, choking back laughter.

"Aye-aye, LPO," said Jackson, running off to get the six-by-six truck the training cell had left for them.

They appeared to sober up as quickly as they got drunk. Ten minutes later Evans and Saleen were alone with the sound of coyotes and the six-by-six was groaning up the road in the distance on its way back to the SEAL camp.

"What do you think, Shooter?" he asked as they walked back to the Blazer hidden in the draw.

"I think they got the makings of an outstanding platoon. They shoot good, they stick together, they listen, and they definitely got a sense of humor. How 'bout you assign me in Masure's place."

Evans chuckled. "Not on your life, Master Chief. You're too damn old for so much fun. Besides, if I did I'd have to take Owen's job."

"Not a bad idea, Skipper," said Saleen. "It'd be a damn sight more fun than dealing with Commodore Cameron."

Dawn was breaking when they slipped past the SEAL camp and headed back to San Diego. Evans was satisfied Alpha Platoon was ready to deploy overseas to an exercise, but he knew they weren't ready for a real-world mission. That was the job of his deployed WESTPAC platoons in Okinawa. Even with experienced men like Masure and Williams in the group, Alpha needed another six months of training before they would be ready to tackle a real mission.

Natila Saraskina took the elevator to the lobby of the Hilton Hotel in Seoul, Korea, and selected a seat where she could watch the tourists come and go. It was a strategic location where she could observe the little Korean girl playing the piano while watching all exits. She ordered a cup of sweet tea and listened to the pianist murder Mussorgsky while waiting for Khasanov to rendezvous for a personal meeting. Before her tea arrived Khasanov quietly slipped into the seat behind her, trying not to draw attention to himself. He liked to sneak up on people, especially Saraskina, and observe them before making contact. Saraskina saw his reflection in the polished surface of the piano and commented, "You are losing your touch, Viktor."

He saw her image and gave her a mock salute with two fingers. "We can't all be as observant as you, Natila," he said, getting up to take the seat next to her. "I like your new look," he commented. "I wouldn't have spotted you if not for your luscious lips and abundant breasts."

She ignored the come-on. Khasanov ordered an OB beer from the little Korean waitress who was circulating around the huge hotel lobby, and slumped back in the plush chair. "So, did your Mexican whore come through?" he asked under his breath, scanning the exit behind her.

"Yes," she said, handing him a travel magazine she had picked up in the hotel rack.

He opened it to find several pictures of Evans and his men inserted within the pages.

"He will be in Chinhae in a few days. It is a small town east of Pusan."

"I know where it is," he said indignantly. "He hasn't

changed much, has he?" The waitress served his beer and he took a big gulp before speaking. "I see he still travels with his shadow," commented Khasanov, studying one of the pictures she had given him. "Will he be with Evans in Chinhae?"

"Yes."

"Good. We will kill him when we kidnap Evans," said Khasanov with a smile.

"Viktor, do not underestimate these men. This will not be easy job. Evans is never alone, and need I remind you he almost killed Karpenko without what you call his shadow."

"You are fantasizing about Java again, Natila Saraskina. Was Evans really that good?"

"Khasanov, I have a job to do. You have a job to do. So let's do it," suggested Saraskina with a bored expression.

"I was only suggesting that we do it together," he said, smiling lasciviously.

"Viktor, you are making light of a very important operation. The big black man is much more than a shadow. He is one of the most highly trained killers in the American military. It will not be easy to eliminate him. And if you are successful, you still have to get Evans alive. If you accidentally kill him during your operation," she said, shaking her finger at him, "Karpenko will skin you alive for denying him the pleasure."

"Not to worry, Natila Saraskina. I have the best men in Korea contracted for this job," said Khasanov confidently.

"What is your plan, Viktor?" she asked inquisitively.

"Ahhh, Natila. You have no need to know such details," said Khasanov with a smirk. "Don't worry. I'll get him."

"Viktor, I don't worry," she said, shaking her head. "My neck is not on the chopping block." She smiled confidently. "Yours is. His schedule is written on the back side of his photograph," she said, standing to leave.

"Natila, let's have dinner and enjoy the city tonight. What do you say, huh?" he pleaded with a look of lust in his eyes. He had secretly desired her for years but had not dared press his luck with Karpenko.

"No. Absolutely not. Besides, I am leaving for Hong Kong in a few hours," she lied. She was going to Chinhae on a little errand and then to Pusan, where she was going to catch a plane to Bangkok, Thailand.

"Very well, Natila. Seoul is full of eager young women who would be able to keep up with a man with my appetite," he crowed with sarcasm.

"Enjoy yourself, Khasanov. If you screw this up, you won't have a dick to play with," she said.

CHAPTER

20

The C-141 Starlifter roared to a stop at Kimhae International Airport in South Korea on the military side of the terminal. Evans stood up and stretched as the ramp at the back of the aircraft began to drop. He looked at Saleen and shouted over the sound of the aircraft groaning.

"Twenty-five hours in the back of a One Forty-One is inhumane. I wouldn't treat a damn animal like this," he shouted as he headed for the exit.

Saleen grimaced with a sour expression and stretched like a big dog. As he climbed down the short steps to the tarmac, he bumped his head on the hatch and threatened an air crewman with death. On seeing the ancient navy bus waiting to take them to Chinhae two hours down the road, he yelled, "Goddamn, Captain, I'm getting too old for this shit. Next trip to Korea, I'm stayin' in Coronado."

"Not on your life, Shooter. Misery loves company," replied Evans, and they walked toward the old bus.

At Chinhae, a small town west of Pusan, Saleen set up camp in an old Quonset hut of World War II vintage and bunked the men in barracks provided by the small U.S. station that serviced the Pacific Fleet when it visited South Korea. Evans and all the khaki in his task group stayed in town in hotels that weren't fit for the rats that inhabited them. Two days after their arrival, Saleen dispatched two convoys that moved off in different directions up each coast of Korean peninsula. The main task group with Evans and twenty officers stayed in Chinhae and joined the ROK SEALs to form a headquarters to fight the mock war. The task group served as command and control headquarters for the operations taking place around Inchön on the west coast and Kisamon on the east coast. Exercise Warrior Spirit was the largest annual special operations exercise in the world, and every year the North Koreans protested by putting their forces on high alert. They controlled the territory north of the 38th Parallel, an area to be avoided like hemorrhagic fever.

After deployment of the convoys, Evans and his counterpart, Captain Chun, had dinner together with their principal officers. From experience he knew how such occasions were conducted. Sitting around a communal table with crossed legs, they shared numerous drinks of *soju,* a clear liquor that tasted like rubbing alcohol. The Koreans would slam down large shot glasses of the liquid and pass the empty glass to an American. Then they would take a bottle of *soju* and with both hands politely fill the glass until it flowed over, expecting the American to slam down the drink and pass the glass back to a Korean. *Soju* combined with leafy green vegetables, pure garlic bulbs, and onions was a powerful concoction that guaranteed inebriation in minutes and dragon breath for days. The Korean SEALs were tough men who drank, smoked, and fought like tigers. *Soju* was their truth serum and part of the glue that bonded the warriors together. Dinner with the Koreans was primitive, like sitting around a campfire in ancient times and sharing food with a rival band of warriors before joining forces to fight a common enemy. *Soju* was the catalyst of the shaky alliance, the firewater of the Korean warrior cult.

Evans hated the occasions but endured them for God and Country. He sat cross-legged in the middle of the low table across from Captain Chun. Chun always gave his officers orders to work Evans over with the firewater. Each of them would pass Evans their *soju* glass and expected it returned. Knowing the culture, Evans would eat heavy foods before the dinner party and drink half a bottle of vitamin E oil and a large volume of milk. With the Korean meal he would chase the *soju* with a large volume of beer, and after the first eight rounds he would excuse himself to the latrine. There he would throw the mess up before it had time to enter his bloodstream, and drink the other half of the vitamin E oil before returning to the party. For years he had been putting six to one to bed with his simple algorithm. It had earned him legendary status among the Korean SEALs.

The night of the first *soju* party Evans returned to his room to find it smelling of perfume. A beautiful Korean girl who was young enough to be his daughter greeted him at his open door. She bowed deeply and offered to take off his shoes. The effect of the alcohol was strong and he readily complied with all her instructions. Chun was a generous man who always saw to his manly comforts. At daylight the young girl got up and dressed quietly. As she left she handed him a small envelope. Alone in his bed Evans read a message that made his blood run cold. Neatly written on the expensive paper was one word, *ambush,* incorrectly spelled *ANBUSH.* It had a slightly Cyrillic character to it, the same as the warning he had received from the dirty little street girl in Surabaya, Indonesia.

Warrior Spirit was a mock war between North and South Korea. It had been played many times and it had a set script. Evans and Chun would walk into the briefing theater together and sit in front of a huge map of Korea. ROK and U.S. officers would alternate, briefing them with artificial intelligence that over several days built up to a North Korean invasion of the South. Then a combined United Nations force would counterattack and drive the hated North Koreans back. From time to time Chun would grunt an order, and his men would scramble like cockroaches trying to please him. It was all show and gamesmanship that Evans knew well. Just before the field exercises began, Commodore Cameron paid a visit. He arrived with Master Chief Humbert by commercial jet from Seoul loaded with packages bought in the marketplace at I'tae won. Evans knew without asking that he was expected to get them back to California, intact, on his military aircraft. The next day during the daily situation briefing, Evans tried to sit in the audience with his men to give the commodore his due honor, but Chun insisted on three chairs at the briefing table in front of the map. Chun entertained Cameron with great cordiality, giving him a gift in remembrance of Korea. He bragged at length about Evans, trying to increase Evans's face with his boss. Face is a unique concept in the Orient, a mixture of honor, pride, and expectation.

"Evans number one! Number one warrior, Commodore Cameron. Thank you very much for sending me Evans."

He told Cameron that Evans had placed first in a closed-circuit Draeger dive, surprising his men because they knew he was an older warrior. He made a joke about Evans landing with his parachute next to the *soju* table during the friendship jump, and he invited Cameron to a dinner in his honor at the finest restaurant in Chinhae. Evans knew Chun paid for the gifts and the dinners out of his own pocket, so he briefed Cameron en route to the party. While they walked, he made small talk about the country and its traditions. From his words Evans was sure that Cameron knew the customs and what was in store for him at the *soju* party.

When they arrived at the restaurant, it was clear Chun had gone all out to please Cameron. ROK SEALs lined the entrance like side boys. The girls serving the party were gorgeous, somewhat unusual for Chinhae, and the table was covered with all the delicacies of Chinhae Harbor. Vegetables and sushi were arranged as flowers and birds. On one side of the table was *soju* supreme, a luxury Evans had never been afforded at his *soju* parties. Cameron was given the seat of honor across from Chun. Evans watched with amusement as Cameron tried to cross his legs under the low table like the Koreans. When he was unable to achieve the Buddha posture he tried to extend his legs in front of him. He kicked Captain Chun under the table and apologized. When the extended leg posture failed he sprawled his legs out on both sides of him with his shins cutting into the table. Fortunately he had his back to the wall for support or Chun would have had to order in a chair. Chun began in English with a speech to honor the occasion. Although he spoke good English, he rarely used it.

"I want to welcome Commodore Cameron to Korea. We hopes your visit will be good one!" Chun eyed Cameron with his moonface. He looked like a caricature of Buddha without a smile. His round belly jutted out from under his plaid coat. Chun was an experienced man but he had no sense of western dress. "This combined exercise prepare men for war with North Korea. We fight together in Korea and Vietnam. By good exercise in Korea, we can be ready for next enemy."

Chun reached for an open bottle of *soju* supreme and filled the glasses around the table himself as a gesture of friendship. When he had finished he said, "I propose toast to Commodore Cameron, warrior spirit, and success of Warrior Spirit exercise."

"We hi yo!" said the participants, downing the firewater in one gulp.

Cameron put his glass on the table, full. As was his custom Chun passed his glass to Cameron, who refused. But Chun wouldn't take no for an answer. As he tried to refill the glass Cameron protested.

"Captain Chun, because of my religion I do not drink," he said, eyeing the Korean across the table.

Chun acted as if he didn't understand and insisted on giving Cameron his glass. He knew of Cameron's likes and dislikes, as well as his religious canons. When Cameron declined he sat it on the table in front of him and filled it to the brim. Again Cameron insisted through an interpreter that he could not drink because of his religion. And again Chun insisted that he drink a toast to warrior spirit. Seeing the impasse, Evans whispered to Cameron. "Just touch it to your lips, Commodore. You don't have to drink it," he said under his breath. Cameron paid him no attention and continued to refuse. The anger on Chun's face was obvious even through the oriental mask of nonemotion. Evans reached over to take Chun's glass, prepared to drink the Commodore's *soju*. With his puffy hand Chun reached across the table and placed it over Evans's hand, preventing him from picking up the glass.

"No!" he snapped in English, and rattled off a string of Korean curses. Chun took the drink and with great ceremony poured it on the floor. He picked up the *soju* bottle and with great show, like an actor in a Kabuki play, emptied the bottle on the floor. Then he looked at Evans long and hard before reaching for a fresh bottle. After a long period of silence Chun poured himself a drink and downed it in one gulp. He passed the empty glass to Evans.

"Evans, my friend!" he said as he filled the glass to the brim.

Evans held up the glass and proposed a toast, "Chun, we warriors are all the same at heart. We hate three things. We hate wet toilet paper." He nodded and they nodded. "We hate warm beer." He raised one eyebrow and they nodded agreement. "And we hate cold pussy! To fallen comrades, *we hi yo!*" he said, downing the *soju* in one gulp. Everyone at the table except Cameron downed the firewater and passed their glass to a partner. Evans passed his glass to Chun, who accepted with a smile. With the friction behind them they traded drinks and ate for two hours without Chun acknowledging Cameron's presence. For the rest of the evening he neither looked at nor spoke to the commodore.

When the party ended, Chun invited them to a karaoke bar where they drank *mecju,* a strong Korean beer. Cameron watched as Chun took center floor and sang a sad Korean song he couldn't understand. Evans knew it as the Dead Warrior song. The Korean officers in Chun's party were drunk to the point of sickness. Every other pass they poured on the floor, trying not to let their boss or the Americans see. Soon the floor was sopping wet with beer. They tried to drag Cameron up to sing a song, but Chun snapped his fingers and blurted out a Korean phrase that roughly translated, "Fuck him!" So they dragged Evans to the floor and before he could speak the kid on the keyboards began to play "House of the Rising Sun," a song Evans had sung for them more than ten years before. This was all the proof Evans needed to confirm his suspicions that his dossier was three inches thick. He sang the song, Eric Burdon style, and returned to his seat beside Cameron.

Evans had caught a few hostile words, so he whispered to Cameron, who was sipping a Coke, "Sir, the situation is about to deteriorate. I'll have someone escort you to your hotel." To his surprise Cameron agreed.

After the commodore had departed, Chun dismissed all of his men and invited Evans to a special bar. As they walked down the back streets of Chinhae, Korean sailors snapped to attention and saluted them. Evans noted that the watch was out and about, taking care of business. Chun took him to a private bar and into a small private booth where two beautiful young Korean girls served fruit and dried squid along with the beer. Chun played with his hostess for a while, fondling her breasts and thighs. When he tired of the amusement he dismissed the girls. For a long time he sat staring at Evans, who said nothing.

"Evans, you my friend. You my friend. I teach you karate on top of hotel in Vietnam. You teach me to box. I go through BUDS training, just like you. You my friend," he said, slurring his words.

"Yes, Chun. We are old friends," said Evans, clasping his hand in friendship. Chun was proud of his U.S. SEAL trident. As an exchange student he had gone through BUDS in San Diego a couple of years after Evans and he had mastered the English language while in the United States.

"Evans, things very bad in Korea. Very bad."

"How so, Chun? Things seem the same to me."

"Evans, you come to Korea many times. You know Kim Il Sung is crazy man. We think he buy nuclear weapons from Russians," he said, studying Evans's face for reaction.

Evans, like Chun, was drunk, but the revelation struck him in the face like a bucket of ice water. He looked at the Korean, trying to read the inscrutable Asian mind. *Why would he tell me such a thing?* he thought. *How would he know?*

"Kim Il Sung making a nuclear weapon at Yongbyong," he continued.

"Do you know these things for true, Chun?" asked Evans, with the weight of the world written on his face.

"We know. Many South Korean people have relatives in North Korea. Evans, can South Korea trust United States?"

"Trust?" asked Evans incredulously.

"If North Korea has nuclear weapon, will United States help us fight dem?"

"Yes. I think so," responded Evans, not sure of himself.

"You will come and fight with me, Evans?" he asked with blurry eyes almost in tears.

"Yes," said Evans without hesitation. "I'll fight the North Koreans with you."

Chun took a deep pull on his OB beer. It spilled out of the sides of his mouth and trickled down his chin. "If the Israelis not bomb Saddam's reactor, Saddam would have used nuclear weapon on you in desert," stated Chun with focused eyes. "You lucky, Evans. You lucky man."

"Yes, Chun. We were very lucky in that war," agreed Evans, wondering what was coming next.

"Now, North Korea have nuclear weapons at Yongbyong. They buying nuclear weapons from the Russians. Maybe we bomb Yongbyong like the Israelis bomb Baghdad," said Chun with a sad face.

"Chun, you can't be serious? That would start a war no one can win," argued Evans.

"Evans, if we wait, North Koreans start war after they have more nuclear weapons. Then, what we do? Can we trust United States?"

Evans sat motionless, looking deep into Chun's eyes. Through the *soju* and *mecju* he could see the heavy Korean was speaking from the bottom of his heart as if he were a brother. He dared not answer affirmatively for fear that his own doubts about the current U.S. administration would show through his own mask.

"Chun, if the North Koreans have a nuclear weapon at Yongbyong, why would they buy them from the Russians? It doesn't make sense," he argued in a solicitous voice.

"They give to the Arabs," growled Chun, staring at him with piercing eyes. "You know why, Evans? You know why?" insisted Chun.

Evans felt hollow in the pit of his sick stomach. His heart leapt into his throat and he swallowed hard. He leaned forward, nodding his head in a positive motion. Sucking air through his teeth, which was a Korean habit for expressing something very bad, he picked up his beer and said, "After the war in the Middle East begins and United Nation's forces are engaged, North Korea will attack." Evans took a huge swallow of beer.

"Nay-nay, Evans. Nay-nay. You understand. Now. We drink to the warrior spirit. No warm beer! No wet toilet paper! No cold pussy!" said Chun with a hearty laugh. He took a big drink and called the two young girls back over to the table.

"We hi yo," said Evans before downing the last of his beer. It smelled strong and thick as it trickled down his chin and into his chest hairs. He looked at Chun and said, "I go sleep now, old friend."

Chun nodded and waved with his hand for one of the Korean girls to go with Evans. Evans picked up on the command and shook his head.

"Thank you, old friend. But I go sleep now. Alone." He turned to look at Chun as he left the private booth, but Chun was too busy molesting the teenager to notice.

Evans walked down the block and turned left along the main street of Chinhae toward his hotel. It was deserted at two o'clock in the morning as he swaggered down the sidewalk. Two blocks from his hotel two men appeared twenty-five yards in front of him. Evans sobered up with a breath of fresh air and puffed out his chest, sensing danger. As he closed the distance between himself and the men he glanced behind him. Two more men were following. They were Korean, so his first thought was that Chun had assigned them to ensure his safety. For a moment he walked on, unconcerned.

Saleen had interrogated Chief Horsecock about the Mexican girl. After further investigation Evans was convinced she was snooping for information and not after Horsecock's vast assets, which consisted of a beat-up Chevrolet and an empty bank account. His second thought was that he was walking into a kill zone. His thoughts turned more ominous when he saw the headlights of a car come barreling around a street corner and head in his direction. It screeched to a halt at the curb fifteen feet in front of him. Two hefty Koreans jumped out of the rear seat of the sedan. Bracketed and outnumbered six to one, he decided to attack. He knew if he went to the ground his chances of escape were nil.

Evans sprinted five yards toward the men in front of him, and at the last second cut to his left up five steps to the front of a small store. To get at him, the six men had to climb the steps. He looked around for a weapon but found nothing. Two of the men walked cautiously up the steps, separated as far apart as possible. Just as they reached the last step Evans attacked. He faked to the guy on his left with a left jab and a right cross but stepped to his right with a low side kick to the other man's leg. His femur snapped with a pop and the Korean rolled down the steps, screaming in agony. Using momentum from the man's leg, Evans stepped quickly to his left and planted his right foot, shooting out his left leg in a low horse kick to the other man's groin. He, too, rolled down the steps in agony. Before the Korean reached the bottom Evans was on his lower leg with a stomp kick that shattered both bones below the knee.

The closest Korean shot out a high side kick, which Evans caught in the air above his shoulder. With his left hand he raised the Korean's leg up while dropping down ten inches to tear the man's testicles loose with his right hand. He caught a foot in the back before he could complete the attack. It sent him to the ground and a forward roll. Evans rolled back onto his feet, and before he could set himself one of the men grabbed him from behind in a bear hug. In a flash Evans stomped down on the man's foot while bucking back viciously with his head into the man's face. Spinning, he stuck his fingers into the man's eye sockets and ripped back with all his power, trying to tear off his face.

Now the fight was two to one. Concerned for their lives, the other two Koreans ran for the car. Evans crashed into the car door like a football lineman, catching one of his assailant's lower legs in the door. Using his right foot like a hatchet he stomped into the trailing appendage as hard as he could, snapping the lower bones like twigs just as the car squealed off. Pumped with adrenaline, Evans spun around into a fighting stance to face ten Koreans ready for action. He was about to attack when he recognized a friendly face. Chun's cavalry had arrived.

Evans took a deep breath and glanced up the street toward his hotel. The huge black man gave him a half salute and holstered the .45 before stepping back into the shadows. Evans quickly glanced in the other direction. As his eyes scanned up and down the sidewalk, he saw Masure standing in a doorway not ten yards away. He smiled and gave Evans an amphibious salute. It had all happened in less than thirty seconds.

Evans walked to his hotel, dashed up to his room, and crashed on his bed, shaking with after-action nerves. A few minutes after he calmed down, Saleen knocked on his door. Evans reluctantly opened the door, and seeing Saleen, said, "Go away, bad dream."

"Sorry, boss. It happened so fast I couldn't get to you."

"Shooter, I need some rest, man."

"I wouldn't have bothered you, boss, but this just came in. CO's eyes only," he said, handing him an official message. It was a communiqué from the embassy in Seoul, Korea. Through blurry eyes he read the contents. Harris wanted him in Seoul.

"What the hell does she want now?" said Evans out loud.

"It says urgent. The commodore is leaving in morning. We can catch the shuttle with him to Seoul," suggested Saleen.

"Roger, tomorrow," said Evans, falling on the bed.

Before leaving the hotel, Saleen doubled the watch.

CHAPTER

21

When they arrived at the airport in Pusan, Saleen and Humbert went to buy the tickets while Cameron and Evans had coffee. Before the brew arrived, Cameron started lecturing Evans on the evils of alcohol.

"Commander Evans, I've seen alcohol ruin a lot of good SEALs. As commanding officer of one of my teams I expect you to set an example. Your little performance last night has left me no choice but to write a special fitness report documenting your substandard performance. I expect you to maintain control of these men, not lead them into every bar in Chinhae. Is that clear, Commander?"

"Crystal clear, Commodore. Excuse me, sir," growled Evans.

Evans walked over to where the two master chiefs were standing in line to buy tickets for the shuttle to Seoul.

"Shooter, book us a flight on the noon shuttle," he ordered with anger in his voice.

"I thought you were traveling with us, Commander," said Master Chief Humbert.

"Not on your life, Master Chief. I intend to finish my career without a court-martial."

"Huh?" said Humbert.

Saleen read Evans's face and voice.

"It's against the UCMJ to stomp the shit out of your boss, Humby," he said with a grimace.

"Oh. Sorry, Commander," apologized Humbert.

Two hours after Cameron and his master chief left Pusan for Seoul, Evans and Saleen took the shuttle. As instructed in Harris's communiqué, he booked a room at the Hyatt Hotel and rushed to the American Embassy in downtown Seoul. He showed his ID card and a marine guard escorted him to a room deep within the building where several people were seated in conference. By the look of the room Evans could tell the meeting had been in session for several days. He recognized the senior man as the ambassador. The crowd of twelve stared as Harris introduced him.

"Thanks for coming, Commander," said Harris, formally getting up out of her chair. "Gentlemen, this is Commander Derek Evans. He has the unique distinction of personally trading blows with General Karpenko and living to talk about it."

She motioned for him to have a seat at the table as she flashed a picture of Karpenko on the screen. He was dressed as a two-star general, seeming to stare arrogantly at the people in the conference room. The cameraman had caught him pointing at some underling with a menacing glare, obviously giving orders. His eyes were glazed like a madman's.

"Major General Dimitri Karpenko is brilliant, ruthless, and completely without morals," she began. "He is a megalomaniac who suffers from severe recurring migraine headaches, stemming from an injury sustained in combat. He is addicted to narcotics and prone to violent mood swings. As I briefed your counterparts in Europe, my job is to differentiate his personality and integrate all information into a predictive behavioral model. My study of his personality leads me to believe he is likely to use one or more of his remaining weapons as bargaining chips. He has the power to hold an entire city hostage, and I believe he will destroy himself and his hostages if placed in a checkmate position."

The men looked at each other with worried expressions, and at the ambassador, but no one spoke.

Harris continued. "Karpenko has two obsessions. His primary obsession is the acquisition of power. By power I mean money, military power, such as the control of weapons of mass destructions, and intelligence, the kind that gives him control over people. His second obsession is to personally kill Commander Evans."

"Why?" asked an army colonel.

"Because Commander Evans defeated him at his own game. He took away his mission, and was successful where he had failed. Then when Karpenko fought back, Commander Evans took away his weapon and defeated him with it. His constant pain is a daily reminder of this man," she said, pointing at Evans, "and he is *obsessed* with revenge!"

Harris looked at Evans for a reaction, as did the others in the room. Evans sat stone-faced like a statue.

"So, no one's safe being in the same city with the Commander Evans?" retorted an army colonel.

"Quite the contrary, Colonel," responded Harris. "Killing Commander Evans is an obsession. It's a very personal grudge. Dimitri Karpenko is compelled to look Evans in the eye before he kills him, and that rules out the use of a nuclear weapon."

"Tries to kill, Dr. Harris!" snarled Evans with a wild-eyed look. The viciousness of his response registered with the ambassador, who raised one eyebrow.

"So how do we get to this guy?" asked a sharp-looking colonel. "If you're correct, Dr. Harris, he'll light off a nuke and take out a couple of hundred thou, and threaten to do it again if we don't let him have his way."

"We have to lure him away from the weapons before we launch any strike or recovery operation," responded a civilian staff officer who was obviously CIA.

"And just how are we going to do that?" protested an older man in civilian clothes. "We don't know where the weapons are and we don't know where Karpenko is. For all we know he's already planted a bomb in a major metropolitan area."

"The coalition is doing everything humanly possible to answer those questions, gentlemen," interjected the general in charge of the Asian task force. He explained the latest

241

intelligence from the joint coalition and the efforts under way to ascertain the possibility of remotely detonating the nuclear devices Karpenko had stolen.

The meeting went on for several minutes of pointless discussion. Finally, the ambassador looked at Evans like a professor studying a petri dish.

"If your study is correct, Dr. Harris, Commander Evans is the key to separating Karpenko from the weapons, perhaps long enough to recover them."

"Sir, you may be correct. However, there are three crucial pieces of information we must know before launching a mission. First, we have to know Karpenko's location. Second, we have to know the location of all the weapons. And third, we have to know if he has the capability to remotely detonate one or more of the weapons," responded Harris.

The ambassador breathed out a sigh.

"We're doing everything possible to answer those question, Mr. Ambassador. The purpose of this meeting is to establish an FOB in your AO and ensure no one charges off like the Lone Ranger. That would be a big mistake," commented the general.

"If Commander Evans is such an important key, why haven't I been notified of plans for his security? For Christ's sake. I didn't even know the man was in my area of responsibility," exclaimed the ambassador, exercised by the knowledge.

"Sir, Commander Evans is the commanding officer of SEAL Team Five. Man for man, he has more firepower than any organization we could possibly assign to protect him. He is literally surrounded by the most capable men in the world. Two of his platoons are in Okinawa assigned as second-tier forces and if I'm not mistaken, General, they have been outperforming the other groups in the task force."

The general nodded.

"I believe if we look carefully outside the embassy, somewhere we'll find a large black man with a big gun and several other men you wouldn't want to tangle with in a firefight. Am I right, Commander?"

Evans nodded at Harris with renewed respect for her and the Agency.

"Commander Evans came into country by military aircraft and he'll leave by military aircraft. He came up by shuttle from Pusan. He'll go back by car or bus or train, but assuredly not the shuttle. He's a very careful man who packs his own parachute. I have vehemently argued against dragging Commander Evans into Operation Fastback. One cannot fish Dimitri Karpenko like a marlin. Luring him with Commander Evans *won't work!*" said Harris loudly.

Harris had accurately predicted Evans's moves. As he watched her control the meeting he readjusted his thoughts about her and the Agency. She was better than he had given her credit for, much better.

He decided to speak. "Mr. Ambassador, may I speak with you and Dr. Harris in private?"

"Certainly, Commander, certainly."

In the ambassador's private chambers Evans told them of South Korea's concern about North Korea and that they were planning a preemptive attack.

"They have been conducting special exercises in preparation for a preemptive strike at North Korea's nuclear capabilities," he explained. Their faces turned white when he told them about Captain Chun's assertion that North Korea intended to precipitate a war in the Middle East by providing the Arabs with a nuclear weapon and then blitzkrieg South Korea while the UN was busy with the holocaust in Israel.

After the meeting, Evans left the embassy and took a cab to the Hyatt Hotel. He made three phone calls and waited for Harris in his room. Just after dark she knocked on his door.

"Let's go," he said before she could even say hi.

He grabbed her by the arm and led her to the elevator for a quick trip to the floor below the lobby of the Hyatt.

"Where are we going," she asked.

"To meet someone. Remember?" he asked.

"Oh," she said, remembering the contacts he had promised her.

When the elevator door opened, he led her to a small bar near the huge staircase that led up to the lobby. Inside, he ordered two big bottles of OB beer and guzzled down half a glass. A large Irishman with an infectious smile sat at an adjacent table.

"Hey, mate! You look a mite familiar," he said with a broad grin.

"I've swilled down a bit of OB in I'Tae Won. Perhaps we've crossed trails there," suggested Evans.

"Can I buy you a beer, webfoot?" he chuckled.

"You can buy me the whole damn bar, if you can afford it, Tank," responded Evans.

"Well, I can't. But I can stand you to a pint of swill," suggested the affable gentleman.

Alysin Harris met Dick O'Niel, ex-Green Beret, MI, MP, and freelance rogue. He spoke fluent Korean, Chinese, Tagalog, Malay, and Vietnamese. Three beers later, she had all the contacts she would ever need in Asia.

Harris and Evans drank with O'Niel until two in the morning. Then they slipped up to Evans's room and made love for two hours. When they awoke she kissed him gently on his shoulder and stroked his back with her fingernails. That's all it took for an instant replay of the first moments of passion. When she finally climbed out of bed it was almost too late for her meeting.

Cross-training with the Koreans was difficult at best. The weather was harsh and unpredictable, and controls were tight because the country was technically still at war with the People's Democratic Republic of Korea in the north. Since the armistice in 1952, there had been numerous incursions by both governments, resulting in hundreds of deaths. The North Koreans had gone so far as to dig huge tunnels under the DMZ that were large enough to drive a jeep through. They frequently infiltrated the shores of South Korea and had even planted bombs that had killed several South Korean ministers on overseas diplomatic missions. They had been caught with the smoking gun after their agents confessed to blowing a South Korean 737 out of the sky over Thailand. South Korean security guards carried live ammunition and they were trained to fire first and ask questions later. Nerves were especially on edge because of North Korean belligerence over Exercise Warrior Spirit.

During the three-week deployment to Kisamon, Lieutenant Owen expected to conduct every type of SEAL operation from closed-circuit diving to free-fall parachuting. They were ready when the first mission came in by secure fax. It ordered them to conduct a strike mission on a transformer that supported the entire east coast electrical power grid. Master Chief Saleen headed the controller group and at each target he stationed two men with radios. Just before the platoon arrived on target the controllers would check the security guard's weapons to ensure they were unloaded and report to Saleen that it was safe to approach the target. Alpha Platoon's first few missions went exceptionally well.

Using Korean fast patrol boats they sailed along the coast to a location twenty-five miles at sea. At that distance they were over the horizon from South Korean radars that were searching for them. They launched their Z-birds and navigated west at low profile through a weak point in the radar coverage. Their success at striking the power grid caused a South Korean bird colonel to lose his job. Security was beefed up along the coast where the radar coverage had been weakest.

In the next two missions, Evans ordered them to infiltrate by helicopter. These missions also went extremely well, even though they failed to penetrate the target areas. ROK soldiers circled the targets at arm's length. Recognizing that their mission plans had been compromised to prevent further firings, Evans ordered an at-sea parachute rendezvous with a Korean submarine. Alpha Platoon and their South Korean counterparts followed the rubber boats out of the cargo bay of the C-130s and descended lightly into the cold ocean. They rigged the boats for transit and motored to the awaiting submarine. Once onboard, the sub ferried them to a launch point off the east coast, to the weakest point in the radar coverage. Leaving the submarine thirty miles at sea, the combined platoon took a satellite fix and navigated to a beach infiltration point just north of Kisamon, an area cleared by Master Chief Saleen. As they neared the coast the Korean officer in charge began to argue that they were too far south. Owen tried to explain that the satellite fix he was using was accurate to within ten meters, but the Korean officer took off toward the beach anyway. Owen's only option was to follow.

Master Chief Saleen spoke with the controller in the Zodiac when they were about a mile offshore, who spoke to the controllers on the beach, who disarmed the beach guard. But Alpha Platoon was a full click to the north. As they approached the surf zone, all hell broke loose up and down the beach in front of them. Tracers were flying and grenades were flashing directly in front of them no more than a hundred meters away. They found themselves in the middle of a firefight loaded with blank ammunition.

"Lock and load," ordered Owen. The men quickly exchanged their blanks for live rounds.

The Korean SEALs tried to explain that the beach patrol was shooting at North Korean infiltrators, but the message was garbled. Owen was discussing his perilous situation with Master Chief Saleen on his HF radio when the lead Zodiac boat struck the North Korean craft. It was a semisubmersible vessel running along underwater with the heads of the infiltrators sticking above the surface. Fortunately for Alpha Platoon their rubber boat nearly decapitated most of the North Korean infiltrators. In the dark and confusion it was impossible to see exactly what sort of obstacle they had hit.

Owen was in the second Z-bird, and just as he approached the first boat to render assistance he used his nightscope for a better look. What he saw made his heart stop. Men were in the water all over the place. Some were facedown, dead. Then a shot rang out. The first shots went wild, missing Lam on the bow of Owen's boat. Lam had no idea that a 9mm slug had just passed six inches from his brain. Owen raised his M-16 and cut loose with several double taps at the figures in the water just as Masure and his crew motored up behind him.

"What the fuck are you doing, Lieutenant?" he screamed, seeing tracers skip across the surface of the sea.

"Get back! Infiltrators in the water!" he yelled. The SEALs peeled away a safe distance and called Saleen on the radio.

"Master Chief, we hit some Koreans in some sort of submersible craft! They shot at us! How copy? Over!" reported Owen, full of adrenaline.

"Roger, good copy, Lieutenant Owen. Stand clear until I can get a PKM on site."

As the men held the three Zodiacs together, Masure whispered to Owen. "Lieutenant, for your sake I hope those were North Koreans and not some of our allies."

"Lieutenant Owen, this is Master Chief Saleen, over?" crackled the radio.

"Roger, Master!" responded Owen.

"There was an incursion just north of the beach controllers. You must have bumped into a group of them trying to exfiltrate. How copy, over?"

"Roger, Master. Good copy. We'll hold this posit until the PKM is on station."

"Watch your ass, Lieutenant. All kinds of shit are breaking loose up and down the beach," he yelled in the radio. By the sound of his voice, Owen could tell he was on the move. "I have two patrol boats on the way. Watch your ass, sir. There may be more out there too. Saleen out."

At dawn the Koreans on the PKMs fished several bodies out of the Sea of Japan. Three had been shot in the head by an M-16. As they pulled the bodies out of the water Owen felt the full gravity of war.

Evans canceled the rest of the exercise and ordered the men to return to Chinhae. For two days he watched Owen mope around before he engineered an opportunity to discuss the incident. As Owen drove through the streets of Chinhae on their way to the U.S. side of the base he initiated the conversation. "How are you doing?"

"Just fine, sir," answered Owen.

"Bullshit. I can read your face like a book."

Owen stopped the car and looked at the experienced commander. "It was all just a big game until I saw the bodies being pulled out of the water. Even then it wasn't real until the guys started to kid me about body count and the placement of rounds. It was macabre, sir, a grotesque nightmare that just won't go away."

"David, I would be very disappointed in you if you took this lightly. Killing a man, any man, is a horrible thing. But you made the right decision, son."

"Yes, sir. I know, but I still feel rotten inside," responded Owen.

"I know the feeling. Just keep in mind, the military is the line between international sanity and insanity. Without people like us, our way of life would come to an end. Killing another warrior is sometimes a necessary evil, David. Imagine what would happen in the State of California if all the cops quit. There would be total chaos, murder, rape, robbery, brutality beyond belief. Without people like us, that's what would happen to the world."

"I know you're right, Skipper. I just feel sick inside."

"Run, David, run. Lift weights. Beat the shit out of that heavy bag in the gym until your lungs feel like they are going to burst. Then think about Thailand and training your platoon. You saved their lives. Whatever you do to ease the pain, stay away from booze! It won't help."

"Thanks, sir," he said, letting out his breath slowly. "Thanks a lot. I needed to talk to someone."

"Anytime, David. Anytime you need to talk, I'll be here."

CHAPTER

22

The Turkish ship *Balikesir* left Istanbul on the evening tide bound for Bombay, India. In her belly she carried a hold full of lignite and chrome, grist for the mills of India. In her staterooms she carried forty passengers of various ethnicities. She was mainly a cargo vessel, but like many ships of her class she also carried paying passengers when they were going her direction. Postcolonial in design, she had a clear foredeck and an aft superstructure that rose up four decks to a pilothouse. The air was clear and hot as she sailed smoothly through the Red Sea and out into the Gulf of Aden.

The first night out of port, Karpenko had noticed the lovely young Greek girl at dinner. On several occasions she cut her eyes at him in that seductive way European women employ to invite attention. He was more than twice her age, which made her fair game. For several days he had bided his time, returning that look of interest, bowing his head slightly as they passed each other in the confines of the ship. He was savoring a Cuban cigar at the railing of the ship when he saw her come out on deck. She looked his way and smiled. She strolled around the deck for a few minutes, speaking to some of the other passengers who were taking in the breeze before dinner. Demurely she worked her way over to where he was standing at the rail.

"Good evening, young lady. Out for a breath of fresh air before dinner?" he asked, gesturing like an English gentleman taking off his hat.

"You're English?" she asked, surprised by his accent.

"Actually, I'm a mongrel of sorts. My father is bloody English. My mother is a German sauerkraut," he said, and smiled.

She held out her hand. "I'm Sofia Skiathos."

"Klaus Van Hessen. Pleased to meet you, Sofia Skiathos," said Karpenko, taking her hand. It was soft, dainty, and warm, and he held it for a long moment to show his interest.

"Are you going to Bombay?" she asked coyly, retrieving her hand from his manly grip.

"But of course, and then on to Rangoon for business."

"Sounds exciting. What do you do for a living, Mr. Hessen?"

"Do call me Klaus. It would make me feel much more comfortable."

"OK, Klaus, if you call me Sofi."

"You are such a beautiful and fascinating woman. Are you traveling with your husband?" asked Karpenko, probing for information he already knew.

"No. I'm not married. I mean, I was. But now, thank God, I am finally free."

"Freedom is such a beautiful feeling, isn't it?" said Karpenko, taking in a deep breath and looking at the sea.

"Yes, and I will never give up my freedom to another man," she said sadly, looking down at the water.

"So your marriage was not so good? That's most unfortunate. But you will meet someone else. That is the nature of life."

"I don't want to meet another man. I'm through with men." She smiled salaciously.

"Perhaps your liberation calls for a drink," suggested Karpenko.

He motioned over the deck attendant and ordered two drinks. Several rounds later he had her in the frame of mind he wanted.

"So, Klaus, do you do everything as well as you make

conversation?" she asked seriously. "I feel like I've known you for years."

"Why, yes, I do, thank you," he said politely.

"I'll bet you do everything well, like play shuffleboard, make love?"

"Shuffleboard is a game, lovely lady. Making love is an art." He smiled knowingly.

"If we hurry, you could show me your art before dinner," she suggested with a hungry look.

Karpenko held out his arm for her and said, "No, my dear Sofi, there is no need to hurry. Shortly you will no longer desire dinner."

She took Karpenko's arm and they strolled off to his cabin. As the ship slowly swayed back and forth in a gentle sea, Sofia Skiathos sang Karpenko her song of passion.

"Ohhhh, Klaus, it feels so good. No one makes me feel like this. Ooooh! Ohh, Klaus, oooooh!"

That night as Sofia entertained the general, Khasanov, Suburov, and the other Spetznaz began quietly to clear decks of unwanted passengers. They began at midnight, silently entering the cabins of the passengers who were careless enough to leave their doors unlocked. Using their spades they killed the younger men first. Then they killed the old people. Most never knew what hit them. One by one the passengers and some of the crew were killed and tossed overboard. The attractive women were spared. They would serve as entertainment. By morning only twenty of the forty passengers were alive. A steward, sent to awaken one of the crew, stumbled on a bloody mess in the man's bed. He immediately alerted the captain, who was taking breakfast in the galley.

With a worried expression the captain ordered a silent head count of the crew and passengers, and upon discovering that half of them were no longer aboard the ship, he went into a state of panic. When he was informed that the missing persons' beds were soaked in blood, he nearly went into shock. His hands were shaking so badly that he was unable to light his cigarette until the third try. White-faced, he stood up from the captain's table and headed for the radio shack. Suburov barred the hatchway.

"Captain! Please return to your seat," said Karpenko kindly.

The Turk turned slowly to face six burly men eyeing him like a pack of wolves. Suburov placed a hand on the back of the captain's neck, like leashing a dog, and said, "Come with me, Captain. You did not finish your coffee."

He escorted the Turk to a side table and rudely jammed him down in a chair. Karpenko took the captain's chair at the head of the table, and when he was seated he said in a loud, gruff voice, "Ladies and gentlemen, this vessel is under new management."

With that statement, Suburov pulled the trigger on his pistol and blew out the captain's brains. The force of the blast threw the man's head forward. Women screamed in horror as his corpse lay quivering spasmodically over an unfinished breakfast plate.

"Silence!" yelled Karpenko. "Or you will be next."

After several minutes of pandemonium, reality set in.

"Sofi, my dear," he said, holding out his cup, "would you be so kind as to fetch me a fresh cup of coffee?"

With eyes wide and a face in shock, she moved like a frightened child. The china tinkled as she took the cup and saucer from his hand. Karpenko looked at Khasanov and Suburov, and nodded. Taking out their pistols, they herded the remaining passengers into a corner and separated them by use. The remaining crew, those not on watch, were ordered to pick up the captain's body and carry it to the poop deck at the stern of the ship. After they had thrown the bodies overboard, they were ordered to follow their captain. Several of the Filipino crewmen refused to go over the rail. Suburov grabbed them in Akido wrist locks and forced them over the side like puppets dancing on a string. Those who clung to the outside railing begging he bashed in the face to break their iron grip on life.

The Spetznaz watched, mesmerized by the sight, as people flailed in the wake of the ship. Several old people looked on with sad eyes and prayed. When Suburov began to shove them overboard one old lady cried out, "May God have mercy on your soul!"

"God does not have mercy," corrected Suburov, "but

Suburov does!" He quickly drew his pistol, put it to her head, and pulled the trigger, killing her instantly.

While his men were busy on deck, Karpenko addressed the remaining passengers and crew.

"I am Major General Dimitri Karpenko, former head of Soviet Covert Operations. You are alive because I allow you to be alive. If you do exactly what I want you to do, you will survive. If you anger me, I'll have you thrown overboard."

Sofia Skiathos's hands were shaking uncontrollably when she handed Karpenko the cup of coffee. It spilled into the saucer.

"Sofi, my dear," said Karpenko in a soothing voice, "I will let you live."

Sofia Skiathos couldn't stop shaking. She knew that if they found the satellite radio in her room she would die a thousand deaths.

Karpenko accepted the coffee and continued addressing the remaining crewmen.

"I have allowed you to live so you can sail this vessel. When I leave you will take her to Bombay, and you will tell the authorities that Major General Dimitri Karpenko spared your miserable lives. Do you understand me?"

The horrified crewmen nodded their heads.

"If you cause me no problems and serve me well, you will live. If you cause me problems I *will* feed you to the sharks."

Karpenko sipped his coffee and looked about the galley.

"You lovely ladies. I have allowed you to live so you can entertain my men. There is no other reason for your existence. If you do not want to service my men, please step forward and you will be killed quickly, with mercy." He looked at a handsome woman who had been preaching the gospel nonstop since leaving Istanbul. She quickly looked down at the deck. None of the six women stepped forward.

Taha Ahmed Mohammed studied the Israeli base through his binoculars. Men with dogs patrolled the fence line and the surrounding heavily mined off-limits areas. He wiped his brow and watched the highly trained troops walk the perimeter. They were vigilant, ever vigilant. They had to be. Armed with infrared and thermal imaging devices they had created an impenetrable barrier to protect the aircraft and weapons within. Minefields and sensors were everywhere. Several goats had lost their lives probing the minefields until he had discovered a way through the mines. The nuclear weapons of Beersheba were stored inside the base behind security walls as strong as the walls of Jericho.

Mohammed had studied the Beersheba facility for more than six years, probing, testing, and evaluating every possible way to get inside. Then it had come to him like a gift from Allah. He needed a trumpet loud enough to make the walls come tumbling down. A nuclear weapon was the answer, and like a message from Allah he knew what to do. They would destroy Tel Aviv with a sound so powerful it would make the walls of Beersheba come tumbling down, like the walls of Jericho. They would sabotage the power grid feeding the base and with the nerve gas provided by Colonel Qaddafi they could kill the guards of Beersheba. The first assault unit would fly above the minefields in small ultralight aircraft. Behind them would come the assault troops bashing through the gates in large trucks. They had practiced the mission a hundred times in the deserts of Iraq and now they were ready to change the course of history in the Promised Land. His Promised Land. He put down his binoculars and unfolded his prayer rug.

"Allahu akbar, God is most great," he prayed, fulfilling one of the five pillars of Islam. "O Lord! Deliver us from the Jews. Grant our land veneration. Deliver our land from oppression. O Lord! Grant those in the struggle for freedom peace and forgiveness. Thou art the peace. Peace is from Thee. So greet us on the Day of Judgment with the greeting of peace. Here we come, O Allah! Here we come! No partner have You. Praise and blessings are Yours. No partner have You."

One hundred and fifty miles south of Cairo at FOB Sword, Gomez and Thompson exchanged war stories as the men of Task Force Blue packed their gear for redeployment. The coalition had outgrown its welcome in Egypt and was headed to sea. Operating off ships was infinitely more difficult than operating from land bases. The big cargo aircraft needed to air-drop the large American speedboats at sea couldn't land on aircraft carriers. Moreover, their special boats were not designed to launch from underway ships. And ships lacked the maneuver speed of aircraft to get out in front of a target vessel's track. And military ships were packed to capacity without special operations forces on board and there was no way for the commandos to practice their perishable shooting skills.

When all the coalition forces were deployed onboard the afloat task forces, sailors would be forced to hot rack or sleep in passageways. But there were few options in the Eastern Mediterranean other than ships. Greece was no longer friendly and Italy was too far north and west. Turkey was openly hostile after news of the failed assault missions became public knowledge. Third-country basing privileges for military operations were difficult to secure at best and impossible when the attention of the media was aroused. Such coverage resulted in terrorist attacks of reprisal. Israel was the obvious choice for FOB Sword, but after coalition forces surrounded the merchant and impounded the missing nuclear weapon for return to Russia, relations chilled. They asked Gomez to leave Haifa. With Savarese in the hospital in Germany, Alex Gomez was only too happy to join his teammates in Egypt.

Gomez dragged his gear off the courier aircraft just in time to throw it on a pallet destined for a flattop at sea. He walked inside the hangar and joined Commander Thompson in conversation as he finished packing his personal gear.

"Hey, Loco, welcome home," he said, cutting his eyes about the near-empty hangar.

"Thanks, Commander."

"Have a seat in my parlor," said Thompson, gesturing to a folding cot. "I got a few questions for you."

"Shoot."

"Did you get laid in Haifa?" he joked. It wasn't a serious question and he didn't expect an answer. "Seriously, how did the Israelis know the nuke was on board that freighter?" asked Thompson, stuffing the last of his personal gear in a parachute bag.

"I don't think they knew, boss, or they wouldn't have

assigned me the mission," responded Gomez, sitting down on a folding cot opposite Thompson. "They seized a bunch of merchants simultaneously. The rest were dry holes."

"Why do you think they let you guys tag along?" asked Thompson.

"They were stretched pretty thin. They had boats scattered all over the ocean," answered Gomez.

"And you two fucks just happened to hit the one with the nuke?"

"Yep, the last one on their list. If we hadn't been there, no one would have taken her down," said Gomez.

"No shit!" commented Thompson. "So it was just dumb luck?"

"Yeah, I think so. The only real op in the last two years and you missed it, sir," said Gomez with a smile, rubbing it in.

"How's Boomer?" asked Thompson, changing the subject.

"Great. When he found out he was being medevaced to Germany he couldn't stop talking about his fur-lined fräulein."

"Knowing Boomer, he's probably jumping her bones in his hospital bed right now," said Thompson.

"Not for a while, boss," responded Gomez with a shake of his head. "The vest stopped the bullets but the impact busted him up pretty bad."

"Well, he's a sight better off than we are. My guess is we'll spend the next three months in the middle of a Turkish desert while our counterparts rock and roll, cutting gator circles in the ocean," said Thompson.

"I thought we were headed to a flattop," said Gomez.

"Me too. But they ordered Delta out to the ships, along with our fuckin' boats."

"What the fuck for?" asked Gomez, exercised by the absurdity of the disposition of forces.

"I don't know, Loco. Not enough room on the ships, I guess."

"So where are we going?" asked Gomez.

"Some shithole place in the middle of nowhere. Some secret Turkish base down near the Syrian border," said Thompson disgustedly.

"We're headed for the desert and the army is headed for the high sea with our boats?" asked Gomez incredulously.

"Yeap. Un-fuckin'-believable, huh? How do you figure it, Loco? We hit three strong signals and come up dry. The Israelis hit a bunch of targets at random and come up with a gusher. How do you explain that?" asked Thompson with an angry expression on his face.

"Well, you know they had a female agent working the big Russian we snatched out of Greece. Maybe she told them which ships to hit or maybe the Ruskie told them more than they told us."

"Or maybe they have a mole inside Karpenko's organization," interjected Thompson.

"One thing's for sure, the Israelis intended to keep the nuke. That's why they're pissed at us," commented Gomez.

"And that's why the task force is movin' to sea and not to Haifa," continued Thompson.

"I thought you said we were headed to—"

"Loco, the fuckin' task force is moving to sea. We're headed for obscurity, man, relegated to the edge of the action," explained Thompson.

"Why?"

"'Cause we're navy, man! But don't worry, Loco; no one's gonna see any action for a long time. We've beat this guy underground."

"I wouldn't bet on it, sir," said Gomez, shaking his head.

"Hey, Commander!" yelled a burly chief petty officer. "We're stacked and packed. We gotta have your shit now to finish racking the pallet."

As Thompson and Gomez picked up the parachute bags, several sailors began to break down the folding cots they were using as makeshift chairs. The life of a commando was as impermanent as the life of a gypsy.

CHAPTER

23

During World War II, the United States developed the atom bomb under the code name the Manhattan Project. The first bombs were large, cumbersome devices that required special handling to deliver to target. They were dropped on the Japanese cities of Hiroshima and Nagasaki, with devastating effect. Both cities were effectively obliterated, ending the war. The explosive force of Fat Boy, the bomb that was dropped on Hiroshima, was about twenty kilotons, the equivalent of twenty thousand pounds of TNT. The bombs Karpenko possessed were five times more destructive. One of them was capable of completely destroying a city as large as New York or Tokyo.

After World War II, a new age of military strategy developed as the United States and the Soviet Union built up massive nuclear weapons arsenals and elaborate systems of delivery and defense. The first nuclear bombs were fission reactions, limited in size by the upper limit of critical mass. Critical mass is the smallest amount of fissionable materials that, once triggered, will sustain a chain reaction. The bomb that devastated Hiroshima was huge in size and relatively small in wallop. The *Enola Gay* was barely able to lift off the runway with just one bomb in her bay. The second generation of nuclear weaponry produced bombs that were small in size and enormously destructive. The hydrogen bomb, a fusion reaction device, forces lightweight nuclei to fuse into heavier nuclei, releasing energy in the process. It is the same nuclear reaction that takes place in the sun. The bombs Karpenko possessed were thermonuclear devices, miniature suns in a bottle. Each was capable of scorching a hundred square miles of the surface of the planet of all life-forms. They were small in size in comparison with Fat Boy, but they were five time more destructive in effect.

In Berlin, the members of the Future Technologies Assessment Group faced near impossible tasks: Locate several thermonuclear bombs, each no larger than an office desk. Recover the missing weapons simultaneously without Karpenko detonating one or more of the weapons remotely and capture Major General Dimitri Karpenko. Boris Yeltsin understood the problem better than most because he understood Karpenko's personality. He assigned his best diplomat to the coalition with orders to cooperate to the fullest measure.

Maksim Litvinov faced an inquisitive but erudite audience at the fourth meeting of the Future Technologies Assessment Group. The meeting began with intelligence summaries provided by each country, each hoping the other would provide a crucial clue. The briefings were bland and whitewashed. After the fiasco in the Mediterranean, Karpenko's trail had grown cold. Even the sophisticated surveillance and reconnaissance satellites of NSA had failed to turn up any clues. Ferret satellites like the one monitored by Sergeant Chaffin couldn't be trusted to provide positive identification of the weapons Karpenko possessed, if and when new signals were acquired.

In executive session, the discussion turned to the general problem of proliferation, and it pointed like a sharp stick at Maksim Litvinov.

"Maksim," said Norton-Taylor in a congenial voice, "with the Ukraine's public defiance over the nuclear weapons issue and its refusal to ratify either the nuclear nonproliferation treaty or the START I Nuclear Arms Control Pact, do you fear that an opposition to weapons controls will spread to the other members of CIS?"

"Yah. This is big problem. The southern and western rim of Russia has big problem. There are not enough forces to ensure positive control. In these new republics there are few controls on the materials they possess," responded Litvinov.

"Isn't that an understatement of the problem?" asked MacFarlane.

"There are many problems, Miles, many, many problems," confessed Litvinov.

MacFarlane pressed his point. "I have information that your bordering territories have become huge bazaars for arms merchants shopping for nuclear materials."

"Yes. This is true. They are courting agents from aspiring nuclear states. Some of the agents are working closely with networks of criminals who have access to nuclear materials, even within Russia," explained Litvinov.

"My agents have purchased zirconium, beryllium, and several other dual-use metals from smugglers operating as far north as the Polish border," interjected von Kessler. "Recently, we arrested two Kazakhstani citizens for selling low-enriched uranium fuel pellets manufactured at the Alma-Ata plant."

"What do you want me to say, Klaus? Money talks," responded Litvinov. "It is free enterprise, no? Most of the nuclear infrastructure and all of the weapons controlled by the Soviet Union are now located in Russia. This we control. However, there are uranium mining and processing facilities in Kazakhstan and elsewhere, we do not control. The Russian government can no longer provide security for materials outside our borders. I must remind you, Kazakhstan is an independent nation," argued Litvinov smoothly.

"Litvinov, is it true the Iranians bought two nuclear warheads from Kazakhstan?" asked Habberman.

"No!" responded Litvinov harshly. "All nuclear weapons have been accounted for," he insisted in a stern voice.

"How many nuclear weapons did the Soviet Union possess at the time of dissolution?" asked Habberman.

"About twenty-seven thousand," said Litvinov.

"My God! Exactly?" asked Habberman incredulously.

Litvinov ignored the accusation.

"And you have accounted for each and every one of them?" demanded Habberman.

"Yah," said Litvinov. They felt the lack of conviction in his voice like sharks getting a taste of blood in the water. "There have been transfers of sensitive technologies, that is true, but no nuclear weapons have been lost," insisted Litvinov, staring from man to man at the conference table. "We have *not* lost any weapons!"

"But, Maksim," said Norton-Taylor, "we are here for precisely that reason. Major General Karpenko, by your own admission, stole three thermonuclear bombs. Do we have your assurance that those are the only nuclear weapons unaccounted for?"

"Yah."

"How many NBC weapons does Russia control?" asked MacFarlane.

"I am not at liberty to provide that information," responded Litvinov.

"Maksim, would red mercury be one of those sensitive technologies that has escaped Russian control?" asked von Kessler.

The Russian took a deep breath and exhaled with a gush. "Yah. We are missing a quantity of this substance," answered Litvinov. He knew the West had acquired red mercury because it had been reported in several European newspapers. The importance of the substance had escaped notice.

"Would you tell us the purpose of this technology?" asked von Kessler.

"I am not authorized to disclose this information."

"You know we have been successful in buying a small quantity of this substance from a ring of smugglers," said von Kessler. "They claim red mercury was the key material for making lightweight neutron bombs."

Litvinov was cornered. The look on their faces made him decide to speak about the subject. "This is true. The red mercury was for the making of neutron bombs."

"Bombs small enough for a man to carry—say, the size of a suitcase? Maybe as small as ten kilos?" inquired MacFarlane.

The poker faces of the men at the conference table gave way to the weight of the revelation. Neutron bombs were designed to kill people and leave buildings standing. A single terrorist with such technology, or a megalomaniac like Saddam Hussein could kill every human being in a city such as New York and not disturb a brick in the Empire State Building.

"Maksim, does Karpenko have this technology?" asked Habberman.

"No one has this bomb! The technology is not proven," he insisted.

"But a neutron bomb small enough for one man to carry is technologically feasible with this red mercury, is it not?" pressed Habberman.

Litvinov rubbed his face like a man exhausted from a long nightmare.

"Yah."

"Does Karpenko possess red mercury?" asked Norton-Taylor.

"Yes, Alfred, we believe he does. But he does not have the plan for the bomb. Nobody have this plan," insisted Litvinov, shaking his finger in the air.

Norton-Taylor took a drink of water while the others stared at Litvinov. "Maksim, is this a fair assessment of the situation? There is a thriving illegal trade in fissionable materials and NBC technology going on on the borders of Russia?"

"Yah."

"There is a rumor that one or more nuclear warheads have been sold to the Iranians or to some other non-CIS state. Can you confirm or deny this rumor?"

"Alfred, to the best of our knowledge this is only rumor," insisted Litvinov. He continued, "Of the three non-Russian republics with nuclear weapons, only Belarus has fulfilled the pledge made in the Lisbon Protocol. Ukraine and Kazakhstan have not yet allowed anyone to do accounting. This is great problem!"

"All of us understand the gravity of the problem, Maksim. Will you help us establish an intelligence apparatus designed to monitor and prevent the transfer of weapons of mass destruction?" asked Norton-Taylor.

"I will take this up with President Yeltsin as soon as I return to Moscow."

Norton-Taylor knew there were two fifty-megawatt nuclear research reactors hidden on military bases at Kazakhstan's Semipalatinsk Test Range and one located at Ukraine's Sevastopol Naval Base. Powerful interests in the non-Russian republics were dreaming of becoming nuclear states and they were still discovering secret "things" in their territories. They had possession, and thus bargaining power. Litvinov looked at the men around the conference table and spoke in a grave tone.

"The realization of the nonproliferation treaty will take a lot of money, proper agreement, and a lot of skilled people. None of these things we have. It's like you want me to play baseball," he continued, "and I have no balls and no—what do you call dem?—bats."

"Maksim, I have a very reliable source, from one of your former scientists, that the Scientific Research Institute for Organic Chemistry and Technology created a new biochemical weapon more toxic than anything previously known to man. Do you know of Airborne Warrior?" asked MacFarlane.

"I know nothing of this, Miles," he said with conviction. "President Yeltsin is doing everything in his power to open the secret doors of the Soviet military. This, too, is very difficult thing. There were programs, and programs within programs, which are secret to only few men. These secret programs were used to develop nuclear, chemical, and biological weapons of mass destruction. They were the mirror image of your own programs, Miles. If you want to know what they are, I suggest you look at your own government."

"But the United States, unlike the Union of the Soviet Socialist Republics, has not disintegrated," interjected MacFarlane. "Our technology is not for sale to madmen."

"Only madmen could develop such horrible things, and I did not participate in such endeavors. I am from the diplomatic corps! Always the diplomatic corps!" snapped Litvinov, raising his voice.

"I'm sorry, Maksim," apologized MacFarlane. "I know you and your president are in a difficult situation."

"Yes. Yes, we are. War now rages in Azerbaijan, Georgia, Tajikistan, Kazakhstan, and other place you cannot pronounce. We are surrounded by nationalists, religious fanatics, Soviet apparatchiks, Bolsheviks, and others who would kill me for being in the same room with you. Mafia rule the streets of Moscow and other major cities, and there are many evils about the Soviet military we know nothing about."

"Gentlemen, we have callously abused Maksim," interjected Norton-Taylor, taking charge. "With your help and President Yeltsin's, perhaps we can apply some resources toward policing this undesirable technology transfer. As for the immediate problem I suggest we have patience and keep our special units at a high state of readiness. Gentlemen, this meeting is adjourned."

The *Balikesir* sailed the Indian Ocean for days under heavy cloud cover as the Spetznaz relaxed in the comforts of the old ship. Off the Maldives, Karpenko ordered a dinner party to celebrate the end of the voyage. With music, wine, and excellent food served by the petrified cook, they dined on the best she had to offer. He sat at the head of the table like a monarch with Sofia Skiathos like a queen at the other end of the table. Throughout the meal Karpenko made small talk with his men and their well-worn ladies. To the sound of a mandolin reminiscent of the songs of the Russian Steppe, he made a short speech and a toast.

"Tomorrow, ladies and gentlemen, our voyage together comes to an end. I would like to propose a toast," he said, holding up his glass. After the ship's steward had poured wine for all, he continued. "To cossacks, the free spirit of the Russian Steppes, not Asian, not Turkish, not Slavic, warriors without country!"

"To cossacks!" yelled his men.

They muscled their women and slugged down their glasses of wine. Suburov, Khasanov, and the others all made toasts. After several minutes of raucous and rude behavior, Karpenko held up his glass for a second time and hit it with his fork to gain attention.

"I would like to propose another toast," he said, smiling at Sofi. The others held up their glasses and muscled their women to do the same. The lady missionary was somewhat recalcitrant, so Suburov backhanded her completely off her chair. With his huge right hand he yanked her back up like a child and stuck the wine goblet in her face. She took it without pause.

"Sofi, I propose a toast! To the Mossad. They have such beautiful spies."

"To the Mossad!" yelled the Spetznaz, slugging down wine.

Sofia Skiathos went faint. The color drained out of her face and she fell out of her chair. She came to as Suburov's huge hands lifted her off the deck and jammed her into her seat at the head of the table. She was too petrified to look at Karpenko so she stared at her plate, sobbing like a child, waiting for the report from Suburov's pistol. It didn't come as she expected.

"Sofi, my dear, what's wrong? The wine go to your head?" asked Karpenko in a joking manner.

The Spetznaz soldiers thought the comment was hilarious. They laughed for two minutes uncontrollably. When Skiathos found the strength to look up she saw he was smiling. Her breathing had almost stopped and she was near fainting again. It came in short little puffs like the breathing of a wounded animal. Her whole body was quivering as if she were in shock from intense cold.

"Sofi, I have nothing against the Jews. Maybe you would like to work for me?" he said with a smile.

For a moment her life flashed before her as she saw a glimmer of hope. She looked up at Karpenko tentatively and slowly nodded yes, like a child who had been bad.

"OK then. I propose a toast to Sofi, the beautiful Jewish spy!"

"To Sofi!" they yelled and gulped down their wine.

After the steward had filled the wineglasses, Karpenko continued. "Vlad, what kind of job opportunities do we have for beautiful Jewish spy?"

Suburov jumped up from the table, unzipped his fly, and pointed at his penis. The others roared with laughter.

When Suburov had resumed his seat, Karpenko shook his head. "Vlad, you are so crude, so crude, but as always you have excellent idea. Sofi, my dear, Sofi, if you wish to survive you will give all my men the same excellent blow job you gave me last night. Under the table. Now!" he yelled.

With eyes wild with fear, she stared at Karpenko in disbelief. When Suburov pulled out his pistol and placed it on the table in front of him, she slowly slid out of her chair and disappeared under the table.

Karpenko continued talking. "You will give each man your services. At random! Soldiers, the objective of this mission is to determine who is receiving the service of this beautiful Jewish spy. Keep straight face!" he ordered.

Suburov held up his glass. "I propose a toast to beautiful Jewish spy."

"We already did that toast, Vlad, you old *stariki*," complained Khasanov.

"Then you make toast, Khasanov," roared Suburov with annoyance. He glared at Khasanov, who only smiled in return.

"OK. OK," agreed Khasanov. "I make de toast. To beautiful Jewish spy who gives great blow job."

Karpenko eyed Khasanov with a menacing expression. "How would you know this, Viktor, without personal experience?" demanded Karpenko.

Khasanov kept wearing his huge grin.

Again they roared with laughter and yelled. "To cossacks!"

CHAPTER
24

The jungles of Thailand were steamy and hot as Alpha Platoon patrolled cautiously through a grove of banana trees. Korea was a distant memory, a blurry *soju* remembrance. Twenty-four hours after breaking camp in Kisamon, every man in the task group had a *soju* hangover and a throbbing headache. The twelve hours they spent in the back of the C-141 on the way to Thailand was hell for them and the aircrew who were forced to endure the odor of used kimchi and garlic paste within the confines of the aircraft. But within a few hours of landing in Thailand the resilient young warriors were ready for liberty. Drinking Singha beer and watching Thai belly dancers pick up baht notes off the dance floor with the lips of their vaginas was every young sailor's dream. Anything was possible in Thailand as soon as the skipper let them have liberty. They approached the mock enemy camp like young lions on the prowl.

Evans had established his tactical operations center in a Thai navy compound southeast of Bangkok, giving the men easy access to the delights of the Orient. He had arranged for their missions to begin as soon as they were acclimated, leaving a lot of free time after the exercise to explore the country before returning to the States. His schedule had not gone unnoticed at exercise headquarters in Bangkok.

Alpha's first mission was to strike a jungle training camp and take prisoners for interrogation. The pressure to perform increased enormously when the marine general in charge of the Exercise Cobra Fang insisted on personally observing the SEAL mission. As Alpha Platoon cautiously prowled the jungle trail outside the camp, General Kris gave Evans a piece of his mind.

"Commander Evans, when this exercise is over I want you to personally ensure your men stay out of trouble. I won't tolerate a liberty incident under my command. Is that clear?" roared General Kris, glaring at Evans.

"Yes, General. Crystal clear."

"You people have a bad reputation. I mean *bad*," he snarled. Kris was a chain-smoker and he spoke through a cloud of tobacco. "Everywhere you people go you leave behind a trail of international incidents. I won't tolerate any shenanigans under my command. I assure you I will hold you personally accountable, Commander."

"Crystal clear, General. Crystal clear," repeated Evans.

From outside the *hootch* a noise disturbed the general's lecture. He looked out the door and saw Saleen skulking about the compound, checking the wire leads to the explosives he had hidden around the perimeter of the *campong*. Evans used the break in the castigation to exit the *hootch*, leaving the general with several of his marine entourage. He walked over to Saleen and pretended to be busy, trying to escape the general's admonition.

Outside the *campong*, Simons cautiously walked the point, leading the platoon toward the target. He was agile and quick and possessed outstanding senses. He smelled the campfire Saleen had built long before he saw its glow.

The moonlight filtering down through the banana leaves and coconut palms was insufficient to see booby traps, and his NVGs distorted his sense of balance. As they drew closer to the enemy camp he took them off and began feeling his way along the jungle path, crawling on his knees inch by inch. The Thai marines integrated into the squad for cross-training kept making noise as they crept down the trail. When Simons held up his fist to halt the patrol, Masure collared the Thai next to him and threatened to smack him, gesticulating with his fist.

Simons looked at Lieutenant Owen. Using his hand, he made an open-fingered gesture covering his face, the signal for enemy ahead. Owen passed it down the line and hit the button on his intersquad radio. Just as he whispered to Masure, a Thai marine dropped his weapon on the ground with a clatter. The noise was distinctively metallic and alien to the jungles of Thailand. The camp came alive with guards. Then a chain of explosions shot fire and water into the air all around them. Master Chief Saleen had planted water shots along the trail. He had used one-gallon plastic milk jugs filled with water to dampen the shock of the explosives he had suspended inside. They create the effect of being in a deadly kill zone without the danger of fragmentation. Explosions erupted one after another all around the enemy camp, filling the air with mist and smoke.

"Center peel," yelled Owen as he started reconning by fire on full automatic with his M-16. The others began shooting, some on automatic and some on semiautomatic. Then the jungle came alive with gunfire pouring in from enemy positions ahead of them. The weapons were loaded with blank ammunition, but the sound and gut feeling was like a real firefight. Robinson's M-60 hammered away, laying down a base of fire as the platoon maneuvered back to a preselected rally point. Concussion grenades began to rain in on them, blinding them with flash and smoke. In leapfrog fashion they worked their way back into the jungle and ran to their second rally point. When the count was sure, they ran to the next rally point, trying to stay one step ahead of the OPFOR.

At the third rally point, Owen took muster and glanced at Masure. He was smiling like a Cheshire cat. "Goddamn, L.T., that was almost real!" he said, pumped up on adrenaline.

"Everything except the fuckin' hot lead," said Williams, smiling with excitement.

"I know how Saleen thinks," coached Masure. "They'll ambush us along the trail we came in on. Let's wade down the side of the canal," he suggested, "and catch 'em moving up the bank after us."

"Roger that," Owen said, motioning for Simons to lead off.

Five minutes later they heard clattering as the OPFOR maneuvered up the bank after them. Saleen was making noise intermittently on purpose, like a ragtag guerrilla outfit moving too fast. Owen quickly formed a hasty ambush along the bank. Squatting neck-deep in the water, covered in foliage, they opened up on the OPFOR with everything they had. Bailey laid a concussion grenade on top of the OPFOR formation.

"Goddamn you guys. Be careful where you throw those fuckin' flashcrashes," yelled Saleen gruffly out of darkness.

Chuckling, they waded up the canal and changed directions, backtracking toward the original objective. Just before dawn they held up on the bank of a small canal in a thicket of nipa palm.

At first light they crossed the canal one at a time, carefully providing cover for each other. Robinson was loaded down with an M-60 and five hundred rounds of ammunition. As he struggled to cross the canal in waist-deep water, his boot became stuck in the soft mud. Struggling to free himself, he squirmed about for a full minute while the men on the banks laughed at his predicament. Out of the corner of his eye, Robinson saw what looked like a log floating in his direction. It got his attention because it was floating up current. As it got closer the sinuous sideways motion made his heart leap into his throat. It was a croc closing in for the kill.

"Hey, you guys!" he whispered in a hushed tone. "How about a hand here!" he said, speaking a little louder. "Hey, you guys! How 'bout a hand!" he blurted out loud. "That's a fuckin' crocodiiiiiile!"

Lam saw the small croc and jumped in the canal between Robinson and the curious predator. Jackson joined him. Not wanting to give away their position with a grenade, they jammed their rifle butts into the head of the small amphibian like a pair of posthole diggers. After several jabs the stunned croc made its way back downstream after easier prey. Once on the bank Robinson shook himself like a wet dog with a shiver of fear and relief. The look on his face caused them to break out in fits of stifled laughter. Simons was rolling on the ground helplessly holding his sides when

Masure shoved him with his foot and motioned him to lead off as point man.

From his perch in a banyan tree overlooking the canal, Evans clicked the safety on his M-16. It was loaded with live ammunition. He surveyed the scene with amusement and watched as the platoon moved off up the trail. He lowered his gear with a line and climbed down to the base of the tree to wait for Saleen. He wasn't in any hurry because he knew back at headquarters he was going to catch a ration of grief from General Kris.

The weekend after the failed operation, Owen and the boys hit Pattaya with a full head of steam. They settled into BJ's bar and lay back for a comfortable stay. It offered all the delights of the Orient. Outside the entrance Lam watched in fascination as a skittish little mongoose nervously circled a cobra hidden in a basket. As a snake handler played music on a flute, the mongoose strained at its leash. Before a gathering crowd the snake handler enticed the snake to rise up repeatedly out of the basket and spread its hood, threatening the mongoose. He was playing to the oohs and ahs of the crowd, and when they had contributed a sufficient amount of money his assistant released the mongoose from its leash. Over and over, with quick deft movements, the mongoose tested the snake's speed until the reptile grew tired. Several times the cobra struck out at the mongoose only to hit the empty spot it once occupied. With lightning speed the mongoose would jump straight up in the air, twist like a cat, and land in a new location just out of reach of the cobra. The men of Alpha Platoon reluctantly left their newfound girlfriends and joined Lam to watch the show.

"What gives, Lam-san?" asked Bailey.

"The mongoose is about to defang the cobra," said Lam.

"What?" asked Jackson, not believing Lam's words.

"Yeah. Watch the mongoose closely," said Masure. "See if you can see it happen."

With a fake attack the mongoose enticed the snake to strike. Then with lightning speed it shifted to the right and struck the cobra so fast and hard the snake was knocked to the ground. When the cobra recovered to a fighting posture, it was missing its right fang.

"Son of a bitch," said Robinson. "It happened so fast I didn't see it."

Before he finished his sentence the snake struck again, and lost its remaining fang. As the crowd dispersed the snake charmer began to auction off the snake to the highest bidder. Lam won.

"Lam, what are you going to do with the damn snake?" asked Simons.

"Not what I do, Simons. What we do. We are going to eat him."

"Not on your life, buckaroo," said Taufaudy.

The mongoose leapt on the snake's head and shook it like a dog with a rag in its mouth. It was over in fast-forward.

Lam issued orders in Thai and held up a fistful of baht notes before entering the bar and taking his seat. The bar girls came back like flies attracted to honey.

"Senior, we sure looked bad on that prisoner snatch op," commented Owen. "I think the captain's still pissed at us."

One of the bar girls served another round of huge bottles of Singha beer.

"You know, L.T., I've worked with the Thai marines before, and they're usually pretty good operators," said Masure. "I think some bastard set us up to look bad in front of the general."

"Someone did," said Lam. They all stared at him incredulously.

"Someone did!" he protested. "That controller major, the U.S. guy with the big ugly nose. He paid the Thai marines to make noise. . . ." The men continued to stare at Lam in disbelief. "He did! I heard the Thai talking. He pay big money."

"Son of a bitch!" cursed Masure. "I knew it. He set us up so his jarhead general would hear us comin' like a herd of water buffalo. Bastard!"

"Yeah, and now even the skipper thinks we operate like shit," said Owen.

"Not!" said Lam. They all stared at him, mouths agape.

"What? What? Come on!" came voices from three directions.

"I hear him talkin' to the Thai," insisted Lam.

"Who?" asked Robinson.

"The captain, dumb shit," snapped Williams.

"He knows what happen. After that, I see him go to the controller shack. So I follow where he cannot see me," said Lam, smiling.

"Yeah, yeah, yeah, and what happened?" demanded Williams anxiously.

Lam laughed out loud.

"What happened?" demanded five voices simultaneously.

"I hear a big scuffle and a big grunt sound. Then the captain say, if that happen again he was going to kick the major's ass from one end of Patpong to the other."

"No shit," said Taufaudy. "He whacked the bastard?"

"Yeah," said Lam, smiling from ear to ear. "He kick his ass good."

"The captain's nobody to fuck with," said Masure. "He could snatch out your eyes as quick as that mongoose ripped off the cobra's fangs. I've seen him do it."

"No shit?" asked Jackson.

"No shit," answered Masure, shaking two fingers like a snake's fangs.

Owen looked at Masure and the boys, "Here's to the skipper."

"*We hi yo,*" yelled Robinson.

"Wrong fuckin' country, knucklehead," said Williams.

"Salute!" yelled Williams.

"Right fuckin' country, Wild Bill," jeered Taufaudy.

"Jesus, my ass is dragging," said Robinson.

"At least you still got one," said Williams, chuckling. "For a minute I thought that croc was gonna eat your big dumb ass."

"At least you weren't fried to death," complained Lam. "Jesus, those explosions were right on top of me last night."

"Lam, you're not supposed to say Jesus. Say Dali Lama or Katmandu, or something like that," said Robinson.

"Katmandu is a place, dumb shit, not a person," said Williams, sneering. They all started laughing, feeling the warm glow of the booze and camaraderie. One of the waitresses approached with a large wooden tray and laid out

273

a feast of fried cobra, fruit, and nuts, and a shot glass for each man. A second lovely girl in a skintight dress held up a large bottle of Mekong whiskey. Lam nodded approval. "We drink to the cobra before we eat him," said Lam.

"Eat him! Eat him! You gotta be shittin' me! I'm not eatin' that slithery, slimy fucker," protested Simons.

"Me neither," chimed in Bailey.

"Hey, Simons, Bailey, get with the program, goddamnit," snapped Lieutenant Owen in a uncharacteristic manner. Owen rarely cursed. He was savoring a moment that comes only once in a lifetime.

"Now what's he doing, boss?" whined Bailey.

"That's the cobra's venom sacks," answered Masure.

Lam squeezed out a little venom in each glass and motioned for the girl to fill all the glasses with Mekong. He took a glass for himself and said, "To Alpha Platoon, in sickness, in health, in bad times and good, to comrades in arms. *Chin-chin, Ho Chi Minh, kong ca chet!*"

They looked at each other and yelled, "To Alpha Platoon," and downed the liquid in one gulp.

"We hi yo," said Robinson weakly.

"Wrong country, asshole," said Williams, sassing him.

"My first drink since BUDS and it's laced with cobra venom," complained Jackson. "I don't believe it. I don't fuckin' believe it!"

"Believe it, jackass. You can believe it, man," Simons said, slurring his words and feeling the booze. "We just drank fuckin' cobra venom, man!"

"Is it gonna kill us, Senior?" asked Robinson in a serious tone.

They all laughed at the way Robinson had asked the question.

"No, Robby. You're too pigheaded to die from snake poison," answered Masure.

The moment was gone as quickly as it had come upon them, the moment Owen knew would come. It was a special moment when a crowd of individuals transforms into one fighting organism.

Simons shouted, "Look at that shit, man."

Two Thai women were dancing nude on the floor holding out a bottle of Coca-Cola. They danced up to the table next to Robinson, causing a flurry of hoots and hollers. One of the girls handed the bottle to Robinson. He tried to pop it open with his thumbs, and failing that he stuck it in his mouth and popped the top with his teeth.

"Robby, you knucklehead," said Lam, "You were just supposed to inspect it."

"She asked me to," he protested.

"You dumb shit! You'll see," said Lam, motioning for another bottle of Coke.

The bartender ran over with another bottle. Robinson tried to open it with his thumbs but couldn't, and handed it to the dancers. The girls danced around the room naked, allowing others to inspect the bottle. With great show and fanfare, the music stopped. One of the girls lay down on a table with her feet up as if ready to give birth. The second girl inserted the Coke bottle into her vagina. With grunts and sounds of pain the girl on the table smacked herself on the stomach several times. To the amazement of the crowd she opened the Coke with the muscles of her pussy.

"I don't believe it," said Robinson with wide eyes. The assistant danced up to the table and poured some of the Coke into a glass in front of them.

"That's some tough pussy, man," said Taufaudy with a shit-eating grin.

"That thing could guillotine your dick," said Robinson, openmouthed. As they laughed a German tourist began to protest loudly. Her boyfriend had to restrain her from taking off her clothes and putting on a competitive show. During the excitement a Thai pimp walked up to the table. He was dressed in a silk shirt and tight denim jeans that looked as if they had been painted on his body.

"Hey, big American man. You like my sister?" said the Thai cowboy, pointing to a beautiful girl standing near the bar. The girl smiled and licked her lips.

"Not tonight, Jack. We're just drinkin' and thinkin'," said Bailey.

"Yeap. I'm thinkin,'" said Williams, eyeing the whore.

"How about you?" he said, looking at Lam. "How long been since you had little yellow pussy?"

Lam shook his head, giving the cowboy an evil eye. The

others also shook their heads as he looked from man to man.

"You half white, half yellow, no dick?" asked the cowboy, hanging around. "Why you not want my sister?"

Simons thought the comment was funny. "Half white, half yellow, no dick! Does that come with french fries?" he sassed.

"That's OK, Lam-san," said Robinson soothingly. "It looks like a real dick, just a lot smaller."

"Son 'n bitch, Robby! Now I know you been looking at my prick. Between the Thai cowboy and you pucks, there's not a hard dick in this whole goddamn bar but mine."

"God!" said Jackson, "Guillotine pussies, AIDS, and hepatitis. The women are dangerous around here," he said, deflecting attention from Lam.

"Jackson, you been good boy. You try Singha now?" asked Lam.

"Not me, pal! No drinky! No pucky! Both could kill you stone dead," responded Jackson.

"How could a little pucky kill you?" asked Robinson seriously.

"Robby, have you ever heard of AIDS?" asked Owen.

"Oh, yes, sir."

"Well, most of these girls have it," said Masure. "If you get crazy and decided you have to live dangerously, just settle for a squeaky-clean sponge bath and a blow job, OK?"

"You bet, Senior," said Robinson, taking a big drink of beer. His dream of three little Thai girls in the rack with him at the same time had just evaporated.

At the bar the Thai cowboys were talking and pointing at the table with the SEALs. The men were busy watching the naked dancing girl feed patrons with chopsticks. The lovely creatures were controlling the chopsticks with the muscles of their vaginas, easier than the SEALs could with their hands. One of the pimp's girls walked over to the table just as the girl with the chopsticks passed by, serving sliced fruit and sticky rice balls with her pussy.

"AIDS," said Robinson. "What a waste of talent."

At the German table the blond girl took off her top. The guys cheered her on as her huge white breasts appeared from under her blouse. They dwarfed the small Asian girl's, who stared on in disbelief. Her boyfriend dragged her outside topless.

The pimp's good-looking creature approached the table and sat in Williams's lap, rubbing her ass into his crotch. She had long black hair that hung down her back, and a sinuous body that drove Williams wild-eyed. Looking at Williams, she said, "You butterfly. You like blow job. For you, big boy, only five dolla. Only five dolla." She smiled.

"No," said Lam. "Not now. Not ever." He shoved the girl off Williams's lap with his foot, sending her across the floor skidding on her side.

"Whoa now. Hold on," complained Williams. "Speak for yourself, Lam-san," he said with a look of genuine interest. "I'm considerin' the offer."

"It's getting dangerous in here, L.T.," said Masure. "That's a *katoy.*"

"A ka-what?" asked Williams.

"You know, a guy dressed like a girl," said Lam.

"Oh, God, let's get outta here," cried Jackson, who was the only sober man at the table.

"You guys are shittin' me? Right? Right?" pleaded Williams. Masure shook his head no.

Owen gave a motion with his hand and they all got up to leave. Out of the corner of his eye, Masure noticed the cowboys heading out the back of the bar.

"Listen, guys, between the ambushes in the jungle and the thieves in here, we be caught in a cross fire. Stay close together and watch each other's back."

Standing to leave, Robinson looked at Williams and asked, *"Katoy?"*

"Hell, I don't know, Robby," complained Williams. "If it looks like a woman, talks like a woman, and gives a blow job like a woman, I ain't lookin' no further no more."

The nude dancer on the bar didn't miss a hip grind as the men left. Americans didn't spend like the Japanese and the Germans who frequented the place. She fired a banana across the bar with her vagina and stuck her muff in the face of a Japanese patron who was watching intently through puffy Mekong eyes.

Outside, the men headed down the narrow street with Simons at point. As they moved away from the bar, the hooligans blocked their path, sitting on their motorcycles in the middle of the alley. The pimp who had approached them in the bar smiled and drew deeply on his cigarette.

"Stick, we got problems. To the right, to the left, and a bunch in front of us," said Owen with a hint of concern in his voice.

Lam walked up beside Simons. As they continued to walk, the cowboys cut them off.

In Vietnamese the pimp said, "Hey, half-breed, too much white blood take away your balls? Maybe you like boom-boom with fat American girls better? Maybe you like boom-boom with fat American boys?"

Jackson walked up behind Lam and said, "What did that asshole gook say?"

"Let's kick their asses," said Robinson, looking around for a big stick.

"Hey, guys, it's five to one and you're forgetting the most important lessen I ever taught you."

"Senior, it's not too late to remind us," urged Owen.

"Surprise!" yelled Masure, pulling out a concussion grenade.

He pulled the pin and tossed it in the middle of the Thai gang. The SEALs turned their backs just as the explosion boomed up the alley. Lam quickly spun back around and planted a front thrusting kick to the solar plexus of the pimp, sending him to the ground gasping for breath. Robinson yanked a support off an empty vegetable stall and waded through the gang like a hockey player in a brawl. The whore who had worked on Williams tried to kick Owen in the balls, but Lam extended his leg and parried the force of the kick away from the lieutenant. Williams poleaxed the creature in the face, sending him to the ground, unconscious. The wig flew off. It was a guy in drag.

Well, I'll be damned. From now on I'm gonna look a lot closer, thought Williams.

Standing in the middle untouched, Masure pulled out another grenade and gave it a toss. Before it exploded he yelled, "Outta here with your swim buddy! Rendezvous at the Pink Pussy!" The grenade exploded, causing the gas in one of the motorcycles to ignite. Fire and explosions boomed as they ran up the alley laughing. Owen and Masure arrived at the Pink Pussy last.

"Williams, take muster," ordered Owen.

He quickly counted heads and reported, "All present or accounted for, sir."

"Thanks. How about a beer?" he said, slumping into a chair.

"You got it, sir. Senior, Singha?" he asked Masure.

"Yeap, and some dried squid. Make sure it smells like a well-used pussy."

"You got it, Senior," said Simons, motioning for a waitress.

"Hey, Senior Chief. That was cool, man, real cool," chuckled Taufaudy. "The most important lesson is the element of surprise. I got it. But I got a question too. Do you always carry concussion grenades around in your pocket?"

"Second lesson, Taufaudy. Proper previous planning prevents piss-poor performance," he said with a grin.

The platoon relaxed for about an hour, watching the dancing girls. Williams kept checking their breasts closely, ensuring no *katoys* were among the bunch. Those with small breasts he sent away just in case. It was Masure who first noticed the strange look on Lam's face when he returned from the john. "Lam, what's wrong, man? You look like you've seen a ghost."

"I see ghost, Senior. Now he is a man but very soon he will be a real ghost." Lam sat down and stared in the direction of the bathroom like a madman. His eyes were crazed and his face had a strange color.

"What the hell are you talkin' about? Has the booze gone to your head?" asked Masure.

Lam didn't respond. But the look on his face struck a nerve. Owen and Masure looked at each other, perplexed.

"OK, men. I think the coast is clear now. We are going back to the base. Simons, lead out," ordered Owen.

"I stay, Lieutenant," said Lam.

"No, Lam. You go with us," ordered Owen.

"I must stay!" said Lam loudly.

Owen looked at Masure, dumbfounded.

"Lieutenant, I'll stay with him and check this out. You and Williams get the men back to base. We'll take a taxi."

"OK, Senior," responded Owen, reading Masure's eyes. "Be careful. Wake me up when you get back."

After the others had left, Masure slid over close to Lam and took in a big gulp of beer. "OK, who we gonna kill?" he asked seriously.

Lam's head snapped around. He stared at Masure in disbelief.

"How you know what I'm thinkin'?"

"It's written all over your face, boy."

For a long time Lam said nothing and Masure let things be. He slowly sipped on his beer and waited for Lam to make the next move. Finally Lam opened up.

"That man in the corner by the john."

Masure looked around nonchalantly.

"Which one?"

"The one with the tattoos," said Lam.

"The old guy with all the tattoos?" asked Masure in disbelief.

"Ya Phai! In Vietnam he killed many children. He beat my friend to death. He almost kill me with a cane."

"How you want to do it?" asked Masure.

"With my hands," said Lam with a vengeance.

"OK. Order two beers and a pot of hot tea. But we pour the beer under the table and drink the tea. You got it? When he leaves, we follow. Agree?"

"You help me?" asked Lam, astounded.

"How many kids you say he killed?"

"Maybe ten. Maybe more."

"You bet. Now order the tea."

When Waa left the bar they followed him to the canal, where he caught a water taxi. From a safe distance they followed. As the longboat skimmed across the surface of the canal at thirty knots, Masure studied Lam's face. His eyes were fixed on the boat ahead like radar tracking a moving target. Hate oozed from his pores. Pent-up rage and anger radiated from his face like rays from the sun.

Over the sound of the longboat's powerful engine, Masure yelled, "What did the skipper teach you, Lam?"

With the wind blowing in his hair and canal spray on his face, Lam yelled back, "He teach me to know the enemy outside and the enemy inside. The enemy inside me wants me to kill Waa. I become a SEAL so I could kill Waa."

"Then do it," growled Masure.

Ten miles up the canal in a quiet residential area south of Bangkok, the water taxi stopped and Waa got out. He paid the driver and walked off without looking back. The SEALs hurriedly jumped off the longboat, throwing a wad of baht notes at the boatman. Silently they followed Waa to an alley similar to the muddy backstreets of Saigon. Masure sprinted to the corner and up two blocks, leaving Lam alone in pursuit. Walking briskly, Lam closed the distance.

"Lai dai, do mae!" he yelled in Vietnamese.

Waa stopped in his tracks as if frozen by the sound. Then he slowly turned to face his pursuer. In the poor light of the alley he tried to make out the person who was following him.

"What do you want, boy?" he growled in a deep, guttural, Asian tone. The metallic click of a switchblade sliding in place sent shivers up Lam's spine. Lam walked closer.

"Do I know you, boy?" he asked in a cold voice of unconcern.

Lam stood silently studying Waa. He had aged a great deal in the eight years since Lam had escaped from Vietnam.

"You are one of those little American bastards. I know you," said Waa with a smirk.

Lam reached out his left hand and Waa struck at it with the knife. Before Waa could recover, Lam caught him with a right-front snap kick that sent him to the ground. From out of the shadows Masure stomped on his knife hand. He picked up the blade and slipped back into the dark, leaving Waa and Lam on equal terms. As Waa got to his feet Lam kicked out with his left foot, using it as a counterweight to snap forward his right foot. Waa went for the fake. The chicken kick hit him squarely in the face, full force, bursting his nose and lips and sending him to the ground. Waa was rolling in the alley in a half-conscious state when Lam stomped on his leg just above the ankle. He pulled himself into a fetal position for protection, but Lam rolled him on his back and sat down on his chest. Using his fists, he hammered Waa in the face over and over until Waa was stunned like a dog that had been hit by a truck. His eyes glazed under the bloody pulp that was his face. Lam stood up, and as he rose he ripped off Waa's shirt.

"I want to see your dragons! For years they have tortured my sleep," yelled Lam emotionally.

Waa was too stunned to hear him. He tried to roll onto his side but Lam grabbed one arm and with an Aikido wrist lock brought him to his knees like a man about to be beheaded. With a quick downward-thrusting motion of his palm, he shattered the older man's locked elbow. As agony racked Waa's body, Lam grabbed his long snakelike braid.

"That was for Skinny Choi and Trinh. And this is for Tran and Nguyen," he said, yanking Waa up high on his knees by his queue.

"I want to see your black snake strike, Waa. Make it strike!"

With his right foot, Lam hook-kicked Waa in the groin. The pain caused him to convulse in spasms and wriggle on the ground like a worm that had been cut in pieces. When Waa stopped flailing, Lam grabbed his queue and yanked him back up on his knees again. From behind he reached his right hand around Waa's head and grabbed his chin. With his left hand at the back of Waa's skull, he paused, prepared to snap his neck.

"The enemy within and the enemy without," he said out loud. "The enemy within can turn you into an animal." He slowly released Waa, who slumped to the ground.

"Let's go, Senior. I not kill this old man."

Masure stepped quickly out of the shadows.

"How many children did you say he killed?"

"Beaucoup," responded Lam in a broken voice. "Beaucoup."

Masure took two quick steps, grabbed Waa's queue, and yanked him up on his butt. With his powerful right hand he reached down for Waa's chin and cranked on his neck in one vicious motion. Lam heard the vertebrae in Waa's neck snapping like twigs. For a moment he watched the body shiver and convulse like a chicken whose neck had been wrung. Masure put his arm on Lam's shoulder.

"Third lesson tonight, kid," he said seriously. "Some people just deserve killin'."

CHAPTER
25

Saleen dashed out of the TOC and hustled straight to Evans's makeshift office door. He knocked twice and rushed in.

"Enter," ordered Evans as Saleen barged through the door.

"Skipper, we just received a op-immediate message from the admiral," he said, handing Evans a stack of messages clipped to a board. "He wants you to meet Dr. Harris at noon at the Oriental Hotel in Bangkok."

"What? Harris? What the hell is she doing in Thailand?" growled Evans, scanning the message. The communiqué was a short "Personal For" that simply promulgated the location and time of the meeting. It was classified secret, for commanding officer's eyes only.

"I'll have a driver standing by in about ten minutes, Skipper."

Evans's TOC headquarters wasn't far from Bangkok, but traffic along the road from Pattaya to the capital was always terrible. The trip sometimes took several hours.

"Anything else on the board?" asked Evans, referring to the stack of messages underneath the "Personal For" from Arlington.

"No, sir. Just routine traffic wrapping up the exercise,"

responded Saleen, referring to the messages coordinating the redeployment of Cobra Fang units. "Not much in the intelligence traffic either," he continued, studying Evans's face.

"Thanks. Tell the driver I'll be ready to go in about half an hour."

"Skipper?"

"Yeah, Shooter," responded Evans, noting the concern in Saleen's voice.

"What's this all about?" asked Saleen. He took a seat in a rickety chair across from Evans and looked at him like a best friend wanting to help. Saleen had heard through the master chief's grapevine that Savarese had been hit on a mission in the Med. So he called around by AUTOVON until he found him. On a secure phone Master Chief Savarese, in his best cryptic symbolic language, had clued him in on much more than he should have.

"It's a classified program, Shooter. SCI."

"It's got something to do with those Spetznaz we locked horns with in Java, doesn't it?" pressed Saleen.

"What makes you think that?"

"The questions Harris kept beating to death. And it's big. . . . I know it's big enough to stretch from Egypt to Korea," he continued.

"You're right as usual." Evans nodded.

"That all you gonna say, boss?" complained the big man, a disappointed look on his face.

"That's all I can say. I'm just a mushroom."

"The kind they keep in the dark and feed a load of shit?" chuckled Saleen.

"Yeah. One and the same." Evans looked hard at Saleen and continued. "It seems some of the Russians we met in Indonesia have turned renegade and they're selling arms to the highest bidder."

"That big ugly Spetznaz colonel?"

"That's the one," confirmed Evans. "Only it's Major General Karpenko now."

"You think he's the one who put the hit on you in Chinhae?" asked Saleen.

"Probably. Those Korean goons were trying to kidnap me, not kill me; otherwise, they would have pumped me full of lead. I suspect Karpenko holds a grudge for what happened in Indonesia and he wants to personally pay his respects," explained Evans.

"You know, skipper, I've been a master chief a long time."

Evans stared at the big man, wondering what was coming next.

"And master chiefs talk to master chiefs," he said. "You know that."

"Nah," sassed Evans, facetiously shaking his head.

"Savarese got popped taking down a merchant in the Med. It had a nuke onboard."

Evans's eyes focused on Saleen's like a radar. He felt a lump in his stomach and a knot in his throat. His mind was working at light speed trying to put together the scattered pieces of information he possessed.

"He was in the hospital in Germany until just a few days ago," Saleen added.

"So much for SCI," commented Evans. SCI was short talk for *secret compartmentalized information.*

"I understand why the SPECOPS community is on high alert. Those Spetznaz are selling nukes. What I don't get is what Harris has to do with all this shit," Saleen said, fishing. "She's not exactly your regular Agency type, if you know what I mean."

"That's right. She's some kind of psychological expert in personality disorders."

"Personality disorders, huh? I guess that explains her attraction to you," laughed Saleen out loud, making light of the situation. The look of concern on Evans's face bothered him.

Evans smiled and shook his head. "Not everyone can get away with that kind of insubordination, Shooter," he snapped.

"I know too much, boss," he said with a smile. "I know too much. Don't you think she's a mite skinny for you?" he asked facetiously.

"She's married, too," added Evans.

"Ohhh man!" Saleen gasped in shock. "You been diddlin' some Agency guy's wife?"

"How do you know what I've been doin'?"

"I've tailed your ass halfway around the world, Derek Evans. I saw that woman sneak out of your room at the Hyatt. Don't tell me you didn't diddle her."

"Depending on your definition of *diddle,* it was momentary weakness on my part," explained Evans with a sly smile.

"Well, you best be real careful or you'll have a crazy Russian and a pissed-off Company man teamed up after your horny ass." Saleen abruptly changed the subject to business. "I'll have the loggy make reservations for you at the Asia Hotel in case you decide to stay overnight. You want me to put a tail on you?"

"No. Not this time."

"All right," cautioned Saleen with a grim expression. "Call me if you run out of ammunition."

"Thanks, Shooter. Just in case something's going down in our AO . . ."

"I know. I know. Make ready for a mission," said Saleen, finishing Evans's sentence. "But what kind of mission?"

"Mine countermeasure, of course," answered Evans with a smirk.

"Roger the fuck outta that. I'll stay in the kitchen and sharpen all the knives, and I'll put that green-ass platoon on a short string. No pucky, no drinky Singha," he chuckled.

The Oriental Hotel was one of the nicest and most expensive hotels in Bangkok, and the price of a room was well beyond Evans's per diem. So Saleen had made reservations at a smaller, less expensive hotel. Evans checked into the Asia, dropped off his shaving kit, and took a cab to the Oriental. He entered the lobby like a returning tourist and worked his way to the soft chairs where several fat Europeans sat listening to a little Thai girl play Beethoven on the piano. Grabbing a copy of the *Bangkok Times,* he took a seat and pretended to read the paper. He had an hour before his meeting with Harris and he intended to use it casing the place. As he peeked over the top of the newspaper, he saw a face in front of the hotel that stopped his breath for a moment. It was Natila Saraskina. She was getting in a taxicab in front of the hotel. She looked older and more sophisticated, but still stunningly attractive. Keeping his eye on her, he walked over toward the concierge, trying to get a better look, and bumped right into Alysin Harris exiting an elevator.

"Ah, Derek, you're early," she said pleasantly.

"Ahh, yeah, yeah. How are you?" he asked, awkwardly looking back at the hotel entrance. The cab pulled away with only Saraskina in the backseat.

"Great," she responded.

"Well, you don't look so good," he said absentmindedly, looking back at her. "You look so tired, Alysin."

"Well, thank you very much, Commander, for the nice compliment." She bristled. "As a matter of fact, I haven't slept in three days."

"Oh," said Evans apologetically for the faux pas.

"And you don't look so hot either, buster. Sort of like you've just seen a ghost."

"It's the water, Alysin. You know, different bacterial flora," he said, trying to regain his poise. He couldn't get Natila Saraskina out of his mind. *What is she doing in Bangkok?* he thought. *And why is Harris so wrung out?*

"Let's go up to my room so we can talk in private," she suggested.

"After you," said Evans, gesturing toward an open elevator.

As the elevator ascended, Evans evaluated Harris's physical condition. Her eyes were blurry and she yawned heavily. She was almost out on her feet. She leaned against him for support.

"People make mistakes when they're tired, Alysin. Big mistakes."

She looked at him with a glazed expression. "That's why I asked for you, Derek. Operation Fastback is all fucked up."

"Mighty strong words for a Ph.D.," he remarked as the elevator door opened onto the tenth floor. Harris glanced up and down the hallway before leaving the elevator. Seeing no one, she walked briskly to her room, opened the door, and bolted it behind them. She quickly turned on the radio and cranked up the volume too loudly. Putting her arms around him, she kissed him. When the embrace ended, she said, "I've missed you."

Evans said nothing. He knew the purpose of the meeting

was more serious than a love affair. The loud music was to cover the sound of their voices in case the room was bugged or someone outside was using a remote listening device. He waited patiently for her to speak.

"We recovered one of the bombs," she volunteered in a whisper.

"Yes, I know."

She drew away from him as if shocked by electricity. Looking him in the eyes, she asked, "Friends of yours in the teams, I suppose?"

"Yes."

"That's not very professional of the SEALs," she commented.

"Alysin, it's impossible to keep a secret like that for very long," he said. "Too many people involved."

Harris almost seemed to collapse in his arms.

"The whole goddamn world is falling apart, Evans, and I can't seem to stop it."

"You're just tired, Alysin. You're taking this too personally. Remember what you told me. We are just a small piece of a very big puzzle."

"We can't locate Karpenko," she persisted. "They tracked three strong signals for several days, and when they took the targets down all they found were emission generators. The weapon they recovered, that was just dumb luck."

"That doesn't surprise me at all, Alysin. You're riding on a camel, not a racehorse," he volunteered.

"Sometimes you are the most insolent asshole, Evans," she said sarcastically. "How do you know what the hell is going on? Rumor? Sailor talk around a bar?"

"Instincts, Alysin. Intuition. Confidence." He paused long enough to push her away and look into her eyes. "Saraskina is in Bangkok," he said.

"You saw her? You spoke to her?" she asked with a gulp.

He looked deeper into her eyes, searching for more clues.

"You saw her?" she murmured in a half-state of shock.

"Yes." He nodded.

"Ahh! Of course! Your ghost. You spotted her in the lobby. She serviced the damn dead drop when I was—"

"Why did you have me ordered here, Alysin?" he asked, already knowing the answer.

"Saraskina," she muttered.

"Go on," he ordered.

"Not long after Karpenko disappeared, the director received a personal letter. It was a simple, concise message composed of letters and words cut out of newspapers and magazines. It read: 'Perisislav, seventeen September. I will talk to Derek Evans. Bonafides: Ambush'—spelled incorrectly: a-*n*-bush."

"Seventeen September was the day the nuclear weapons were snatched?" he asked.

"Yes. The letters and words used in the message were cut out of articles we traced to East Germany. They were there, all right, but we couldn't locate them in time to run an op."

"So that's why you're so interested in me? You thought she might try and contact me on the sly, without Agency knowledge. You're my personal fuckin' handler, aren't you, Harris?"

"Personal? Yes! Fucking? No! I resent that characterization, Evans! I goddamn resent that!" she snapped. Harris was exhausted and her nerves were frayed.

"I'm sorry, Alysin. I'm really sorry. I was out of line. I didn't mean it like it sounded," he apologized.

After an awkward moment, she continued.

"We have suspected for some time that the Mossad has a mole inside the Karpenko organization. We believe Saraskina is their mole. Our people in Russia think she is Jewish, that she is the sole survivor of an entire family that was wiped out in one of Stalin's pogroms. She is alone, not really Russian, not really Jewish, surrounded by the most vicious men in the world. You are her fantasy. Her means of escape."

Evans stared at her, stunned. Images of Natila flooded his mind, images of her deep, dark eyes, memories of feverish lovemaking. For a moment he could hear her voice echo from past heated moments of passion: "I love you! I love you!"

"Perhaps she saw in you something special, the same things I see and feel."

Harris melted in his arms and kissed him desperately. When the kiss ended, she took a deep breath and laid her head on his chest.

"I believe she warned you in Indonesia because she loved you. You believe it was her. You told me so. The letter to the director was simply a way of reestablishing contact in case she has to bail out of the Karpenko-Mossad vise."

"And that explains why you sent for me, to meet with her?"

"Yes, of course. Maybe she knows where Karpenko is. Maybe she knows where the other two weapons are hidden. Maybe she will tell you something crucial that will end this nightmare. Do you realize Karpenko could have planted a thermonuclear bomb in Washington or New York or Los Angeles? We believe he has the capability to detonate the bombs remotely. Maybe she will confirm or deny this."

"Why didn't you people just level with me?" snapped Evans.

She breathed in heavily and leaned on him for support.

"Not my decision, Derek." After an awkward moment she continued. "This sort of information could cause widespread panic. Maybe they were afraid you would put all the pieces together. Everything is so damn compartmentalized we are tripping over each other."

"Somehow that doesn't surprise me, Alysin," said Evans with concern. He knew the score. Dimitri Karpenko wasn't the kind of man to limit himself to three nuclear bombs. The theft at Perisislav was just the tip of the iceberg.

"I have a load signal and a dead drop she arranged through Langley."

"Here in Bangkok?" he asked, referring to a secret communications drop.

"Yes."

"And that's why you're exhausted. You've been watching the drop for several days," he said, almost laughing out loud at the thought of Harris trying to catch Saraskina servicing a dead drop.

"Yes. And please don't laugh at me," she said in a hurt voice.

"Again, I apologize," he said sincerely. "But she's an expert at tradescraft. How do you think she's survived? You can't make contact like that. As long as you're watching she'll avoid the drop."

Harris glared at him with tired eyes. When she finally spoke it was in an exhausted voice.

"I don't even know what the bitch looks like. The pictures we have are several years old and in each one she looks like a different person. She serviced the damn drop with me staring right at it."

"You can't make contact like that, Alysin. What was in your message?" he asked.

"That you are in Thailand and I can arrange a meeting with you."

"Hummm."

"I'll watch my drop for a reply and as soon as she answers I'll arrange a meeting."

"Sure. But you're out on your feet. Get some rest," he ordered. "We'll make contact with her," he said, knowing that Saraskina wouldn't agree to a rendezvous arranged by dead drop.

"Not yet," she smiled.

"And why not?"

"I'm your personal fuckin' handler, remember?"

She pulled him into an embrace and kissed him with renewed desire. As she kissed down his neck he asked, "What about your husband?"

"My marriage won't survive this job," she said, kissing down his chest.

"I'm sorry to hear that."

"Don't be! Enough talk, Evans. Enough talk."

She worked her lips up his neck to his ear and bit his lobe. He returned her interest, wondering if she was really capable of separating her job from her personal life or if this was part of the game plan. Thoughts of deceit haunted him all through their lovemaking.

Alysin Harris was exhausted, and soon after achieving orgasm she fell into a deep, almost comatose sleep. As she lay in the crook of his arm he listened to her breathing for half an hour. She was a fascinating woman, brilliant, beautiful, and dedicated to her work. Evans liked that in a woman. After all his fantasies about Dr. Alysin Harris, the real thing was no disappointment. She was one in a million and she had leveled with him in violation of U.S. security regulations. She had included him in on high-level briefings and he could tell by the look in her eye she wanted to tell him everything she knew. Duty compelled her to deceive him. But he knew that sooner or later he would be the bait for an elaborate trap and it was her job to handle him when the time came. Thoughts of deceit invaded his mind again.

CHAPTER

26

Before sundown Evans got out of bed and dressed quietly. Harris needed rest; when he left the room, she was in a deep sleep. He walked around the hotel for an hour, making sure he was noticed. He bought a couple of drinks in the bar and chatted with the bartender, hoping Saraskina would spot him. Finally, not wanting to disturb Harris, he walked to the Asia Hotel. He knew it wasn't likely he would see Saraskina again, but maybe she would see him. He took a seat in the lobby of the Asia that afforded a good view of the street and watched. For hours he watched. At midnight he gave up and went to his room. In keeping with his nature, he cautiously opened the door and scanned the darkness. A faint scent caught his attention, a distantly familiar smell. It wasn't the smell of the Orient, not some maid who had freshened his room, and it wasn't the scent of jasmine. His stance widened instinctively as he stepped quickly out of the doorway where his body was silhouetted against the light from the hallway. As he moved to the side he pulled the door closed, drew out his pistol, and dropped to one knee, peering into the darkness toward the window. Before his eyes adjusted to the dark, his ears tuned in on the faint breathing of a human being on the other side of the room.

"Did you have fun with your skinny CIA bitch?"

"It seems you've worn her out with the chase, Natila," responded Evans to the voice behind the curtain.

Saraskina opened the drapes slowly and looked down the barrel of Evans's Colt .45.

"Oh, dat's too bad, Ebans. I am so sorry for her," she said sarcastically. She was standing unafraid in the moonlight that poured through the window.

"You looks good, Ebans. Strong, manly. Just like I remember."

"You too, Natila. I saw you today," he said, putting away the pistol.

"Ah, so you spotted me in front of the Oriental?" she said with mock surprise.

"Yes. And you are as beautiful as I remember."

She responded to Evans's flattery almost facetiously. "You are so clever and so handsome. I wish I had run avay with you in Java."

"But for duty the decision would have been easy," he commented.

"Yah, but for duty."

Evans crossed the room and leaned against the dresser, facing her. She walked slowly toward him, moving like a cat in the moonlight, sensuous, sexy, and deadly.

"What do you want, Natila?" he asked, staring at her.

"No, Ebans. You tell me what you want."

"I want to know where Karpenko is. Where the weapons are hidden. Can he remotely detonate one of them?"

"So you know everything?" she said inquisitively.

"I know you saved my life in Indonesia," he said seriously. "You warned me in Korea. Thank you."

"A momentary weakness for my pretty American lover boy."

"Do you know where the weapons are hidden?"

"I told the Mossad everything I know. But then, they are not ones to share their information, are they? They want the weapons for themselves."

"Natila, if you are working for the Mossad, why do you want to see me?"

"I don't trust them, Ebans. Soon one of my associates will move to take my place or Karpenko will kill me. Maybe someone in the Mossad will blow my cover. I have taken too many chances. It is only a matter of time now."

"Kill or be killed, or disappear?" he asked more as a comment.

"Yah."

"The Israelis can give you a new identity," he insisted.

"If I go to the Mossad, they will treat me like the traitor I am. My parents were Jews, Ebans, but I feel nothing for such stupid archaic religious thoughts. I am only a Jew because I was born of Jew. In Russia that is a curse."

"What do you want from me?"

"Help me to disappear, Ebans. Help me disappear forever. I helped you. Return the favor. Life for life."

"But Harris can do that for you much better than I can," responded Evans.

"Yes. Maybe. Maybe not. Like the Mossad, the CIA would torture me with a million questions for years and years. And with all the spies selling out on both sides, Karpenko would find me. Death for me would be very slow and painful, Ebans."

"Why don't you help them eliminate Karpenko?" he asked seriously.

"You don't understand. No one can eliminate Karpenko. He is a master of *maskirovka*. He speaks many languages, has many safehouses, businesses all over the world, and lots of money. More money than you can imagine. Even the scar you put on his face is gone."

"Surgery?"

"Yah." The scar is gone but not the pain. It still drives him to madness. You must disappear, too, before he finds you and kills you slowly."

"When will he come after me?"

"He has already come after you. In Korea. As soon as he finishes the deal with the North Koreans and the Khmer, he will try again."

"When is that?"

"In a few days they will make the transaction," she replied.

"Will you help me get Karpenko?" he asked.

"No one can get Karpenko. No one! He is a master of *maskirovka* and he has a secret power," she declared.

Saraskina moved closer to Evans. The moonlight coming through the window illuminated her face and caused her eyes to twinkle. She had a special beauty about her that affected Evans profoundly. Through her eyes, he could see the beauty deep within. He could see the loneliness, rage, and fear, and the desire to do good despite her situation. Her eyes were like pools of black liquid as she stared at him like a lost child. The deeper he looked the more he saw himself, trapped in a system he no longer believed in, used by those around him. It was like looking into the eyes of a magnificent mako shark half out of the water, half dead. It killed to survive, not for sport or pleasure. Her eyes softened and teared up as she stared at him without speaking.

"So many nights I have dreamed of you. So many times I have made love to you to the grunts of a drunken brute."

With those words of surrender she collapsed in his arms. She felt as if she were on the island of Bali and he was again perceiving her inner soul as no other man had ever done.

"I wanted to run avay with you," she whispered.

"Why didn't you, Natila? I would have protected you," he said, drinking in the scent of her body. He could feel the heat rise. He could feel her breasts rise and fall with each breath.

"Because you were trying to recruit me for your CIA. They are all the same, you know. KGB, CIA, Mossad, all the same. They use people and when they are through with them, they throw them avay," she said, gently touching his face as if trying to touch a dream. He didn't respond to the comment verbally, but nodded his head in agreement. Slowly she sensuously stroked his face without taking her eyes off him. She ran her fingers through his hair as if touching a thing of great value, and then down his shoulders to his spine, where she dug her fingernails into his flesh. As she pulled him close she sighed with emotional release and clung to him like a child seeking safety. Evans could feel the passion of Bali come alive in his loins. The heat and scent of her body moved him. He wrapped his arms tightly around her and squeezed. There was something about her that profoundly affected his sexuality, like eating forbidden fruit. It unnerved him emotionally. He was a man dedicated to the control of his emotions in the face of danger, but in the face of passion he was inexperienced. A flood of feelings engulfed him as he responded like a teenager, abandoning reality for a time. When the real world returned, he found himself bathing in the warmth of her body, refusing to let her go. As he replayed in his mind the love song she sang him in orgasm, the fire in his body reignited. Gently she worked her lips down his neck to his nipples while caressing his manhood. Again his excitement was so intense he lost his sense of time, as if thrust into a dream. Passion possessed his soul. When he came down he held her in his arms for the rest of the night, unconsciously trying to make the affair last forever. Just before dawn she stirred.

"I have to go soon."

"Where do you want to live?" he asked with a sigh.

"Idaho."

"Idaho?" he said, surprised.

"Yah. I want a *dacha* in the mountains of Idaho. One with a private *banya.*"

"OK. How do you want to do it?" he asked.

"I defect to Harris if she is professional. I will exchange all the information I know for a new identity. I insist on going to U.S. with her, and when we reach U.S. I disappear from her. Then I will find you. You arrange through third party for my *dacha* and help me get new identity."

"Natila, I'm only a commander. I don't have the money for a *dacha* in Idaho."

"Ebans, I have lots of money. I want small, warm dacha in the mountains, where I can grow garden. You ever go to public *banya?*"

"Yes," he answered.

"Then you know why I want private *banya.* I want a place deep in the mountains where nobody goes."

She pulled away from his embrace.

"I have to go."

She was silent for several minutes as he watched her dress and comb her hair.

"Tell your skinny CIA bitch she is being watched. But I will meet her. I want to play the game with her, to meet her myself, to test her myself."

"She is very good. Much better than I first thought," he volunteered.

"Good. I will meet her at nine o'clock this morning in the restaurant at the Oriental Hotel. The recognition signal will be an orchid on my dress, here," she said pointing to her left breast. "Bonafides is, 'Thailand grows the most beautiful orchids in the world.' If I like her I will respond with, 'The only orchids that grow on the Steppes are snowflakes.' Countersign is, 'I like wildflowers because they have to be strong to survive.'"

"Natila, why play this silly spy shit? You know who she is," complained Evans.

"I want to see how she plays this game. Call it curiosity."

Evans knew that if Harris played the game poorly, Saraskina would put into effect an alternate plan.

"Where is Karpenko?" he asked coldly.

Saraskina leaned over and kissed him. "He and several men boarded the Turkish ship *Balikesir* in Istanbul. The ship's destination was Bombay. But Karpenko is going to Cambodia."

"The Khmer Rouge? Earlier you said the Khmer?"

"Yes. They pay very well in gold, jewels, and narcotics. They also give him a small island for safehouse."

"What the hell do the Cambodians want with a nuke?" he asked, frustrated.

"Ebans, you forget the Mekong River flows down from Thailand through Cambodia before it goes to Vietnam. They'll float the bomb down the river and end their problems with the Vietnamese in one blinding flash."

"But what about the fallout?"

"No, no, no, no. The wind blows always to the east, like the monsoons," she insisted.

"Cambodia! For Christ's sake. It's a forgotten country."

"Exactly. All Russians dream of beautiful warm beaches with coconut palms. Karpenko would be czar, and no one will dare threaten him for fear he will explode another bomb."

"Where are the bombs?" he asked, taking a deep breath.

"Karpenko hid them somewhere in Romania, I think. He will give them to the North Koreans and the Khmer. Maybe they are on the *Balikesir*. I don't know what he do with others."

"And the North Koreans will help deliver one to the Arabs?" asked Evans.

"Yes. You are so clever too. You know why?"

"Certainly. A world at war is easy to hide in. The Khmer will use the weapon on the Vietnamese. The Arabs will use one on the Jews and when the fighting is at its worst, the North Koreans will invade South Korea," he responded.

"Horrible people, these Koreans. They smell. I will tell your CIA woman what days to intercept the North Korean plane. That's all I know."

"Thanks, Natila. Thank you for everything," he said seriously.

She stared at his naked body and sat back down on the bed. She kissed him tenderly and said, "We must not wait so long before we do this again."

For several seconds he held her tightly. When she sat up she looked at him for a few seconds before speaking.

"He has the red mercury, but not the plans to make the neutron bomb. If he is successful with his current transactions, he'll get the plans from Moscow. There will be a coup in Russia if Karpenko is successful." She watched his face carefully for a reaction. "He has friends in Moscow. Many friends who want to go back to the old ways. I will tell the CIA woman everything I know. He also has Airborne Warrior." Again she watched his face for a sign.

"A viral weapon?" he asked, guessing.

"Yah. You know this?" she said, surprised. "It is like a biological weapon and a chemical weapon combined. The virus dies in only a few days because it replicates only a specific number of times. The disease kills eighty percent of the people who are exposed, but it quickly runs its course. They tested a strain in Africa and hundreds of people died a horrible death."

"The Ebola River virus?"

"No. Not that. Worse than the Ebola virus. Infection is by air, like influenza, so you must have a *dacha* far away from people. So now you know everything," she said with finality.

"No," he growled. "You haven't told me where Karpenko is going. Cambodia is a big country, Natila."

"I don't know where he is going," insisted Saraskina. "The Turkish ship was going to Bombay. Karpenko is going to Cambodia. Maybe he has hijacked the ship. I don't know."

Evans grabbed her arms forcefully. "I'm going to kill the crazy bastard this time."

"You cannot! You cannot win!" she shrieked.

"Bullshit!" snapped Evans.

"Ebans, Karpenko has the mistake of Airborne Warrior, a virus that has no cure. Everyone who was exposed to this virus died a horrible death, very quickly. It was abandoned by our scientist because it was too dangerous. If released it will spread by the wind. Maybe it will kill everybody on the Earth."

"A doomsday machine in a bottle?" he thought out loud.

"Yah. A bottle. A very small bottle he keeps on a chain around his neck."

"And if he is caught he will use it, like holding hostages?" inquired Evans.

"Like holding billions of hostages. If you attack him he will use this weapon before he dies. You see. He can become a czar. Czar of Cambodia, and when he has everything in place he will return to Moscow as the czar of Russia."

"Pleasant thought," said Evans. "A madman who has a doomsday device, controlling the world's largest army."

A feeling of complete hopelessness flowed through Evans's body as he contemplated the information she had revealed.

"Now kiss me quick. I must go," she insisted.

They kissed long and deeply as if it were their last. When she stood to leave, he asked, "Would you ask the concierge to send up a pot of hot coffee?"

"Anything for you, sugar," she said in a perfect Southern accent. She turned and walked to the door.

"Hot black coffee for my pretty American lover boy," she said, dripping with Georgia peaches.

Evans had two cups of the strongest coffee in Thailand before heading for the Oriental Hotel.

* * *

Evans knocked lightly on Harris's door and waited patiently for her to answer. When he saw the light change in the peephole, he knew she was still in her room. She saw him in the hall, opened the door, and headed directly for cover in the bathroom, still groggy from too much sleep.

"Alysin," he said, speaking through the bathroom door.

"Yes," she said, yawning.

"Hustle it up. We have to talk."

He heard the water in the sink running and the toilet flush. A few minutes later she emerged with puffy eyes. She yawned heavily and asked the most obvious question. "Where have you been?"

"You have a meeting with Saraskina at nine in the lobby restaurant."

"You saw her?"

"Yes."

"Where?"

"At the Asia Hotel."

"How did you find her?"

"I didn't, Alysin. She found me."

Harris stared at Evans, mouth agape, not really believing him. She had searched the planet for Natila Saraskina and couldn't find her. A few hours after she had enlisted Evans's help, he had made contact.

"After you fell asleep I walked around for a while, hoping to spot her. When it got late, I didn't want to disturb you so I went to my room at the Asia. She was waiting for me."

Harris's eyes were focused like radar. She was wide awake and bristling with electricity. "Did I put that mark on your neck or did she?" She glared.

"Alysin, let's keep this conversation on a professional level. OK? She wants to meet with you. She'll trade everything she knows for a new identity, and she knows a lot. Karpenko is on his way to Cambodia."

"Cambodia? That doesn't make sense, Evans. Not one damn bit of sense," argued Harris.

"That's what I said. Wait till you hear what she has to offer, Alysin."

Harris turned the volume down on the TV. Evans had the news channel blaring to cover their conversation.

"OK." Harris sat down on the bed and rubbed her face

with her hands. "OK. Does she know where the weapons are hidden?"

"No."

"Does she know where Karpenko is?"

"No."

"Then what the hell use is she?" snapped Harris, glaring at Evans.

"She knows the approximate time the North Koreans will make the move. She knows the name of the ship Karpenko boarded in Istanbul, and some other rather startling information."

"All right, Evans."

"Alysin, if you don't handle this like the consummate professional, she'll disappear, and with her a treasure of information. If you gain her confidence, she'll open up."

"Well, at least we'll have something in common to *chat* about," snapped Harris, glaring at Evans.

"Bad idea. Bad subject," cautioned Evans, referring to himself.

Harris was crumpling under the pressure. He didn't tell her about Airborne Warrior or the vial around Karpenko's neck. He gave her the recognition signals.

"Good luck, Alysin. And be careful. She told me you are being watched."

"Where are you going?"

"To find the fastest nondescript boat in Bangkok."

"What for?"

"Instincts, Alysin. Instincts," he said, leaving the room.

Natila Saraskina was sitting in the coffee shop of the Oriental Hotel when Harris walked in. She intended to judge her performance, and if she didn't like the chemistry she planned to use the ticket in her purse. It was a one-way ticket to Perth, Australia. She watched out of the corner of her eye as Harris coolly scanned the room, spotting her instantly. She took a seat near Saraskina and ordered the continental breakfast.

"That is a lovely orchid you are wearing," said Harris, eyeing the exquisite flower on Natila's dress.

"Why, thank you," said Saraskina in a deep Southern drawl. She carefully watched the self-doubt cross Harris's face and wondered if she should respond. She gazed at Harris for several seconds, undecided as to whether to make contact. Finally she decided to respond. "Thailand grows the most lovely orchids in the world."

"The only orchids that grow on the Steppes are snow-flakes," said Harris.

"What a strange thing to say," responded Saraskina with a knowing look. "I like wildflowers. They have to be strong to survive."

"I love all types of flowers, especially the wild ones," said Harris.

"Me too. Say, would you like to join me for breakfast?" asked Saraskina pleasantly.

"Why, thank you, miss," said Harris, mimicking Saraskina's Southern drawl. "My name is Donna Devoir. What's yours?"

Natila Saraskina made a deal with Alysin Harris.

Evans scoped out the junks in Bangkok Harbor. He knew what was coming. When he called Saleen for the return trip to Pattaya, he finished the conversation with one word. "Shipboarding!"

"Roger that, boss. We be ready."

CHAPTER

27

Evans and Saleen arrived at the American embassy in Bangkok after a ride from hell. The Thai driver Saleen called Parnelli Sawan floored the old jeep when he left Pattaya and didn't let up until he reached the embassy. Driving was a national sport in Thailand, and careening around an oxcart to face an oncoming bus was part of the game. The fact that it was played on the wrong side of the road gave Saleen heart palpitations. When the jeep screeched to a halt at the gate of the American embassy, Saleen looked at Evans, rolled his eyes back in his head, and took a deep breath.

"Captain, I ain't ridin' with this maniac again! I'm walkin' back," he insisted.

Inside the compound they were escorted to a restricted area and offered seats at a desk containing several red telephones. It took the communicator nearly twenty minutes to establish the secure phone link with Okinawa. When the call went through, the voice on the other end of the line grunted.

"Arlington here."

"Good morning, Admiral," responded Evans cheerfully. Arlington ignored the greeting.

"Evans, we have an emergency situation. I've just released a top-secret message with orders for you to conduct a highly classified mission."

"Sounds serious, Admiral."

"It is serious, Commander," said Arlington gravely. "Very serious."

"Sir, all I have here is a green-ass platoon. Several of them are right out of BUDS."

"That can't be helped. You are the only special forces with shipboarding experience within five thousand miles of the target vessel."

"But sir, shipboarding is last on my list of training priorities," responded Evans. "These men aren't ready for—"

"Evans," Arlington said, interrupting. "I don't want to hear your bullshit about mine warfare. I know what you've trained that platoon to do and I know what has to be done. Do I make myself clear?"

"Yes, Admiral. Crystal clear."

"No, I don't think so. But I'm going to make it perfectly clear even for a mule like you. There is no other choice. You have the only men in the AO with the experience to board an underway vessel and *you will* conduct this mission by any means at your disposal. Now is that crystal clear?" said Arlington gruffly.

"Yes, sir."

"I'm sending you the latest imagery and all available HUMINT. It should be there within the hour by secure fax. Agent Harris briefed you on Operation Fastback, so you know what's at stake here. In the last few days we've hit ten targets and no joy. Your target is probably another ruse, but it has to be investigated. How copy, over?"

"Good copy, Admiral. I understand. But I don't have much to work with—no boats, no helicopters."

"That's why you're at the embassy, Evans. The ambassador has been ordered to put all the assets in the area at your disposal."

"Admiral, I'm outranked by at least ten people. I saw General Kris's car in the compound. You know how these things go. I'll be getting marching orders from a bunch of heavyweights that don't know squat about SPECOPS."

"Just play the game, Evans," he said in an exasperated

voice. "Right now we've got ten other high-priority targets to worry about and they're scattered all over the goddamn planet."

"I get the picture, Admiral."

"Look, Evans. Do the mission your way. Improvise. You're famous for that. If you're true to nature, that's what you'll do no matter what I say. If they give you too much shit, call me and General Ashton will fix it with the NSC. And, Evans."

"Yes, sir."

"Just make it look like they're in charge, OK? do you know what I mean?"

"Yes, Admiral. Believe me, I understand."

"One more thing, Evans."

"Yes, sir."

"Keep Lieutenant Owen out of harm's way. Put him in charge of the task group or something."

Evans exploded.

"For Christ's sake, Admiral, he's the fuckin' platoon commander!"

Arlington interrupted with an equal explosion of words. "Do I need to remind you we are talking about the CNO's one and only son? And that I just gave you a direct fucking order?"

"No, you don't, *sir!* I copy, *sir!* Good copy, *sir!* I'll do it my way, and I'll make it look like all the assholes that outrank me are in charge! Evans *out!*" he yelled, slamming down the receiver. This was his last mission and his last tour of duty in the United States Navy. He was committed.

The young marine escort stood by silently with eyes wide open. He knew by Evans's one-sided conversation that he was talking to an admiral, and he knew that commanders weren't supposed to hang up on admirals, much less yell at them. When he saw that Evans had calmed down, he spoke.

"Sir, would you please follow me, sir?"

"Yeah!" snarled Evans, still bristling with anger.

Taha Ahmed Mohammed surveyed the remote airstrip in the Syrian Desert. It was typical. Nothing more than a huge area of tarmac in the middle of the desert floor. Such remote strips were common in Syria, Iraq, Iran, and Korea.

307

They were enormous wide areas along remote highways where aircraft could take cover in times of war. All that was needed to create an airfield were a few fuel trucks, a portable air-traffic control station, and a few remote landing lights.

The heat of the Syrian Desert was almost palpable. The temperature was 110 degrees Fahrenheit and the pavement on the highway was oozing tar. The air rose in shimmering waves off the tarmac, bathing the men in a desert sauna. Mohammed ordered teams of men out on each flank of the landing strip to build signal fires for landing lights. Using his truck he checked the position of each fire pit to ensure they were in the proper locations. Then he questioned them to verify they knew the exact time to light the fires.

Using his old American radio he called the two team leaders he had stationed at opposite ends of the desert road to check that they were still in position. Their mission was to stop all road traffic after midnight, what little there was in the middle of the Syrian Desert. Satisfied with his preparation, he realized that it was time for prayer.

Evans followed the young captain to a conference room where several staff personnel were seated. Two colonels were hovering over a map of the area.

"Hi, Commander, I'm Colonel Talbert, army liaison to the Thai military," said a leatherneck colonel who looked fifty-five. The way he sucked on the cigarette incessantly, Evans figured him for about forty-five. Evans introduced himself and Saleen to Talbert. The other men in the room stiffly introduced themselves.

"Colonel Reynolds, Marine liaison to the Thais," said a sharply dressed marine colonel in khakis. His uniform looked as if he had just taken it off a hanger. The spit shine on his shoes was like black glass. Evans was dressed in a well-worn camouflage uniform that looked as if it had been to war in Vietnam. The marine looked at him with disgust. A fat air force lieutenant colonel introduced himself to Evans, but ignored the master chief.

"Commander Evans, do you know what this is all about?" asked the stone-faced army colonel.

Evans glanced at Saleen. "Not exactly," he said noncommittally.

It was obvious the men in the conference room were completely in the dark. On the table in front of them and on the walls were maps and charts of Southeast Asia. Just as the air force lieutenant colonel opened his mouth to ask another question the door opened and the ambassador entered with General Kris and Alysin Harris. Everyone jumped to their feet. Harris looked as if she hadn't slept in a week. As they took their seats the ambassador looked at Evans, sizing him up.

"Gentlemen, thank you for coming. This is Alysin Harris, Central Intelligence Agency. You all know General Kris, I believe."

The ambassador looked at Evans again. "Commander Evans, I presume?"

"Yes, sir."

"Thank you for coming on such short notice," he said. "I have been informed you have the necessary expertise to conduct this mission."

"Yes, sir. I do."

The ambassador turned his attention to the men in the room.

"Gentlemen, Dr. Harris is going to brief you into a classified program that must remain close-hold. We have been assigned a very difficult mission that could have grave consequences for thousands of innocent people. The object of this meeting is to pool our collective brains and solve this problem. Dr. Harris," he said, ending his mandatory introductory speech.

Harris stood and addressed the men in a professional tone that left no doubt she was in charge. "Gentlemen, about a year ago a cabal of Russian soldiers stole three nuclear weapons from an arsenal in the Ukraine." There was silence in the room as everyone stared at Harris, anxious to hear more. "Their intentions are to sell the weapons to the highest bidder."

"Excuse me, Agent Harris," interrupted Evans. "I see no reason to review history. Our mission is to board and seize a merchant vessel in the Gulf of Thailand."

"As you were, Commander!" snarled Kris. "You're out of line!"

"I don't think so, General. We're wasting time, so let's cut to the chase," growled Evans.

"I said, *as you were,* Commander!" snapped Kris, bug-eyed with anger.

Harris interrupted the exchange.

"Perhaps Commander Evans is correct. I'll try to be brief, Commander," she said apologetically. "A coalition of special forces is attempting to prevent delivery of nuclear weapons to North Korea, Syria, Libya, Iran, and Iraq. However, recent information indicates that the Khmer Rouge may be a possible buyer. As Commander Evans indicated, the vessel in question is nearing the Gulf of Thailand as we speak."

There was a hush in the room. They all knew that Pol Pot was a maniac who was capable of anything. He had murdered millions of his own people for no apparent reason and had gotten away with it.

"Unfortunately coalition forces are too far away to prosecute this target," she said, pointing to the map. "The only special operations forces in the area belong to Commander Evans."

"Unfortunately with the end of Exercise Cobra Fang most of my assets have returned to the States," commented Kris with a glazed look. "I hope these forces of Commander Evans's aren't the ones I observed during Exercise Cobra Fang."

"General, they are one and the same, and I suggest you have a long talk with your Major Oceanbine, who paid good money to have the Thai marines embarrass my men," snapped Evans.

The general looked taken aback. Evans and Saleen sat emotionless as the ambassador and the other men stared at them. Harris continued her briefing before anyone escalated the verbal skirmish.

"Several weeks ago, the survivors of a Turkish vessel put into Bombay. The story they related was horrible. General Karpenko seized the vessel on the high seas. Somewhere off the tip of India, he transferred some cargo to a second ship of unknown registry and let the people go. The vessel we acquired on satellite two hours ago in the South China Sea is one of several potential targets. It appears to be on course for Cambodia. At present it is located here," she said, pointing to a chart on the wall, "about two hundred miles off the tip of Vietnam."

The ambassador spoke up. "If they are successful in getting a weapon ashore in Cambodia or Vietnam it may be impossible to retrieve it without great loss of life."

"Yes, sir," responded Harris. "We're trying to move a specially trained unit into the region, but we're running out of time and options. It takes a couple of days to break down and build up their special boats and helicopters. Besides, this may be another false target."

"I see," said the ambassador.

"The ship has been traveling at about eight knots. She can make land in Vietnam in about twenty-four hours and the coast of Cambodia in less than thirty hours."

"Mr. Ambassador," said General Kris, "since time is of the essence, I suggest we commandeer a fast patrol boat from the Thais and use the embassy helicopter to put Commander Evans and his troops aboard the vessel as soon as possible. I have several outstanding marines still in the country that can assist in seizing the vessel."

"No," interjected Evans. "The helicopter doesn't have long enough legs to reach the ship."

"And a military patrol boat would eat a rocket at a hundred yards if the Spetznaz are on board," chimed in Saleen.

"Then what do you suggest, Commander?" asked the marine colonel, somewhat cynically.

"The fastest junk in Bangkok Harbor," responded Evans instantly.

"Why, that's preposterous!" shouted General Kris.

"No, it's not," argued Evans. "The fancy ones with the handrubbed teakwood decks can make fifteen knots in good weather and they are large enough to carry all my men and several sampans and Zodiacs."

Harris stared at Evans. A smile of realization crossed her face. "Of course," she said. "Be sneaky. Do the unexpected. A junk could pull alongside a merchant in these waters and not arouse attention."

"Trying to get aboard a defended steel ship in a wooden boat is preposterous," reiterated a marine colonel, echoing his general.

"Ambassador, she is four hundred miles south of here, headed this direction at eight knots. Khmer strongholds are in the north of Cambodia. If the Khmer are the customer, the ship has farther to travel than we do. If you have the money, sir, gold, I can depart within three hours and close the ship in less than twenty-four hours."

"And how do you propose to find the ship once you are at sea?" asked the ambassador curiously.

"We'll establish a satellite radio communications link between the embassy and the junk, and you can keep me continuously updated on the ship's track."

"I see," responded the ambassador. "Clever."

"We'll plot an intercept course and after dark we'll board her underway using Z-birds. If possible, we'll board her at anchor off the coast of Cambodia or Vietnam with sampans," continued Evans.

"And then what do you propose to do, Commander?" asked the marine colonel sarcastically. "Beat on the hull with your fists?"

Saleen slammed his massive fist down on the conference table. His face froze as if he intended to reach across the table and snatch the colonel out of his chair. With a wild-eyed look he growled in a deep resonant voice, "We'll kill everybody onboard that vessel if we have to, and we'll put her to sea, Colonel!" Saleen glared at the marine until he looked away. It was clear he was annoyed with the amateurish nature of the questions being directed at his boss.

"Ambassador, this is ridiculous. What if the junk breaks down or Commander Evans and his men get shot up? Why don't we request an F-18 to bomb the ship?" suggested the fat air force lieutenant colonel.

"No!" snapped Harris. "That would scatter radiation for miles and poison the entire South China Sea. That is preposterous!"

There was silence for a minute before Harris spoke.

"Mr. Ambassador," said Harris, "Commander Evans's orders are to board and seize the vessel. He has the men and the experience. Our orders are to assist him."

The ambassador looked from man to man, slowly rubbing his chin. He paused at Evans and for the first time noticed the worn uniform and the thickness of the muscles bulging beneath the camouflage.

"You are quite right, Ms. Harris. Gentlemen, we are wasting time. I'll release the gold immediately. Good luck, Commander," he said, standing to leave.

Evans dispatched Saleen to Pattaya to get the men, munitions, and equipment ready while he, Harris, and an entourage of embassy staff personnel bought the sleekest junk in Bangkok. He knew the vessel he wanted, and with gold bullion, it was his with little negotiation.

CHAPTER

28

"Delta Tango Niner, Delta Tango Niner, this is Delta Oscar Three, over?"

"Delta Oscar Three, this is Tango Niner, roger over."

"Tango Niner, Pigeon Eight Five is in descent. Vicinity, Bacău. Traffic Control Tokyo verifies planned route of Pyŏngyang, Novosibirsk, Moscow, Novosibirsk, Pyŏngyang. How copy? Over."

"Good copy, Oscar Three. I have track. Pigeon Eight Five is on descent. Vicinity of Bacău. Not on flight plan. Break! Tango Foxtrot One, Tango Foxtrot One, this is Delta Tango Niner, over?"

"Delta Tango Niner, this is Tango Foxtrot One. I copy all. Maintain track. Report changes in course and speed. How copy, over?"

"Delta Tango Niner, good copy, roger out."

Thompson, Gomez, Savarese, and the forty members of Gold Team sat around the aircraft hanger listening to the airborne chatter. The two AWACS aircraft were tracking a North Korean 737 that had deviated from its flight plan. Tango Foxtrot One was the call sign for the European headquarters of the coalition. It was located in Italy, where a huge antenna farm linked the whole operation together.

One aircraft, stationed over South Korea, was orbiting at thirty-seven thousand feet. It was in communication with a second aircraft over Europe at thirty-six thousand feet. Another AWACS bird was in position over the Persian Gulf. For several days the coalition had maintained special aircraft aloft, monitoring all traffic remotely related to North Korea. Thompson looked at Savarese with a gleam in his eye when the AWACS confirmed that the North Korean 737 was off course and descending into Romania. Commandos all over Europe, the Middle East, and Asia did the same. They were like cats sitting at a mouse hole waiting for the mouse to make a move.

Gomez looked at Thompson. "I'll see if there's anything new in the spook shack."

"When you come back, Loco, bring me a cup of coffee and a lot of action," said Thompson with a grin.

By accident, the SEALs were in excellent position for the call. Their location was in southern Turkey just north of the Syrian border. They had been given the remote sector of the earth because everyone in the plans department of the coalition staff thought all the action would occur in Northeast Asia or at sea, boarding ships. Army special operations forces were even in position to conduct an interdiction at sea, a job the SEALs were specifically trained for. The coalition was dominated by army and air force personnel, most of whom knew little about special operations. All the choice assignments, the ones likely to see action, were give to the army special forces and the British SAS. The SEALs, specially trained for underway shipboarding in rough seas, were relegated to obscurity in the Turkish desert. There wasn't a body of water for six hundred miles. The look on the faces of the fat staff officers at coalition headquarters in Italy turned to awe when the 737 lifted off from Romania and headed south across the Black Sea. As Gomez got up to leave the card table, Thompson nodded his head to Master Chief Savarese.

"Shit, boss! I've checked the fuckin' gear ten times in the last four days. We're locked and cocked, sir!"

"Humor me, Master," he said, smiling. "I feel it coming, day by day," he sang in a lighthearted mood. Savarese was losing the card game. Thompson knew he wasn't complaining. He was just bored stiff. They were isolated in a desert with no booze, no women other than their support personnel, who were off limits, and there was nothing to do but play cards. Gold Team's gear was staged onboard the two Blackhawk helicopters sitting twenty meters outside the hangar next to a C-141 Starlifter. Their weapons were at their sides. Thompson was winning the hand with his pilots when Task Force One got excited about Pigeon Eight Five's southerly track. They listened to the airborne conversations like students listening to music, picking out only the information they wanted to hear. Pigeon Eight Five caught their interest.

Gomez walked out of the hangar toward several metal cargo containers sitting inside a razor-wire compound. They were specially configured shipping containers outfitted with state-of-the-art communications equipment. Outside the razor-wire was an antenna farm that linked them to Task Force One in Italy and allowed them to listen to the chatter coming from the trackers orbiting above Europe, Asia, and the Persian Gulf. Gomez looked at the young guard in front of the metal container and strolled by without showing his badge.

"Lieutenant! Sir! I have to see your badge," said the young sailor dressed in camouflage fatigues.

Gomez stopped and grimaced. "How many times have you seen my badge in the last two weeks, Johnson? How long have we been stuck in this shit hole?"

"Sir. You know the rules. I'm supposed to see everyone's badge."

"Johnson, your job is to stop the bad guys. The bad guys are the ones you don't know. You know *me!*"

"And you know the rules, Lieutenant. I'm supposed to check everyone's badge to see if they're on the list," said Johnson, "or Commander Thompson will kick my ass."

"Johnson, there's no one out here but us, for Christ's sake."

Gomez had left his badge on his cot and he didn't want to go back to get it. He saw the sailor's right hand move slightly toward his pistol.

"If you put your hand on that pistol, Johnson, I'll knock you on your ass," snarled the stocky Cuban.

"OK, Lieutenant Loco. Go on in. But when the commander kicks my ass I hope you feel bad," said the sailor with a worried expression. Loco wasn't called crazy for nothing.

"The commander's a probable, Johnson. I'm a sure thing," said Gomez, walking inside the wire compound.

Outside Washington, D.C., Staff Sergeant Steven Chaffin was busy at his desk tracking ten emissions with the geosynchronous satellite when the sexy voice programmed into his computer broke his concentration.

"Oh, Stevie, I have something new to show you."

Chaffin looked at his CRT and saw a new firefly glowing in eastern Romania. It was near the same area where the false emissions had originated before the failed operations in the eastern Mediterranean. He reached for the phone and called his lieutenant.

"Chaffin, this had better be a goddamn good signal," yelled Lieutenant Vernon loudly into the receiver. "I'm tired as shit of all your false signals," she complained.

"Lieutenant, it's coming from that same area in Romania."

"I'll be right there, Chaffin."

Chaffin confirmed the coordinates and tracked the signal for two hours to a remote airfield near Bacău. From there the signal began to move south at almost six hundred knots across the Black Sea.

Gomez was walking into the spook shack just as Chaffin's information was transmitted to Task Force One. The communications station in Washington, Task Force One, and two of the AWACS were all trying to talk on the same net at the same time. Gomez caught Delta Tango Niner's report of the 737 simultaneously with the order from Task Force One to start turning up their birds. He ran out of the spook shack in a sprint.

"Put your hand on your pistol, asshole," he yelled over his shoulder at Johnson. "The bad guys are on their way."

317

Johnson watched Gomez sprint toward the hangar. His eyes got big as saucers as he scanned around the desolate airfield.

Taha Ahmed Mohammed always prayed before a mission. When he was satisfied with the preparations, he took his prayer rug out of his truck and carefully placed it on the ground. Facing Mecca, he prayed to Allah for deliverance from the Jews. Mohammed invoked the name of his father and six brothers, all dead from Israeli bullets. He said a special prayer for his mother and sister, killed by an Israeli bomb in a Palestinian refugee camp in southern Lebanon. Then he said a silent prayer for his lost comrades in arms.

Before each mission he always invoked the names of his fallen comrades one at a time, ending with his boyhood friend, Ahmed El-Sayed Farouk. The ritual took him more than half an hour just to say the names. It was his way of remembering them. He always ended with Farouk, because his boyhood friend had died of torture in an Egyptian prison, keeping the secret of Allah's revenge and prokaryotes. He would have a special place of honor at Allah's side. And the traitor Arabs who had tortured him to death would die a thousand deaths. Even after his body had been reduced to pulverized flesh, Farouk hadn't talked. Farouk was a martyr.

"Allahu Akbar. O Lord! Deliver our land from oppression. O Lord! Grant those in the struggle for freedom peace and forgiveness. Greet us on the Day of Judgment with the greeting of peace. For peace is from Thee. Here we come, O Allah! Here we come. No partner have You. Praise and blessings are Yours; the Kingdom too. No partner have You."

When Mohammed's prayers were finished he carefully folded up his rug and put it back on the seat of the truck, over the top of his loaded pistol. He lit a cigarette and leaned against the fender to rest his mind for a few minutes before continuing the struggle. For some reason a shiver ran down his spine. An omen in a hot desert. The heat of the day was giving way to the cold of night that comes quickly in a desert. His mind flashed back to the face of the Egyptian magistrate he and Farouk had executed in Cairo. That face of fear had always haunted him, maybe because it was an Arab face. In all his long years of struggle against Jewish oppression he could not understand why his Arab brothers failed the Palestinian cause.

The Jews had come to the land of Palestine out of Egypt and killed the Palestinians like dogs. Then the Romans dispersed them to all corners of the earth, where their Jewish ways invoked the wrath of all peoples. The curse of the Palestinian people was that the Jews had returned to kill them like dogs again, to take their land and scatter them to the other Arab lands. It was an Arab diaspora, not the creation of a Jewish state. But soon, very soon, Armageddon would befall the Jewish city of Tel Aviv. The Blood of the Lamb smeared over the door was the signal for all Arabs to quietly leave the cursed city. It was a signal delivered as a religious proclamation to all the faithful. When the Blood of the Lamb appears above the door, visit the holy places in Jerusalem, or die. When Tel Aviv was destroyed, the invasion would begin, an overwhelming flood of Arab peoples from all directions. It would be over before the satanic American forces could do anything about it.

Now that Iran had a Russian nuclear weapon and Libya had chemical weapons, success was assured. Colonel Mohammed finished another cigarette and ordered his men to light the fires, creating a pattern that could be seen from outer space. He thought it funny that both the Arabs and the Jews were begat from Abraham. The Arabs were from the first son and the Jews from the third.

The covenant is the root of all the problems, he thought. *If only the Jews would stop insisting they were the only chosen people of God, perhaps there could be peace between the children of Abraham.*

Near midnight, Mohammed's thoughts changed. He took out the radio the Korean agent had given him and began calling in poor English. "Airplane, airplane, this is ground, over."

Over and over he called until the thickly accented voice of an Asian answered.

"Ground, this is airplane. I see you. OK to land?"

319

"Yes. OK to land the plane," answered Mohammed excitedly.

"Stand by for landing," returned the Asian pilot.

The landing lights of the jet came on five miles west northwest of the desert strip. Mohammed was facing Mecca when the aircraft magically appeared in the sky. He was on his knees praising God.

"Path Maker, this is Tracker One Zero, over?"

"Path Maker, roger, over?"

"Path Maker, vector right ten degrees, direction one-zero-five degrees, slow to four-five-zero knots. Maintain altitude six-zero-zero feet AGL."

"Roger, Tracker, vector right ten degrees, course one hundred and five degrees, slow to four hundred and fifty knots, maintain altitude of six hundred feet AGL, Path Maker out."

"Break. Falcon Leader, this is Tracker One Zero, over?"

"This is Falcon Leader, roger, over?"

"Falcon Leader, slow to niner-zero knots, maintain altitude one-zero-zero feet AGL."

"Roger, I copy, same course, ninety knots, one hundred feet AGL."

"Roger that, Falcon Leader, Tracker One Zero out."

"Break. Starlifter, this is Tracker One Zero, over?"

"This is Starlifter, I copy all."

"Starlifter, vector left ten, course one-zero-five, slow to two-zero-zero knots, maintain altitude one-zero-zero-zero feet AGL."

"Roger, Tracker. Understand course one hundred and five degrees, speed two hundred knots, altitude one thousand feet AGL."

"That's a rog. Tracker One Zero out."

Tracker continued vectoring and timing the approach of several sorties of jets, helicopters, and a cargo plane toward the remote desert target, while simultaneously talking to UN headquarters in Italy. Updates provided by Sergeant Chaffin's geosynchronous satellite fixed the true target precisely in relation to the runway in the desert. A ROARSAT passing overhead sent imagery of the landing strip flickering in the darkness of the desert below. The coordinates were linked instantaneously to Tracker One Zero. The old men in the Pentagon ordered more coffee and crossed their fingers as the images on the screen converged.

Colonel Taha Ahmed Mohammed watched the 737 screaming toward him down the road, and for a moment he thought that the big bird would overshoot the desert strip and be unable to turn around. But it whined and shuddered to a stop directly in front of him. The pilots looked out from the cockpit and hurriedly ordered the crew to open the hatch. As the ladder dropped down from the plane, Mohammed praised Allah again for the gift of deliverance. When he had finished his prayer he ordered his heavy truck to back up slowly to the plane's open cargo door, and thirty men began to struggle with a huge metal container. When the container was loaded on the truck he praised Allah again, just as Path Maker roared up the desert strip at four hundred knots, less than fifty feet off the deck. The wedge formation of five planes ripped up both sides of the tarmac, narrowly missing the wingtips of the 737. The shock and blast from the low-flying aircraft were sufficient to knock every man to the ground, and with the added noise and blast of the ordnance the scene was a nightmare straight out of hell. The warthogs disappeared as quickly as they appeared, like phantoms in the night. They were tank killers designed to fire explosive bullets that penetrated armor. They routed and tore up the ground like warthogs in a muddy field. Mohammed's men on the flanks of the 737 were ripped to shreds like pieces of meat in a butcher's grinder. The 20mm cannons had passed within twenty feet of the 737's wingtips.

Mohammed regained his senses and pushed himself up on his knees. For a few seconds the desert was quiet, and then he heard the moans of the dying. Before he could decide what to do, the second wave of warthogs blazed up the desert strip, lighting the night sky. Like giant ray guns blasting out of the sky they set the pavement on fire with tracers.

"Loco, this is Big Dog, over?" called Thompson. His voice sounded metallic and distantly distorted through the short-range radio. He was only a hundred yards away in the lead helicopter, screaming along five hundred feet off the desert floor.

"Roger, Big Dog," responded Gomez, yelling over the whopping noise of chopper blades.

"You guys ready?" asked Thompson over the whine of the engine.

"Roger, dodger, Big Dog. Ready, willin', and able," responded Gomez.

"You see the path those warthogs blazed up that road?" asked Thompson.

"Yeah. I don't think the greedy bastards left anyone for us to kill," replied Gomez.

"Watch your ass, Loco. There'll be tangos shooting at it in three Mikes," said Thompson. "I'll set down two hundred meters this side of the runway to the west of the bird. You do same two hundred meters east, this side of the runway."

"Roger, Big Dog. I copy my posit to be two hundred meters east of the runway, this side."

"Roger. Good copy. Can you tell which way the wind is blowing?"

"Roger, Big Dog. Wind is blowing smoke toward the south."

"Roger, I concur. As soon as you clear your bird make comms with me. Set paraflares overhead on my command."

"Roger, Big Dog. Good copy," responded Gomez.

Thompson ordered the choppers in behind the warthog's second pass. They jumped off the birds as soon as the wheels touched the ground and began to move toward the 737. Halfway to the jet they dropped to the ground.

Thompson spoke to Gomez through his throat mike. "Loco, you in position?"

"Roger, boss. Let's do it."

"Paraflares aloft!"

"I copy!"

Two men in each group began shooting 40mm illumination grenades in the air in ten-second intervals. On line the SEALs began to wade in toward the jet. As they walked, weapons at the ready, the nervous Korean crew tried to button up their aircraft for takeoff. Thompson ordered the sniper with the fifty-caliber rifle to waste the jet's tires.

Several huge explosions pierced the night as the tires ruptured over the sound of turning rotors and whining jet engines. Sporadic gunfire from Mohammed's surviving men was met with awesome firepower directed low and away from the jet. The snipers on the flanks used exploding rounds on the muzzle flashes of their enemy. Grenadiers pummeled the flanks with high-explosive grenades. In the eerie light from the parachute flares, Colonel Taha Ahmed Mohammed saw a phalanx of commandos cautiously working their way toward the jet. He made a decision. The jet engines on the 737 above him were screaming as the pilot tried to move his aircraft on flat tires. In desperation he leapt to his feet and ran to the cab of the truck. Jamming the heavy vehicle in gear, he lurched away from the jet, bumping over the bodies of his dead men. Thompson ordered the front tires of the truck shot out. They exploded with a hiss, but Mohammed continued to drive on the rims. Then Thompson ordered the snipers to shoot out the rear wheels. Several shots rang out and the rear tandem tires exploded, but still Mohammed ground on down the road. Thompson carefully fired several bursts from his M-16 into the cab of the truck, but Mohammed ground on. It was traveling no more than ten miles per hour, wobbling on its rims, when it approached Gomez's position.

Gomez yelled into his mike, "Cease fire!"

No one was firing, because the truck had a nuclear weapon on its bed. Gomez threw down his rifle, ran up alongside the moving truck, and timed his approach so he could jump up onto the running board. Holding the door handle with his left hand, he drew his pistol with his right and stuck it through the open passenger side window. Mohammed found himself staring down the muzzle of a 9mm pistol. For a second the image of the Egyptian judge popped into his mind. But Mohammed didn't beg like a cowardly Egyptian magistrate. He slipped his hand under his prayer rug and in a flash pulled out his Beretta pistol. As the truck wobbled along on its rims, Gomez shot first, drilling Mohammed through the head. Death was instantaneous. The warrior of a thousand battles slumped over the steering wheel as the truck ground to a halt like a gut-shot water buffalo.

"Loco, you crazy son of a bitch. You OK?" yelled Thompson into his radio.

"Roger, sir. But the driver of this rig has got a bad headache!" came the response.

Thompson went back to action, ordering Starlifter to land.

"Tracker, Tracker, this is Big Dog, Big Dog, over? Tracker, you copy, over?" said Thompson, pumped on adrenaline.

"Big Dog, this is Tracker, roger, over."

"Bring in Starlifter on the double. Make sure he doesn't overshoot the runway. I got a seven-thirty-seven blocking the west end."

"This is Starlifter. I copy all, Big Dog. I have a visual on the bird and the truck," interjected the pilot in the C-141.

"Roger, Starlifter, Big Dog out," said Thompson, ending the transmission.

The big cargo plane landed and taxied smoothly down the road toward the Korean jet. A hundred yards from the 737 the pilot turned her around and brought her to all stop. The ramp dropped down and crewmen began to rush around the rear section of the cargo bay.

Thompson kept close guard over the Korean aircraft while the men loaded the weapon from the battered truck into the cargo bay of the C-141. The Koreans had buttoned up their bird and refused to deplane. Not wanting to stir up another firefight, he left them aboard the plane to their fate. When the 141 lifted off, Thompson ordered the Blackhawks back in for the trip back to Turkey. Before the helicopters lifted off he took muster and radioed Gomez, standing outside the other bird.

"Loco, this is Big Dog."

"This is Loco, over."

"What's your count?" he asked, taking muster.

"All present, sir."

"We got 'em all, Loco. Head 'em up, move em out," he said, climbing on the helo. Then he ordered the pilots to take off.

A mile from the target Gomez and Thompson looked back at the jet as the warthogs made their third and final pass directly up the center of the road. The jet exploded with a flash when the 20mm cannons ripped into its fuel cells. A huge red ball of flame leapt into the night sky, lighting up the desert as the SEALs helicopter screamed away from the holocaust at five hundred feet AGL.

"Another tragic airline disaster, Loco," said Thompson into his radio mike.

Gomez keyed his radio. "Yes, sir. I'd say no one survived that crash."

"They just don't build 'em like they used to," commented Thompson, spitting his chaw of tobacco out the side of the open helicopter.

"You know, I'll bet they're watching this in the Pentagon," said Gomez through his mike. He was right. They were and they were cheering.

Sergeant Chaffin was watching the desert, too, with his satellite. But what he saw wasn't something to cheer about. It was a cometlike signal spreading out slowly from the Korean aircraft. As one signal left the target area at several hundred knots in the cargo bay of the C-141, the other spread out like Chernobyl, spewing radiation across the floor of the desert. He picked up the phone.

"Lieutenant Vernon, you'd better come look at this!"

CHAPTER

29

Within four hours of the gold's changing hands, Evans was under way with twenty-five men and women dressed in local clothing. The vessel he had secured was shaped like a Chinese junk, but it was far from an old clunker. She was constructed of the finest teakwood in Asia and powered by a huge Cummings diesel that was so clean it could pass a white-glove inspection. The yacht belonged to a wealthy Chinese businessman who used her for weekend cruises in the Gulf of Thailand. She had all the amenities, from a wet bar to an Italian radar.

Before leaving dock in the Chao Phraya River, Saleen quickly established a tactical operations center in the galley. He strung an antenna wire from the mast for HF communications and set up a SATCOM antenna on deck. When the satellite communications link was established, he cranked up a secure fax and a voice net. Before the junk cleared the mouth of the Chao Phraya River, Evans had a fully functioning TOC, complete with a chart of the target ship's track and current position. Frequencies, satellite positions, and weather projections were plastered on the galley bulkheads. Lieutenant Kelly, Team Five's intelligence officer, pulled down the latest satellite imagery using the secure fax. She put together a real-time overhead picture of the target vessel and, with the assistance of DIA in Washington, D.C., compiled the necessary data on ship type and ship configuration for mission planning. The merchant was a forward-hold freighter with an aft superstructure that rose up three levels to the pilothouse.

While Saleen organized the TOC, Masure set up an armory and munitions area belowdecks. As soon as the junk was in open water in the Gulf of Thailand, he began drilling the boarding parties in close quarters battle, shipboarding, and weapons handling. Using the junk's cabin, Alpha Platoon practiced entry procedures and room clearance. They checked each other's web gear and rigged the climbing ladders to the mast to test them.

Even the Junkyard Dawg played his part as sheriff by directing the preparation of food and coffee and ensuring the decks weren't fouled with sampans, Zodiac boats, and unnecessary gear. By sunset, the junk was shipshape and the men were ready for action. All Evans had to do was watch, plan, wait, and think. The thinking part was the hardest, because he knew too much. It was anguish.

As the sun set, the junk was making a good twelve knots running before the wind, with the diesel wound up tight. At Sattahip they would hit the first way point and turn southeast toward Cambodian waters. In a little more than twenty-four hours the young men in his charge would meet the greatest challenge of their lives. They were bound for a killing ground, and someone was going to die. Evans stood at the railing, appearing to savor a gorgeous vermillion sunset. The last rays of the dying sun had turned the Gulf of Thailand to gold, but he couldn't see the beauty. His handsome, confident face hid the turmoil inside.

How am I going to do this, he thought, *without getting these kids killed? Without getting everybody killed. They're not ready for this kind of mission. This is insane. The whole damn op is insane.* Self-doubt consumed him.

If I trip the crazy bastard's trigger, he may wipe out the whole world just for spite. Then he thought, *Karpenko doesn't want to die. And he doesn't know that I know about the vial around his neck. He won't break it until the very last second of his life. To do otherwise would be an act of suicide. Not in character. I have to use his desire to live to my advantage. I have to use the element of surprise. Yes. Be sneaky and do the unexpected,* he said out loud, mouthing the words of his first master chief. The lessons of the past supported him.

But what do I do if it comes down to a standoff? he thought. *I wait. I wait until the very last moment before I let him win. That's what I'll do. I'll look for a weakness, take my best shot if it's clean, and if not I let him win. And losses? What about losses? He's willing to lose all his men to win. Can I stomach that?*

Evans looked at the men moving about the vessel. He saw Robinson joking with Jackson and Simons up on the bow. They were scared. Joking around was their way of hiding the fear. *They just got out of training. They're not ready for this mission,* he said to himself.

Owen, Masure, and Williams were sitting on top of the cabin talking quietly, taking in the sea breeze. At the stern Lam stood at the helm taking his turn at watch. *What's he thinking?* thought Evans. *Just a few hundred miles to the east of here are the people who starved and beat him as a boy. He nearly died right here in the Gulf of Thailand trying to escape. I wonder what he's thinking.*

The pressure of the mission was weighing on Evans's mind when Harris joined him with two cups of coffee. She handed him one without speaking, reading his face like a book.

"Thanks," he said, unable to smile.

"You're worried. I can see it on your face," she said.

Evans smiled to cover his inner anguish. "Aren't you?"

"You know, this is probably another false alarm," suggested Harris.

"I don't think so. Instincts, Alysin. Instincts. There are targets all around his most likely customers, and none have proven out. The special operations forces that are trained to do this mission are strung out so far they can't possibly take down every target. He abandoned the Turkish ship off India for another of unknown registry. Where is he going? Saraskina was working Southeast Asia under Karpenko's orders. I think she is correct. I think he's coming here to wait out the holocaust. What did she tell you, Alysin? The

North Koreans, the Palestinian Freedom Council, and the Khmer?"

"Yes."

"Anything else? Anything I didn't mention in my debrief? We need to confer here," he pleaded, looking closely at her face.

He hadn't told her about Airborne Warrior or about the vial around Karpenko's neck. She was exhausted and he didn't think she could handle the pressure. Three ninety-five-kiloton thermonuclear bombs were enough pressure. She had been working nonstop for months supported by coffee and catnaps. He had chosen not to tell her, and now wasn't the time either.

"No. Just the day the North Korean jet was supposed to pick up the bomb in Romania. Last night," she said, deep in thought.

Evans looked back at the sea. The sun was below the horizon and night was falling like a shadow over his soul. Time was running out. Saraskina hadn't told her about Airborne Warrior or about the doomsday vial around Karpenko's neck. If she had, Harris was deceiving him.

"What happened between you two at the Asia?" asked Harris.

"I sensed someone was in my room, Alysin. I slipped through the door like a cat burglar and stuck a pistol in her face," he growled. "She doesn't trust you. She doesn't trust anybody."

"She trusts you. Why?"

"I don't know."

"Yes, you do," insisted Harris.

"No, I don't."

"Well, I'll spell it out for you. She fell in love with you in Indonesia. She helped you and now she thinks you will help her. What did she ask you for, Derek? A new ID? A new life?"

Harris paused in her interrogation. She studied the sea and then Evans's face. "When this mission is over, I'm going to meet her in Jakarta and escort her to the States. She going to get a new life. Do you want to see her again, Derek?"

"No. She's a beautiful mako shark, fighting for her life. A man could be torn to shreds by a predator like that."

"Derek, I love you. When this is over, I'm going to rearrange my life. I hope you'll be a part of it."

She moved closer to him, seeking assurance.

"Alysin. Do you know what PDA is?" he asked.

"Ahh . . . no."

"In leadership, PDA means public display of affection. It's one of the cardinal sins of a leader," he said, looking at the men on deck. "It's kind of like crying before going into battle. It doesn't instill confidence."

"I understand," she said, taking a step back.

Evans wasn't just deflecting Harris's questions. He was keeping her at arm's length. He didn't trust her. And he didn't trust Saraskina. He didn't trust anyone but Saleen and his men.

"Alysin, would you take the helm for a few minutes? I want to talk to my crew."

She looked at him with a lost expression.

"They don't know what this is about. They are going into battle and they don't know what the hell the score is. I'm going to tell them."

"I understand. You realize this is probably just another merchant ship. And if you tell them what's going on, you will be violating your security agreement with the United States government," said Harris flatly.

Evans exhaled heavily. "Take the helm, Alysin," he ordered.

When all hands had gathered in the galley he told them about the missing nuclear weapons. He told them about the Spetznaz. But he didn't tell them about Airborne Warrior. Fear permeated the cabin. Then he told them the reason the Khmer wanted the weapon. To destroy Saigon. He read the fear and doubt on their faces.

"A warrior follows his instincts, men. There must be integrity in his actions and control over his emotions. Fear is the enemy. A warrior consciously chooses the things that make up his world so he can be exquisitely aware of everything around him, to attain control. Then he must act with controlled abandon for a cause higher than himself.

Duty calls us. If anyone wants out, see me by midnight. I'll let you have one of the Zodiacs. Sattahip will be ten miles to the east. Dismissed."

Several men and women came and talked to him, expressing their fear and confidence. He waited until one in the morning before going to sleep. No one quit.

Using updates from satellites tracking the merchant ship, and the global positioning system to plot their location, they sailed the junk to the northern coast of Cambodia near Kompong Som. They were in position well before the freighter arrived. Evans watched her drop anchor four miles off the coast. Before last light, she lowered a brow on the port side and began receiving boats. Evans studied the situation carefully with his binoculars and called the men around the galley table for a briefing. When they had gathered round, he described the plan of attack.

"This is what we're going to do, men. It's simple, because simple is best. Lam, when I give you the word you will pilot the junk three hundred meters north of the anchor chain, as if we are a fishing boat returning to port. Lieutenant Owen, Assault Unit One will enter the water up current and swim to the anchor chain. Don't, I repeat, don't climb until you see Lam approach the port brow. Establish comms with me as soon as you're on deck. Got that?"

"Yes, sir," answered Owen with wide eyes.

"After we drop off Assault Unit One, we will circle around the starboard side of the ship at about five hundred meters and drop off Assault Unit Two. Stick, paddle the sampans slowly like natives coming out from port. There is no moon, so unless they have NVGs they won't be able to see you. Sneak up on the starboard quarter and take cover under the curve of the stern. Maintain comms with me if you can. Listen for Lam's approach and don't begin your climb until we've attracted the attention of whoever's on deck. Got that?"

"Yes, sir," said Masure, grinning eagerly. The smile covered the fear he felt inside. Fighting Spetnzaz with AKs was one thing. Fighting them with a nuclear bomb onboard was quite another matter.

"Assault Unit Three will remain onboard the junk under

331

cover of the gunwale. Lam, we will continue around the ship at five hundred meters and approach the gangway. Everyone wait until Lam tries to sell the men on deck his catch. I'll keep talking to you over the inner-squad radio. At the first sign we have been made, I want Lieutenant Owen and Assault Unit One to cover the foredeck. Masure, you and Assault Unit Two cover starboard side and forward. Make sure of your targets, gents, before pulling the trigger. Assault Unit Three will hose the deck from the junk, and on my command will run up the gangway to the port side. Assault Unit One, *don't shoot any friendlies!* Is everyone clear on the plan so far?"

"Hoo yah!" said Robinson too loudly. He gulped like a child when everyone looked at him as if he had gone nuts.

"The first objective is to take the weather decks. Masure, I want you to take out as many guards as possible with the silencers. Shut and zip-tie all hatches as you go. Once they are on to us, we'll have to work fast to button up the ship. Assault Unit Three, at the sound of the first shot, we'll rush up the gangway and storm the port side of the ship. Be careful of your target. Be aware of what's behind your target. Once the shooting starts, work your way to the nearest open hatch. Toss in a concussion grenade and bolt the hatch closed. No fragmentation grenades! Concussion grenades only!"

Evans didn't want fragmentation bouncing off the bulkheads of the ship. A sliver of metal might break the vial around Karpenko's neck. He was hoping for a lucky break. Perhaps a concussion grenade exploding inside the confines of the ship would knock Karpenko unconscious.

"Once we control the weather decks, we will own the ship. Then we'll take our time clearing the inside, level by level, compartment by compartment. OK, does everybody understand how we're going to do this?"

The men nodded in the affirmative, eyes filled with fear. This was the real thing, the thing they had been training for. There were men on the freighter who would kill them, given the least opportunity. Evans asked for questions and spent several crucial minutes clarifying the plan of attack. He knew the plan was flawed. It was pure improvisation, ad lib, but it was the best he could do under the circumstances.

"One more thing. Rules of engagement. Don't shoot unarmed men. Force them overboard. We still don't know that the bad guys are on that freighter. OK. Let's get ready," he ordered with a grim face.

"Assault Units One and Two, weapons check," said Masure.

"Assault Unit Three, weapons check. I want to see your shooting positions," said Saleen. "All hands stay below the gunwales."

As the men prepared their equipment Evans talked to Lam.

"Do you understand the mission?" he asked.

"Yes, sir. I understand," he answered quietly. "I go toward port and make big circle like coming out of port behind the ship. Then I try to sell them fish."

"OK, then, what's wrong?" asked Evans, seeing a strange look on his face.

"The Khmer Rouge wants to blow up Saigon," said Lam. "I know why."

"Why?"

"Because they hate the Vietnamese. The Vietnamese invade Cambodia and put many people to death. They hate them like I hate them. They want the nuclear bomb so they can destroy them. The Mekong River flows through Cambodia and into Vietnam. It very easy to get to Saigon by big river junk," he explained. "I want them to blow them up."

"Why?" asked Evans clinically.

"Because I hate dem! What makes me angry is, maybe I die to save the people who make a scar on my mind. They starve me and call me dust of the earth. Why should I save the Vietnamese, the people I hate?" he asked.

"You're a warrior. This is no place for hate or anger. The babies in Saigon didn't hurt you," said Evans. "They didn't beat you."

"I understand what you mean, Commander. I think I achieve warrior enlightenment when you make me run to IB three times. You and Senior Chief Masure help me a lot. But how do you say, ei-ronee?"

"You mean irony?" asked Evans.

"*Ya Phai.* Irony. They try to kill me and I try to save dem.

And now I only afraid of letting you and Alpha Platoon down. Maybe I cop out again, sir, like Hell Week."

"Oh, I don't think so," said Evans with confidence. "The secret to unit integrity is creating a mind-set where one is more concerned with letting his buddies down than he is with his own safety."

"I not really understand what you mean. But I not cop out unless you make me crash into giant oil rig at night. OK?" He smiled.

"OK. No giant oil rigs," agreed Evans. "Just a seagoing freighter."

Evans looked forward. Harris was dressed in black pajamas like Saleen, who looked ridiculous because he was twice the size of a Cambodian and he was jet black. Harris crossed the deck at a low crawl and climbed down the ladder into the open galley. She looked back at Evans through the open hatch at the back of the cabin. There were deep worry lines on her face. He smiled at her from the stern of the vessel like the captain of a yacht on a weekend outing, but she didn't smile back. Her face was contorted with fear and worry.

Does she know about Airborne Warrior? he thought. *What does she know? If she knows, why hasn't she told me?*

Evans watched the movement on deck. It was all below the level of the gunwales. He nodded to Owen, Saleen, and Masure, who gave him a thumbs-up. In the waning light it was difficult to see Assault Unit Three in their covered positions on the starboard side of the big junk. Owen and his unit were low on the port side.

"OK, Lam. Let's go do it. Slow and steady like a fisherman headed home."

"Aye-aye, sir."

"Di mau," said Evans in Vietnamese, with a smile.

With Lam the only visible person on deck, he made for the harbor, keeping the merchant on his starboard side. Wearing black pajamas, the local clothing, and a cone hat, he looked like a Cambodian fisherman. Only the perfect condition of the junk gave him away. Three hundred meters north of the anchor chain, Evans gave a hand signal and Owen and his men slipped over the port side of the underway junk. They used the cabin for cover in case anyone on the freighter was watching them with binoculars or NVGs.

The water was warm and the seas were calm. With their partially inflated life jackets they half floated, half swam toward the freighter. She was tending bow on, and from their perspective in the water she looked as if she were under way toward them. In silence, they slowly closed the distance to the anchor chain.

Lam continued on his course toward the harbor for another three hundred meters before turning slowly south and sweeping the ship at five hundred meters. On her starboard beam he slowed his speed so Masure and Assault Unit Two could put their long wooden sampan in the water. Dressed in black pajamas and cone hats, they looked like natives. Evans lost sight of them fifty meters from the junk.

When Lam was five hundred meters south of the ship he turned and headed west until he could see the merchant's port brow hanging down the side of the ship to the water's edge. A junk was tied up alongside, taking on cargo.

From Owen's perspective at water level, the brow looked far away down the side of the ship. Spotlights on the deck above lighted the dark, undulating sea in huge splotches. He could see a large junk secured to a sea painter and steve-dores walking up and down the gangway carrying bundles. He waited until he saw Lam come alongside before making his climb up the slippery anchor chain.

Masure couldn't see Lam's approach on the opposite side of the ship, but he could hear Evans's play-by-play account through his earpiece. When he heard the junk back down hard, he knew it was time to climb. He reached up from under the curve of the ship and hooked a caving ladder to the railing with an old painter's pole and quietly began scaling the side of the ship.

"Robby," whispered Simons in the back of the sampan.

"Yeah," he said, watching Jackson climb up behind Masure.

"You scared?"

"Man, I've never been so scared in my whole life."

"Me too," whispered Simons.

Robinson grabbed the caving ladder and pulled himself up. Simons held the bottom until Robinson was halfway up the side of the ship, then he followed, letting the sampan drift free.

From the deck of the junk Lam yelled in Thai, "Fresh fish, crab, and shrimp."

The guard on deck hollered back in rough English, "Stand away."

Lam ignored him and yelled in Vietnamese, "Fresh fish, crab, and shrimp!"

"Go away," shouted the guard, holding up an AK so Lam could see it. He spoke to one of the men on deck, who yelled in Vietnamese for Lam to go away.

With a big, toothy grin Lam yelled in broken English. "You buy shrimp. You buy fish. Fresh fish," he shouted, holding up a stringer of fish that had begun to stink from the tropical heat.

"Go away!" yelled the guard more belligerently. He walked to the top of the brow and shook his finger at Lam. Lam smiled and held up the fish.

Evans held his breath as he waited for the sound of voices in his earpiece.

"Assault Unit Two in position, Skipper," whispered Masure from the stern of the freighter.

"Roger, Stick," he responded immediately.

Time stood still as he waited for Assault Unit One to report. The five men with Lieutenant Owen had climbed the anchor chain without difficulty. They slid through the hawse pipe onto the foredeck and quickly removed the waterproofing from their weapons and communications gear. As they took aim with their sniper rifles, Owen reported to Evans. "Assault Unit One in positions, sir."

"Roger, Good copy, Lieutenant," responded Evans. "The guard on at the brow is carrying an AK. This is not a dry run. I repeat. There are bad guys on target."

"Assault Unit One, roger, out," acknowledged Owen.

"Assault Unit Two, roger, out," reported Masure.

"Stick, silent approach. Take out everyone you can before the shit hits the fan."

"Roger, boss," he responded immediately.

Masure, Robinson, Jackson, and Simons move silently up the starboard unlighted side of the ship like one bristling organism peering in all directions simultaneously. They moved in step, in constant contact with each other, weapons pointing in all directions. Masure dropped two men standing at the railing smoking cigarettes. His MP-5 made less noise than the bodies thudding on the deck. Robinson rolled the corpses over the side of the ship. The noise of the ship's generators masked the sound of the bodies hitting the water.

Taufaudy looked through the scope on his Remington sniper rifle and began whispering target information to Lieutenant Owen. Owen repeated the information to Evans on the radio. Masure monitored and whispered the information to Jackson, Robinson, and Simons.

The guard on the rail of the freighter began walking down the gangway, yelling at Lam. "I said, go away!" he demanded, shaking his rifle.

"Two tangos on the foredeck with AKs, one tango on the oh-one level. I can't ID the weapon. Three tangos in the pilothouse," reported Owen.

"Roger, Lieutenant," whispered Evans as the guard neared the bottom of the gangway. "How copy, Stick?"

"Good copy, Skipper," whispered Masure.

"Roger, stand by," breathed Evans.

Harris, under cover of a big cone hat, handed Lam a sea turtle from the galley way.

"You buy? You buy?" begged Lam, holding up the stinking turtle.

Masure motioned Simons and Jackson up a ladder to the 02 level of the ship while he and Robinson rounded the starboard side of the superstructure. He peeked through the athwart ship's passageway and saw another guard headed his way. As the man stepped through the hatch, he caught two 9mm rounds in the middle of his forehead and dropped to the deck with a thump.

Jackson and Simons drilled two guards on the 02 level in the backs of their heads, dropping them to the deck like rag dolls. As Jackson dragged the bodies back out of sight, one of the soldiers inside the ship saw a boot slide by the hatch. He walked over to investigate and Simons drilled him in the hatchway, knocking him back with two rounds in the chest.

"Boarders!" he screamed, frothing blood from his mouth.

Alarmed by the cry, the three guards on the foredeck began running toward the superstructure. The snipers cut them down from the bow. Then Owen cut loose with his MP-5 on two men running down the port side toward Masure's position at the stern.

With the report of the sniper rifles the guard on the gangway looked up for the last time in his life. Evans rose up from the cover of the gunwales and blasted him with two rounds to the head. The coolies on the deck of the adjacent junk began to scramble for their lives. Evans jumped over the gunwale and dashed across the junk at the gangway with Saleen, Ryeback, Harris, and the Junkyard Dawg right on his heels. Halfway up the gangway he ran into two coolies frightened out of their minds. Using his weapon and his forearms, he shoved them over the side. As he did, he glanced back and saw Harris cut loose on five coolies on the bow of the junk. They were unarmed.

Lam, using an M-14 from the stern of the junk, sighted in on top of the gangway and let loose with a few rounds before turning the weapon on the open hatch to the pilothouse on the 03 level. He and the security team on the junk kept up a steady barrage of fire, pinning the Spetznaz inside the ship.

Evans reached the top of the gangway, followed closely by Saleen. He opened up on three men near the front of the superstructure. Saleen was shooting from behind Evans, so closely his bullets were passing two feet from Evans's skull. The three men dropped like dead meat as Owen, Taufaudy, Bailey, and Williams joined them and caught the Spetznaz in a deadly crossfire. With the foredeck clear of Spetznaz, Owen ordered Taufaudy and Williams to shoot out the ship's lights. Then they began maneuvering down the deck toward the superstructure, leapfrogging as they advanced.

A pitched battle raged on the weather decks of the ship. Evans and Assault Unit Three covered starboard side and aft from the superstructure. Masure and Assault Unit Two covered port side and forward on the 01 and 02 levels. Owen and Assault Unit One covered the foredeck in front of the superstructure. Lam and the security team on the junk peppered the 02 and 03 levels port side. The only weak point in the kill zone was the starboard side 03 level off the pilothouse, and that's where the Spetznaz attacked from. Several Spetznaz found the hole and poured out onto the high ground of the 03 level. From the bridge wing they shot down on the men on the foredeck, pinning them behind cargo containers. Green tracers danced all over the deck, preventing Assault Unit One from taking aim with their sniper rifles. One of the Spetznaz cut loose with a thirty-round magazine, ricocheting bullets off the deck and hatch near Lieutenant Owen. Fragments of lead peppered his leg. One round careened off a hatch and smashed into his thigh. Owen grabbed his leg and screamed, "I'm hit!" Williams dashed through a hail of bullets to Owen's position and pulled him to better cover. He ripped a field bandage out of his pocket and bound the wound.

Assault Units Two and Three threw flashcrashes into every hatchway in their area of responsibility and bolted them shut. Evans and the Junkyard Dawg climbed a ladder to the 02 level port side and began to work their way aft to link up with Robinson and Simons. Saleen and several men worked their way aft on the 01 level, sealing the ship as they went.

Masure and Jackson killed two men on the 01 level starboard side and made visual link-up with Assault Unit One, pinned down on the foredeck. Above them, Spetznaz rained bullets down, reconning the deck by fire. Masure stepped out into the open and tossed a concussion grenade up on the 03 level. But one of the Spetznaz picked it up and tossed it back before it exploded. It went off ten yards from Masure and Jackson. When they recovered from the blast their ears were ringing.

"Damn it!" yelled Masure. "They've got us pinned down!"

Jackson climbed up on the rail of the ship, grabbed a stanchion, and leaned out far enough to get a glance at the bridge wing. He looked back at Masure and pulled a concussion grenade off his belt. "Try another, Senior."

Masure nodded, grabbed a grenade, and tossed it up toward the pilothouse. Jackson pulled his pin, leaned out over the side, and followed Masure's grenade by two seconds. The first one landed on top of the pilothouse and exploded above the heads of the Spetznaz. The concussion caused the entire 03 level to shudder. Jackson's grenade landed on the bridge wing. As the concussion of the half-pound block of TNT smashed into the exposed men on the bridge wing, Masure tossed up another. After the third explosion, several men inside the pilothouse threw down their weapons, ran out on the bridge wing, and dove overboard. They knew the situation was hopeless and were taking their chances with the sea.

"Stick, I'm climbing the ladder to the port-side 03 level. I have Robinson, Simons, and Ballard with me," said Evans.

"Roger, boss. Several men just jumped overboard. I think we've got them on the run."

Evans ran up the ladder and crossed to the starboard side of the ship. He peeked out around the side and let loose with a three-round burst toward the pilothouse hatch. He followed the rounds in and slammed the hatch shut. Standing up, he took a quick peek through the hatch porthole. The pilothouse was empty. When Masure joined Evans at the 03 level, the SEALs controlled the weather decks of the ship. Anyone inside was locked in a steel prison. Evans quickly regrouped the men, and with two teams began to clear the ship top down, level by level, using flashcrashes. With each explosion, the ship shuddered and reverberated in agony. Using personnel from the task group, Saleen ordered certain hatches spot-welded closed. The two units methodically worked their way through the ship, pausing at each passageway or compartment, peeking inside, and when in doubt, tossing in a concussion grenade before entering the space. Anyone armed was shot dead. The prisoners were assembled on the foredeck and cinched up with nylon zip ties for interrogation.

Inside the ship they found a few crewmen and several female passengers still alive. Evans's intelligence officer, Lieutenant Oakley, separated the survivors, isolating them on the deck by category. Slowly she began to put together an intelligence summary of the voyage. By cross-checking the information between the survivors, she pieced together the events that had occurred since the ship had departed port in

Genoa, Italy. One of the younger women who was suffering from severe acid burns to her face recounted a tale of horror. She identified herself as Sofia Skiathos, one of the passengers of the ill-fated Turkish ship, the *Balikesir*. As the corpsman treated her burns, the lieutenant listened to her story. At moments Oakley was overwhelmed with waves of nausea. Sofia Skiathos's facial skin was peeling off in huge black chunks.

When Harris rushed up to the pilothouse, Evans could tell by the look on her face there was something wrong.

"The bomb is not on board!" she said frantically. "Do we have any Russian prisoners?"

With his intersquad radio Evans questioned Oakley, Saleen, Owen, and Masure.

"Yes, Masure just secured several prisoners in the galley. He thinks they're Russian."

Harris rushed out and down the ladder toward the galley.

"Stick, Harris is on her way to question your prisoners. Give her a hand."

"Roger, boss. I copy."

Harris entered the galley cautiously. Smoke and cordite filled the ship.

"Senior Chief Masure," she yelled. "Alysin Harris here."

"Enter," he boomed through the smoke left by the flashcrashes he had used to clear the large compartment. Masure and his team had zip-cuffed five men who lay on the galley floor. Their hands were cuffed behind their backs and their feet were zip-tied together. They were all bleeding from their ears and noses from the trauma of the concussion grenades. Two of the men were still unconscious. Harris grabbed one of the men by his shoulder and spun him around on the slick tile deck. In Russian she asked, "Where's Karpenko?" He just stared at her with a dazed expression. Then she spotted Suburov, whom she recognized from a photo.

"Sergeant Suburov," she said in Russian.

The big man slowly looked up to meet the eyes of his interrogator. He spit at her and cursed. "Fuck you, bitch," he said in Russian, with a vicious look.

Harris stepped back and with incredible speed kicked

Suburov full force in the face. With his hands zip-tied behind him and his legs bound, he could do nothing to avoid the full impact of the blow.

"Where's Karpenko? Where is the bomb?" she screamed in Russian. Blood was streaming from Suburov's nose and mouth. Through swollen and bleeding lips he growled, "Your Russian sucks, you American whore!"

Harris had memorized his file. She reached down and grabbed Suburov's right boot and felt for the knife she knew would be there. She pulled it out of its scabbard and carefully felt the edge. Turning to face Masure, she gave Suburov a side kick that laid him out on the deck. Planting a knee in his chest, she took the knife and put it to his throat.

"Where's Karpenko and where is the bomb?" she demanded.

Suburov tried to curse, but Harris stuck the blade a half inch in his throat. His eyes were wild with bitterness when she asked him again. She released the pressure and Suburov let loose a string of curses. He cursed her again, and he cursed her mother and her father and her father's father. Harris ended his litany by jabbing the knife two inches deep into the big man's thigh. With a scream he yelled, "Fuck you, you American bitch."

She waited until he had caught his breath.

"Where is Karpenko? Where is the bomb? You will tell me *now* or," she said calmly with an evil look in her eye, "I will cut off your dick."

Suburov was in shock from the flashcrashes and the kicks to the head. He stared at Harris in disbelief.

"Masure, hold 'im," she ordered.

Masure stepped forward and planted his boot on Suburov's neck, choking him with the pressure. He eased off enough for him to breathe. Harris felt the edge of the knife and quickly reached behind her, placing the point of the knife at the base of his penis. Suburov's eyes were wild.

"Last chance, Mad Wolf! Last chance!" she screamed.

Suburov knew by the look in her eyes she was going to cut off his dick. He said to himself, "Don't trust, don't beg, and don't show fear."

Harris waited for an answer, and when it didn't come she

pushed down hard on the handle of the knife, but it wouldn't move. With a twist and an Aikido wrist lock, Evans stood her to her feet as if yanking up a child by its arm. He looked her squarely in the eyes.

"No! Not on my watch!" he said with authority. "You'll not do this under my command."

"I'm not under your command, Evans. You're under my command!" she screamed.

"Not anymore. You're relieved," he said, shoving her back.

Suburov looked up at Evans. As their eyes met, he recognized the commander from Indonesia.

"What's your name?" he growled, blood streaming down his nose. "I know you," he said. "Yes. Evans. We drank that shitty Indonesian beer together, no? And you! I recognize you, too, pretty boy," he said to Masure. "If I am to die, I want it to be at the hands of a warrior, not a bitch with a shitty haircut."

Suburov's words rolled off his tongue with arrogance and vile contempt for Harris. As Evans stared at Suburov's face, he yelled at Masure.

"Get a corpsman in here and clean these men up. *Now!*"

"Evans." Suburov paused, looking up at him with a cold stare. "Karpenko got off the ship fifty miles south of here. He has one bomb with him."

"He's lying!" yelled Harris.

"No, he's not," said Evans. "The surviving passengers told Lieutenant Oakley the same information," he said with a cold stare, *"without torture!"*

"Thank you, Sergeant Suburov. I will see your wounds are tended to properly."

Evans walked out of the galley and began issuing orders into his throat mike.

"Masure, get all the prisoners on deck as soon as possible."

"Roger, sir. I copy. Masure out."

"Break. Shooter, get the troops ready to travel in the junk. Check ammo. We need M-sixties, M-fourteens, and M-sixteens."

"I'll have 'em ready in five Mikes, Skipper," responded Saleen.

"Lieutenant Owen, can you take command of this vessel?" asked Evans, still growling over the radio.

"Yes, sir," responded Owen immediately. The corpsman had dressed his leg wound and he was hobbling around the pilothouse, eager for something meaningful to do.

"Very well. Use the support personnel and get the ship under way. Steam her offshore twenty-five miles and maintain radio contact with me. Be careful. There may be more Spetznaz hiding aboard."

"Aye-aye, sir," responded Owen.

Just before Evans put the junk to sea, Harris ran up to him, excited. "Derek! Derek! I just received a report from the embassy. All three bombs have been accounted for!"

"Great. That's just great," he replied, still making preparations to leave.

"Don't you understand? You don't have to go after Karpenko. Suburov was lying. They've accounted for all the missing weapons!" she exhorted.

"Who told you there were only three bombs? The Russians?"

She understood the question. Her mouth fell open and her face lost its color.

"I'll go with you," she offered.

"No!" snapped Evans with a bitter expression. "I'm going to stop the crazy bastard, if I have to chase him all over Cambodia. And I don't need your help," he snarled. Evans continued to ignore her halfhearted efforts to dissuade him. She stared at him with a blank expression as he walked down the gangway toward the junk.

CHAPTER

30

Evans and most of Alpha Platoon got the junk under way and headed south for the Krong River. It was the only water course large enough to carry heavy traffic inland to the capital of the fractured country. Since the Vietnam War, Cambodia had been a country in turmoil. First the Chinese-backed Lon Nol government had seized control of the capital, Phnom Penh. Then, Pol Pot and the Khmer Rouge emptied the city. More than a million people were murdered in bloody factional purges. Skulls were stacked in piles, Attila-the-Hun fashion. Under Pol Pot, Phnom Penh became a ghost town. Then the Vietnamese invaded and established a puppet government. Fighting had continued nonstop for three decades, with four factions involved in a bloody civil war. Karpenko intended to capitalize on the divisions. One thermonuclear bomb would effectively wipe out the Vietnamese. He intended to pick up the pieces as a shadow ruler.

At first light, as Lieutenant Owen and the task group got the freighter under way for international waters, Evans and crew entered the mouth of the Krong River. He was only minutes behind Karpenko. Lam immediately began questioning the local fishermen and discovered that a group of white men had departed only minutes before their arrival.

With the diesel at maximum rpm, they headed inland, hugging the banks of each meander. Twenty minutes into Cambodia, Evans spotted his target. Through binoculars he studied the vessel riding low in the water and moving slowly. Onboard were a dozen Spetznaz soldiers and several Cambodians.

"Lam, stay close to the bank, and when we round that bend crash our bow into their stern as hard as you can," he said, pointing out Karpenko's junk from the other traffic on the river.

Evans could see the fear in Lam's eyes. "You can do it. Just bash into her rudder. Disable her. Shove her against the bank if you can."

"I can do it, Captain. I not cop out," said Lam with more bravado than he felt. Evans ordered the men down low, but before they could close the distance Karpenko sensed their presence. The Thai junk was in too good a condition for Cambodia. He studied her polished teak hull and her constant bearing and decreasing range and knew he was being chased. He let the SEALs get within rifle range and took them under fire with AKs and B-40 rockets. All hell broke loose as the SEALs and Spetznaz exchanged fire. One of the soldiers stood up to fire his B-40 and Taufaudy cut him down with his sniper rifle. With their scopes the SEALs ran the Spetznaz to the front of the junk's cabin, killing several of the soldiers in the skirmish. Round for round they traded blood. Bailey took a round in the chest and collapsed in a heap on the deck. Masure took a shower of wooden splinters in the head as AK rounds ripped through the wooden railing next to him. Blood ran down his face in rivulets, covering his chest and legs.

When the two junks collided, Saleen was reloading his M-16. The force of the collision slammed him forward on the deck, knocking him unconscious. Evans stood up and raked the deck of the junk on full automatic. He leapt onto the stern and tossed a concussion grenade forward of the cabin. As he ducked down, a Russian grenade appeared at his feet. He grabbed it and tossed it overboard, eating a shower of river water as it exploded. Then his grenade exploded, hammering the Spetznaz on the foredeck. The tide of battle changed with just one explosion. His grenade had gone off next to a Spetznaz soldier taking cover on the deck. It caused a sympathetic detonation of one of the fragmentation grenades on the soldier's belt, sending a shower of hot metal whirling through the air like tiny buzz saws. Evans followed the explosion, shooting through the haze as he rounded the junk's cabin. With quick three-round bursts, he finished off the bloody men scrambling around the deck and tossed a concussion grenade inside the junk. Contained inside the boat, the force of the explosion demolished the cabin and blew a hole in the bottom of the vessel. As Evans searched for Karpenko, out of the corner of his eye he saw him scrambling up the muddy bank with several soldiers. He took them under fire as they disappeared into the jungle.

When Evans calmed down enough to survey the scene, he saw the bomb. It was housed in a large metal container, tied down in the center of the deck. He yelled to Lam, "Come alongside!" Back onboard the Thai junk he found a gruesome scene. Williams, Bailey, and Taufaudy were dead. Masure had lost so much blood he was near unconsciousness, and Saleen was groggy. As the corpsman worked on Masure, Evans worked on Saleen.

"Shooter, Shooter! We have to get the bomb off the other boat! It's sinking!" he shouted. Saleen slowly regained his senses and began stumbling about deck.

"Robinson! Jackson!" he called. "Take a line over. Lash the boats together!"

When Robinson secured the line, Saleen hollered, "All hands heave around. Lam, ease her forward!" With the power of the engine and the strain of the line, the two junks bumped together side by side.

"Lash them together," he yelled to Simons and Jackson.

As soon as the boats were tied up he grabbed an M-60 and bellowed. "Stand back!"

Using the machine gun like an ax to chop out the wooden railings, he blasted away until they were just splinters and stomped out a path between the two decks. It took all hands to pry and heave the container across. When the transfer was completed, he cut the sinking junk free.

"Shooter, rendezvous with Lieutenant Owen. I'm going

to take some men and track Karpenko. I'll stay in touch by radio."

"Aye-aye, Skipper," Saleen said, grimacing in pain. "Ryeback, set up firing positions for the two sixties, there and there," he ordered, pointing at the forward gunwales.

As Saleen got under way, Evans, Lam, Jackson, Simons, and Robinson slipped over the side and scrambled up the muddy bank. Like an instant replay from Indonesia, Evans found himself chasing Karpenko down jungle trails and across rice paddies. From time to time he paused long enough for Lam to ask for information in the small campongs that clung to the banks of the canals. As they neared a Buddhist *wat* nestled in a clump of coconut palms, Evans's sixth sense went wild. It was like an alarm bell going off. He halted the patrol and scanned the pagoda for signs of life. The monkeys were nervous and there were no birds in sight. Seeing no one, his senses told him this was the killing ground. Evans looked at his young warriors with sadness, knowing what lay ahead. The men were exhausted and out of breath from jogging, but there was no time to rest. They were several miles inside hostile territory.

"Jackson," he ordered. "Take Robby and Simons, and work your way to that clump of trees," he whispered, pointing out a cluster of coconut palms at the far end of the Buddhist *wat*. "Make sure you have a clean shot down both walls of the compound. Stay away from the wall. Bullets travel down them like a rock skipping on a pond. And watch out for an ambush. Lam and I will cover the south and west walls," he said, pointing to the opposite corner. "Maintain radio contact."

"Yes, sir. I understand," said Jackson excitedly.

"They're in there and they know we're out here," commented Evans.

"Hoo yah," said Robinson.

They all stared at him in silence. Robinson was so scared the only way he could relieve the tension was to say "hoo yah." Evans and Lam covered Jackson, Robinson, and Simons as they leapfrogged their way along the east side of the compound. The religious sanctuary was about the size of a football field, surrounded by an eight-foot stone wall. Inside was a large pagoda encircled by trees and statues.

With hearts pumping and muscles tense, Jackson and crew patrolled to the far corner. Jackson motioned Simons to take up a position behind a tree where he could see down the north wall. Just as Simons crouched down behind the tree, a grenade landed among the trees. Both Jackson and Robinson saw it hit the ground and they both dove for cover. Before it exploded, the Spetznaz inside the compound threw two more grenades.

Evans saw the grenades go off, he heard the rattle of AKs barking, and he knew the troops were in big trouble. Leaving Lam at the corner of the compound, he ran up far enough to peek through an arch in the wall. He saw a Spetznaz soldier run from the wall toward the pagoda in the center of the compound. A grenade flew over the wall behind him and exploded among the statues. The soldier took cover at the base of a stone statue, facing Evans. Evans took careful aim with his M-16 and squeezed off one round from seventy-five yards. It pinned the soldier to the stone statue like an arrow. The man slumped to the ground, motionless. Evans ducked back behind the cover of the wall and whispered, "Jackson, this is the skipper, over?" into his throat mike.

There was no answer.

"Jackson, Jackson, this is the captain, over!"

"Captain, this is Simons. Jackson's dead and Robby's hit bad!"

"Simons, treat Robby as best you can, but keep them pinned inside the compound."

"Aye-aye, sir."

"You got good cover?" asked Evans.

"Yes, sir."

"Good. Evans out."

"Captain."

"Yes."

"Robby's not going to make it, sir!" he said sadly.

"Simons, keep your cool. We've got to kill these bastards, right here!"

"Yes, sir! Anyone who comes out of that compound is fuckin' dead!" said Simons, filled with anger. He was scared and he was angry. He lay Robinson's head on the ground and lay prone behind a tree so he could kill anyone who ran out of the *wat.*

Evans scurried back to Lam's position and motioned for him to follow him to the opposite corner of the rectangular compound. With Lam in one corner and Simons in the other, Evans had Karpenko in a trap. He worked his way back to a gate in the wall and threw a fragmentation grenade inside the compound. It landed near the pagoda and exploded with a crash, sending metal slivers ricocheting off stone and rattling through the trees. When the sound had echoed away, Karpenko called.

"So, Evans! We meet again!"

Evans ignored the greeting. He knew Karpenko only wanted to fix his position so he could toss a grenade on his head.

"I see you are still working for that socialist government of yours," he yelled, shifting his location inside the pagoda. Each time he spoke, his voice seemed to come from a slightly different angle. "I'm into free enterprise, Evans! Let's make a deal like good capitalists!"

Evans remained silent.

"There is a lot of money in the arms business! You could join me! We could make lots of money, you and me!"

Evans knew by instinct not to answer. Somewhere hidden inside the compound was another Spetznaz soldier with a grenade in his hand. He knew the soldier was close, just inside the compound on the other side of the heavy stone wall. So he threw another grenade into the compound. It exploded with a crack, ripping frag through the coconut palms.

When silence reigned, Karpenko yelled, "Free enterprise! That's the capitalist way, isn't it, Evans?"

Evans motioned for Lam to take better cover and whispered into his throat mike. "Lam, when I answer him, a grenade will come over the wall. See if you can spot where it comes from."

Lam moved back behind a large banyan tree.

"No deal, Karpenko! No deal!" yelled Evans.

With his last word, he ran down the length of the wall and took cover in a small ditch. The grenade exploded in the exact location of Evans's voice, throwing shrapnel through the trees. Karpenko changed his location as soon as his soldier threw the grenade. For several minutes the pagoda was silent as each man tried to locate his enemy by sound.

"Captain," whispered Lam.

"Yeah!"

"The grenade come from northwest corner by big elephant statue," reported Lam.

"Roger," whispered Evans. "On my command throw a grenade between the statue and the pagoda. *Break.* Simons, you copy?"

"Yes, sir!" reported Simons from the other side of the compound.

"Can you get a grenade over the northeast corner of the wall?" he asked.

"Yes, sir. Captain, I've only got one left."

"I've got two," said Evans. "How many do you have, Lam?"

"I got one, Captain," reported Lam.

"OK. Let's use 'em well. On the count of three, let 'em fly. Ready, *one, two, three,*" he counted into his throat mike and let loose with a grenade toward the northeast corner. The three grenades exploded at slightly different times, sending a shower of fragmentation all around the statues. Evans heard the moans and gurgling of death. Through the arched entrance of the compound, he saw a soldier crawling toward the pagoda. Evans took careful aim and fired one round into the soldier's torso, finishing him off.

Karpenko ran out of the pagoda and down the path toward the compound wall on the opposite side of the building from Evans. He was tired of the chase. The years of smoking black tobacco was affecting his stamina. Using statues for cover, he moved toward Lam's position at the southwest corner. Through an entrance in the west wall he made contact at twenty yards, exchanging bursts of full metal jackets. From the entrance in the south wall, Khasanov, the last of Karpenko's men, caught Lam in a crossfire, hitting him with several rounds. As Khasanov peeked out of the compound, Evans fired one round. Khasanov's head exploded like a melon from the impact of the bullet, sending brain matter all over the open gate. Karpenko was alone.

Evans ran toward Khasanov's body and took cover at the entrance to the compound.

"Well, old friend, it's just you and me. Just like Indonesia, no?" Karpenko shifted his position in the west entrance just as a grenade exploded in the compound. Shrapnel cut through his left thigh and calf muscle. In shock, he slumped against the stone arch and began dressing his wounds.

"Evans," he bellowed. "I have a virus weapon. If you break it everyone in the world will die."

He held his breath, listening for a grenade hitting the ground. None came. Evans was out.

"You're bluffing, asshole!" yelled Evans, standing up against the wall. He listened and watched for a grenade, ready to duck inside the compound. They were both out of grenades.

"I'm going to kill your sorry ass this time!" yelled Evans.

"I have Airborne Warrior, Evans. You know what it is. Let's make a deal? No more grenades, OK?" asked Karpenko, shifting his locations from one side of the wall to the other, staying near the entrance so he could quickly trade the inside of the compound for the outside.

"OK!" yelled Evans, and ran toward the cover of the banyan tree.

Karpenko shouted back, "Evans, do you know the teachings of the Buddha?"

Evans scurried down a ditch and headed for Lam's position at the base of the tree.

"The Buddha taught mind control. You must keep your mind free of fear, greed, and anger. I'm not scared! Are you?" taunted Karpenko.

Evans didn't answer. He was trying to fix Karpenko's changing position.

"I'm not greedy. I will share with you!" he shouted. "I am not angry because you killed all my men. Let's make a deal, you and me."

Evans kept scanning the direction of the voice for grenades and watching his back for a spade. He couldn't be sure how many men Karpenko had taken ashore and he wasn't sure where Karpenko was. He silently worked his way toward Lam, slumped at the base of the banyan tree.

Lam was bleeding badly. His eyes were glazed and his

breathing was shallow and labored. Evans automatically began treating his wounds while scanning his surroundings like a radar.

"I not cop out, Captain. I not cop out," whispered Lam, gurgling blood.

"No, son. You didn't cop out. Hang in there. I'll get you out of here as soon as I kill this bastard."

"I not cop out," repeated Lam in shock.

"No, son. You saved thousands of innocent lives. That's what warriors do, save lots of people by killing a few bad ones."

Evans worked frantically on Lam's wounds while watching for the mad Russian.

"You might be my fadder, sir," said Lam, closing his eyes. "Maybe you my fadder?"

"Yes, maybe I am. I left a few wild seeds in Vietnam. Maybe I am. Any man would be proud to have a son like you," he said, feeling the life leave Lam's body. "You're a SEAL, a real warrior," he whispered. Lam's pupils changed, like the eyes of an animal when it takes its last breath.

Leaning over Lam, Evans peeked around the tree just as Karpenko kicked at his head. Evans snapped his head around and felt the blade of a boot knife skid down his cheek. It buried up in the trunk of the tree with a clunk. With his left hand, Evans grabbed the toe of the boot and slammed his right palm into the heel. With a vicious twist he snapped the blade off in the tree trunk and tried to twist off Karpenko's foot. Karpenko spun and caught him in the head with the heel of his right boot, stunning him with the blow. Jumping to his feet, Evans faced Karpenko, circling for advantage.

"I'm going to kill you slowly, pretty boy," he growled.

"Talk's cheap, asshole!" snarled Evans.

Evans attacked first with a fake kick, which Karpenko blocked with a bloody fist. With his hands down, Evans sneaked in a tiger claw to Karpenko's face, sending him to the ground with blood and tears. Evans stomped down as hard as he could, trying to catch Karpenko's lower leg on the ground, but the big man moved at the last second. As Evans stamped on the ground, Karpenko threw another kick with the boot knife. The remnant of the blade sliced into Evans's calf, leaving behind a bloody gash. Before Evans could recover from the kick, Karpenko was on his feet, circling. They traded blows over and over until they were both completely exhausted.

"I'm going to kill you!" growled Karpenko in a mad rage.

Bloody and panting for breath, he tried a desperate kick, which Evans trapped. He twisted the Russian's leg, sending him to the ground in a spin, and he moved in for the kill. Evans tried to stomp on Karpenko's stomach, but the big Russian rolled on the ground, trapping his leg. As the Russian took him to the ground, Evans hammered at Karpenko's head with a spinning back fist. Evans fell on his back and thrust out his heel, kicking Karpenko in his side. Flat on his back, Karpenko drew his Sukorov pistol and began shooting wildly at Evans as he rolled along the ground, trying to reach cover behind the tree trunk. When Evans came to a stop, luck was with him. He was lying on Lam's M-16. Grabbing the rifle, he let loose with a burst of rounds that stripped bark off the tree.

"Evans," growled Karpenko, out of breath.

"Fuck you, you goddamn animal!" yelled Evans, popping off a couple of rounds on each side of the tree.

"Evans! I have the virus weapon!" he yelled. "I am not bluffing. Don't shoot or you will be the destroyer of worlds!" he ordered.

Evans kept the rifle pointed at the center of the tree, ready to shoot on either side. Karpenko's hands slowly appeared. They held a small vial against the barrel of a pistol. For several seconds he sat motionless, holding the viral weapon in view.

"Evans!" he said, still panting for breath. "I am a cossack, not a fucking Buddha!" he said, gathering his strength. "I will pull this fucking trigger and kill every man, woman, and child on this planet." Karpenko held the pistol steady, finger on the trigger, vial against the barrel. "We are men who understand the transiency of life and the unjustness of the world. You know I will pull this trigger, Evans! And you know what it will do!"

Karpenko stood up slowly, using the tree trunk against his back. He turned and stepped into the open, looking down at the M-16 aimed at his head.

"My country has turned from socialism to capitalism," he growled. "Yours has turned from capitalism to socialism. Let's make a deal, you and me. For now, let's live and let live. You go your way and I go my way."

Karpenko staggered against the tree trunk for support, oozing blood down his leg. He was covered in mud and blood. He knew that if he took his finger off the trigger or the vial off the barrel of the gun, he was a dead man.

"Evans!" he growled like a madman. "You know what's in this tiny bottle, don't you? You know or you would have killed me already. This tiny bottle is more powerful than all the nuclear weapons in Russia!" He smiled maniacally. "Inside are horrible little creatures you cannot see. They are real airborne warriors who travel on the wind and kill everyone they meet." As he talked he staggered toward Evans, pistol in hand and barrel against the vial, until he was just a few feet away.

"Before they kill they make a man bleed from every hole in his body. I have seen it, Evans. In Africa! Blood . . . blood slowly oozing from the eyes and ears and mouth. Thick, oozing, deadly, infectious blood."

Karpenko stared down at the M-16 pointing at his brain, knowing Evans couldn't pull the trigger.

"Evans! If you shoot me, my finger will pull this trigger, and every man, woman, and child on this planet will die!" he yelled with contempt. "Now! I am leaving this killing field. I am tired of your company," he grunted.

"You're bluffing, asshole. There is no such thing as Airborne Warrior," goaded Evans.

"Oh! Shoot me and become the destroyer of worlds, pretty boy."

They stared at each other eye to eye for a long moment. Sighting down the M-16, Evans saw the hate and rage in his eyes. He knew he could pull the trigger. He had taken the gamble too far already.

"You are a worthy adversary, Evans. Is this what they call a Mexican standoff?" asked Karpenko.

"Maybe I can shoot you through your warped fucking brain and your finger won't pull the trigger," goaded Evans. "And maybe there's nothing in that vial but colored water."

"And maybe I shoot you quickly through your fucking brain," said Karpenko, bristling.

"Try it, asshole!" Evans said with a smile. "Go ahead and try it!" Evans was hoping Karpenko would remove the vial from in front of the pistol for just one second. All he needed was just one second.

Karpenko turned the pistol toward Evans, keeping the vial in front of the barrel. His nostrils flared and he sniffed the air like an animal seeking scent. With an evil glare he stared at Evans, studying the M-16, calculating his chances.

"We will meet again, Evans," he said with a look of pure hate. *"Do svidaniya, asshole,"* he said with a snarl.

Karpenko limped past Evans and down the dirt road, dripping blood from his leg. Evans kept his front site focused on Karpenko's head as he staggered down the road and out of range. He held the sight picture until Karpenko was well beyond the range of the M-16. When the pistol dropped to Karpenko's side, Evans took a deep breath and let it out slowly. Sighting well over Karpenko's head, he slowly squeezed the trigger ever so gently until the weapon discharged as if by accident. His mind was racing in fast-forward as he watched the bullet arc out the distance to the Russian in slow motion. It struck with complete surprise. Karpenko spun violently and looked back at Evans as he slumped to the ground. Evans watched him crawl into the foliage at the edge of the dirt road.

"Simons!" yelled Evans.

"Yes, sir."

"Get your ass over here on the double."

"Aye-aye, sir!"

Evans and Simons carefully patrolled down the dirt road. At the location where Karpenko had gone down they found a pistol and a bloody trail that led off to a muddy canal fifty yards in the jungle. Exhausted and frustrated, they searched in vain for more than two hours. Finally Evans gave up and commandeered a sampan to take them and the lifeless bodies of his men back to the mouth of the Krong River. Saleen was waiting to ferry them to the freighter standing by twenty-five miles off the coast of Cambodia.

EPILOGUE

Commander Derek Evans, USN, retired, sat in the bar at the top of the Charthouse and nursed a Scotch and water while waiting for Alysin Harris. The day had been an emotional roller coaster. The downhill run ended with his change of command. At ten o'clock he had been properly relieved as commanding officer, SEAL Team Five, and another man now occupied his office. He took a gulp of the Scotch and let it work its magic, feeling a deep sense of loss, as if another man were sleeping with his woman. There was no going back in the navy. SEAL Team Five was gone forever, like the men he had lost in Southeast Asia.

In addition to relinquishing command, he had retired, ending a career that spanned more than two decades of military service. His sense of personal loss combined with uncertainty. Evans belted down the Scotch and ordered another. If they had demoted him and made him the XO of a SEAL team, he would have stayed in the navy. But that wasn't the navy way. His career was planned. On to bigger and better things, like making coffee in the Pentagon or serving on some joint staff with a bunch of fat army tankers. The captain of a SEAL team was the most senior operational billet in the SEAL community, the last stop in the operational world of the SEAL warrior. Evans couldn't see himself as a Commodore Cameron, playing the politics of self-promotion, so he had retired. Moreover, Arlington would never allow him to be promoted after letting Lieutenant Owen go into combat with his platoon. He was, after all, the CNO's only son.

Evans's bags were packed in the back of the Porsche, but he didn't have the foggiest notion of where he was going or what he was going to do when he left the Charthouse. All he knew for certain was that he was leaving Coronado. A lot of water had passed over the dam since he had walked out of a Cambodian jungle with the lifeless bodies of his men. Telling the parents their sons had been killed on a training mission had been the hardest part, because it had been a lie forced on him by operational security. Six months had passed since he had buried Williams, Taufaudy, Jackson, Bailey, Robinson, and Lam. Six months to think.

The life of a man is a journey, he thought, *a journey that must be traveled, however bad the roads or shitty the accommodations along the way. Each of us comes for a short visit not knowing why, yet seemingly for a divine purpose. The only thing I know is that we are here for the sake of others . . . for the countless unknown souls with whose fate we are connected by the bond of empathy.*

"Here's to you, Wild Bill," he said out loud before taking a gulp of Scotch, "and to you, Taufaudy. Hear, hear."

"You want something, Commander?" asked the bartender.

"Nahhh! I'm just talking to myself."

Evans gulped down the Scotch and ruminated over the past. *I was privileged to watch the professional lives of young men grow and develop,* he thought. *I saw them suffer through Hell Week and explode with pride at graduation. I watched them train hard and play hard. Then they died. The silent option. What a crock of crap!*

"Here's to you, Robinson and Bailey and Jackson and Lam, wherever you are," he said out loud. The bartender looked at him with a puzzled expression. He had never seen the commander talk to himself before.

The thread of time remains with us in the form of a succession of abiding facilitation, he thought. *It travels through each man's waking hours from the cradle to the grave. On that thread are memories strung like pearls in unending succession, the meaningful patterns that can still recall the vanishing content of former awareness. I wish some of those pearls would hurry up and disappear.*

"Here to you, boys," he said out loud. "Bartender. Bring me another."

"Are you all right, Commander?" the man asked.

"Hell, no. What a stupid question to ask. I just retired."

"Oh. I thought that was good," commented the bartender.

Evans gave him a dirty look, as if he were looking at a communist. He needed to get his head screwed on straight. He was meeting Harris in a few minutes. Her invitation to dinner had dredged up an assortment of painful memories, such as deceit and duplicity, and the death of comrades in arms, things he had suppressed since the funerals. He had seen her in the crowd during the change of command, but they hadn't talked since the operation in Southeast Asia. When she called and invited him to dinner at the Charthouse he accepted, only because he thought it was a fitting way to end his career. He got up and went to the table in the corner that overlooked the bay. He was admiring the boats at the dock when she arrived, dressed to kill.

"I'm glad you accepted my invitation," she beamed.

He held her chair and took his seat without speaking.

"I wanted to see you after we returned from Thailand, but my boss wouldn't let me out of D.C.," she said in apology.

"Nice to see you again, Alysin," he said, not sure if he really meant it. "You look marvelous," he said, somewhat subdued.

"Thanks. Admiral Arlington invited me to your change of command. I hope you didn't mind me being there."

"No. Not at all. Thanks for coming," he responded without enthusiasm.

"I'm really sorry you retired. The country needs men like you," she said seriously.

"No, it doesn't, Alysin. It needs people like me to get out of the way for people like you. The face of war is changing and I no longer fit in."

"Oh, I disagree, Derek. This country desperately needs

people like you. In fact, my boss asked me to talk to you. He wants to meet with you. Maybe we could work together?" she said with a bright smile. He answered the invitation with a serious expression of doubt.

"Alysin, I'm a combat leader, nothing more. . . . I have too many traits that are inconsistent with high rank, and I'm certainly not cut out for your line of work," he said with conviction.

"Derek, after what you did in Thailand we can fix it so you can stay in the military or the Agency, or whatever you want. The director is interested in putting together a new counterproliferation force under the direct control of the Agency, and he wants you to be a part of it."

"You're kidding me," he said, as thoughts raced through his head.

"No. He wants me to set up the meeting."

"Is that why you're here?" he asked.

"It's one of the reasons," she said with a salacious smile.

"Not on your life. The whole goddamn system's poured in concrete. It's designed for ticket-punchin' assholes and bureaucrats who play politics in the locker room. I'm neither, and I'm out of here."

She stared at him in shock.

"But I'm talking about something new," she insisted.

"Yeah! I'll bet. A new unit driven by spooks with a quota for women and gays," he replied. "Not my idea of a combat unit."

"You are really bitter, aren't you?" she asked soothingly.

"Yes, I am. I saw the U.S. military turned from a fighting machine into a social laboratory with just one election. I've had enough of government service for a lifetime."

The waiter approached and they ordered dinner, which softened the conversation. After the meal she approached the subject with more finesse.

"I was hoping you would call me," she said in a sultry feminine voice.

Evans didn't say anything. He sipped his wine and looked at the boats in the bay.

"Tom and I are getting a divorce, and I was hoping that we could start seeing one another."

Evans continued to stare at the bay as if in a trance.

"OK. You're angry with me. I can sense it. Why?"

"I'm angry at everything. For starters, you deceived me with your Agency bullshit," he said, giving her a hard look.

"Derek, I was just doing my job, for Christ's sake," she pleaded. "I was one of several hundred people desperately following loose ends all over the planet."

"And I was a loose end, huh?" he said with a mock laugh.

"Yes. A remote possibility. You were a very small part of one of several plans conceived to neutralize Karpenko."

Evans shook his head and stared out the window at the bay bridge linking Coronado with San Diego. His gut instinct was to get up and head out across the bridge.

"Like it or not, Derek, there has been a power shift in the world. It's no longer bipolar, communist and noncommunist," she argued.

"You're right, Alysin. Clever rulers have discovered how to play the media and manipulate their own people with just a touch of mythology, religion, ideology, chicanery with words. We're not immune in this country, are we?"

"We still have the best country on earth," she retorted.

"Yeah. On that we agree," he growled.

"OK. You said the face of war is changing. On that we agree too. That's why we need to come up with a counterstrategy and a counterforce. Join us," she pleaded.

"You don't get it, do you? I don't trust anyone. Not you. Not the admiral. Not your boss, and certainly not the President of the United States," he said emphatically.

"I'm sorry to hear that, Derek. Next there will be a biological weapon that poisons a major city's water supply. Then some crackpot organization will let loose with a chemical weapon in the name of Allah or Vishnu, or some god. If we don't do something, some nutcase will explode a neutron bomb in New York or London. The battlefield is the world and the troop carriers are international airlines. You said it. Not me. Like the drug war, taken to the fifth power. Join us, Derek. You can't stand by and let it happen."

Evans's mind was racing. *Did she know about Airborne Warrior?* he thought. *Does she know about Karpenko's little vial?*

"What's the code for your new generation of warriors,

Alysin? Does the end justify the means?" he asked, boring holes in her head.

"Do you prefer . . . do you accept the alternative?" she shot back. "Ten thousand innocent people incinerated."

"Alysin, I stopped you from cutting off a man's dick. I saw you shoot five innocent coolies who just happened to be in your way, and for what . . . expediency? That's a war crime in my world. You've been promoted. I was berated for endangering Lieutenant Owen's life," he said with scorn.

"I couldn't take a chance, Derek. There were too many lives at stake!" she mumbled, feeling guilty.

"Justify it anyway you want, Dr. Alysin Harris, but what about integrity, morality, and justice? I'm not going to abandon my values. Whether it's ten thousand North Koreans coming across the DMZ with blood in their eyes, looking for my head on a platter, or five coolies on the deck of a junk in the Gulf of Thailand. It all boils down to the same thing."

"And what's that, Commander?" she asked viciously.

"Principle, Alysin. Principle," he snapped back. "It's not right to shoot innocent men. It's not right to torture another human being. It's not right to cut off a man's dick."

The waiter approached the table, defusing the heated conversations. "Commander, you have an urgent phone call. You can take it over there," he said, pointing to an office phone.

"It's just Derek Evans now, Johnny. No more commander, huh? I retired today."

"Sir, you'll always be the commander to me. I'll send over a bottle of wine to celebrate the occasion," he replied with a grin.

As Evans walked to the office, he thought, *Life is fired at us like a bullet and there is no escaping it short of death. What the hell does she really want?* He didn't trust Harris and he no longer trusted the U.S. government.

Evans picked up the phone, expecting his relief to ask for the combination to the safe, or a well-wisher like Shooter or Stick to say good-bye. "Evans here," he said gruffly into the receiver. The voice that spoke sent a chill down his spine.

"Derek Evans? Is this the famous Commander Derek

Evans of SEAL Team Five?" asked a man with a heavy English accent, obviously from a long distance.

"Yes."

"I had a great deal of trouble locating you, Commander. On this day of your retirement I wanted to send you my personal congratulations," said the limey voice on the other end of the line.

"Who is this?" demanded Evans, already knowing the answer.

"Let's say I am a distant associate who has established a very large Swiss bank account for you."

"Karpenko?"

"Yes, my handsome friend. I'm here in Saigon, in the best hotel, of course. With me are three lovely and very naked ladies," he chuckled. "If you sum their ages, they are still younger than me," he said, and laughed.

"What do you want?" snapped Evans.

"First, let me say I am not angry because you killed most of my soldiers. That is the price of business in the arms trade. I still have merchandise, Evans." Karpenko paused for dramatic effect. "There were six bombs, not four as your people believe. I also have numerous other resources, such as Airborne Warrior. So you see I am still very much involved in free enterprise. You might say I am a happy man, Evans."

"Cut to the chase, asshole. What do you want?"

"Now, now, now! Don't be so rude. Second, I wanted to tell you I don't blame you for splitting my skull in Java. That was your job. I understand that now. But I do take offense to you shooting me in the back. That wasn't very chivalrous, old chap."

"What do you want, Karpenko?" asked Evans with a tone of impatience.

"I want to invite you to join my organization, and as proof of my sincerity I have established an account for you to play with. How does two million U.S. dollars in a Swiss account sound to you?"

Evans was stunned.

"You are shocked, my warrior friend?" asked Karpenko.

"What's the catch?"

"No catch. I just need a little help locating one of my most trusted associates, who has disappeared."

"Who? Suburov? He's in a CIA dungeon," said Evans, knowing Karpenko was referring to Saraskina.

"No, no. Saraskina. I miss her warm feminine touch," said Karpenko. "You did enjoy her warm touch, didn't you?"

"I don't know where your ruthless bitch is, Karpenko," lied Evans.

"Well, I think you do. When you remember and want to retrieve your numbers, leave a message for me at the President Hotel in Saigon. I am part owner there, you know. Let's say this is a standing offer," he chuckled. "And Evans. There is no pussy in the world worth two million dollars."

"You'll have to find your murdering bitch by yourself, Karpenko." Evans slammed down the phone and stared at the receiver as if he were looking at a snake. "Principle," he said to himself. "Principle!" He had lived up to his bargain with Saraskina. As far as he was concerned Saraskina didn't exist. The woman who lived in Idaho was just another potato. Evans walked back to the table wondering what he would do with two million dollars.

Harris poured him a fresh glass of wine and reached across the table for his hand. Her touch was warm and soft.

"Derek, let's order another bottle of wine and go back to my hotel room."

He looked deep in her eyes and asked, "Where is Saraskina?" He knew she was in Idaho. He had taken her there. The question was truth serum.

"Derek, I'm not authorized to divulge that information. She's . . . let me just say that she's been taken care of."

Evans stared into Harris's eyes until she looked away. When she looked back, he shook his head no. "Alysin, it ain't the size of the balls, it's what's in the heart that counts." He stood up to leave. "You know something, Dr. Alysin Harris? You are going to make one hell of a match for Comrade General Dimitri Karpenko. Just make sure you don't blow up the world or gut-shoot our national values along the way. 'Bye!" he said with a smile. He handed the waiter a fifty-dollar bill and walked out the door.

Man-eater? Man-eater? he thought as he unlocked his car door. *How about Circe?*

As Evans climbed into the comfortable leather seats of his car, he heard the concussion of artillery simulators going off at the Naval Special Warfare Center. Another group of young men were in Hell Week. He paused for a moment before turning the key.

Life goes on. But for how long, boys? he thought. *Until Karpenko decides to check out and take everyone with him.* He fired up the car and rumbled down Orange Avenue on the way to the Coronado Bridge.

Special Operations Consultants, Incorporated, he thought. *Yeah, Sock Ink! That has a catchy sound. The world needs a new corporation, one dedicated to special things,* he thought. The white Porsche 928 moseyed across the Coronado Bridge and headed north on Interstate 5. There was no reason to hurry. Evans had the rest of his life to go anywhere he wanted, how ever long that happened to be.